Padraig O'Malley is senior associate at the John W. McCormack Institute of the University of Massachusetts at Boston, editor of the *New England Journal of Public Policy,* and author of *The Uncivil Wars: Ireland Today* (Blackstaff Press, 1983).

D1065701

BITING
AT THE
GRAVE

The
Irish Hunger Strikes
and the
Politics of Despair

PADRAIG
O'MALLEY

THE
BLACKSTAFF
PRESS

BELFAST

First published in hardback in 1990 by
Beacon Press, Boston, Massachusetts

This paperback edition published in September 1990 by
The Blackstaff Press Limited
3 Galway Park, Dundonald, Belfast BT16 0AN, Northern Ireland

Reprinted October 1990

Printed by The Guernsey Press Company Limited

Portions of "Sixteen Dead Men" and "Meditations in Time of
Civil War" by W. B. Yeats are reprinted with permission of Macmillan
Publishing Co. from *The Poems of W. B. Yeats: A New Edition,*
edited by Richard J. Finneran, © 1924 and 1928 by Macmillan
Publishing Co.; © renewed 1952 and 1956 by Bertha Georgie Yeats;
and by permission of A. P. Watt Limited, on behalf of Michael B. Yeats
and Macmillan (London) Ltd. Portions of *The King's Threshold* by
W. B. Yeats are reprinted from *The Collected Plays of W. B. Yeats*
(New York: Macmillan, 1989).

Text design by Dennis Anderson

British Library Cataloguing in Publication Data
  O'Malley, Padraig
    Biting at the grave: the Irish hunger strikes and the
    politics of despair.
    1. Lisburn (District). Prisons: Maze Prison. H Block.
    Prisoners. Hunger strikes
    I. Title
    365.44
ISBN 0-85640-453-5

King. Persuade him to eat or drink. Till yesterday
I thought that hunger and weakness had been enough;
But finding them too trifling and too light
To hold his mouth from biting at the grave,
I called you hither, and all my hope's in you,
And certain of his neighbours and good friends
That I have sent for. While he is lying there,
Perishing there, my good name in the world
Is perishing also. I cannot give way.
Because I am King; because, if I give way,
My Nobles would call me a weakling, and, it may be,
The very throne be shaken.

William Butler Yeats,
from *The King's Threshold*

CONTENTS

ACKNOWLEDGMENTS

Many people helped make this book possible: my thanks to Pat Johnson, who transcribed the hundreds of hours of taped interviews, met demanding schedules for herself and set demanding ones for me; my thanks also to Robert Bell who made the facilities of the Linenhall Library, Belfast, available and who gave me full access to the library's unique collection of data on the conflict on Northern Ireland, and to Don Jennings, and Lou Richards, who did heroic work in Belfast during the summer of 1986. I am especially indebted to Kirsten Thomsen for research assistance and for her encouragement and warm friendship during hard times. Also, my thanks to Kate Burns, Alex Moon, and James Hooton, who tidied up loose ends, and to Lionel Shriver, who provided invaluable criticism and insights that immeasurably improved the text. My thanks to Winnie Burns and Eliza McGrand, who also provided research assistance, to Robie Macauley for having faith in me, to my brother, Peter, to James Thompson, Jr., and Patricia Keefer for critical readings, and to Ed Beard, director of the John W. McCormack Institute of Public Affairs, for his understanding and patience. I am further indebted to Patricia Keefer for her steadfast interest and unflagging assistance, and for her perceptive comments on an early draft. My thanks to Dr. Vamik Volkan for sharing his insights into the psychological dimensions of political conflict with me. The manuscript benefited enormously from the sharp eye and sharp mind of Sarah Flynn, who provided editorial direction and valuable advice. Marcy Murninghan's equally sharp eye and mind and meticulous attention to the small details often overlooked made the difference between a good and better manuscript. But I am particularly indebted to her for introducing me to the works of Alasdair MacIntyre, and for the numerous discussions we had on questions of morality, violence, and values. The opinions expressed are, of course, entirely my own. My thanks, too, to my editors at

Beacon Press, Wendy Strothman and Thomas Fischer, and my special thanks to Mary-Beth McGee who deciphered my almost indecipherable handwriting and typed the entire manuscript, and her one-year-old daughter, Meaghan Rose, for the useful diversions she provided. My sincere thanks to all my interviewees who gave their time and thoughts many more than once over a number of years. And finally my thanks to the families of the hunger strikers—the O'Donnells, McCreeshes, O'Haras, Devines, Lynches, Hursons, and McElwees who received me into their homes and shared with me what they had gone through—experiences that have indelibly marked them for the rest of their lives. Because of their willingness to share, these experiences have also indelibly marked me.

CHRONOLOGY OF EVENTS

27 October 1980 Seven Republican prisoners in the H-blocks of the Maze/Long Kesh prison—Raymond McCartney, John Nixon, Sean McKenna, Brendan Hughes, Leo Green, Thomas McFeeley and Thomas McKearney—refuse meals on the first day of a "fast to death."

2 December 1980 On the thirty-seventh day of their fast, the seven Maze/Long Kesh hunger strikers are moved to the prison hospital for closer surveillance of their health.

12 December 1980 Six UDA prisoners in the Maze/Long Kesh, serving sentences for murder and arms offenses, begin a hunger strike for "political status" and segregation from Republicans.

13 December 1980 An eye specialist visits Sean McKenna on the forty-seventh day of his hunger strike.

15 December 1980 Twenty-three more Republican prisoners start a hunger strike with Provisional Sinn Fein announcing another six would join, meaning the largest number ever on hunger strike.

16 December 1980 Seven more Republican prisoners join the Maze/Long Kesh hunger strike.

17 December 1980 The six UDA hunger strikers "suspend" their fast to give the Northern Ireland Office the opportunity to act on their demands.

18 December 1980 The seven original Republican hunger strikers end their fast after fifty-three days.

1 March 1981 Bobby Sands, age twenty-seven, from Belfast, refuses food on the first day of a new hunger strike campaign for "political status" for Republican prisoners.

15 March 1981 Francis Hughes, age twenty-five, from South Derry, joins the hunger strike.

22 March 1981 Raymond McCreesh, age twenty-four, from South Armagh, and Patsy O'Hara, age twenty-four, from Derry city, join the hunger strike.

5 May 1981 Bobby Sands dies on the sixty-sixth day of his hunger strike.

9 May 1981 Joe McDonnell, age thirty, from Belfast, joins the hunger strike to replace Bobby Sands.

12 May 1981 Francis Hughes dies on the fifty-ninth day of his hunger strike.

14 May 1981 Brendan McLaughlin, age twenty-nine, from North Derry, joins the hunger strike to replace Francis Hughes.

21 May 1981 Raymond McCreesh and Patsy O'Hara die on the sixty-first day of their hunger strikes.

22 May 1981 Kieran Doherty, age twenty-five, from Belfast, joins the hunger strike to replace Raymond McCreesh.

23 May 1981 Kevin Lynch, age twenty-five, from North Derry, joins the hunger strike to replace Patsy O'Hara.

27 May 1981 Brendan McLaughlin gives up his hunger strike on "medical grounds."

29 May 1981 Martin Hurson, age twenty-four, from East Tyrone, joins the hunger strike to replace Brendan McLaughlin.

8 June 1981 Thomas McElwee, age twenty-three, from South Derry, joins the hunger strike.

15 June 1981 Paddy Quinn, age twenty-eight, from South Armagh, joins the hunger strike.

22 June 1981 Micky Devine, age twenty-seven, from Derry city, joins the hunger strike.

29 June 1981 Laurence McKeown, age twenty-four, from County Antrim, joins the hunger strike.

8 July 1981 Joe McDonnell dies on the sixty-first day of his hunger strike.

10 July 1981 Pat McGeown, age twenty-four, from Belfast, joins the hunger strike to replace Joe McDonnell.

13 July 1981 Martin Hurson dies on the forty-sixth day of his hunger strike.

15 July 1981 Matt Devlin, age thirty-one, from East Tyrone, joins the hunger strike to replace Martin Hurson.

31 July 1981 Paddy Quinn becomes the first hunger striker to be given medical treatment on orders of his relatives, and ends his fast after forty-seven days.

1 August 1981 Kevin Lynch dies on the seventy-first day of his hunger strike.

2 August 1981 Kieran Doherty dies on the seventy-third day of his hunger strike.

3 August 1981 Liam McCloskey, age twenty-five, from North Derry, joins the hunger strike to replace Kevin Lynch.

8 August 1981 Thomas McElwee dies on the sixty-second day of his hunger strike.

10 August 1981 Pat Sheehan, age twenty-three, from Belfast, joins the hunger strike.

17 August 1981 Jackie McMullan, age twenty-five, from Belfast, joins the hunger strike.

20 August 1981 Micky Devine dies on the sixtieth day of his hunger strike. The family of Pat McGeown agree to medical intervention to save his life on the forty-second day of his hunger strike.

24 August 1981 Bernard Fox, age thirty, from Belfast, joins the hunger strike.

31 August 1981 Gerry Carville, age twenty-five, from South Down, joins the hunger strike.

4 September 1981 The family of Matt Devlin agree to medical intervention to save his life on the fifty-second day of his hunger strike.

6 September 1981 The family of Laurence McKeown agree to medical intervention to save his life on the seventieth day of his hunger strike.

7 September 1981 John Pickering, age twenty-five, from Belfast, joins the hunger strike.

14 September 1981 Gerard Hodgins, age twenty-one, from Belfast, joins the hunger strike.

21 September 1981 Jim Devine, age twenty-four, from Strabane, joins the hunger strike.

25 September 1981 Bernard Fox ends his hunger strike after thirty-two days because of medical complications.

26 September 1981 Liam McCloskey ends his hunger strike on the fifty-fifth day after talking to his family.

3 October 1981 Republican prisoners in the Maze/Long Kesh end their hunger strikes.

1 HUNGER STRIKES

. . . there is a custom,
An old and foolish custom, that if a man
Be wronged, or think that he is wronged, and starve
Upon another's threshold till he die,
The common people, for all time to come,
Will raise a heavy cry against the threshold,
Even though it be the King's.

William Butler Yeats
The King's Threshold

1   On 1 March 1981, Bobby Sands, acting on behalf of 361 Republican prisoners at the Maze/Long Kesh prison outside Belfast, went on hunger strike. It was the opening scene in the final act of the prisoners' campaign for political status, a campaign that had begun four years earlier with the "blanket" protest when prisoners convicted of what would, in other times, be described as politically motivated offenses refused to wear prison clothing, the badge of an ordinary criminal, and covered themselves with the only clothing at hand—their blankets. The blanket protest became the "no wash" protest, then the "no slop-out" protest, and finally the "dirty" protest. Prisoners smeared their excrement on the walls, floors, and ceilings of their cells. And when this didn't work, seven prisoners embarked on a hunger strike in October 1980, vowing to fast to their deaths until the British government agreed to meet their five demands, which were ostensibly the cornerstone of their protest: the right to wear their own clothes; to refrain from prison work; to associate freely with one another; to organize recreational facilities and to have one letter, visit, and parcel a week; and to have lost remission time restored. The hunger strike lasted fifty-three days, ending a week before Christmas when the prisoners announced that they were satisfied that the government had agreed to meet the substance of their demands.

But the government had not, hence Sands's hunger strike and the ones that followed. Over a three-month period, ten hunger strikers died, their deaths coming staccato-like in clusters of twos and threes, and for each hunger striker who died, another prisoner stepped forward to take his place.

The media of the world gathered in Belfast to chronicle his slow deterioration, eager to capture the violence they had confidently predicted, their presence ensuring it would follow, adding to the forebodings of menace that accompanied the death watch.

He died sixty-six days later, his body having digested itself, his name known in the most obscure corners of the world. He was hero, martyr, Bobby Sands, M.P., lonely agitator. He had pitted his fragile psyche against the impersonal power of a government and he had won.

In death he was accorded the political recognition he had sought. Over 110,000 dock workers, members of the International Long-shoremen's Union, boycotted for twenty-four hours all British ships entering U.S. ports. All the major U.S. dailies put the story on their front pages; for most, it was their main headline. Even the *New York Times* paid attention: "By willing his own death," an editorial read, "Bobby Sands has earned a place on Ireland's long roll of martyrs and bested an implacable British Prime Minister."

Attention—and empathy—were worldwide. Members of the Portuguese Parliament observed a one-minute silence. The highly influential French daily newspaper *Le Monde* condemned the British. The Iron Lady, it said, had been "faithful to her legend to the point of caricature." In Spain the mass-circulation liberal paper *El Pais* predicted that "implacable toughness would only lead the matter toward an open civil war and the eventual situation of violence between Britain and the Irish Republic." The Soviet Government newspaper *Izvestia* blamed the British government for "increasing terror and repression in Northern Ireland." In Mexico, the smiling face of Sands was put on the front pages of all the national dailies. In Mozambique, the semiofficial daily newspaper *Noticias* said that Sands died because the British government had refused to accept "the simple and indisputable fact that he was a freedom fighter," and the *Sowetan,* South Africa's main black-run newspaper, devoted a full tabloid page, which it headlined "Belfast Pays Tribute to Martyr Bobby Sands," to Sands's funeral. The *Hindustan Times* said that Mrs. Thatcher "had allowed a member of the House of Commons, a colleague in fact, to die of starvation. Never had such an incident occurred in a civilized country." Anti-British demonstrations took place in cities all over the world, including Athens, Antwerp, Milan, Oslo, Brisbane, and Chicago. And Lech Walesa, leader of Poland's independent trade union Solidarity, called Sands "a great man who sacrificed his life for his struggle."

When Sands died I found myself reacting in anger and near despair: anger because his actions were calculated to require me to respond in a predetermined way—sympathy for the perceived victim of injustice, admiration for the fallen hero, antipathy for the perceived oppressor; near despair because it appeared that the prison dispute could have been resolved some time earlier had the British government been inclined to use a modicum of common sense.

You could outline it like a story: a chosen few, the elite of the elite, resolve to take matters into their own hands, prepared to sacrifice their lives to achieve through the shedding of blood what they cannot achieve through physical force. Their noble gesture fails and they die, their lives taken from them by the callous, almost indifferently methodical oppressor. The nation, once unresponsive to their cause and dismissive of their efforts, now rises up in furious anger on their behalf, and thus aroused it throws off the yoke of serfdom. The cause prevails.

The story, of course, had been written. It was history, old stuff, part of the national mythology. It had been memorized, categorized, eulogized. But no matter. In Ireland, history collapses itself; analogy is a substitute for analysis; replication is more important than invention; a sense of the inevitable overwhelms the sense of the possible. "It is often said there is too much history in Ireland," I wrote in the *Boston Globe* the day after Sands's death,

but there is no history now, just lies, distortion and sham. And it is to this that the sad and awful death of Bobby Sands will add. He is myth now, part of an elaborately cultivated contrivance about the past to conceal an ugliness about ourselves we [the Irish] dare not face; it is the Irish who are doing the damage to the Irish. We are our own oppressors.

We have, of course, constructed ingenious stratagems to evade the truth, even to the point of changing the past. We have instead a set of myths, a set of ideas about Ireland that compensates for the harsh, uncomforting reality of what we are doing to each other in the name of God and in the name of Country.

We need England. We need it to disguise the sordid and sad reality of our murderous designs on each other. We need it to give life to the lie, we need it to escape the reality of our condition—and we need it because we need an enemy.

Poor Ireland. Poor Bobby Sands. On his headstone we should inscribe the words of Yeats: "Out of Ireland have we come / Great hatred, little room / Maimed us at the start."

But even when I wrote these words I knew that they were inadequate—a spontaneous emotional response to an event that profoundly upset me, a bellow of frustration, a cry in the forsaken night, not a considered response to the historical moment.

When the hunger strikes ended, grinding with an exhausting tenacity to their inevitable halt, they continued to preoccupy me. There was something both noble and perverse in a conscious decision to fast until death, especially when the decision was carried through with the bitter certainty that death, not vindication, lay in store, unless death itself and the triumph of will it required could be considered vindication. I was attracted and repelled by the hunger strikers' actions: attracted by the heroic element, the steely determination to sacrifice life itself on behalf of conviction, the impulse to transcend the daily petulance of stuporific resistance; repelled because I was tired of the small gestures of impotence, the fusing of the praxis of suffering and the pretensions of idealism to evoke the easy sentimentality that too often is the hallmark of the Irish response to questions of life and death. And perhaps deep within myself I was dimly aware of something far more disturbing. For I, too, Dublin-born and raised, with deep roots in the subsistence farmlands of the West, was a product of the culture I so scathingly and easily assailed, and some small voice buried in the subterranean mind would whisper to me that if I had been born in the Catholic ghettos of Republican Belfast, I, too, perhaps, would have found myself inexorably but easily drawn into the Republican fold, a willing disciple of the theologians of violence. To borrow a phrase, "There but for the grace of God go I," for it is easy for the observer who stands outside the culture he observes to make judgments about right and wrong and what is normal and abnormal when he does not run the risk of being killed. "Different and incompatible conceptions of justice," the moral philosopher Alasdair MacIntyre writes in his magisterial work *Whose Justice? Which Rationality?* "are closely linked to different and incompatible conceptions of practical rationality."[1]

Indeed. In the summer of 1986 I returned to Northern Ireland one more time to examine the hunger strikes in detail, to explore the lives of the ten young men who had starved themselves to death in the summer of 1981, to learn about the culture's responses to the crisis. Who were we, I wondered, who could incubate and breed such merciless young who would prefer to do right by denying life instead of affirming it, whose sense of victimhood had become such an integral part of their personality that they needed to reaffirm it by destroying identity itself? And who were they, I wondered, who could harden themselves to abandon life with a casual disregard for the terminal consequences of their actions, eyes fixed on a star in a galaxy of patriot-ghosts imploding in their imaginations, their bodies sacrificial offerings to the glutinous gods of a degenerative nationalism, minds impervious to the importunings of those who did not inhabit their closed universe. And who were the others, I wondered, who wished them dead, who saw the media attention lavished on the hunger strikers as evidence of a conspiracy to defraud them of their own grief, who cried out in anguish and isolation for recognition of their own victimhood?

Whose justice? Which rationality? When Mary McDermott, a close family friend of the hunger striker Kieran Doherty, tried to reassure him nine days before he died, she told him that "everybody is doing what they can, you know; we are contacting that one and the other one and so forth and I am sure that they will give in to your demands." But Doherty, with the lucidity of one for whom the certainty of his own death has become a matter of comfort rather than regret, turned his once splendid body, now almost diaphanous in its thinness, toward her and said, "Oh, the demands, there is a lot more to it than that."

Doherty was right. The hunger strikes polarized Northern Ireland to an extent that no single event in the twenty-year-old conflict had or has since. During the 217 days of the second hunger strike, sixty-four people died, including thirty-four civilians, and the divisions between the Catholic and Protestant communities were expressed in ways that exposed the psychic undercurrents of religion and tribe, which the parties to the conflict go out of their way to deny, preferring to attribute their divisions to more civilized causes—if only to make them more acceptable to themselves.

Within the Catholic community the hunger strikes cruelly exposed the ambiguous relationship between militant Republicanism and mainstream nationalism, between militant Republicanism and the Catholic Church, between the ancient mythologies carefully nurtured for decades, an idea of Ireland imbued with memory traces of blood sacrifice, and the newer mythologies of money and status and the affluence of the filthy tide. Within the Protestant community they exposed the depth and intensity of Protestants' rage, their fear of the repercussions of the hunger strikes at once unfounded and real, having more to do with an imagined reality than with an imminent threat. Their hatred of Republicanism became fused with their fear of Catholicism, their efforts to assert their own humanity thwarted by their insistence on denying the humanity of others. Confronted with events they could not understand, they took comfort in their own sense of supremacy, their marginal advantages becoming the reward of moral superiority rather than the legacy of entrenched privilege.

For the first time since the conflict erupted anew, in the late 1960s, the churches emerged as the surrogate spokesparties for their respective constituencies. The Irish Catholic Church refused to call the hunger strikes suicide. The Protestant churches—and even the English Catholic Church—were unanimously of the opposite opinion: the hunger strikers were committing suicide, had earned the censure of their church, and should be denied burial in sacred ground. The Irish Church was unmoved, resting its case on its obligation to its community and its duties as pastor rather than on the doctrinal niceties of the Fifth Commandment. But this argument was merely the surface manifestation of a more deeply rooted difference, as much ideological as theological, over the nature of right and wrong and the meaning of an ambiguity that was, in the eyes of Protestants, at the heart of Catholic teaching and the root of their distrust of Catholics in general and Irish Catholic nationalists in particular. For once, the churches, despite the carefully worded statements of their leaders that concealed the ugly insinuations under the surface, appeared to barter their integrity and independence for the support of their congregations, making them, in effect, one of the major sources of sectarianism. They became the mouthpieces for the political importunings of their constituencies rather than exemplars of the Christian ethos they professed. They were unable to lift themselves out of the moral entropy they had succumbed to, unable to put the hunger strikes in a moral context that would illuminate rather than divide.

In the Republic, the hunger strikes exposed the ambivalence of the country's attitudes toward the North, its less than enthusiastic adherence to the myths of the past, its unwillingness to acknowledge essential elements of these myths, its anger at being forced into a situation where that acknowledgment was called for, the bankruptcy of its ideation of Irish identity, and its impotence in matters relating to the management of its own affairs. Finally, the hunger strikes exposed Britain's overwhelming arrogance where questions of Ireland are concerned, its insensitivity seasoned with an ingrained residue of superiority, its chronic postcolonial hubris, its predilection for an imperial righteousness that saw every British action as being self-evidently justified, making the small and rather hapless neighboring island the unwilling recipient of its domination.

But perhaps more than anything else, the hunger strikes exposed the extent to which Northern Ireland is a paradigm for what political scientist Robert Elias calls a "political economy of helplessness,"[2] a victim-bonded society in which memories of past injustice and humiliation are so firmly entrenched in both communities and the sense of entrapment so complete that the hunger strikes are a metaphor for the entrapment of the larger society. Moreover, this sense of victim-hood extends to the South, the pervasive passivity there a product of an inherited sense of powerlessness. Responses to the hunger strikes—whether on the part of the hunger strikers themselves, their families and supporters, the prison community, the IRA leadership on the outside, the Protestant community, the churches, Catholic nation-alists, their coreligionists in the South, or both governments—illu-minate the nature of that entrapment and the pervasiveness of the sense of victimhood, allowing us to understand how those who re-member the past are especially condemned to repeat its mistakes.

2   History is a matter of starting points, and for Irish nation-alists, especially Republicans, the roots of the conflict in Northern Ireland can be traced back to the year 1170, when Norman warriors speaking Norman French crossed from England to Ireland with the approval of King Henry II and at the invitation of the Irish chief Dermot McMurragh. For the next four hundred years the English tried with limited success to conquer Ireland but the range of their rule was confined to a small area around Dublin with perhaps a thirty-mile radius. In the late sixteenth century King Henry VIII tried to bring Ireland more firmly under the control of his Crown, primarily for strategic purposes (the advance in technology that vastly increased the range and capability of long sailing ships had made England more vulnerable to attack through Ireland by her continental enemies) and the subsequent attempts by his successors to secure the Crown's au-thority resulted in a major uprising led by the Ulster chieftain Hugh O'Neill. O'Neill's rebellion, however, collapsed with the defeat of the Gaelic chiefs at the Battle of Kinsale in 1601.

Kinsale spelled the end of the old Gaelic order. Within years the defeated Gaelic chiefs had fled to the continent in what came to be called the Flight of the Earls—thus giving King James I an opportunity to secure the most rebellious part of Ireland by colonizing much of Ulster with English and Scottish settlers. The new settlers who began to arrive in 1607 were different. The Scots were Presbyterians of the most strict and doctrinaire kind, the English Episcopal Protestants. From the beginning, land and religion were inextricably linked and religion remained the barrier to assimilation because the settlements took place in the larger context of the Counter-Reformation.

Twice in the course of the seventeenth century the native Irish, in attempts to win back their confiscated lands, aligned themselves with an English monarch, and on both occasions they chose the losing side in an English civil war. They aligned themselves with Charles I in his dispute with Parliament in 1641 and for their efforts brought down on themselves the wrath of Oliver Cromwell, who arrived in Ireland in 1649, laid to waste the towns of Drogheda and Wexford, dispatching the native Irish to the impoverished west of Ireland. One-third of Irish Catholics perished in the eleven-year war, and after Cromwell's settlements three-quarters of the land was in the hands of the Protestant minority.

For Protestants, 1641 had a different significance. They had long anticipated an uprising by the native Irish to reclaim their lands. Actual events exceeded their worst expectations, and when a number of Protestants were slaughtered by vengeful Catholics, the myth of siege was reinforced by the myth of massacre. The massacres, of course, were exaggerated in the telling but their extraordinary symbolic significance transcended exaggeration. They became a vindication for fearfulness, vigilance, and distrust.

In 1685 the Catholic Irish allied themselves with James II, the Catholic monarch who had been deposed from his throne by Parliament in favor of his brother-in-law, the Protestant King William of Orange—William III. The forces of James with his French and Irish allies were decisively crushed by the armies of William at the Battle of the Boyne in 1690. The conquest of Ireland seemed complete.

For the better part of the next one hundred years, the Protestant Ascendancy ruled. It legislated the penal laws in 1695, laws that were designed to ensure a permanent Protestant hegemony. Catholics were banned from public office, the legal profession, and the army. They could not vote, teach, or own land. The penal laws were the apartheid of their day, isolating Catholics in an inferior identity, causing the percentage of land owned by Catholics to fall steadily—to 15 percent by 1703 and to just 7 percent by mid-century.

During the latter part of the eighteenth century secret agrarian societies, which tenants used to control the savage competition for land, began to proliferate. In Munster the Catholic White Boys terrorized the countryside, burning the houses and killing the livestock of Protestant landlords. In Ulster Presbyterians used a network of secret societies, the most notorious being the Oak Boys and the Steel Boys, to keep Protestant landlords from raising rents. The competition for land between Catholics and Protestants was even more intense in Ulster because of a system of land tenure unique to the area. Under the "Ulster Custom," tenants had fairly comprehensive rights including freedom from eviction as long as they paid their rents. Accordingly, Protestant tenants were better off than most tenants in the rest of the country. However, when the Catholic Relief Acts of 1778 and 1782 were enacted, Catholics were allowed to purchase and hold leases on an equal footing with Protestants. Catholics became more attractive tenants to landlords since they were used to a lower standard of living and were prepared to pay higher rents. Protestant tenants were not. Their secret societies turned their attention from Protestant landlords to Catholic tenants. The "have littles" fought the "have nots" along strictly sectarian lines. The Peep O'Day Boys, made up primarily of former Steel Boys and Oak Boys, emerged in the mid-1780s to terrorize Catholics. In response, the Catholics formed their own protection society—the Defenders. The distinctive feature of both was their sectarian orientation.

The paradigm was set. In the nineteenth century, when the rapid influx of new residents, especially Catholics, transformed Belfast from a Presbyterian town of some 19,000 at the turn of the century to a teeming polyglot of some 400,000 residents at the century's end, competition for jobs took the place of competition for land. The sectarian rioting that sporadically ravaged the city had its roots in the rural agrarian violence of the previous century. The cleavages of the nineteenth century have been reinforced by the events of the twentieth. Even today, the main locations for sectarian clashes have remained remarkably unchanged since the riots of the nineteenth century.

The eighteenth century was the age of the Protestant nation. In the later part of it, Protestant nationalism began to emerge in its own right. At issue was the power of the British Parliament to override legislation passed by the Irish parliament and the extent to which it engaged in this practice to ensure that Britain's mercantile interests were always put before Ireland's. The Irish Volunteers, founded in 1778, ostensibly to protect Ireland from a possible French invasion when British army resources were stretched during the war in the American colonies, were in fact an army the Ascendancy could deploy to back up its demands for legislative independence. The threat that Ireland might go the same way as the American colonies was enough to persuade the British Parliament to grant independence to Ireland in 1782. The Act of Renunciation of British legislative rights in Ireland declared there would be two nations—one Irish and one British, each with its independent parliament under a joint crown. Two kingdoms, one crown.

In 1791 the Society of the United Irishmen was formed, largely by Presbyterian Republican separatists. It took its mandate from the French Revolution and began to articulate a broad-based form of Irish nationalism that would unite to "end the English connection, assert the independence of the country and unite the whole people of Ireland." Its leader, Theobold Wolfe Tone, attempted to forge an alliance with the Defenders and organize a national uprising with the help of the French. The uprising in 1798, however, was a dismal failure, degenerating into sectarian violence in Wexford where a number of Protestants were murdered at Scullavogue, and failing to take place in Ulster, where it was expected to be most successful. Its significance, however, was that it marked the birth of the Irish Republican separatist tradition, the tradition of physical force to which the Irish Republican Army (IRA) today sees itself as being the legitimate successor.

The attempted uprising made the British aware of how vulnerable they were to attack by their continental enemies launched through Ireland. Accordingly, in 1800, the Act of Union, abolishing the Irish parliament (which was, of course, exclusively Protestant), was passed. Britain and Ireland were united in one kingdom with one parliament. The history of the next 120 years is the history of the attempts to undo the Act of Union, and to give Ireland a parliament of its own. However, the granting of Catholic emancipation in 1829, which gave Catholics the right to sit in Parliament, ensured that either repeal of the Union or Home Rule (self-rule within a United Kingdom) would have a most deleterious effect on the status of Irish Protestants: they would go from being part of a Protestant majority in the United Kingdom parliament to being a permanent minority in an Irish parliament.

Twice in the late nineteenth century—in 1886 and 1893—the Liberal prime minister, William Gladstone, who needed the support of the Irish parliamentary party (the Home Rulers) to form his government, brought Home Rule Bills for Ireland before Parliament, and on both occasions they went down to defeat. Protestant opposition to any form of Home Rule was vociferous, widespread, and militant. In 1912 they formed the Ulster Volunteer Force, an army of some

100,000 men who were prepared to resist Britain with force of arms to prevent the implementation of Home Rule. Nearly half a million men and women signed the Ulster Covenant, a declaration to use "all means which may be found necessary to defeat the present conspiracy to set up a Home Rule parliament in Ireland." Herbert Asquith introduced a third Home Rule Bill in 1912 which passed its third reading in January 1913, but its implementation was delayed when World War I broke out. It was clear, however, that Home Rule for the entire island was not on—even nationalist leaders were prepared to grant parts of Ulster at least a temporary exemption.

If the nineteenth century was one in which the great mass constitutional movements—for Emancipation, Repeal of the Union, Land Reform, Home Rule—flourished, the parallel tradition of the unconstitutional also emerged, a tradition which held that only physical force could resolve Ireland's problems. Uprisings in 1803, 1848, and 1867 were all easily put down. None of them enjoyed any kind of mass support nor did the majority of people subscribe to what they stood for. However, they fed the myths of unending rebellion, of ennobling failure—and the failure of the people to respond to the message of Republicanism became subverted in time by the larger myth of heroic failure in the face of overwhelming English superiority. And the distinguishing characteristics of militant Republicanism began to emerge: elitism (to a chosen few fell the burden of freeing Ireland; had the men of 1916 waited for the apathetic nation to catch up to them, there would have been no War of Independence); suspicion of politics and the democratic will; a belief in physical force as the only means to secure Ireland's independence; a hatred of England; and separatism. Moreover, the founding of the secret Irish Republican Brotherhood (IRB) in 1858 would have an impact beyond its size. When the Irish Volunteers were formed in 1913 (nationalists were only following in the footsteps of the Unionists in forming their own "army") it was rapidly infiltrated by members of the IRB, and when the movement split in 1914 the IRB's control of the smaller Sinn Fein Volunteers became even more pronounced. (The National Volunteers supported volunteers enlisting in the British army in support of the war; Sinn Fein Volunteers opposed enlistment.)

The Easter Rising of 1916 was mythic. Planned in secret by a small cabal in the IRB, itself a small cabal in the Sinn Fein Volunteers, it was designed to fail, to be a blood sacrifice that would redeem the Irish nation and rouse it to action. Led by Patrick Pearse, a group of about 1,400 Volunteers took over the General Post Office and several other strategically placed buildings in Dublin and proclaimed the establishment of a provisional government of the Irish Republic on behalf of the Irish people. Ill prepared, ill equipped, without any apparent plan of action, they were more like the occupants of besieged garrisons ready to resist assault rather than the vanguard of a national uprising. In less than a week of fighting, 220 civilians, 64 volunteers, and 134 British soldiers were killed. When Pearse surrendered, the Volunteers were jeered by the people of Dublin as they were led away. But when the fifteen leaders of the uprising—including the seven signatories of the Proclamation of Independence—were summarily executed over a nine-day period between 3 May and 12 May, the public mood was transformed. Outrage at the Volunteers turned into outrage at the authorities, and those who had been executed became martyr-heroes. "Every student of the Rising, reluctantly or otherwise, has reached the conclusion that it was a cardinal event— *a cardo rerum,* a hinge or turning point of fortune, after which all recourse to Home Rule on the part of the English government became impossible," the historian George Dangerfield writes in *The Damnable Question.* "This did not dawn all at once. It appeared first as sympathy with the rebels, then as a martyrology; then as a growing rejection of the sober promises of constitutionalism. Had Home Rule been accepted by the Tories in 1912, this constitutional path would have led in the long run to independence without partition. . . . The great political effect of the Easter Rising was that it generated impatience in a living generation."[1] The public expressed its impatience in a more forceful way in the 1918 general election when it gave its overwhelming electoral support to Sinn Fein. The party founded by Arthur Griffith in 1905 had become an alternative political option, if only by virtue of its existence, for all those, radical or conservative, who were disillusioned with the National party (formerly Home Rulers). The repudiation of the National party, the voice of constitutional nationalism that had represented nationalists in the Westminster Parliament under one name or another since 1873 for failing to deliver Home Rule, paved the way for the War of Independence, spearheaded by the Volunteers—now the Irish Republican Army—under the leadership of Michael Collins between 1919 and 1921.

In 1920 the British government passed the Government of Ireland Act, creating two Irish states within the United Kingdom framework: a Northern state composed of six counties that would ensure a per-

manent Protestant majority, and a Southern state of twenty-six counties. However, this arrangement was superseded by the Anglo-Irish
Treaty of 1921, which established the Irish Free State, an independent
country in its own right, albeit with dominion status, with its own
parliament, and the Northern Ireland state, with its own provincial
parliament, which would remain part of the United Kingdom.

The IRA split over the treaty—some wanting to hold out for the
Republic they had sought, others arguing that the treaty gave "the
freedom to win the freedom," in Michael Collins's memorable phrase,
and that the Boundary Commission established by the Treaty would
redraw the border in such a way as to make Northern Ireland eco-
nomically unviable. A bitter civil war followed in 1922 and 1923,
pitting the Free State army (largely made up of former members of
the IRA) against their erstwhile comrades, before the "Irregulars"
accepted that they could not prevail. Most of those on the losing side
in the civil war put aside their arms, formed the Fianna Fail party in
1926, and entered constitutional politics under the leadership of Eamon De Valera. A few remained in Sinn Fein and gave their allegiance
to what was left of the IRA, to the Proclamation of the Republic in
1916, to the historically ordained mandate for a united Ireland. For
them the establishment of the Irish Free State in 1921, with its Dominion Status and the Oath of Allegiance to the Crown, was an illegal
act, and all subsequent Dublin governments were, therefore, illegal.
The IRA, they held, was the true political and military heir to the
1918 parliament. They did not accept the right of the minority created
at the time of the plantation of Ulster to secede from the nation.

When de Valera himself assumed power in Dublin in 1932 he
proscribed the IRA. During the next thirty years the IRA made periodic attempts at mounting bombing campaigns in Britain and armed
attacks on military and police installations in the North, its most
sustained effort being the Border Campaign of 1956–62. The movement enjoyed little popular support and was caught totally surprised
when Northern Ireland finally erupted in 1968. In *The Provisional
IRA,* authors Patrick Bishop and Eamonn Mallie estimate that there
were perhaps fewer than sixty men in Belfast in 1969 who would
have regarded themselves as being members of the IRA, and at least
half of them had lapsed.[2]

Irish nationalists—Catholics for the most part—maintain that the
partition of Ireland in 1920 was contrary to the desire of the great
majority of the Irish people and that Northern Ireland was an arti-

ficially created entity, its borders drawn to maximize an area that would ensure a permanent Protestant hegemony. The British maintain that Home Rule for Ireland would have resulted in civil war. One million Unionists—Protestants for the most part, concentrated in the northeast of Ireland, who thought of themselves as British—would have gone from being members of a majority within the Union of Great Britain and Ireland to being a minority within an all-Ireland Catholic state. They had indicated not only their intentions but their capacity to fight any attempt to impose Home Rule—"Home Rule was Rome Rule." Britain's solution therefore: partition Ireland into two separate political units, one of which—Northern Ireland—would maintain its own parliament within the United Kingdom.

And thus the irony: Northern Ireland came into being because no one wanted it. Protestants did not want it—they sought only to preserve the union of Ireland with Britain; Catholics certainly did not want it since the new arrangements prevented the one-third of Northern Ireland's population who were Catholic from expressing their national identity. Catholics in the North never gave their allegiance to the new Northern Ireland state but instead proclaimed their allegiance to the South. At its most basic level, therefore, the conflict pits the one-million-plus Protestants, who believe the maintenance of the Union with Great Britain is the only means of securing their future, against the one-half million Catholics, who believe they can secure their future only within a united Ireland.

Even though they formed a permanent majority in the new Northern Ireland state, Protestants felt besieged, from within by the recalcitrant Catholic minority and from without by the new state to the South that laid claim in its constitution to Northern Ireland as a part of its own national territory. The Unionist government established a special paramilitary police force, the "B Specials," in 1920 to protect the state against the assaults of Republicans and introduced a Special Powers Act in 1922 that gave the government draconian powers to intern people without due process. The Unionists concentrated all power in their own hands, and being a permanent majority they never had to relinquish it or share it with Catholics. Increasingly, Protestants came to see all Catholics as subversives, and to interpret all Catholic actions in that light; any compromise with Catholics in anything that had a political dimension to it was seen as undermining Protestant hegemony. The result was widespread discrimination against Catholics, especially for jobs and housing; a concentrated attempt to keep their numbers down by keeping their emigration up; stereotyping; gerrymandering with the electoral process at the local level; and a society that put the utmost premium on geographic divisions and that used religion as the badge of political allegiance.

Ever since the 1920s, Protestant response to partition has been reflexive; behind every Catholic demand was the intent to destroy the Northern Ireland state. Accordingly, when Catholics organized a civil rights movement in the late 1960s, demanding impartial police protection, an end to electoral abuses, equal employment opportunity, fair allocation of public housing, and the disbanding of the "B Specials," Protestants responded according to their prior perceptions. Since any organized Catholic effort was thought by many to be an act of subversion to bring about a united Ireland, their response was predictable: violence in order to thwart the perceived threat. When the police could no longer control the situation, the British government had to deploy its army troops on the streets of Northern Ireland in August 1969 to protect the Catholic community.

By early 1970 the civil rights movement had achieved its major objectives, but the army's presence had become a symbol of old hatreds—a symbol that at last provided a renascent Irish Republican Army, which sought to unify Ireland through force of arms, with a situation to exploit. By mid-1970 the Provisional IRA had fifteen hundred members, six hundred of whom were believed to be in Belfast.

By the middle of 1972 violence in Northern Ireland was escalating at an unprecedented rate. The IRA responded to the British government's introduction of internment in August 1971 with a military campaign of unparalleled ferocity. In the seven months prior to internment, eleven soldiers and seventeen civilians died; in the five months following internment, thirty-two British soldiers, five members of the Ulster Defence Regiment (UDR), and ninety-seven civilians were either shot dead or blown to bits. On Bloody Sunday— 30 January 1972—British army paratroopers shot dead fourteen civilians during a civil rights demonstration in Derry, provoking an even more murderous response in the form of an unrestrained all-out bombing campaign. The bombing of the Abercorn Restaurant in downtown Belfast on a Saturday afternoon in early March, when it was sure to be crowded with shoppers, left two dead and nineteen injured. Weeks later massive car bombs in Lower Donegal Street killed four civilians and two policemen, leaving many of the 190 who were seriously injured handicapped for life. Car bombs and the threats of car bombs immobilized Derry and Belfast, stretching the security forces to breaking point. In April, the British government abolished Northern Ireland's parliament at Stormont and established direct British rule, and the IRA, perhaps with some sense that it could now force the next step—British withdrawal—reached for the pinnacle of excess. During April and May sixteen British soldiers were killed. In May there were 1,223 shooting incidents and ninety-four explosions. And in the first three weeks of June the army's casualties—nineteen dead and several dozen injured—were worse than in any previous complete month since its troops were deployed on the streets of Northern Ireland in August 1969.

In the middle of this IRA juggernaut, with Belfast engulfed in war and terror and destruction, with civilians petrified for their lives and increasingly the victims of the random bomb and the bullet of the unseen assassin, with the social order in disarray and the political order in collapse, Billy McKee, formerly the IRA leader in Belfast, led forty fellow prisoners in the Crumlin Road Jail on a hunger strike for prisoner of war status.

There were two classes of prisoners in Northern Ireland at the time. One class, internees (persons imprisoned under the Special Powers Act) were not charged with any offense or convicted of any crime. These prisoners, Republican and Loyalist, were segregated according to paramilitary allegiance and housed in Nissen huts at Long Kesh, a one-time air base outside a small village called Maze. Prisoners were able to wear their own clothes, drill, hold classes, and behave, in most respects, like prisoners of war. Within the compounds there were usually three huts housing about eighty men to a cage. Prisoners ran their own affairs and organized themselves on military lines. Each cage had an officer commanding (OC) who acted on behalf of the prisoners, organized classes on subjects ranging from history to explosives handling, and dealt with the prison authorities.

The second class of prisoner—persons, like McKee, convicted in the ordinary way of terrorist-related offenses—were treated as ordinary criminals. They were confined to their cells in Crumlin Road Jail, had to wear the standard prison uniform, were not free to associate, and were not segregated from one another according to paramilitary affiliation.

William Whitelaw, the newly appointed secretary of state for Northern Ireland, adopted the usual hard line: there would be no question of the government knuckling under to McKee's demand. Within weeks, however, he reversed himself. Several reasons are given for the about-face: Whitelaw was convinced that McKee was about to die; he became greatly alarmed at the disturbances that surely would follow McKee's death, especially when rumors that he was about to die had been sufficient to provoke a riot; and, most important, the granting of special category status was part of a deal between Whitelaw and the IRA, a precondition for a ceasefire and talks between the two sides.[3]

However, in the eyes of the prisoners protesting in 1980, the real reasons for Whitelaw's capitulation on the issue were irrelevant: the hunger strike had been the instrument of their success. McKee's action became an essential part of prison folklore and the rationale for subsequent hunger strikes. When the 1972 strike ended, the prisoners in Crumlin Road were transferred to separate cages at Long Kesh, and prisoners subsequently convicted of political-type offenses were given special category status and assigned to Long Kesh's compounds. All prisoners could wear their own clothes, were free to associate within their own cages, and received special visiting privileges. In short, within the compounds, the prisoners had control of the prison system.

Having what amounted to de facto prisoner-of-war status for its prisoners was of immense propaganda value to the IRA. It allowed the movement to describe the conflict in Northern Ireland on its own terms—the army of the Irish Republic declared in 1916 pursuing its unfinished war with the British army to end the British presence in Ireland—and to claim that the British government accepted the IRA's legitimacy and hence the legitimacy of its cause.

In the mid-1970s, however, the British government moved to change the context of the conflict. It sought to redefine the problem in terms of law and order and to label militant Republicans as terrorists, criminals without a political dimension to their actions. Anything suggesting that there was a war going on was either revamped or replaced. More authority was given to the police, the role of the army was reduced, and the emphasis was put on "normal policing" and "normal police procedures" to deal with a terrorist element that was now regarded as no different from the Red Brigade or the Bader-Meinhoff gang.

Internment was abandoned in 1976 for a new policy. Henceforth, suspected terrorists would be dealt with through the criminal court system: the one judge, no-jury Diplock courts introduced in 1973. There would be no more special category status for persons convicted of so-called political offenses. Anyone convicted after March 1976 would be treated as an ordinary criminal according to the new policy of criminalization. He would be jailed in the newly constructed prison facilities—quickly dubbed the H-blocks, since they were built in the shape of the letter H—erected alongside the compounds in Long Kesh. The legs of each H comprised a wing of twenty-five centrally heated eight-by-twelve-foot cells, a toilet area, and dining, recreation, and handicraft rooms; the central bar of the H was used for medical and administration quarters. Long Kesh, in keeping with the new order of things, was renamed the Maze Prison.

According to the British government the facilities were better— more modern, better equipped, more congenial, if one can use the word *congenial* in conjunction with the word *jail*—than any prison facility in Ireland or the United Kingdom. Indeed, in the propaganda war during the years of the ensuing dirty protest, and especially during the hunger strikes, the government repeatedly and with some satisfaction would point to the deluxe prison accommodations and extensive facilities available to conforming prisoners, as though the expenditure lavished on the prison should somehow compensate for whatever indignities the system might impose. "The Cellular Maze Prison [is] one of the most modern in Western Europe," it would later boast in *H-Blocks: The Reality,* a publication especially prepared to counteract IRA propaganda. It was "most comprehensive in the facilities it provides . . . administered in humanitarian fashion"; it was "the government's intention" to keep the prison regime "in the forefront of modern prison practice."

With the abolition of special category status the Maze/Long Kesh became, in effect, two prisons. The compounds, with their Nissen huts, continued to hold the declining number of special category prisoners, since anyone convicted of a political offense before 1 March 1976 continued to hold this status, while prisoners convicted after that date were confined to cells in the H-blocks.

From the start the prisoners would have no part of the new policy. Ciaran Nugent, the first person convicted under the new regime, refused to wear the prison uniform. Put in a cell without clothes, he covered himself with the only thing available, the blanket for his bed. Several hundred prisoners—at any given moment between

one-third and one-half of the men arriving at the Maze/Long Kesh—
followed Nugent "on the blanket," their protest drawing its inspiration from the tradition going back more than 100 years when Fenian
(Republican) prisoners went naked rather than wear a prison uniform
that would mark them as criminals. By September 1980, there were
approximately 1,400 prisoners at the Maze/Long Kesh. Of these, 370,
half Republican and half loyalist, had special status. Of the others,
about 700 were Republican and 300 loyalist, and close to 450 were
on the blanket.

And from the start, the prison authorities were determined to break
the protest. Nonconforming prisoners were subject to a punishment
regimen every fourteen days. They were confined to their cells
twenty-four hours a day; they were deprived of their three "privileged" visits per month; they lost the fifty percent remission of their
sentences so that their prison terms were doubled; they were denied
access to radio, television, books, newspapers, and all reading materials other than the Bible; they were also denied writing materials,
letters, parcels, pens; and if they refused to wear the prison uniform
for the once-monthly statutory visit to which they were entitled, they
lost that, too.

Every gesture of noncooperation on the part of the protesting
prisoners brought a harsher response: further punishment and stric-
ter enforcement of the prison regulations. Allegations and counter-
allegations of mistreatment were rife: when prisoners smashed their
furniture, their cells were stripped of everything, including beds and
footlockers, leaving only mattresses and blankets; when prisoners
baited warders, refusing to comply with even the simplest of orders,
warders beat prisoners; when prisoners in turn tried to defend
themselves against warders, or assault them, warders administered
savage retaliation; when the IRA, which had added prison officers
to their list of legitimate targets, shot prison officers (eighteen prison
officers were shot during the period), warders took their revenge on
prisoners.

The blanket protest escalated, at first to the no-wash protest, when
prisoners refused to leave their cells after they were denied a second
towel with which to cover themselves while they washed. (The towel
they used to cover themselves when they left their cells to slop out
or use the toilets was officially a wash towel, and when the prisoners
insisted on being allowed to use the washup facilities, the prison
administration insisted that this towel had to be placed on the towel

rack while they washed, leaving the prisoners naked.) The no-wash protest became the dirty protest, when prisoners were refused buckets to slop out into after they were denied permission to use the toilets unless they wore a prison uniform. They broke the windows in their cells and threw packages of excrement wrapped in whatever was at hand out into the yard below; warders outfitted in special suits threw it back in. When the windows were blocked, they smeared the feces on their cell walls and the ceiling or shoved it under the bottom of the cell doors. It was disgusting, putrid, and repulsive—and it didn't work.

As conditions in the H-blocks deteriorated the relationship between the prisoners and their keepers also degenerated into violence and viciousness. Random cell searches, invariably accompanied by resistance on the part of the prisoners and assaults on the part of the warders, became increasingly frequent. The dreaded mirror searches, for which prisoners were forced to squat naked over a mirror before and after visits and during wing shifts, became increasingly degrading. Wing shifts, forcible bathings in scalding water, and delousing were carried out with force and often vengeful brutality.

At every turn the warders were out to break the prisoners and the prisoners were out to thwart the warders. Every exchange became a confrontation, pitting the authority of the warders against the resistance of the prisoners, and though the prisoners had unequal means with which to resist, they had their own power. They drew the warders into their world, made them work in conditions of unrelieved filth, of putrid smells repugnant to the warders' physical senses and to their psychological sense of self. They forced the warders to become part of an environment of deprivation, making them, if only psychologically, the targets of excremental assault, so that they, too, became prisoners of the conditions the blanketmen had created. Insofar as the prisoners dictated the environment in which the warders had to work, they were in control. "The conspiracy between the degraders and the degraded became so close," the poet and critic Seamus Deane observes, "that the filthy nakedness of the prisoners and the space-suited automatism of the disinfecting jailers[4] seemed to be an agreed contrast of what they represented—vulnerable Irish squalor, impersonal English contamination."[5]

There was an element of taunting in the psychological battle: for every hardship the prisoners had inflicted on them they were prepared to inflict a hardship of at least equal severity on themselves, thus devaluing the system's power to intimidate them. Their willingness to deprive themselves undermined the authority of the regime to do so. Whatever debasement or humiliation the regime might impose on them in the form of punishment was nothing compared to what they were prepared to impose on themselves in the form of protest. The struggle over the cell windows was a case in point. In an effort to get rid of the pungent odor of the disinfectant used to clean their cells, the prisoners repeatedly smashed the windows, no matter how many times they were repaired, thus enduring the cold of one of the hardest winters in memory rather than submit themselves to the periodic aftereffects of the disinfectant's fumes.

"The blanket protest brought about an 'equality amongst us' even if it was an equality of brutal existence," writes former blanketman Laurence McKeown, who would later spend seventy days on hunger strike, in an article smuggled out of the Maze/Long Kesh and published in *An Phoblacht/Republican News* in 1986.

Each man had three blankets, a mattress and a chamber pot. He also had his thoughts and his comrades.

Everyone was an individual in his own right, with all his peculiar characteristics, abilities and talents, and no one was given any special social status. . . . What mattered was how individually and as a unit we were to get through another day. The common bond of struggle over and above everything else was to provoke thought in anyone willing to open his mind to it and, for those who did, resulted in a critical look at oneself and a reassessment of previously held beliefs. Such a process was to identify very clearly superficial and materialistic aspects of life and to focus beliefs which really mattered.

Endurance had therapeutic value. "I salute courage and sacrifice whenever I find it," Father Raymond Murray, a leading advocate of prison reform, told a meeting of Cumman na Sagart (the Society of Priests) at Maynooth College in December 1978.

Whatever the past deeds of the men in H-blocks may or may not have been and whatever the justice or injustice of the sentences, one has to admire their courage, fortitude and endurance against impossible odds. The Athenian prisoners in the stone quarries of Syracuse could not endure their deprivation for two months. The American and British soldiers collapsed in Korea. The men in H-block . . . have already created a place for themselves in the records of human endurance.[6]

Confrontation alleviated boredom and monotony, lessened the sense of isolation and confinement. Hatred gave meaning, forged camaraderie, boosted morale, became a tool for survival. Need created the ingenuity to fill it. Unable to leave their cells, the prisoners opened small holes between the prefabricated slats of their cells and communicated with each other. Unable to receive educational or reading materials, they taught themselves Irish history and Gaelic, shouting the words and phrases from one cell to the next. Unable to send or receive letters, they used the statutory visits to smuggle out notes—"comms," short for communications (the smuggled letters, often written on scraps of toilet paper, sent by the prisoners to the outside leadership)—and to receive contraband: tobacco and letters, wrapped in plastic wrap, pens, and sometimes larger items such as radio parts, all of which were invariably secreted in the rectum.

In June 1980, the European Commission on Human Rights (ECHR) unanimously rejected a series of complaints from four protesting prisoners who claimed that their conditions of imprisonment were being imposed on them by the British government in violation of a number of articles in the European Convention of Human Rights. "The protest campaign was designed and co-ordinated by the prisoners to create the maximum publicity and to enlist public sympathy and support for their political aims. That such a strategy involved self-inflicted debasement and humiliation to an almost sub-human degree must be taken into account," it reported.

Amnesty International largely eschewed the issue. In its report for 1980, it took official note of the protest for the first time, but confined itself to observing that "although Amnesty International does not support a special status for any prisoners and strongly condemns political assassinations [a reference to the IRA campaign of assassination of prison guards], it has expressed its humanitarian concern to the government on a number of occasions, urging in particular that the prisoners receive adequate exercise and occupational facilities." In 1979 Amnesty wrote to the Board of Visitors of the Maze/Long Kesh Prison (a supervisory body of members of the local community appointed by the secretary of state for Northern Ireland), noting that "the availability of those facilities that are essential for the maintenance of the physical and mental health of prisoners should be *unconditional* and afforded to all prisoners at all times. Insofar as certain facilities may be temporarily withdrawn as punishment, Amnesty International is concerned that the frequent repetition [of the withdrawal of such facilities] or even continuous deprival of such facilities through regularly repeated punishments may have effects that can adversely affect the health of the prisoners." And that was it. In short, the situation of the prisoners at the Maze/Long Kesh Prison did not compel Amnesty International to pursue the matter more diligently. It did not support the aims of the protest; it opposed the granting of political status. On the scale of human abuse, the Republican prisoners' condition ranked low; it merited attention but not action.

Increasingly, faced with more long years of living in stench and filth, in the detritus of their own waste, bereft of any comfort that would reduce the appalling bleakness of their existence, the prisoners wanted to force the issue, and increasingly they began to discuss a hunger strike, for had not a hunger strike been the instrument that had secured special-category status in the first place?

3   **Hunger** striking is not especially Irish: between 1972 and 1982, there were at least 200 hunger strikes in 52 countries, including 23 deaths spread over ten countries. Twelve of the 23 deaths, including the deaths of the 10 hunger strikers who died in 1981, were of Irishmen in United Kingdom jails.

"A hunger strike," says Father James Healy, S.J., who monitors hunger strikes around the world, "is an interaction between two parties. What is so distinctive when this interaction is between Irish and British? Perhaps it is a combination of great determination in both parties, mutual incomprehension, fear and distrust, and in each an unshakeable conviction that any death which occurs will be the responsibility of the other party. In the Irishman there is also likely to be the conviction that he is showing great love in laying down his life for his friends." And, he concludes, "from reading a great deal about Irish hunger strikers I am convinced that any suggestion that they are taking, rather than giving, their lives would sound absurd to them, a plain mistake."

In Ireland the myth of hunger striking is more powerful than the history of hunger striking itself. Hunger striking fuses elements of the legal code of ancient Ireland, of the self-denial that is the central characteristic of Irish Catholicism, and of the propensity for endurance and sacrifice that is the hallmark of militant Irish nationalism. In pre-Christian Ireland the less powerful fasted against the powerful in order to redress a perceived injustice or recover a debt. Indeed, it was the duty of the injured person, when all other remedies had been exhausted, to inflict punishment directly on the wrongdoer. Responsibility for ending the hunger strike rested with the perceived wrongdoer. If he allowed the plaintiff to starve himself to death, he was held responsible for it and had to pay compensation to the victim's family. Thus, from the earliest times, this tradition of passive-aggressiveness, of taking injurious action against oneself for which another was held to be responsible, was given favor.

Fasting quickly established itself in Christian Ireland. The early saints regularly engaged in prolonged fasts to move God on their behalf, and God, it was believed, invariably capitulated in the face of such determined self-sacrifice. Pilgrims to holy places were required to fast—either as penance for their sins or as part of a larger invocation to have their prayers answered; thus the Lenten fast preceded the Easter Resurrection, the communion fast the receiving of the Holy Eucharist. Suffering had value, especially when it was "offered up," united with the sufferings of Christ.

The use of hunger striking for political purposes in Ireland came into vogue after the 1916 Easter Rising. In late 1917, Thomas Ashe, an imprisoned veteran of the 1916 uprising who had refused to work or wear prison clothes, died after being force-fed during a hunger strike Republican prisoners at Mountjoy Prison had undertaken in support of their demand that they be either treated as political prisoners or released.

Ashe's death was immediately seen as martyrdom, part of the heroic legacy of the 1916 rebels whose execution had transformed the political situation in Ireland. His funeral procession, which upwards of forty thousand people, including nine thousand uniformed members of the Irish Volunteers, followed through the streets of Dublin, became an occasion for an outpouring of nationalist grief, providing a rallying point for Sinn Fein, itself coming under increasing criticism for its failure to articulate a national policy.

Three and a half years later, on 24 October 1920, Terence McSwiney died in Brixton prison after a seventy-three-day hunger strike that all of Ireland and much of the world had followed for two months. McSwiney's lonely defiance, and the sense of vicarious participation that the long death vigil engendered, became a symbol of what lengths small Ireland would go to, of what pain she would bear, to assert her independence in the face of the military power of the mighty Empire. His famous words, first uttered during his inauguration as Lord Mayor of Cork in 1920—"It is not those who inflict the most but those who suffer the most who will conquer"—became the theology of mystical Republicanism, the philosophy of nonviolence of physical force separatism, the embodiment of the warrior without weapons, the fighting man as the apostle of passive resistance.

Other hunger strikes followed: in 1923, during the Civil War, antitreaty prisoners staged a massive hunger strike involving at one point eight thousand prisoners. The government responded by having the Dail (parliament) pass a resolution to allow anyone who used the hunger strike against the government to die. The hunger strike resulted in two, and possibly three, deaths. After Fianna Fail came to power in 1932 it proscribed the IRA and began to crack down on former comrades. Eamon de Valera—the new head of government who had led the antitreaty forces during the Civil War—was unyielding: there would be no political status for Republican prisoners. In September 1939, Patrick McGrath, a 1916 veteran, was imprisoned, but the public outcry that followed his hunger strike forced the government to release him after forty-three days. However, it allowed two other IRA men, Tony D'Arcy and Jack McNeela, to die in 1940. (Government censors restricted press coverage of their hunger strike and hence its impact on the public.) "The government have been faced with the alternative of two evils," de Valera declared. "We have had to choose the lesser, and the lesser is to let men die rather than the safety of the whole community be threatened." Six years later, in 1946, Sean McCaughey, the IRA chief of staff at the time of his arrest, went on a hunger strike for political status and was allowed to die after seventeen days.

Billy McKee's hunger strike in 1972 was the first in twenty-five years in Northern Ireland, and the first successful one. Less successful hunger strikes followed. In 1973, the then chief of staff of the IRA, Sean MacStiofan, was arrested in the South, imprisoned, and went on hunger strike. However, he ended his fast after fifty-seven days, and although he maintained that he did so on the orders of the Army Council (the governing body of the IRA), his decision to come off was met with some derision in Republican circles, and he never again held a position of prominence in the Republican movement. ("A hunger strike is a two-sided weapon," he writes in his autobiography, *Revolutionaries in Ireland,* "and it does not work well unless those inside and outside the jail play their part with equal determination. Mine was not getting the usual degree of support given to a hunger strike in the Republican movement. The regular press statements and bulletins about my progress and condition dried up.")[1] The following year two sisters, Dolours and Marian Price, who had been imprisoned in England for a car bombing in London, went on hunger strike demanding the right to serve their sentences in Ireland. After fasting for 200 days, during which they were forcibly fed, the government gave in and they were repatriated. In 1976 two members of the IRA, Michael Gaughan and Frank Stagg, died on hunger strikes in English jails, demanding political status.

In March 1977 about 100 Republican prisoners at Port Laoise Prison in the South embarked on a hunger strike in protest against their conditions of confinement and in pursuit of a number of demands, among them the right to free association. From the beginning, the Irish government adopted an uncompromising stance. "Any adverse consequences to the life or health of a prisoner would be the responsibility of those who ordered the hunger strike," Patrick Cooney, the minister for justice, warned at the onset of the hunger strike, and nothing that followed led to a softening of the official attitude. Public demonstrations on behalf of the prisoners were never very large and only seemed to make a noticeable impact when they sparked off a confrontation with the authorities. After five weeks, hopes that the government would introduce concessions began to fade when prisoner solidarity began to crumble. On 15 April, five weeks into the fast, two hunger strikers, Dan Sullivan and Robert McNamara, ended their protest. Two more men, Philip O'Donnell and Seamus Swann, followed suit a few days later, and the hunger strike itself was called off on 22 April, forty-seven days after it had begun.

However, the fact that hunger strikes had a decidedly less than successful record of accomplishment was of no concern to the blanketmen in the H-blocks in 1980. Their options had narrowed. They either escalated their protest, continued the dirty protest indefinitely, or ended it. The third option was unthinkable, the second unacceptable, leaving only the first, with McKee's singular achievement in 1972 to guide them.

A hunger strike was an instrument of last resort to which the prisoners turned in order to prevent a sense of impotence from taking hold, to counteract the dehumanization that threatened to envelop them. They saw no other way to act. Conditions within the blocks had become intolerable, with the psychological exhaustion as devastating as the physical confinement, the prospect of interminable confrontation distressingly daunting. Emptiness had become complete in itself, the tedium of identical days indeterminate, the rhythms of change lost in the dissolution of time, in the oppressive permanence of the increasingly unbearable present. A hunger strike would allow the prisoners to take action in their own behalf, to empower themselves, to see themselves as something other than victims.

Thus, on 27 October, declaring that there was "no prospect of compromise in sight," seven Republican prisoners—Raymond McCartney from Derry, John Nixon from Armagh City, Sean McKenna from Newry, County Down, Brendan Hughes from Belfast, Leo Green from Lurgan, County Armagh, Thomas McFeeley from Claudy, County Derry, and Thomas McKearney from Moy, County Tyrone—began a hunger strike "to the death" leaving "our lives in the hands of the Irish nation and [our] souls to the most high God." On the Falls Road, almost ten thousand marched in support of the hunger strikers' five demands.

Both the timing and the detail of the hunger strike were planned with meticulous care: the timing to ensure that the fast would peak at Christmas, the choice of seven hunger strikers to provide symbolic union with the seven signatories of the 1916 Declaration of Independence. All seven occupied positions of leadership in the prison command structure. They were mature, prison-wise, and protest-tested, their stamina and endurance proven by long periods on the dirty protest. Six were members of the IRA, one a member of the Irish National Liberation Army (INLA). Three were serving life sentences for killing members of the security forces.

Decisions relating to the hunger strike were taken by the seven and then approved by a committee of the block OCs; a decision to end the fast was not, therefore, the hunger strikers' alone to make. They had surrendered their individual autonomy to the welfare of the larger prison community when they had agreed to undertake a hunger strike. The fast was led by the prison OC, thirty-two-year-old Brendan Hughes, from the Falls area of Belfast. Hughes came from a family with a rich Republican tradition: his father and uncle were former internees and he had a brother who was also imprisoned in the Maze/Long Kesh.

The issue hardened right away. The Social Democratic and Labour Party (SDLP), the voice of constitutional nationalism, called for prisoners to be allowed to wear their own clothes. The Unionist parties condemned the government's offer of civilian-type clothing as "the first step of capitulation to the evil men of the H-blocks." The National H-block Committee, which spearheaded the public campaign on behalf of the prisoners and covered a wide spectrum of nationalist opinion, pressed the prisoners' case: if there were two kinds of law, two kinds of court, two kinds of justice, there were two kinds of prisoners. And British Prime Minister Margaret Thatcher put herself unambiguously on the record: there would be no concessions to the hunger strikers, there was no such thing as political murder. Both communities in Northern Ireland, however, had rather jaundiced views of British "nevers."

Inside the prison it was a different story: the government encouraged dialogue. It allowed Bobby Sands, who became prison OC in place of Hughes, to sit in on discussions Hughes had with officials from the Northern Ireland Office (NIO); it allowed Hughes to contact outside advisers; and it allowed a procession of would-be intermediaries to visit him. Father Brendan Meagher, a Redemptorist priest from Dublin who had contacts with the IRA, the Republican movement, and the NIO, was allowed into the prison in early December and became an unofficial go-between, the conduit for messages or hints of messages from one party to another. The authorities' behind-the-scenes eagerness to facilitate negotiations, to find some basis of compromise, stood in paradoxical contrast to their public posture: the repeated and insistent announcements that there would be no concessions, no response to attempted blackmail, no granting of any kind of special status. Their willingness to accept Sands as the spokesman for the prisoners-at-large amounted to an unofficial if expedient acknowledgment that the prisoners were in fact somehow different.

The circumstances in which the first hunger strike ended remain murky. The governor of the prison, Stanley Hilditch, and John Blelloch, a senior representative of the NIO, met the hunger strikers on or about 12 December and attempted to spell out what was on offer. They presented Hughes with a thirty-four-page document from the NIO outlining what would be available once the hunger strike ended. Prisoners coming off the protest would be put in clean cells; within a few days they would be given clothing provided by their families, which they could wear during association and visits. As soon as possible, they would be provided with civilian-type clothing to be worn during the working day. Prisoners would also be able to associate within each wing of the blocks in the evening and at weekends; "work" would not be narrowly interpreted—it might even be defined to include educational activities. It should be possible, the document went on, "to work out for every prisoner the kind of available activity which we think suits him best."

The contents of the document were circulated in the blocks, debated for several days, and a consensus arrived at: despite strong reservations and misgivings in some quarters, the block OCs, Sands told the hunger strikers, felt that if the hunger strikers themselves believed that the document provided the basis for a solution, they would defer to the hunger strikers' decision, especially in view of Sean McKenna's deteriorating condition. However, they also felt that several clarifications were called for to pin down precisely what was on offer, the understanding being that if satisfactory clarifications were forthcoming the hunger strike would be called off. The hunger strikers believed as a result of their discussions with Hilditch and Blelloch and from their reading of the NIO documents in their possession that they were heading toward what they called a Port Laoise-type solution; but they also knew that there was no question of their being granted full political status. (Under the prison regime in operation at the Port Laoise Prison, Republican prisoners—like all prisoners in the South—can wear their own clothes at all times; they have special rights of association; there are broad definitions of what constitutes work; each Republican grouping—Provisional, Official, and INLA—is segregated; the prison governor meets with the men's elected OCs on an occasional basis to discuss grievances and problems; but there is no question of the prisoners having a special status or of their being treated as prisoners of war who run their own affairs.) Hughes, according to Pat McGeown, one of the block OCs, sent word back to Sands: clothes did not appear to be a problem but problems continued to exist in other areas. Further clarifications would be required.

At this point a number of events conspired to force the hunger strikers' hand. First, Hughes was informed that the Republican movement had been in contact through an intermediary with a senior civil servant at the Foreign Office. It appeared that a second, more sympathetic channel of communication had opened up, that the Foreign Office would propose additional clarifications regarding a post–hunger strike prison regime that would go beyond NIO proposals. (The Foreign Office traditionally has been assumed to be more sympathetic to Irish aspirations than the NIO.) Father Meagher was instructed by Sinn Fein to go to Belfast Airport on the evening of 18

December to meet a man—he would be wearing a red carnation—who would have with him copies of the additional clarifications prepared by the Foreign Office. (Even as this was happening, SDLP leader John Hume was telling Cardinal Thomas O'Fiaich that on the morning of 18 December the British Cabinet had considered and then turned down two proposals—one that would have allowed the prisoners to purchase their own civilian-type clothing, and a second that would have provided for a broader form of association—despite Northern Ireland secretary of state Humphrey Atkins's backing of both.)

However, on the morning of the eighteenth Sean McKenna, who had been going downhill for days (his eyesight had begun to fail) began to sink rapidly, lapsing in and out of consciousness. Late in the afternoon he was given the Last Rites and transferred to Royal Victoria Hospital. Hughes faced a crisis. McKenna, it was clear, had not long to live, and might be either dead or have entered a stage of irreversible decline by the time the Foreign Office clarifications reached the prison and a decision was made regarding their efficaciousness.

One doctor told Father Tom Murphy, one of the prison chaplains, that McKenna had probably less than twelve hours to live. Hughes had made a promise to McKenna: he would not let him die if he was convinced that they were at the point of winning their demands. In Hughes's view they had reached or were about to reach that point. His promise to McKenna bound him and he would honor it. He moved to call the hunger strike off. Not all the hunger strikers agreed with him, however. Tom McFeeley, in particular, strongly argued that the hunger strike should be allowed to follow its natural course, that the British couldn't be trusted to negotiate in good faith, that once the hunger strike was called off the outcome of their discussions with the British would be entirely dependent on British good will, that they had, in short, to maintain the pressure of the hunger strike to the very end, even if it meant some of them dying, or lose the only leverage they had. At first he refused to abandon his fast, and it took the better part of an hour to convince him otherwise.

Hughes was immovable: the clarifications they sought were on their way, the Foreign Office initiative clearly indicated British eagerness to settle the issue, and if McKenna died needlessly, there would be hell to pay in their own communities—and the other hunger strikers backed him.

At 7:46 P.M. on 18 December, they called off the hunger strike. (Strictly speaking, they didn't have the authority to do so. According to the protocol established before the hunger strike started, a decision to end it would have to be approved by the hunger strikers themselves, a committee of block OCs, and the outside leadership.) At the suggestion of Father Tom Toner, another prison chaplain (at this point the hunger strikers were somewhat at a loss for an explanation for their abrupt action that would not leave the impression that they had simply given up) they issued a statement saying they had come off the fast in response to the request of Cardinal O'Fiaich, and indeed, the following morning, in its lead story, the *Irish Times* duly reported that "the strikers said they were responding to the appeal to them from the Primate of All-Ireland Cardinal Thomas O'Fiaich to end their protest."

Meanwhile, however, Father Meagher had picked up the additional documents at Belfast Airport and taken them to Sinn Fein, who made copies of them, and then he went directly to the prison, where he delivered them to Hughes and Sands hours after the hunger strike had ended. It was clear that the clarifications on offer did not meet the prisoners' specifications, but there was, of course, no undoing what had been done. The hunger strikers' official statement, drafted by Sinn Fein and sent into the prison with Father Meagher for their approval before it was issued (Meagher had been with Sinn Fein when news that the hunger strike had been called off came through) fudged the issue. They had ended their hunger strike, they said, "after . . . having been supplied with a document that contains a new elaboration of our five demands." But they warned that "in ending our hunger strike we make it clear that a failure of the British government to act in a responsible manner towards ending the conditions which forced us to a hunger strike will lead not only to inevitable and continued strife within the H-block but will also show quite clearly the intransigence of the British government."

Whatever the exact circumstances surrounding the ending of the first hunger strike, one thing was clear: the prisoners' demands were not met. The widespread perception was that the prisoners had backed down when they saw that McKenna's life was on the line. Indeed, the organization of the hunger strike—seven prisoners undertaking their fasts simultaneously—had a built-in structural weakness: the chain of fasting prisoners was only as strong as its weakest link. The threat to it came not from the outside from the refusal of the authorities to negotiate their demands, but from within, from the unwillingness of the prisoners to allow one of their own to die when the first of them weakened and his physical condition began to deteriorate. They were prepared to force others to be the instruments of their deaths, but they themselves would not be the instruments of one another's deaths. When the burden of the decision to allow one another to die became theirs and not others, they could not bear the burden, and group cohesion collapsed.

The prisoners, however, tried to seize the moment. The ending of the hunger strike was to be treated as if there were a settlement—the intention was to see what the government was prepared to concede now that there was no longer any question of its having to act under duress.

The intention simply dissolved. Protesting prisoners were confused: what appeared to be on offer seemed no different from what had been an offer all along; the assumption that they would be supplied with their own clothes prior to the issue of prison-issue clothing was mistaken, and hence their strategy—to ignore prison-issue clothing once they were in possession of their own—became irrelevant. Prisoners who had joined the dirty protest in large numbers during the hunger strike in anticipation of a favorable resolution of the status issue began to abandon it in equally large numbers, threatening to undermine the solidarity of the protest. In contrast, other prisoners, including the INLA inmates, categorically refused to consider the wearing of prison-issue clothing before being given their own. The hunger strike had solved nothing. The circumstances of its ending eroded morale.

4   Initially there was euphoria on the blocks when the hunger strike ended. The British, Sands told the block OCs, had agreed to a settlement, an agreement had been hammered out, and the British had sent in a document agreeing to certain interpretations that would give the prisoners the essence of the five demands. But he knew this wasn't the case. In private conversations with members of the prison command he would maintain that what was on offer "wasn't what we were fighting for." "I'm going around," Jake Jackson recalls him confiding to Brendan McFarlane—Jackson and McFarlane occupied

the cell next to Sands and McFarlane would become the prison OC
when Sands went on hunger strike,

and I'm looking at people and their faces are staring out the [cell-door] windows
and they're all waiting on you bringing good news and I'm giving them what
is apparently good news but I know that we're going to be forced into another
hunger strike because the Brits will renege: there's no way that they are going
to give. I'm going around and I should be bringing good news to everybody
and I know on the surface it all sounds like good news but it's not. I know what's
happening, the ground's been cut out from under us and there's no hunger strike
anymore.

In his heart Sands knew they had lost, and the loss devastated him.
He held himself responsible, blaming himself for being wrong-footed
and outwitted by the authorities, for being too trusting of their gestures of good faith, for being duped by their willingness to deal with
him, for trusting promises made by the British when he should have
known better, for the breakdown in communications between the
hunger strikers and the prison command. He was the first to raise
the question of a second hunger strike. Within a day of the hunger
strike's end he was importuning the IRA leadership to be allowed to
restart the protest himself immediately. But the leadership was inflexible: for the time being the movement would follow the strategy
that had been agreed on—the prisoners would claim victory, call the
authorities' proposals a satisfactory expression of the five demands,
assert that appropriate assurances had been given where there appeared
to be differences in interpretation, claim the moral high ground, and
hope that the public climate of relief that accompanied the end of the
strike would force the government to respond favorably.

But Sands was not mollified, and his resolve hardened as events
unfolded. Within the prison he was under pressure from Patsy
O'Hara, the OC of the thirty INLA prisoners on the dirty protest,
who vowed that he would start another hunger strike for political
status irrespective of what the IRA prisoners might do. Governor
Hilditch's new policy of dealing with the prisoners on a one-to-one
basis began to erode Sands's authority, the steady trickle of prisoners
to conforming status was undermining solidarity, the recriminations
over how the first hunger strike had ended (some argued that if the
hunger strikers had held out another twenty-four or forty-eight hours,
even if it meant Sean McKenna's death, they would have won a clear
victory) and the disputes over what was on offer—all these pressures

called for mediating skills he did not possess. "Bobby didn't rely an awful lot on too many people," says Jake Jackson. "He would have bounced ideas off certain people but he led from the inside out."

The fragile boundaries of the closed universe of protest in which Sands had lived for the better part of his adult life began to deconstruct, compelling him to take action to reassert control, to hold it together, to save the protest. Sands became insistent: he would assume the burden of a new hunger strike. There would be no misunderstandings because there would be no negotiations. Either the government would capitulate, giving in to the five demands, or he would die. If he died, the public furor would compel the government to bend. If the hunger strike collapsed, the government would have won, protesting would be over, the prisoners would have lost. The hunger strike, therefore, would not collapse—he would see to that.

Once again there was the same attention to detail. Three other prisoners—two IRA prisoners selected by Sands himself and Patsy O'Hara, the INLA OC—would follow him on the hunger strike at fixed intervals to keep the maximum pressure on the government; the strike would start on 1 March 1981—the fifth anniversary of the date on which the government had started to phase out special status; it would climax at Easter, the anniversary of the 1916 Uprising and symbol of redemption and resurrection. "I am standing," Sands wrote in a diary he kept when he began his fast, "on the threshold of another trembling world. May God have mercy on my soul." Sands's private imagination would become a public event.

It was, of course, the manner of his dying for which he was remembered, not the circumstances of his life. But it is these circumstances—the deceptive surface ordinariness of Belfast, a city that concealed but could not quite contain the hate-filled sectarian disease that infected suffocating working-class rhythms, where the young grew up with no expectation of escape and no prospect of something better—that shaped Sands's life. When those circumstances changed, when the familiar became threatening and the threatening overwhelming, Sands became a victim: the circumstances simply devoured him and spat him out again in their own image.

He was born in 1954, the eldest of four children, in Rathcoole, one of the huge, dreary, sprawling housing estates that cordon Belfast. His family was neither Republican nor especially nationalist. His father worked for the Post Office; his mother, not unlike many

Irish Catholic mothers, was devout to a fault. They lived in Abbots Cross, a predominantly Protestant suburb of Newtownabbey. But when Sands was seven, they were forced to move when their neighbors learned that they were Catholics (their name was not obviously so). (According to a BBC program, "Old Scores," a documentary on a local Catholic youth club called the Star of the Sea, which had a mixed soccer team on which Catholic boys, including Sands, played alongside Protestant teammates, the Sands's marriage was a mixed one. The father, it claims, was Protestant, but even if the report is true—and there is some reason to doubt that it is—it would have been at least more accurate to say that the father was a convert to Catholicism. Many dispute the BBC's account; it was Sands's grandfather on his father's side, they maintain, who was Protestant; still others dismiss the entire matter, but there are some who attributed Sands's highly developed sense of individualism, his stress on individual conscience and his own direct relationship to God—standards of morality he would later challenge the Catholic clergy with—to his having the leftovers of an inherited Protestant mentality, the residue of Protestant genes somewhere in the bloodlines.) Mrs. Sands became the target of an orchestrated campaign of harassment by her nextdoor neighbor, according to Sands's sister, Bernadette, and when the choice came down to either taking the woman in question to court or leaving, her parents, says Bernadette, "being so quiet and not wanting to bother anyone, gave up the house." The family moved back to Rathcoole, also a predominantly loyalist district, kept to themselves, and though they were living again amid Protestant neighbors, there were no problems.

Many people who knew Sands when he was growing up in Rathcoole or during the time he lived in Twinbrook later on are reluctant to talk about him. Most will do so only with the assurance that their names will be held in confidence. Their reluctance stems in part from the fact that they appear to be afraid they might say something that will contradict or detract from the accepted mythology about Sands that has become a standard part of Republican lore since his death, something that could be interpreted as being derogatory or at least not sufficiently reverential, or something not sufficiently supportive that might be traced back to them—and also in part because there is so little to remember. Moreover, those who knew him now tend to filter their memories through their perceptions of his later actions: they frequently look for the qualities of leadership and single-mindedness he later displayed, and because they cannot locate them in their memories they blame themselves for some defect of the mind, for failing to see in the child the qualities that would later distinguish the man. They want to apologize for their own lack of memory, for their prior inattention, for being unable to come up with some anecdote that would shed light on the inner workings of his character.

But if it is difficult to reconstruct the whole of Sands's past, it is easy to deal with what little there is to reconstruct—he had spent one third of his twenty-seven years in jail at the time of his death—because it was so ordinary; indeed, the most extraordinary thing about Sands was his unremitting ordinariness. He had no special gifts, he did not stand out, shine at school, show special leadership qualities, do anything that would attract anything more than passing attention.

He did have one consuming passion: he loved sports of every kind. Whether it was soccer or Gaelic football, basketball or cross-country running or table tennis, Sands was both an avid participant and observer. Sometimes his enthusiasm made up for his lack of natural ability, but that was of little consequence: what mattered to him was the game itself, the involvement. He mixed easily but was a loner of sorts. "He had a lot of friends," says one school teacher who was close to him, "and he was thought very highly of by the rest of the boys but to an extent he kept to himself." He got involved but he held back. There was a part of him, even as a child, that he kept to himself.

Two images, perhaps, capture the essence of both his vulnerability and his stubbornness, qualities that would give a special poignancy to his later actions. One former primary school teacher has a vivid memory of him, a young boy at the Stella Maris Secondary School, who always wore a blazer that was too tight for him. "I can always remember this young man," she says, "very trim, not too tall, with dirty sort of sandy colored hair and the sort of skin that freckles easily and he always had this blazer that seemed a bit tight and wore a scarf and sometimes he wore the scarf under the blazer which made it tighter still." And then there is Father Denis Faul's recollection of Sands on his way to meet the Governor of the Maze/Long Kesh Prison some weeks before the second hunger strike got under way. (Faul was a frequent visitor to the prison and a staunch advocate of prison reform who would eventually bring the relatives of the hunger strikers together to end the strike.) "It was," he says, "extraordinary to see this thin, emaciated-looking character in a ragged pair of trousers, bare feet, bare chest, going out, so to speak, to dialogue with the representative of the almighty British government."

Filling the space between these two images is Sands's life—the young boy who ran errands for his teachers, who hung endlessly around the school after hours either playing games or watching others play, a fitness fanatic; a boy of average scholastic ability not considered sufficiently promising by his teachers to be put forward for O-level examinations, but one who, nevertheless, was given lots of responsibility and who responded with an earnestness that suggested a desire to oblige rather than a need to ingratiate; a boy who could be depended on, trustworthy, well liked, integrated into the school's activities, at ease with himself and with others; the young man without a political thought in his head who came to see himself as a freedom fighter; the prison propagandist and fledgling writer; and finally, Republican martyr.

The words "average" and "ordinary" and "easily fitting in" keep cropping up in conversation with those who knew Sands before his involvement with the Republican movement. If anything, he is remembered as being a follower. He was the closest friend of Tommy O'Neill, the star football player, the boy, people believed, who would make it into First Division English football—the natural player who attracted the kind of attention from his peers that young "star" athletes attract. "Tommy led the way. Tommy got the girls," one former teammate recalls. "Tommy did all the stuff and Bobby followed, it was as simple as that." The two were almost inseparable. They went to the Stella Maris Secondary School together and they played soccer together on the same team at the Star of the Sea Youth Club.

The club, if not perhaps typical of its time, provides a good insight into Belfast in the mid-1960s, of how the signs of surface normality could easily be mistaken for social cohesiveness, of how easily things fall apart when the social organism itself is diseased and inherently unstable. Catholic and Protestant boys played on the same team, were friends with each other, went to the same discos. Two or three times a year they would travel to Dublin to play clubs there and would pass the travel time singing each other's rebel songs: "Sean South of Garryowen" alternating with "The Sash My Father Wore." It was all in good fun, and politics of any color—green, orange, or other hue—were the furthest thing from anybody's mind. No one minded if you were Catholic or Protestant: if you were a half-decent football player you were on the team, if you weren't, that was it. Yet within a few years three members of Sands's team would be in jail for paramilitary activities—Sands himself for his involvement with the IRA, and two young Protestant teammates, Terry Nichols and Michael Acheson, for having gotten caught up in the Protestant paramilitary Ulster Volunteer Force (UVF). Getting involved was an accident of circumstance, especially in working-class areas, not evidence of social deviancy.

Sands might not have been a great football player—many of his teammates remember him as being a "hacker," a physical player who made up for his lack of skill with his aggressiveness—but good enough to make the team. (In time myth would transform even this. In a memorial piece that appeared in *An Phoblacht/Republican News* after Sands's death, Danny Devenny, who had done time with Sands in the compounds in the mid-1970s recalls that Sands was "a fantastic footballer, not of the George Best dribbling mold, but a thinker, a planner, a tactician . . . one of the best footballers I have ever played against in jail, not only at soccer but Gaelic as well.") But above all, former teammates remember Sands as a team player, a player who would run the length of the field to come to the assistance of a teammate who had gotten into a fight. The team always came first. He would come to your aid not because he liked you but because you were a member of his team. Other than that he was just "Sandsy," one of twenty-plus football players.

At home he displayed the same kind of protectiveness toward his two sisters that he provided for his teammates on the football field. "When we were kids he was always protecting us—myself and Marcella," his sister Bernadette would recall in *An Phoblacht/Republican News* the week before he died. "If anyone went to hit us he would jump in. He was always small for his age and he used to get murdered by different fellows on the street and still he would go out and beat them back." And he was stubborn, she recalled: "If we had done something wrong in the house, my mother would put us outside to play and then when she called us in Bobby wouldn't come. He would wait until she asked him. There was always this stubborn attitude the whole time."

Although he mixed easily he didn't belong to any particular group. One of his favorite sports was cross-country running and he was good at it, running for the Willowfield Temperance Harriers, a predominantly Protestant running club, and winning many prizes. At fifteen he left school, worked for a while as a barman at the Glenn

Inn in Glengormley, and then started as an apprentice coach builder with H. W. Alexander on the Antrim Road in March 1970, when he was sixteen.

But already the world in which he had grown up had begun to disintegrate. Belfast was at war. The underlying divisions between the two communities had exploded in violent confrontation in 1968. Whole areas were under attack; vigilante defense committees patrolled the streets of their respective neighborhoods. Families in mixed areas were routinely burned out, atavistic territorial imperatives once again reasserting themselves. The largest displacement of a civilian population in peacetime Europe was under way as people sought the protection of their own tribal enclaves. The British army, originally sent in to restore order and protect lives in August 1969, had become one more source of disorder from whom Catholics in particular sought protection. Internment without trial solidified support in the Catholic community for the IRA. Within two years Sands was intimidated out of his job (some co-workers threatened to shoot him and he found a note in his lunch box telling him to get out) and in Rathcoole the situation became intolerable.

Rathcoole was the largest housing estate in Northern Ireland. In 1952 construction began on a site of 366 acres on the lower slopes of Carnmoney Hill, six miles north of Belfast. Eventually 3,800 dwellings with a population of 10,000—one-quarter of whom would be Catholic—were built. By Northern Ireland standards it was an exceptionally well integrated estate, but from the beginning it had problems: a lack of recreational and community facilities. Although it represented a genuine attempt to build a balanced mixed community, there was no real feeling of community: Rathcoole was apart from Belfast, but it was never independent of it, and people's primary sense of where they were from invariably focused on their Belfast origins, their tribal roots.

In 1969, when violence exploded in Belfast, Derry, and other places, Rathcoole was free of disturbances. But the peace didn't last. By mid-1971 the Provisional IRA bombing campaign was under way, and the character of the estate began to change, imperceptibly at first and then with a vengeance. Protestant families intimidated out of their residences in West and North Belfast began to move in, altering the delicate demographic balance of the estate, bringing with them tales of the horrors to which they had been subjected and a largely unarticulated desire for revenge. The Protestant paramilitary Ulster

Defence Association (UDA) set up a branch in Rathcoole. It was a blatantly sectarian organization that set up barricades at entrances to the estate and assumed the duties of policing. The "Tartan" gang and other teenage hooligan elements would congregate at the barricades and harass and intimidate Catholic residents of the estate as they came and went about their business. Following the introduction of internment in August 1971, intimidation of Catholics became an everyday occurrence and the situation steadily grew worse there in the absence of adequate protection by either the police or the army: the collapse of communal order was increasingly evident. Barricades went up again in June 1972 and for three days entrance to the estate was barred to all vehicles except those approved at the barricades. Because there was an inadequate police presence, intimidation went unchallenged. Families sat up late into the night tuned into the police channel to find out exactly where the mob was, which street they were heading toward, waiting for the anonymous fire bombs that would come hurling though the window. Children, exhausted from being up all night, fell asleep in school. ("The mob was outside his door last night, sir, he was up all night," children would tell their teachers.) But in Stella Maris there was little talk in the school itself about what was going on. The denial of the reality outside its doors was a complicity of sorts, as if silence itself were the incantation that would exorcise the demons of sectarianism that possessed the mobs prowling the streets, encircling homes. Parents invariably kept their troubles to themselves, often arriving, distraught, at the school in the middle of the day to take their children away. Flight of Catholic families from Rathcoole became commonplace, squatting by incoming Protestant families was organized by the UDA, and as squatting became more frequent, the pressure on the remaining Catholic families to get out became more intense.

The six Catholic families on the Sands's street came under increasing threats from the UDA. Mobs of chanting youths would gather outside their houses, petrol bombs came through windows at all hours of the night, and in the end, according to Sands's sister Bernadette, many of Sands's Protestant friends were among those who helped to force his family out of its home: "It ended up when everything erupted that the friends [Sands] went about with for years were the same ones who joined the Tartan gangs, pointed him out and got him beaten. When we were put out of Rathcoole we found out afterwards that it was our own neighbors who helped to put us out."

It was something Sands would not forget. Some years later when he was a special-category prisoner in an IRA compound at Long Kesh, Terry Nichols, his former teammate from his Star of the Sea soccer days who had joined the UVF, was a special-category prisoner in a UVF compound adjacent to Sands's. One day he saw Sands across the open space separating the two compounds. "I called him over [to the wire]," Nichols says, "and he refused to come. I think he didn't want his friends to know that he actually associated himself with any Protestants. I was shouting at him and calling his name and he kept on looking at his friends, as if to say who's that, I don't really know him, you know." Nichols may not have realized it fully, but they were now playing on different teams.

"The whole world exploded and my own little world crumbled around me," Sands would later write in *An Phoblacht/Republican News*. "The TV did not have to tell the story for now it was on my own doorstep. Belfast was in flames but it was our districts and humble homes which were burned. The Specials came at the head of the RUC and Orange hordes, right into the heart of our streets, burning, shooting, looting and murdering." The Sandses finally did what so many families on both sides of the religious divide did. They fled, found an empty house in a Catholic neighborhood, and moved in.

Sands grieved for their "humble" home. Years later in prison he wrote a short essay entitled "Once I Had a Life." In it he recalls looking down at Rathcoole, "a massive concrete jungle," one summer afternoon from a perch, "an earthen mound" on Cave Hill, the mountain in whose shadow Rathcoole stands. "There were deck-chairs in the gardens where the sunworshipers gloated in contentment," he wrote. "I retraced my gaze and found with ease our old house. Nobody I knew was there any more, just strangers, who trimmed the lawn around the ash tree that I grew up with. The fence needed a coat of paint and the front garden had been deflowered of its colour— my mother's and father's pride and joy. An old dog chased its tail on the street where we once played 'kick the tin' and the old fellows made their way to the bookies for the first two across the card."

"Any severe loss may represent a disruption in one's relationship to the past, to the present and to the future," Marc Fried writes in *Grieving for a Lost Home*. "It is a disruption in that sense of continuity which is ordinarily a taken-for-granted framework for functioning in a universe which has temporal, social and spatial dimensions." The loss of an important place "represents a change in a potentially significant component of the experience of continuity."[1] The sense of belonging is severed; the focus of meaningful interpersonal relationships is destroyed; the sense of spatial identity—that sum of experiences that are grounded in spatial memories, spatial imagery, and the spatial framework of social activities which is fundamental to human functioning—is traumatized; the sense of group identity, of communality with other people, of shared human qualities, is undermined.

Within months of the family's move in June 1972 to Twinbrook, a Catholic estate on the outskirts of West Belfast which had lost its Protestant population in much the same way that Rathcoole had lost its Catholic population, Sands joined the IRA, his search for structure in part a search for his lost self. He didn't do so because of some burning belief in the ideals of Republicanism, or a commitment to Irish unity, or even a hatred for the British. The reason was almost a nonreason and, therefore, more disturbing, because many young people like Sands, who had just turned eighteen, didn't make decisions to join paramilitary organizations—they simply drifted into them, with consequences out of all proportion to the level of motivation that led them to join in the first place. It seemed like the thing to do. A brother, a cousin, a friend, a neighbor had been picked up and interned, and getting involved became a way of getting back at the actions of the army, of protesting the house searches, street harassment, checkpoints, random arrests, casual intimidations, the sense of being invaded and under collective arrest, of acting out what were often intensely held feelings of personal affronts. Even the knowledge that friends or neighbors had joined up was sufficient. You were helping out, lending a hand to those protecting the community. The impulse to join up had its roots in the day-to-day happenings on the streets of your own neighborhood rather than in the sacrosanct ideology of militant Republicanism. It was a way of adjusting to the extreme conditions of everyday reality when existing beliefs were no longer sufficient to sustain a sense of coherence, when the need to reconstruct and reinterpret the world around you became a matter of survival. Our sense of self is deeply entwined with a sense of ethnicity and nationality,[2] and in times of stress during political crises, we adhere more stubbornly than ever to a sense of ethnicity[3] in order to maintain that sense of self. "I had seen too many homes wrecked, fathers and sons arrested, neighbours hurt, friends murdered. Too much gas, shooting and blood, most of it our own people's. At eighteen and a half I joined the Provos," Sands wrote.

Less than six months after he had joined the IRA, Sands was arrested when four handguns were found in a house where he was staying. In prison he blossomed. He was assigned to Cage 11, where Gerry Adams, who would later become president of Sinn Fein, was OC. Cage 11, Adams recalled in a lecture he delivered on the fourth anniversary of Sands's death, "was a different kind of Cage with the development of a discipline which owed more to comradeship and collective commitment than it did to square-bashing." "As soon as you walked into our recreation hut," said Jake Jackson, an internee there at the time, "there were murals, it was just an ordinary portocabin with a lot of desks and chairs and a blackboard, and on the left side of the blackboard was a massive proclamation, the Proclamation of the Irish Republic with the heads of the signatories drawn around it, and on the opposite side was a big portrait, the red face, black beret, and star of Che Guevera. So you had Guevera and 1916."

Sands easily fitted in. He eagerly participated in the lectures and discussion groups on history, politics, and culture that Adams organized. He discovered the poet Eithne Carbery and began to experiment with his own verse. He developed an avid interest in the Irish language, spending months in a special hut in the Cage where only Gaelic was spoken and becoming within a short period of time a fluent speaker, a teacher of the language to others, and the proud possessor of a "fainne"—the Irish language movement's gold pin, official confirmation of one's fluency in the language. (Eamonn Mallie, a reporter for Downtown Radio and himself a fluent Gaelic speaker, recalls visiting Sands along with two other journalists in late 1979 when the dirty protest was in full swing. When Sands learned that Mallie spoke Gaelic he immediately switched languages and spoke only Gaelic for the duration of the meeting. "His Irish," Mallie says, "was unbelievable. He was so fluent he embarrassed me. His use of language, turn of phrase, total control of the language was quite remarkable. I knew I was in the presence of someone who was a first or second honours student in University in terms of ability to achieve.")

It was part of a process of transformation: he was reshaping himself in a new cultural mold, remaking his identity. He became Riobard O'Seachnasaich, not Robert Sands—O'Seachnasaich being the closest

Gaelic approximation to the name Sands that he could come up with. (The name Sands originates in England from the name Sandys, and in Scotland its use dates from approximately the end of the fifteenth century. It was "imported" into Ulster in the 1660s. It has, therefore, no Gaelic equivalent. Cardinal O'Fiaich tells of receiving a letter from a prisoner in the H-blocks written in Irish and signed by Riobard O'Seachnasaich. The cardinal, translating O'Seachnasaich into its English equivalent, believed the letter had come from a Robert O'Shaughnessy, and when he asked the prison authorities the whereabouts of a prisoner with that name they were nonplussed, having no record of an O'Shaughnessy.)

Other transformations followed, among them an eagerness to compensate for the lack of proven Republican credentials in his own past. Later, when he was on the blanket, he would take his quest to authenticate his Republican antecedents a step further when he described how he imbibed Republican stories from his mother. "From my earliest days," he wrote in *An Phoblacht/Republican News,* "I recall my mother speaking of the troubled times that occurred during her childhood. Often she spoke of internment on prison ships, of gun attacks and death, and of early morning raids when one lay listening with pounding heart to the heavy clattering of boots on the cobblestone streets, and as a new day broke, peeked carefully out of the window to see a neighbor being taken away by the Specials." And so, "although I never really understood what internment was or who the Specials were, I grew up to regard them as symbols of evil. Nor could I understand when my mother spoke of Connolly and the 1916 Uprising, and of how he and his comrades fought and were subsequently executed—a fate suffered by so many Irish rebels in my mother's stories." In his new identity his mother's enthusiastic support for his involvement with the IRA was unequivocal: "At eighteen and a half I joined the Provos. My mother wept with pride and joy as I went out to meet and confront the imperial might of an empire with an MI carbine and enough hate to topple the world."

The characteristics that would dominate his later personality also came into sharper focus. An iron determination to do what he set out to do, a stubbornness to adhere to his own point of view, an intensity that later in the H-blocks would become more focused still, an unwillingness to concede anything in argument, little time for small talk, a certain ill-humor when crossed, an impatience that alternated between an edgy nervousness and boundless energy, a single-

mindedness that made him often impervious to what others felt
or said—and above all else a loyalty to his fellow prisoners. He was
at all times the team player, although still very much the loner, a
prickly personality who nevertheless always went out of his way to
entertain, to energize, or otherwise cheer on his prison comrades.
Eventually, he became OC of one of the three huts in the cage, and
later training officer for the cage itself.

The uncertainty of life outside the prison—where neighbors and
friends could turn on you, where ordinary events like walking the
street or going to work or even living in your home were occasions
of potential menace, where there was no order or logic or explanation
for the way things worked, where control of what was going to
happen was always in the hands of others, where meager ambitions
were the limits of your horizon, where your sense of the reality of
things was not to be trusted—was replaced with certainty, with a
coherent framework that provided an interpretation for what was
happening, with the context of a history that identified the villains,
pinpointed the scapegoats, and spelled out the panaceas, with a sense
of belonging, of trusting, of meaning, with a structure that provided
security, comradeship, and support.

He became an articulate debater, a voracious reader, immersing
himself in the writings of Frantz Fanon, Che Guevera, George Jackson, and Camilo Torres, revolutionaries who called for the empow-
erment of the downtrodden, the wretched, the forgotten. For these
writers a shared dialect of perceived oppression provides the context
in which everything is a question of "us" versus "them," of "good"
versus "evil," pitting the undifferentiated masses of oppressed people
against the collective forces of an imperialistic, antihuman social order
teetering on collapse, propping itself up through violent repression.
The solidarity of the oppressors has to be matched by the solidarity
of the oppressed, by their unity of purpose as they struggle to recover
their identities.

Each of these writers adheres to a cult of violence: violence has a
positive value; it is an act of meaning rather than an act of destruction.
For Guevera death is the reality, victory the dream. For Fanon, "violence alone, violence committed by the people, violence organized
and educated by its leaders, makes it possible for the masses to understand social truths and gives the key to them."[4] Violence "is a
cleansing force. It frees the native from his inferiority complex and
from his despair and inaction; it makes him fearless and restores his

self-respect."[5] Fanon's views on revolutionary violence, with their emphasis on "the good [for natives] is quite simply that which is evil for 'them,' [colonists]"[6] had special appeal for Sands. They bore striking similarities to the views of Patrick Pearse, who resoundingly endorsed bloodshed as "a cleansing and a sanctifying thing," and resoundingly condemned "a nation which regards [bloodshed] as the final horror" as having "lost its manhood."[7] For Jackson, "if people are to understand and relate to revolutionary violence they must first be educated into an acceptance of the fact that there is no alternative. . . ."[8]

Each harps on the oppressor's obsession with destroying the self of the oppressed, with murdering his consciousness, erasing his identity, destroying his language, obliterating his traditions, emasculating his culture. Each emphasizes the necessity to expurgate the false consciousness the oppressor imbues the oppressed with. Each recalls loss and asserts that only through the use of violence can innocence, the idealized past, be discovered, that only violence can restore, only violence can eradicate the fatalism that is the hallmark of the colonial experience.

Each idealizes revolutionary death and the redemption of identity through violent struggle. Each subscribes to what Huey Newton, who drew heavily on their teachings in developing his own revolutionary theories, called "revolutionary suicide"[9]—the belief that it is better to oppose the forces that would drive you to self-murder (reactionary suicide) than to endure them. And each romanticized violence as a way of resolving the tensions in their own personal crises of identity. "The ideal of revolution as an irreconcilable opposition of classes," writes Peter Marris in *Loss and Change,* "has a . . . powerful appeal for those who have lost their sense of belonging." It "relieves the threat of personal disintegration, because the structure of conflict offers a side to take, a reference for behavior, a meaning to the experience of loss: and with this reassurance, life becomes manageable again."[10]

When Sands was released in 1976 he was no longer a naïve eighteen-year-old but a committed proponent of Republican separatism with a newly developed sense of self-awareness. He returned to Twinbrook, where he lived with his wife and their three-year-old son, Gerald. According to his sister Bernadette, he threw himself exuberantly into community activity, joining the local tenants' association, persuading the Black Taxis to run in the area, setting up a branch of Sinn Fein, launching his own Republican newsletter, which she typed, and starting social and cultural evenings in a parochial hall. But in Twinbrook today it is difficult to find many community activists who remember Sands from those days or who were aware of his community activities. For most their first recollection of him dates from the time of his hunger strike. One thing is certain, though: he rejoined the IRA and became the leader of an active service unit in Twinbrook.

Within six months, however, he was back in jail. He and three others, who were part of a nine-person unit carrying out a bomb attack on the Balmoral Furniture Company at Dunmurray, were caught with a gun in a car. They spent eleven months on remand (in jail without bail), were charged with possession of firearms, and although the prosecution could not link them to the bombing each of them was sentenced to fourteen years. At the time of his arrest Sands was interrogated for six days. Later he would maintain that he was the victim of extreme physical and psychological ill-treatment during this period, that he was denied sleep, forced to undergo constant interrogation throughout the six-day period with only short breaks in between, and that he was repeatedly punched, spreadeagled, and verbally abused. In September 1977 he was sent to the Maze/ Long Kesh and immediately went on the blanket, and from that on to the dirty protest.

His talents were put to good use. He became public relations officer, in effect an aide to Brendan "The Dark" Hughes, the prison OC, with whom he shared a cell. He was responsible for communications both between the blocks and with the outside. Writing became the main outlet for his energies, and his poems and descriptions of life on the blanket were published in *An Phoblacht/Republican News* under the pen name Marcella—his sister's name. He wrote with a ballpoint refill tube (which was, of course, contraband) in tiny letters on cigarette paper or toilet paper, and these were smuggled out.

Sands was a writer learning to find his own language. Given the constricted world in which he lived for the last five years of his life and the conditions under which he wrote, and the fact that he had no access to books or reading materials of any kind, his accomplishments are considerable, the raw energy of his talent compensating for an awkward propensity to imitate. In many of Sands's essays, descriptions are forced or artificial—they appear to be descriptions of things he has not so much seen as imagined or read about, written in a way he supposed a writer would write about them. But when he turns to prison themes and descriptions of prison life, his voice finds a surer pitch, and his prose, now rid of superficial adornment, sparse and to the point, strikingly conveys the harsh, turbulent world in which the H-block prisoners lived, where periods of pure terror randomly interrupted long periods of boredom and isolation. Certain themes emerge: He refuses to allow his captors to impose their view of him on him.

I am now in H-block, where I refused to change to suit the people who oppress, torture and imprison me, and who wish to dehumanize me. It is my political ideology and principles that my captors wish to change. They have suppressed my body and attacked my dignity. To accept the status of criminal would be to degrade myself and to admit the cause I believe in and cherish is wrong. When thinking of the men and women who sacrificed life itself, my suffering seems insignificant.

He asserts his link with the historical past, the connection the prisoners have with the Republican dead and the sustenance they draw from the memories. "I remember, and I shall never forget, how this monster took the life of Tom Ashe, Terence McSwiney, Michael Gaughan, Frank Stagg and Hugh Coney, and I wonder each night what the monster and his black devils will do to us tomorrow." He evokes the mythological symbols of Ireland's eternally self-renewing spirit with their resonances of sacrifice: "Yellow and white are the colours of God and Easter." Yellow and white roses "portray the purity of freedom." Their scent "has been drunk by the bondsman, arousing his heart." They have "blossomed into murderous rebellions . . . bled in pitiful agony before the callous winds of a foreign land. They are Pearse and Connolly, this terrible beauty."

The conditions in the H-blocks are beyond imagination; they are forced on the prisoners; waiting for the inevitable to happen is worse than having to endure it. The H-blocks resemble "a pigsty." You are "crouched naked upon the floor in a corner, freezing cold amid the lingering stench of putrefying rubbish, with crawling, wriggling white maggots all around you, fat bloated flies pestering your naked body, the silence is nervewracking, your mind in turmoil." You are "locked up naked in solitary confinement, twenty four hours a day, and subjected to total deprivation of not only common everyday things, but of basic human necessities, such as clothes, fresh air and exercise, the company of other human beings." You are "entombed, naked and alone." He has watched his own body and the bodies of his comrades "degenerate to pure white shells of skin and bone." Their stomachs "are bloated out by white bread." Their eyes "that once held a glimmer now stare insanely and seemingly at nothing." Their faces are "sunken . . . long-matted hair and untamed beards complete the naked, ghost-like skeletal figures of what are referred to as 'blanket men of H-block.' "

Abuse, physical and psychological, is a constant, the impending threat of what is about to happen or what one hears is happening down the wing instills as much terror as what actually happens. "It is inconceivable to try and imagine what an eighteen year old naked lad goes through when a dozen or so screws [warders] slaughter him with batons, boots and punches, while dragging him by the hair along a corridor, or when they squeeze his privates until he collapses, or throw scalding water around his naked body." It is also "inconceivable for him to describe the blanketmen's state of mind just sitting, waiting for this to happen." The torture in the H-blocks "has brought many men to the verge of insanity."

Boredom, isolation, and the monotony of the sameness of things are the most insidious enemies, threatening to undermine morale, destroy hope. "The greatest part of each seemingly eternal day that I face is filled with thought. I have nothing else to help pass the time during the long never-ending hours. Boredom and loneliness are terrible things, continual and unrelenting." Monotony "depresses and demoralizes." Each day he and his comrades "face a psychological battle for survival." It is "a very intense struggle," the enemy "is unmerciful."

He is preoccupied with images of death. The cells are "tombs," he is "entombed," his body "is dying before its time," he will "never grow old," he wakes up "like a corpse in a grave," he "is being tortured to death in this quiet tomb," he feels like "a living corpse," but a corpse "doesn't fear torture and doesn't wake up in the middle of the night terrified and feel the pain of humiliation, degradation, torture, and inhumanity," he will "die in a tomb," he "fears he will never see [his parents] again." In "the gloom of the prison tomb / Men crave for mother earth," the time has come "To walk the lonely road / Like that of Calvary / And take up the cross of Irishmen / Who've carried liberty."

He has to fight despair. "This night will be another night, huddled up in the corner, fighting the intense cold amid despairing thoughts when pain and depression become almost overwhelming." "Dear

God, I wonder how things are in Siberia." And sometimes he succumbs to it. "The bowl in my hand is cold, it contains some sort of porridge or gruel. The smell from it revolts me. I set it down on the floor. Pacing the floor in total darkness, I become engulfed with depression and despair. I wish I was dead. 'But I am dead' I say aloud. I can't even kill myself, I think."

But the will to resist remains unbreakable, even if the consequence is death itself.

The monster is shrewd. It plays with me, it humiliates me, and tortures me when I resist, it doesn't understand . . . it doesn't even try to comprehend why I resist. My spirit says, "No, no you cannot do what you want with me. I am not beaten. You cannot do what you want with me." I refuse to be beaten. This angers the monster. It goes mad. It neutralizes me to the point of death. The monster keeps me naked. It feeds me. I know why it won't kill me. It wants me to bow before it, to admit defeat. If we don't beat it soon, it will murder me.

Murder the physical self, perhaps, but not the psychological self. "Over the months I know that bitterness has grown inside me," he writes. "A hatred so intense it frightens me." But Sands has no outlet for his hatred, no means to take his aggression out on the monster; it is almost inevitable that he will take it out on himself. To kill the monster, he has to kill himself; to escape psychological death, he has to submit himself to physical death. In the end he and the monster become one.

Ultimately the pain and suffering he has had inflicted on him become fused with the pain and suffering of Christ.

> Blessed is the man who stands
> Before his God in pain,
> And on his back a cross of woe
> His wounds a gaping shame
> For this man is a son of God
> And hallowed be his name.

At other moments Sands idealizes his own life, summing up images of domestic repose that had ceased to exist. "The smile, the soft warm tender smile of my wife kept coming up out of the darkness in front of me," he wrote, "and I heard her plaintive gentle voice: I miss you, and I love you, come home." His son lay "sleeping like an angel, innocent and unaware of his mother's hardship and loneliness, with no father to tuck him into bed, to love or emulate as he grew." But there was no home to go home to. The loving wife had left him shortly after his arrest in 1976. She did not share his dedication to the Republican cause and when their second child was born prematurely and died shortly after he was imprisoned, she couldn't go on. She went to England; his son Gerald would be raised in the country Sands had grown to hate.

The lark was both Sands's metaphor for his own imprisonment and a symbol of release. He recounts the story of the man who incarcerates a small lark in a cage. The lark "would sing no more and when the man demanded that the lark sing, the lark refused." The man became angry and violent. "He starved [the lark] and left it to rot in a dirty cage but the bird still refused to yield. The man murdered it." The lark had "longed to be free and died before it would conform to the tyrant who tried to change it with torture and imprisonment." The lark and the freedom fighter were interchangeable. "[He had] been captured and imprisoned, but like the lark, [he] too had seen the outside of the wire cage." And what of the man "who imprisoned, tortured and murdered the lark?" One day "he caught himself on one of his own traps, and no one would assist him to get free. His own people scorned him, and turned their backs on him. He grew weaker and weaker, and finally toppled over to die upon the land he had marred with such blood. The birds came and extracted their revenge by pecking his eyes out, and the larks sang as they never sang before."

But Sands was more than a poet in the making or a writer who could movingly convey the horrors of the conditions the blanketmen endured. He was also the IRA's prison press relations officer, the official propagandist, so to speak, responsible for creating the public imagery, especially through his column in *An Phoblacht/ Republican News,* of the details of daily life in the H-blocks. He was also more than a mere propagandist, however. He was a strategist with a talent for clear-sighted, penetrating analysis who understood that the struggle within the prison had to have its counterpoint in the political struggle without, that the two struggles had to complement and enhance each other. "For Sands," says Jake Jackson, "the battle in the H-blocks wasn't so much about conditions in the jail, it was two ideologies fighting each other. It was two cultures fighting each other. It was the crystallization of the whole struggle"—a crystallization that he distilled with extraordinary clarity in a comm that he sent to the Republican leadership in August 1979 in which he outlined in a clinical, wholly dispassionate way the failures of the public campaign for the prisoners' demands to capture public attention, detailing with equally clinical dispassion a new strategy. "We have failed to reach a broader base of support," he noted, "therefore we have failed to engage any active support outside of our own immediate hard-core." Two things had to be done: "One, we must make more people aware and engage their help. Two, to get these other people, we must organize our own people effectively and massively on the ground." They had to prepare "an army of propagandists" who would be ready to move "in a massive co-ordinated attack." The key: "The idea to reach people is to pass a simple message to them. Our simple message to everyone will be 'Smash H-blocks,' that is what we shall build around." They should get this message to everyone, "to make it impossible for people to forget it." The medium should be "a massive Paint and Poster Campaign," one that would ensure an H-block poster in "every window in a nationalist area" and a painting spree "that would cover the countryside with it [Smash H-block]." "By continually pushing 'Smash H-block,' " he went on, "we believe that we are pushing a small message and making people aware through their wee jobs and those who they reach will learn something if its only that H-blocks exist." They had to "broaden the battlefield— nationally and internationally." "If we do this," he said, "and ap-proach a massive amount of people, it helps us pass the message, pick up support." It would also help "the progress of politicizing in a simple fashion," for it would "open up avenues of contact between us and everyone who is anyone and at the same time it's politicization on both sides." The prisoners needed lists of names, of "anybody who's anybody." The idea: "one of us in here can write to whomever in a very emotional and disturbing letter." He envisaged, "creating an atmosphere of mass emotion [and] trying to use it as best we can and as soon as we can." Posters, therefore, should "be eye catching, with black type with 'Smash H-block,' a small run down on the blocks and a call for action." They should prepare a poster "with a child on it, emotional, The Year of the Child, 'Don't let my Daddy Die in H-block.' " (1979 was the International Year of the Child.) The "Smash H-block" posters should be up everywhere in time for the pope's visit to Ireland that October and when the pope celebrated an open-air mass in Dublin's Phoenix Park, they should "send our kids in blankets." All of what he proposed, he said, had come out of an hour's discussion on one wing. More would follow.

A little over two months later, on 21 October 1979, the National

H-block Committee was established at a conference in the Green Briar restaurant and dance hall in Andersonstown. The strategy Sands had outlined in such compelling detail became the national strategy.

Danny Morrison, national director of publicity for Sinn Fein, calls Sands's writings the "raw literature of the H-block protest." Every evening after lock-up Sands would entertain the block with his compositions, articulating what many of the prisoners could only feel, providing them with images and interpretations of their behavior that reassured and helped them to persist, making the world in which they lived less sordid and less obviously degrading, imbuing their situation with hope and rationality and the prospect of victory, linking their actions to the larger history of Republican resistance. "Bobby," Jake Jackson recalls, "was always giving, he was always organizing, he was always saying, 'here's a thought, try this or that out, do this or that or what about this,' and he'd have been firing things out. He'd be doing books, writing poems, reading his poems out the door and encouraging other people to write stuff. He was convinced that everybody had a book in him."

Leon Uris's novel *Trinity* was one of Sands's principal mainstays of escapist support. He knew whole parts of the story by heart and would recite it to his fellow prisoners over a period of days. *Trinity* is a romantic, sentimental fiction about Ireland's fight for independence. It feeds the myth of heroic opposition in the face of impossible odds. It is a paean to blood sacrifice, to the idea that the chosen few who are prepared to take upon themselves the burden of history can themselves make history, that blood sacrifice is a noble and a cleansing thing, that a glorious defeat is a prerequisite to prevailing, that in death there is victory. The novel's heroes plan revolution in the face of hopeless odds; they gladly lay down their lives, eager to embrace a defeat that may somehow "stir the ashes of [the] people into a series of even more glorious defeats" so that "over the land long dead stirrings"[11] will at last be heard.

Trinity is bad history but powerful propaganda. It became more powerful still in the stench-ridden wings of the H-blocks, where for nights on end the heroic exploits of Long Dan Sweeney and Conor Larkin and Brendan Sean Barrett, who, in their epic pursuit of Irish freedom, had been incarcerated and abused in captivity, who had endured hunger striking itself—"a silent defiance"—became for the prisoners fictional role models with whom they could identify, investing their protest with a political leitmotif that mirrored their own lives.

"No crime a man commits on behalf of his freedom can be as great as the crime committed by those who deny him freedom," Long Dan Sweeney declares. "We engage in a fight vulnerable to scathing propaganda, unloved by most of our own people, but God and God alone will eventually decide which side was just in its aspirations and which side was evil." "Remember," he exhorts his fellow revolutionaries, "the British have nothing in their entire arsenal of imperial might to counter a single man who refuses to be broken. Irish words, Irish self-sacrifice, and ultimately Irish martyrdom are our weapons. We must have the ability to endure pain to such an extent that they lose the ability to inflict it. This and this alone will break them in the end. Martyrdom."[12]

Fact and fiction reinforced each other. *Trinity* had its historical counterpoint in 1916, the H-block protest its fictional counterpoint in *Trinity*. The primitive, repelling circumstances of the H-blocks were often more unimaginable and less real than the imagined circumstances in *Trinity*. Fantasy fed the heart, and there grew among a number of the blanketmen a belief that a hunger strike would provide the catalytic momentum that would make 1916 come again.

For Sands, the situation had become even more precarious, the necessity for some action to alleviate his psychological distress more urgent. His predicament was not at all unlike the predicament Patrick Pearse had to face in the run-up to the Easter rising. Sands, like Pearse, was driven by what William Irwin Thompson describes in *The Imagination of an Insurrection* as "an intense consciousness of failure,"[13] and like Pearse he had the capacity to be extraordinarily single-minded. Pearse had vowed to free Ireland, but when "the Irish Revival dragged on year after year without ever coming to a point," Pearse began to despair. Thompson writes: "he would never be given his chance and still another generation would pass into old age without having taken arms against the British." And so, as Pearse moved into middle age, "he became more desperate and violent." Whereas "the tone of his earlier writings is meditative, the tone of his later writing is not personal at all. The human voice is replaced by the shrill screech of crowd rhetoric." His imagery shows "almost a pathological lust for violence." The desperation reveals just how much was at stake for Pearse psychologically, "for if he slipped into old age without having taken arms, then his whole life . . . became meaningless and absurd.

In the face of that threat, even action that failed was to be a welcome relief from futility."[14]

Sands had vowed "to set the prisoners free," to win them the right not to have to accept the badge of criminality, and yet as year after year went by, as the smash H-block campaign, which he had brilliantly conceived, continued to drag on without a resolution anywhere in sight, he, too, began to despair. The lyrical tone of his earlier writings fades and his later writings, especially his poetry, reflect an almost pathological preoccupation with sacrifice and death as the one inescapable release.

Liam McCloskey, a former hunger striker, says that Sands confided to his fellow blanketmen that he wasn't prepared to die for the five demands only, but for "the wider thing," for "more support for the IRA"—for the glorious defeat. He accepted that he would die. Before he started his hunger strike he became "withdrawn, wrapped up in himself," according Pat McGeown, who would himself join the hunger strike. "You got the impression that you were talking to someone who was one step removed from life already."

Sands's diary, which he kept for the first seventeen days of his hunger strike at the request of the outside leadership, reflects his detached involvement in what he had undertaken. He is passive observer, incurious commentator rather than active participant. He states his case—"I am a political prisoner because I am a casualty of a perennial war that is being fought between the oppressed Irish people and an alien, oppressive, unwanted regime that refuses to withdraw from our land"—and rests it. He does not mention the five demands or indicate what he might settle for. Only that he will die, that the Republic of 1916 will never die, that he is sustained by the memories of Thomas Clark, Terence McSwiney, Frank Stagg, Michael Gaughan, Thomas Ashe, Sean McCaughey, and above all, James Connolly. "I am dying," he concluded, "not just to attempt to end the barbarity of H-block or to gain the rightful recognition of a political prisoner but primarily because what is lost in here is lost for the Republic and those wretched oppressed whom I am deeply proud to know as the 'risen people.' " He and the collective past were part of the same organic whole; all Republicans were linked to one another and to the past and future generations, itinerants in the diaspora of the dispossessed. Living and dying were not separate. In death he would become intertwined with the mystical body of the Republican movement, his imminent martyrdom what philosopher Richard

Kearney calls "a sort of leitmotif recapitulating the eternal song of sacrifice and rebirth which subtended and harmonized all [the] dead generations of Irish heroes."[15] Mythological repetition would redeem Ireland, would "negate present history in favor of some holy beginning, some eternally recurring past."[16] The diary is a statement for posterity, not a record of his fast. On 2 April, he wrote Adams, "I'm afraid I'm just resigned to the worst, so *sin sin* [that's that]. People find this hard to grasp."

Sands's hunger strike was initially met with little enthusiasm. Fewer than four thousand people turned out in West Belfast on 1 March to mark its beginning. The crowd was quite undemonstrative, lacking in the atmosphere of excitement and apprehension so apparent during the much larger march that had launched the first hunger strike the previous October; speeches were mechanical, platitudinous, arousing indifference rather than emotion; speakers conveyed their own sense of misgiving, conscious that they were reenacting events that had already failed, unable to muster the urgency to suggest that this time the hunger strike would prevail under even less propitious circumstances. However, all that changed on 5 March, when Frank McManus, nationalist MP for Fermanagh-South Tyrone, died suddenly.

In the tribal politics of Northern Ireland, Fermanagh-South Tyrone occupied a special place. Suspicion between Catholics and Protestants ran deep. In the previous ten years more than sixty people had been gunned down in appallingly vulnerable circumstances in Fermanagh alone, almost all of them Protestant, part-time members of the Royal Ulster Constabulary and Ulster Defence Regiment, lending credence to the Protestants' angry assertion that the IRA was engaged in a campaign of genocide specifically aimed at the only sons of elderly Protestant farmers. Unable to work their farms after their sons were murdered, they invariably would be forced to sell, and invariably they would have to sell to Catholics. Land was changing tribes, and hence political allegiance. The frontier was being pushed back.

Catholic voters in the district outnumbered Protestants by about five thousand, so that a Protestant candidate could in fact only win against a divided opposition. What mattered most to Catholics was not letting the Westminster seat fall into Unionist hands. Accordingly, even though there was a long history of disunity between constitutional nationalists and Republicans in the district, there was also a tradition that the two factions would unite behind an agreed candidate at election time. It was of no account who the agreed candidate was or what he stood for or even that he would attend Westminster, as long as he fulfilled his tribal duty—denying the seat to Unionists.

The mathematics were simple: elections were merely a matter of tribal headcounts. The tribe, of course, could not act against its own—something the SDLP, the majority voice of constitutional nationalism, learned to its regret in the February 1974 general elections when it fielded a candidate, split the Catholic vote, and cost Frank McManus, the old-time nationalist who had been the Westminster MP since 1970, his seat. The recriminations were bitter, the finger of blame pointed angrily at the SDLP, whose candidate had finished third. And so, when a second general election was held later that year, the SDLP, not wanting to become the nationalist scapegoat once again, declined to contest the election in Fermanagh-South Tyrone and McManus, who rarely attended the Westminster Parliament, regained his seat. In the general elections of 1979, the party again bowed to internal pressure, and again gave McManus a free ride.

At the time of McManus's death in 1981 the SDLP still had not managed to resolve its dilemma of how to honor its commitment to contest all elections without becoming the instrument that ensured the election of a Protestant. Accordingly, when it appeared certain that Frank McManus's nephew, Noel Maguire, would run for the seat now vacant in the wake of his uncle's death, the party executive overturned the local constituency's decision to field a candidate. Other factors, however, also entered its decision: a coalition of anti-H-block forces had nominated Sands for the seat.

Sands's selection as a candidate added to the SDLP's quandary. On the one hand, its commitment to constitutional nationalism, its advocacy of the ballot box as the instrument of political change, its adherence to the electoral process, and its repeated condemnations of the IRA were all persuasive arguments for it to field a candidate. On the other hand, there were overwhelming arguments for not contesting the election: to stand against either Maguire or Sands would be to split the Catholic vote, thus ensuring the election of the Protestant candidate, and one way or the other the SDLP would be accused of undermining the H-block protest campaign, taking the pressure off the British government, and possibly costing Sands his life.

The SDLP played it safe. It withdrew from the race, leaving the field to Maguire, Sands, and Harry West, the Protestant candidate who had the backing of both the Democratic Unionists and the Official Unionists. But the pressure on Maguire to give Sands a clear shot at the seat was intense, and in the end, distraught and unhappy, he withdrew, giving the Republican movement what it wanted: a one-on-one contest with Harry West, tribe versus tribe. (Maguire withdrew his nomination fifteen minutes before the deadline for doing so. If he had not withdrawn, the anti-H-block/Armagh Prisoners' coalition, which had nominated Sands, would have pulled Sands's name out of the election. Asked some time afterwards by Peter Gillman of the London *Sunday Times* how the Republican movement got Maguire to step down, Danny Morrison, then the national publicity director for Sinn Fein, was succinct: "Intensive pressure and moral blackmail," he replied.)[17]

The election attracted international attention. Sands's campaign message was simple: the Catholic community should not stand by and let prisoners die. Elect Sands and you would save his life. There was no call on the voters to endorse the five demands or political status. With the world media watching the count, the Catholic and Protestant communities closed in on themselves and voted their tribal allegiances on 9 April. Sands polled 30,092 votes, beating West by 1,446 votes. It confirmed to Protestants—not that much confirmation was needed—their suspicions that the SDLP's condemnations of IRA violence were a charade, that most Catholics supported the IRA, and that there were in fact no differences among the various "brands" of Republicanism. In the Maze/Long Kesh, the news of Sands's election was met with jubilation, but for Mrs. Thatcher the result changed nothing. "A crime is a crime is a crime," she said, "It is not political, it is a crime." Sands, too, was fatalistic: "It's still going to be a major hunger strike," he wrote in a comm to Pat McGeown that was passed around the blocks. "There are still probably going to be people coming after me. In other words—I'm going to die."

The Fermanagh-South Tyrone election, however, transformed the context in which his hunger strike was conducted. The media coverage of the election, the fact that Sands was not expected to do well, and that his victory confounded the expectations of even his most ardent supporters, fixed the issue indelibly in the public mind. Sands became a public figure, the focus of intensive scrutiny and attention. The sense of drama and suspense that the election and its aftermath engendered—Would Sands win? Would Mrs. Thatcher respond? Would a British government allow an elected member of the British Parliament to starve himself to death?—created an ambience of shared participation in the unfolding events.

This was in contrast to the level of public attention during the first hunger strike. Then, the fact that there were seven hunger strikers resulted in a certain anonymity. They were referred to collectively and their collectivity made them faceless. There was no one with whom the public could easily identify, no human touch to compel the critical mass of attention that transforms exposure to information into identification with either its message or its messenger. The hunger strikers were abstractions, not personalities in the public imagination. If the public had any impression at all it was that they were hard men: four were doing time for murder and the gravity of their crimes tended to cast a shadow over the purity of their actions.

Not so Sands's hunger strike. Sands's picture was everywhere. The relative inseverity of the crime for which he had been convicted and the severity of the sentence he had received, the fact that he had already spent one-third of his young life in prison, that he had spent every Christmas since he was eighteen behind barbed wire or locked up in a cell, that he was not associated with any acts of violence, that he had a visible family—father, mother, and sisters—transformed his persona. He became a son, a brother, a victim of discrimination and the inequities of the criminal justice system, a young writer whose powerful descriptions of the H-block prison conditions conveyed a sensitivity that was difficult to associate with the hard men of violence and brutal acts of murder.

Four days after the election the Northern Ireland Office (NIO) announced that Sands's death was imminent; on Holy Saturday—17 April—he received the last rites. From that point, the hunger strike, more than ever, resembled McSwiney's. The death watch became a communal vigil; each change in Sands's condition was front-page news, every rumor of his death intensifying fears on both sides of the divide and provoking riots and violence. As Sands edged closer to what had now become his inevitable death, his stature grew. His hunger strike now fulfilled the criteria of mythology. It was in the ancient tradition of the heroic quest, embedded in the hidden recesses of the Celtic consciousness. He had become a hero, retaining control of his destiny even beyond death. He was history because "history was the performance of myth . . . the embodiment of transcendence."

The almost incomprehensible finality of his protest, a gesture of profound impotence in the face of insurmountable opposition, could be understood only in the context of imagination, imagination that caught "the music of infinity and [made] the individual bear witness to it in his own moment of time."[18] Sands not only bore witness; he was seen to bear witness.

The hunger strike continued its inexorable progress. Three other hunger strikers joined Sands—Francis Hughes, when Sands was two weeks into his fast, Raymond McCreesh and Patsy O'Hara a week later—and although there were a number of interventions, there were few real efforts to mediate a solution. Both the government and the hunger strikers stuck tenaciously to their respective positions: on the one side, a simple refusal to consider any concession on all five demands; on the other, a simple refusal to consider anything other than concessions on all five. "For the prisoners in the H-blocks and in Armagh women's prison, the hunger strike is the pinnacle of the struggle to secure not only the five demands but also to establish the legitimacy and worthiness of fighting for a united Ireland," Jim Gibney, a leading Sinn Fein hunger strike strategist, wrote in the *H-block/Armagh Bulletin*.

They see their prison struggle as an integral part of the overall struggle to overthrow a system which has colonized our country, our minds, our language, our culture and our attitude to life for centuries.

The prisoners draw from our historical fight for independence and are strengthened, not weakened by those whose lives are martyred. The British government, no matter how dogmatic or how many forces it has at its disposal will never conquer this spirit.

Charles Haughey, the Irish prime minister, persuaded Sands's sister Marcella to sign a complaint to the European Commission on Human Rights over the treatment of Sands in prison, but when a delegation from the commission subsequently went to the Maze/Long Kesh, Sands refused to meet with them unless his "advisers"—Brendan "Bik" McFarlane, who had replaced him as OC, and Gerry Adams and Danny Morrison of Sinn Fein—were also present, a condition the prison authorities would not agree to. Sands met with a stream of visitors: Sile de Valera, a member of the Irish Parliament, and Neil Blaney and John O'Connell, members of both the Irish Parliament and the European Parliament. O'Connell appealed to him to come off his fast; Blaney would not, believing it would be an insult to

Sands's convictions to do so. Newry-born Monsignor John Magee, Pope John Paul's personal secretary, implored him on the pope's behalf to try and settle the dispute by other means. And Don Concannon, the British Labour Party spokesperson on Northern Ireland, visited Sands during his last days to impress upon him his party's full support for Mrs. Thatcher's no-concession policy.

Father Sean Rogan, the curate in Twinbrook, was a special case. In a comm that Sands sent out just before he went on hunger strike, he warned the Republican movement to stay clear of the "sagarts" (priests) in Twinbrook, especially Rogan: "If he weighs in I'll ask him to leave for he'd say things that weren't okay." But he did see Father Rogan on two occasions, the last just ten days before he died. "I remember," Rogan says, "going in and sitting beside his bed and he was very weak at the time, very gaunt but absolutely determined. And I said, 'You know, Bobby, there's one man for whom I have great respect as a poet and for what he eventually did.' " And Rogan recited the opening lines of a poem in Irish by Patrick Pearse. Rogan quoted the first verse and translated it into English as best he could. 'That's beautiful, that's gorgeous,' is how Rogan recalls Sands's response and Rogan asked him if he knew who wrote the poem: Sands didn't. "It was Patrick Pearse," Rogan told him.

I said I have great respect for Patrick Pearse for something else and that was when Patrick Pearse saw too many lives were going, it was he who surrendered, he who said enough is enough, that he didn't want any more deaths to result from what he was doing, that he wanted to spare the people of Dublin. "Bobby," I said, "if you die there could be many people who would die too because of that. Patrick Pearse did what he thought was right so that others would not suffer." And I remember he turned to me, he was very angry and he says, "Father, you're trying to give me a conscience." He said, "Look, if I die and anything happens, the British are responsible for that and not me," and the conversation ended.

It would be a point constitutional nationalist opponents of the IRA would make repeatedly. When Patrick Pearse saw that a continuation of the Easter Uprising would only inflict more casualties on the people of Dublin, he surrendered, "in order to prevent the further slaughter of Dublin citizens and in the hope of saving the lives of our followers now surrounded and hopelessly outnumbered," according to the orders he issued to his subordinates.[19] He would be the cause of his own death but not theirs. So, the argument went, if the IRA, who claimed to be the legitimate heirs of Pearse, really believed they

were, they should follow his example and order an end to the hunger
strikes to forestall the violence that would surely follow Sands's death
and result in the killing of innocent people.

All the intercessions were to no avail. "He saw himself as the
Messiah, Christlike, and he was determined to go ahead," says Father
Denis Faul. On Tuesday, 5 May, at 1:17 A.M., Bobby Sands died.
"He took his own life by refusing food and medical treatment for
sixty-six days," the NIO said in a terse statement, and in West Belfast
the women took to the streets to spread the news. The clamor of
banging dustbin lids, dirgelike in its metallic monotony and lifted on
the night winds from street to street, called on the people to gather,
for the ghetto to mourn its dead and to vent its grief and outrage.
Some 7,000 police, 5,000 reservists, 7,000 UDR men, and 11,000
soldiers were put on standby.

In the succeeding months, nine others followed in Sands's
deathsteps. On 12 May, a week after Sands's death, Francis Hughes
died. Nine days later, on 21 May, Patsy O'Hara and Raymond
McCreesh died. Then there was a hiatus for seven weeks followed
by the deaths of Joe McDonnell on 8 July and Martin Hurson five
days later on 13 July. After a respite of two and a half weeks there
were three more deaths in quick succession: Kevin Lynch on 1 August,
Kieran Doherty on 2 August, Tom McElwee on 8 August. And
finally, Micky Devine died on 20 August.

Efforts to reach a settlement got nowhere. The Irish Commission
for Justice and Peace (ICJP), established in 1968 by the Irish Bishops'
Conference, had a series of talks with the NIO in late June and early
July, and met with the hunger strikers to discuss its proposals. But
the ICJP initiative fell apart when Joe McDonnell died and the commission accused the NIO of reneging on promises it had made and
proposals it had agreed to. Later in July, the International Red Cross
sent a delegation to the prison, but after two days of talks with
Humphrey Atkins and the hunger strikers and McFarlane, the prisoners asked the Red Cross to withdraw, claiming the attempt had
failed because the British were not prepared to enter discussions with
them. Otherwise, there was little official movement on either side.
Both were impervious to the pleas for compromise, obsessed with
the manipulation of the propaganda war, determined to prevail no
matter what the cost. Each mimicked the other's behavior.

However, the pressure, especially within the Catholic community, for the hunger strikes to be called off increased when it became manifestly obvious that the hunger strikers' demands would not be met. Each hunger striker's death had a lesser marginal impact on public opinion. The international media attention lavished on Sands diminished after his death and evaporated by the beginning of August. The story had become repetitious. TV montages of coffins coming out of the Maze/Long Kesh, of grieving relatives and moving funeral orations, had become reruns, yesterday's drama. The feared backlashes in both loyalist and Republican areas had not materialized. In the South, when the fears that the hunger strikes might somehow foment destabilization were seen to be unfounded, the new government of Garret FitzGerald adopted a tougher line with the families of the hunger strikers: there would be no question of unilateral action by the Irish government to express its displeasure with Mrs. Thatcher's uncompromising position.

Creeping attrition—Paddy Quinn's mother intervened to end his fast on 31 July when he lapsed into unconsciousness; Pat McGeown's wife took him off on 20 August, the day Micky Devine died—created its own momentum. On 4 September Matt Devlin's family ended his hunger strike, and Laurence McKeown's family followed suit on 6 September, reinforcing a pattern of family intervention. The families had had enough and when they collectively announced that they would intervene when the hunger strikes reached a critical point, the hunger strikers themselves accepted the inevitable: it was over. On 3 October 1981, 217 days after the protest started, they abandoned their fast.

5   In the prison Brendan "Bik" McFarlane ran the hunger strike. McFarlane was from Ardoyne. Born in 1951, he was the eldest of three children. His father worked in a Michelin tire factory. The family, especially the mother, was very religious, and from an early age Bik (he got the nickname at school after a brand of biscuits called McFarlane's) was an altar boy at Holy Cross Cathedral in Ardoyne, eventually becoming a vice-president of the altar boys' association, one of the senior boys entrusted with training the younger boys, always called on for the important ceremonies at Christmas and

Easter. He attended Holy Cross Primary School and later St. Mala-
chy's College, and then joined the Order of the Divine Word (SVD)—
a missionary order with posts in fifty-two countries. He spent a couple
of years at their seminary for late vocations in Carrog in North Wales,
bringing his educational standing up to the level where he could study
philosophy and theology.

The conflict erupted when he was in Wales and McFarlane came
back to Ardoyne on holidays to find it under siege from the Protestant
communities which encircled it and the British army which policed
it—enemies without and enemies within. He left the seminary in 1970
and returned to Ardoyne. Jake Jackson says McFarlane told him that
"[my] choices were either to come back and confront imperialism in
Ireland or to go to join Camilo Torres with a breviary in one hand
and an AK-47 in the other." This identification of McFarlane and
Camilo Torres, the Colombian-born revolutionary priest, "the people's priest," who was one of the leading exponents of liberation
theology ("I took off my cassock to be more truly a priest / The duty
of every Catholic is to be a revolutionary / The duty of every revolutionary is to make the revolution / The Catholic who is not a
revolutionary is living in mortal sin"), is an essential part of the
McFarlane myth.

The mention of McFarlane's name in Ardoyne brings warm smiles
of recognition. Even those who disapprove of his later actions
remember his charm, his unfailing pleasantness, his devil-may-care
attitude, his propensity for making himself the center of attention not
because he consciously set out to do so, but simply because his for-
midable personality exuded the kind of energy that commanded
attention. A Gaelic footballer, a hurler, a terrific tin-whistle player,
an avid devotee of Irish traditional music, both as boy and man, a
person for whom almost everyone had praise—he was responsible,
dependable, trustworthy, and he didn't take himself or life too seriously. "He took things as they came," recalls one person who knew
him well, "and when something went wrong he just kept on going
as if nothing had happened." The sacristan of Holy Cross puts him
in the top ten percent of the altar boys he has trained and worked
with.

He is remembered as a highly intelligent young man, who had all
the accoutrements of leadership yet did not consciously seek to put
himself ahead of others, as someone, nevertheless, who might have
been easily led, who would want to prove himself, if only to show

that he was his own man: he sought acceptance so that he could assert his independence. He was fond of a good time, was always up for "the crack" (having fun for fun's sake). He had, as one longtime friend put it, "a buzz about him." "He was a guy who loved fun, having a good time. He was tremendous fun to be with as drinking companion, a music companion or anything else."

His name evokes phrases like "outgoing," "immensely likable," "very pleasant." He was the extrovert with a rogue element, an unlikely candidate for the priesthood. However, he would, says one friend, "have made a smashing priest because he would have done it all as a lay person." But if he had become a priest, says the same friend, he "would never had made Monsignor." In Ardoyne he followed a different course, getting married, losing a child before birth, watching his marriage drift and finally fall apart.

There are different accounts as to when McFarlane actually got involved with the IRA. Some say that in the early seventies he was involved with a loose-knit Ardoyne defense committee, which was affiliated with neither the Official nor Provisional IRA but was tolerated by both, an association that put its primary emphasis on defensive and often retaliatory operations against both the British army and the Protestant paramilitaries, that he did not join the IRA until late 1974 or early 1975. Others say that he joined the Provisional IRA shortly after internment began. Either way there appears to be little doubt that McFarlane was active and that his carefree nonchalance concealed a deadly seriousness of intent and ruthlessness of purpose.

He inspired confidence in others even if the risk sometimes did not seem to justify the possible consequences. One friend recalls that McFarlane and the adjutant of the Provisional IRA in Ardoyne "had conned" ten sticks of gelignite out of the Official IRA, and that McFarlane carried the gelignite, wrapped rather carelessly in old newspapers, right through a para patrol they ran into on the way back to Ardoyne. McFarlane, he says, "whistled his way right through them." It was the kind of derring-do that appealed to his sense of self, bravura masquerading as bravery, a quixotic transmogrification of the real and the unreal in which everything, even in extreme circumstances, became part of the "crack."

He worked first in a printing firm in Belfast and then as the driver of a forklift. Many of his friends were killed: two close friends in a shoot-out with the British army in 1972; a neighbor on his doorstep one evening where he stood smoking a cigarette; friends on the Ardoyne Kickhams, the local Gaelic Athletic Association club whose members were becoming with increasing frequency the victims of sectarian attacks; and then in October 1974 another close friend, Ciaran Murphy, who was assassinated by an organization calling itself the Ulster Protestant Action Group. Ciaran Murphy was the sixteenth person and the tenth Catholic to be killed in the preceding six weeks, the fifty-ninth Catholic to be killed since the beginning of 1974. McFarlane went with Ciaran's brother Pat to identify the body, and according to many people who knew McFarlane, Ciaran's death changed him. Pat Murphy, for one, detected a hardening in him after Ciaran's death, a tendency to be more uncooperative with the army patrols that would often stop them, to be that little bit more confrontational, that little bit less discerning.

At the start of 1975 the Provisional IRA had called a truce and during the following months the conflict increasingly degenerated into sectarian warfare: loyalist assassination gangs randomly killing Catholics, the Provisional IRA retaliating, targeting the hang-outs of loyalist paramilitaries. The Bayardo—a bar on the Shankill Road in West Belfast—was considered to be one such hang-out, a frequent haunt of UVF members. On 13 August 1975 the pub was firebombed. Three men and a woman died and forty-four others were injured after gunmen drove up in a car shortly before closing time and hurled a ten-pound bomb into the packed bar where customers were having a sing-song. Two of the people killed—fifty-six-year-old Samuel Gunning and forty-five-year-old William Gracey—were brothers-in-law who were standing outside the bar when it was strafed with machine-gun fire before the bomb itself was hurled. The two others—twenty-one-year-old Hugh Harris and twenty-nine-year-old Joan McDowell, a mother of four—died when the bomb exploded inside the bar. The Provisional IRA immediately denied any involvement in the bombing, leading the *Irish Times* to speculate that it was a freelance operation "carried out with the tacit approval of a larger unnamed organization which felt bound to avenge [the sectarian murders of Catholics]."

Within twenty minutes of the explosion, McFarlane was arrested when he was spotted driving a car similar to the one used in the attack. He, along with two others, Peter Hamilton and Seamus Clarke, were charged and convicted in connection with the bombing, receiving life sentences with the recommendation that they serve a minimum of twenty-five years.

(McFarlane's arrest for the bombing devastated his parents. Rubie Harris, mother of Hugh Harris, the young man who had died in the bombing, made her way, at the suggestion of a friend who told her of the McFarlanes' anguish, to the McFarlane residence in Ardoyne, introduced herself and consoled them. "I felt sorry for them," she explains. "I think it was my duty to go and try and comfort those people. There's no mother or father sends their child out to commit murder. I told them, it could have easily been me in the same situation as they were. I'm the mother of five sons and it could have been that that son of mine who was killed could have been up on a murder charge. I don't think I could have faced it. I would have been like the McFarlanes.")

McFarlane qualified for special category status and was sent to Cage 11, where he became battalion officer responsible for organizing education lectures. Among his fellow prisoners were a number who would play key roles in the hunger strikes: Brendan Hughes, Bobby Sands, Gerry Adams. However, McFarlane lost his special category status when he and two other prisoners, Pat McGeown and Larry Marley, were caught trying to escape. Once sent to the H-blocks he immediately went on the blanket—and later, like the majority of the blanket men, on the dirty protest. And so it came to pass that in 1980 Bobby Sands and Brendan Hughes shared one cell and Brendan McFarlane and Jake Jackson occupied adjoining cells in H-3.

McFarlane took his religion seriously. "There was a woman who was a Baptist and a member of the Board of Visitors and she used to come in around the wings and hand out wee mass leaflets and tracts and stuff like that," says Jackson,

and Bik specifically asked her to get him a Good News Bible, published by Collins. The Bibles that we had were the Revised Standard Version, the Catholic edition of the King James Bible, and Bik specifically asked for the Good News Bible because it was an updated, modernized version of the Bible in layman's language instead of stilted language, and every morning his routine was, we'd wake up, eat the breakfast and he'd then pull his mattress up and he'd set his runway out on the floor—your runway's just a blanket folded and set out on the floor so you could walk up and down on it—and sit back and do his daily reading of the Bible and then he'd just sit there and I'd imagine he was praying.

Pope John XXIII was a McFarlane favorite. In his Bible he carried a card that had been inscribed to him by one of his friends at the SVD seminary, with Pope John's last testament:

> Love one another, my dear children
> Seek rather what unites, not what may separate you from one
>   another,
> As I say "till we meet again," let me remind you of the most
> important things in life,
> Our Blessed Savior Jesus; His good news,
> His Holy Church; truth and kindness,
> I shall remember you all and pray for you.

The wellsprings of McFarlane's faith could be found in the Acts of the Apostles, especially chapter 2, verses 44 and 45: "The believers all met together and held everything jointly; they sold their property and belongings, and distributed them to all, as anyone might have need." He and Jake Jackson frequently occupied themselves with discussions of what Christ would do if he came back to earth now, of how he would berate the Church establishment just as he had berated the Pharisees, for being hypocrites, for having the form of religion without the truth of it.

For McFarlane, the contradiction from which all others arose was the insistence by Britain that it had a right to interfere in Irish affairs: the only logical thing to do was to wage a struggle against that system. He was at peace with himself, secure in his mission, identifying fully with Torres's message: "Change implies violence for those who retain power. But violence is not excluded from the Christian ethic, because if Christianity is concerned with eliminating the serious evils which we suffer and with saving us from the continuous violence in which we live without possible solution, the ethic is to be violent once and for all in order to destroy the violence which the economic minorities exercise against the people."[1] In Colombia, the economic minorities were the small number of families who owned most of the land; in Northern Ireland they were the agents of British imperialism.

According to Jackson, whereas Sands was a political animal "total and absolute," McFarlane was more reflective. Sands had a very short fuse, McFarlane a very long one. Sands had a fair degree of animosity toward the prison warders, McFarlane didn't—"he [McFarlane] had worked out a lot more in his head." On the surface "he seemed to have reconciled himself a lot more to what was the enemy and not to react to the servants of the enemy as much as Bobby would. Bobby would have reacted to the screws [prison warders]." (Alfie Watson, a former prison officer who served on the blocks during the dirty protest, found McFarlane affable and approachable. On one occasion, he recalls that when the warders were trying to forcibly bathe the prisoners, McFarlane approached him saying, "Do you mind if I bathe myself? I'll still keep shouting." "He lay down in the bath," says Watson, "and bathed himself, all the time shouting away about the prison officers and all.") Sands was "very systematic in his thinking but he would often let snap judgments or snap reactions override [his] thinking." McFarlane was "rigid in his thinking, very reflective and analytical, he wouldn't let anything deflect him from a chosen course of action." McFarlane had "massive qualms about the human cost of things." To Sands these were "incidentals which were usually overridden by political considerations." Sands "always led from the front. He didn't rely an awful lot on too many people. McFarlane "led by consensus to a larger degree. He would have taken counsel." Sands was an organizer, McFarlane more easygoing. McFarlane was a "brilliant singer," Sands had only "a fair enough voice." But the two collaborated once, Sands writing the words and McFarlane putting them to music for a tune called "McIlhaltton," a song about a poteen maker which ended up being recorded by Christy Moore. Sands was into Irish culture in a big way, McFarlane wasn't. Sands was very idealistic, McFarlane was pragmatic.

The circumstances of McFarlane's initial offense—a bomb being thrown without warning into a public house, the civilian deaths, and the overtones of sectarianism—and the fact that McFarlane never denied having participated in the Bayardo bombing disqualified him from being considered as a hunger striker. As Jake Jackson puts it, McFarlane was a "propaganda nightmare." But when Sands stepped down as OC to begin his hunger strike, the outside leadership turned to McFarlane to take over.

McFarlane was the link between the hunger strikers and the movement, a bulwark between hunger strikers and would-be mediators, who were often, he believed, unwitting accomplices in the government's designs to break the strike. When necessary, he was a cushion between the hunger strikers and their families, who were caught between being supportive of their sons and husbands, even to the point of promising not to intervene when they lapsed into unconsciousness, yet wanting to save their lives. He attended to the hunger strikers' doubts, kept their resolve firm, persuaded them of the less than altruistic motives of outside mediators and the shortcomings of proposed settlements, outlined their options, reinforced their sense of purpose, and reminded them constantly that they were in fact the front-line soldiers.

But there was no strategy—no clearly defined plan of how to proceed, no contingency arrangements, no back-up cover. There was no agreement as to how long the hunger strike should last or how many should be allowed to die. Sands himself, we are told by some, wanted no one other than himself to die or at least for there to be no escalation beyond the initial cluster of four. Others, including Jake Jackson, clearly recall Sands anticipating fourteen or fifteen deaths before the British would accede to the prisoners' demands. McFarlane himself in a comm to Gerry Adams (Adams, then vice-president of Sinn Fein, was head of a Sinn Fein committee, which also included Danny Morrison and Jim Gibney, that monitored the hunger strike on the outside and provided counsel) was of the opinion that "if public pressure failed to move the government by the time the first four had died, that they would effectively have shot their bolt," that after four deaths "with the authorities still adamant, more deaths would start to look like suicide, which would be damaging for the movement." Both the IRA and Sinn Fein opposed the hunger strike. They believed it would not succeed in moving the British government and that the movement could not stand another defeated hunger strike. "We are tactically, strategically, physically and morally opposed to the hunger strike," Adams wrote Sands. Yet Sands and the others were obdurate: they would press ahead regardless, and the Army Council, the ruling body of the IRA, found itself overruled by the prisoners but unwilling publicly to order the prisoners to desist, hesitant to test the limits of its own authority—in effect, losing control of the prisoners who were trying to gain control of the prison.

Even the hunger strike's beginning was less than auspicious. "In the end the fact that there was going to be a second hunger strike was leaked," says Pat McGeown, one of the block OCs who would himself wind up on the hunger strike, "and that committed us to the second hunger strike once it was leaked. Then the ball started to roll and it was near enough impossible to pull it back." From the onset the atmosphere in the prison bordered on the passive; there appeared to be a mute acceptance that the hunger strike was inevitable, that it might be, in fact, the only way for the prisoners to maintain the unity of their protest. McGeown wrote to Sands: "We're going at this with the most depressive sort of view. We're going at it saying 'look we're going to die' as opposed to going on it saying 'there's a very strong possibility that we're going to die but what have we got in between to play with, what cards have we got to play.' " On the following Sunday at mass—the last time McGeown would see Sands—he again raised the issue of the need to "put the whole hunger strike in a more positive frame of mind." Sands, he recalls, was almost uninterested and said, "That's up to you. I've already committed myself to going on hunger strike. Bik will be cleared as OC, so the problem actually goes on your shoulders."

The plan of action called for Sands to lead off the hunger strike, for Francis Hughes, who was insistent on joining the strike, to follow Sands, for Patsy O'Hara, the INLA leader who was equally insistent on embarking on a hunger strike, to follow Hughes, and since O'Hara was one of "the others" (the INLA was never quite accepted by the IRA as being an equal partner, fully legitimate, or entirely trustworthy) he had to be paired with one of their own, and thus the fourth hunger striker, Raymond McCreesh.

From the beginning, their resolve would be made clear. They would convince the British that, unlike the prisoners who had undertaken the first hunger strike, they were not engaged in an exercise in brinkmanship, that when the abyss loomed each man would willingly leap into the void. In the struggle pitting raw resolve against imperial might, their resolve would not be broken, the British would have to face an unending procession of funeral coffins coming out of the Maze/Long Kesh, an inflamed nationalist population thirsting for justice and revenge; they would make the British into an international pariah, the policeman of dead men, a misanthropic monster—a government impervious to compassion, losing its political legitimacy by misusing its moral authority.

At the time the logic seemed sound: if Sands died and the British were prepared to ride out the furor that would surely follow his death, they would just as surely ride out whatever furor would follow any subsequent deaths. And thus the argument for a breathing space during which the British could come to realize, without being under the pressure of an imminent death, that the prisoners had proven their resolve, that their determination was no idle indulgence of willful gamesmanship. The British, it was argued, would have room for maneuver before a second series of deaths would start, time to search for an honorable way out. A short-list of standby hunger strikers who would replace those who had died was drawn up, although no actual decision was made that the first four hunger strikers should be followed by four more. "What we didn't know and couldn't take into account," says McGeown, "was the personality of Margaret Thatcher. There was just no way we were aware of the personality of that person. I think naïvely that the way we looked on the British government was that they were politicians, that politicians don't like points of crisis, that politicians negotiate their way out of crisis. We had this in our heads—we were being so flexible, so there'll be flexibility on their side. Whenever it comes to a crisis between the two we'll sort it out."

Within the prison things either got out of hand or were part of a clear-cut, albeit ad hoc strategy, depending on whom you listen to. Each view represents fissiparous reflections from a kaleidoscope, in which the spectrum of colors on display at any given moment is ephemeral, a glimpse into what isn't rather than a guiding light into what is.

On 29 April, six days before Bobby Sands died, the full weight of what Sands had said to McGeown in February and the awful implications of the hunger strike itself began to overwhelm Mc-Farlane. "I think it's becoming increasingly more obvious that the Brits are going to hold fast. It's a nightmarish thought, comrade," he wrote Adams, "which is taking on the form of cold hard reality with each passing day. There [is] every possibility the Brits will not say anything at all or make any attempt at dipping in attractive offers, but just stand back and let things run their course. Their stupidity is unbelievable."

McFarlane's fears arose in part from the fact that although Sands from the start had insisted that he would have to die, the prisoners, and even the outside leadership, seduced themselves into believing their own propaganda: that Sands's election to Westminster would change things, that Margaret Thatcher would not allow a sitting member of the Westminster Parliament to starve himself to death in the face of world opinion. The realization that Thatcher would simply do nothing raised the one question the hunger strikers could not address: What if the government continued to stand firm no matter how many hunger strikers died? It challenged the underlying rationale of the hunger strike itself—that at some point the sheer moral force of their protest, their demonstrated willingness, some would say eagerness, to simply follow one another onto a conveyor belt of death, would compel the British government to reach an accommodation. Later, when the government was unresponsive to the Irish Commission for Justice and Peace proposals—proposals that McFarlane himself felt were grossly inadequate—he exploded. "No changes! Are they serious? What sort of people are we dealing with? It appears they are not interested in simply undermining us but completely annihilating us."

There were assumptions, that at some point, whether it took two deaths or twenty, the British would have to give ground, although assumptions were no substitute for strategy. "The problem arrived," says McGeown, "whenever we actively talked about where the hunger strike would lead if people died. We had picked the initial four to go on it, and we said, 'Right, there's four people. What do we do afterwards if they die?' and there was an air of unrealism because Bobby had this thing in his head that if anybody had to die it should only be one person and it should be him, that he should carry it for everybody else."

The emotion on the blocks was intense. After Sands died, the IRA sent in comms ordering an end to the hunger strike, but Hughes and McCreesh as well as Joe McDonnell, who had taken Sands's place, refused to go along, disobeying what was in fact a military order. "Outside [the IRA] had adopted the position that Bobby should be the only one to die on hunger strike," says Pat McGeown.

They said, "Look, we can't change your decision to go on hunger strike, we disagree with it, if Bobby Sands dies our point's been proved that you aren't getting anywhere with it. What we're prepared to do because we can't do anything else is back it the whole way. If Bobby dies then we look at the whole situation again." We decided, then, that's as far as the strategy goes. What happened when Bobby died is that the outside [the IRA] issued an order saying "That's it, the point's been proven." Frank Hughes said no. All the hunger strikers at that point said no. The people who were waiting—we had then begun to categorize people as to who was going on hunger strike, people who knew they would be going on fairly quickly afterwards—were saying no. . . . Even I [McGeown opposed the hunger strike] got caught up in the emotionalism of it and I remember when we got the comm from the Army Council saying no, writing back and saying I disagree with that and what's going to happen in here is that if you try and implement that order, you're going to get people going against it. Even I felt the need to go against them. [We were] caught up in the whole emotionalism and caught up in the whole commitment to each other. They [the IRA] maintained the line and over a period of weeks, they argued, they thrashed it out, and in the end we were just terribly immobile. We weren't changing our mind. Frank Hughes died and then you went into the whole process of having no way out. At that point the strategy actually collapsed, nobody knew who could take a decision to end the whole thing.

The prisoners' first loyalties were to each other; their universe, already closed, now sealed itself off—in their world of death they had become self-sufficient.

There was no shortage of would-be hunger strikers. Upwards of seventy prisoners sent their names to their wing OCs volunteering to go on a fast to the death. The wing OCs would ask them to supply details of their arrest, interrogation, and sentence. The nature of the offense for which a prisoner had been convicted was a major consideration in the selection process—some were immediately ruled out because their offenses were such that the British could use them to portray the hunger strikers as murderous terrorists who had committed heinous crimes. The wing OC made a recommendation with respect to each volunteer and passed it on to McFarlane. The volunteer would be informed if he was rejected and given the opportunity to argue his case. The final decision was made by McFarlane in consultation with the volunteer's wing OC.

Selection for the short-list was based on a number of other considerations: there had to be a proper geographic spread, and volunteers who were due to be released within a short time were rejected, not because their commitment to the hunger strike might be suspect, but on the grounds that they would be more useful to the movement by reinvolving themselves in the struggle when they were released. Volunteers who had broken under interrogation were usually but not always ruled out. It was McFarlane's decision alone to short-list prisoners and to specify the order in which they would go on the hunger strike. Once a volunteer had been short-listed he was told to send a comm to the Army Council declaring his intention to go on hunger strike and explaining his reasons for doing so. He would receive a comm back from the Army Council instructing him not to go on hunger strike, reiterating once again that the Army Council was on principle opposed to the hunger strike. Some volunteers followed the Army Council's order and opted out, but most did not. They simply ignored the order and waited for their turn to come, their commitment to each other superseding their oath of obedience to the IRA.

"We [Pat McGeown, Brendan McFarlane, Brendan Hughes, Richard O'Rawe, and Jake Jackson] had a meeting with the OCs," says McGeown,

and we told them, "We believe we're going to have to terminate the hunger strike sooner or later—not that we're going to do it within a period of weeks or months, but sooner or later we're going to have to do it—how do we do it?"

And we just let that out and left it to come back. What came back from the OCs was—what the OCs did, probably because we didn't explain it well enough to them—was they actually took a vote among people as to whether they should terminate the hunger strike or not, and a fairly overwhelming number of the prisoners were saying no, we're committed to it, we'll have to continue it. (The hunger strikers were asked in a way "that wouldn't demoralize them.") That became Bik's position, and he being representative of the prisoners was tied to that position.

Death had altered the context in which further deaths were a consideration. McFarlane shared the view that if the pressure of Sands's hunger strike hadn't generated enough of a crisis for the British to welcome an accommodation, then the prisoners, he confided in a comm to Adams, were in for "a very long string of deaths," but that these deaths "would eventually break the Brits." With one death following on the next, the majority view became the barometer of the internal and external pressures facing the prisoners, its exact position at any point registering the level of emotion, giving the temperature of the prevailing view, not a forecast of where their emotions would lead them.

Among McFarlane's command a new consensus emerged: a realization that giving the British a breathing space had been a poor tactic. Intimations that there were moves, once again, toward direct negotiations brought pressure to steer clear of intermediaries, to make the issue become a question of the British having to negotiate directly with the hunger strikers and their representatives on the grounds that only they had the command of the details of the prison's administration that would make any agreement stick.

Sands's logic had been simple enough: if he died it would arouse the Irish people, provoke their anger, and increase support for the IRA; if he lived it would show that Margaret Thatcher could be beaten, and again increase support for the IRA. Either way, he reckoned, the IRA would win. This, however, was hardly a long-term strategy. The weakness of the first hunger strike was that the prison leadership had not worked out in advance what it would settle for, and hence couldn't convince either itself or the prisoners at large that their demands had been satisfactorily met. But a similar weakness afflicted the second hunger strike—it failed to settle on the set of procedures that would oversee implementation of a settlement, despite the presence of Adams, Morrison, and McFarlane on the hunger strike committee.

Nor were the electoral interventions in the Fermanagh–South Tyrone election in the North in April and again in August and in the general elections in the South in June part of a considered strategy. (Two H-block candidates, the blanketman Kevin Agnew and the hunger striker Kieran Doherty, were elected to the Irish parliament; a third, Kevin Lynch, narrowly missed election; collectively the nine Republican candidates polled 15 percent of the first-preference votes in the constituencies they contested.) They were the product of opportunity, and once the moment had been seized there was little leeway to improvise further, to capitalize on what had been achieved. Both interventions were predicated on not unreasonable assumptions: Fermanagh–South Tyrone on the assumption that the British government would not allow an elected member of Parliament to starve himself to death; the elections in the South on the assumption that in a close election the victory of one or two H-block candidates might result in a hung parliament, putting pressure on either Fianna Fail, led by Charles Haughey, or Fine Gael, led by Garret FitzGerald, to press the hunger strikers' case more forcefully.

Both interventions did make a difference: Fermanagh–South Tyrone focused the attention of the world media on the question, attention that was uniformly favorable and inclined to portray Sands on his own terms; the South's election almost produced a hung parliament. However, the main effect of that intervention was to take two seats away from Fianna Fail, deprive Haughey of victory, and bring into power a Fine Gael/Labour coalition that was less sympathetic to the prisoners' protest. The net effect, therefore, was to punish Haughey for his government's failure to be more supportive of the prisoners, while ensuring the victory of a coalition that would be less supportive.

Both interventions could, of course, be viewed as an attempt to force a crisis in constitutional nationalism, to co-opt its important constituencies, compelling the Catholic Church, the SDLP, and the political parties in the South to put pressure on the British government. But the level of political skill and manipulation this effort would have required was beyond the Republican movement, and there were always the old fears that any alliances the movement formed with the standard-bearers of constitutional nationalism would somehow undermine it, dilute its moral purity, contaminate it with convictions that were less than absolute, and, therefore, suspect.

Moreover, once the hunger strikes were under way, it became almost impossible to discuss ways of ending them. The hunger strikers had to know what they were dying for: their own, absolute, immutable commitment depended on there being an absolute, immutable objective. Discussions about which of the five demands might be dispensed with and which modified would introduce an element of uncertainty, destroy the delicate equilibrium between being and nonbeing the hunger strikers had to achieve in order to balance their sense of hope—which prevented despair from destroying their morale—and their sense of surrender—which sustained itself with the sure knowledge they had of what they were dying for.

"My own opinion after the first four lads died," says McGeown,

was to find a cut-off point. Bik was in agreement. I was saying that what we need to do is to grab people in different blocks and say to them "More than likely this hunger strike is going to fail. What do we do when it fails?" and begin to get them thinking about it. Bik, I think, was open to it but because of the pressures he was under to actually make the decision he needed to be able to go along to the hunger strikers and say that. The problem with doing that was that you could demoralize the hunger strikers. It could collapse within an hour of you saying that, so you couldn't do it.

But McGeown persisted in challenging the hunger strikes' logic:

I still didn't think people were taking into account what was really going on. I noticed people beginning to come to terms in the blocks [with the deaths]. When Raymond McCreesh and Patsy O'Hara died it didn't have such a great impact. Certainly there was a sense of great loss and grieving but it didn't have the impact the first two had. So I was saying to Bik, "Look, I don't think that people here are really taking in what's going on. I think one of the problems with it is that we've been through the whole blanket thing, we've put that much effort in this that the protest is now the principle and not how to solve it. I think what we need to do is to begin to say the solution is the principle, not the protest, and if that means we change from a hunger strike to going into the system we need to be able to say that. Otherwise we're going to continue to lose people."

But McFarlane had had his fill of McGeown's second-guessing and took him to task. "[I] had a long yarn with Pat Beag [McGeown] this morning," he wrote Adams on 26 July, "and impressed upon him the necessity of keeping firmly on the line. I explained that independent thought was sound, but once it began to stray from our well-considered and accepted line then it became extremely dangerous." Some weeks after that, when McGeown himself had joined the hunger strike, he and McFarlane went at it again, only this time

McGeown was more direct. How, he wondered, could the British know what the hunger strikers wanted, when he didn't even know himself. For his part, McFarlane kept referring to a "flexible settlement"—something he couldn't quite spell out but which, he insisted, the hunger strikers themselves would recognize once it was offered by the British.

But when it came time for McGeown to go to the prison hospital (McGeown took Joe McDonnell's place on the hunger strike when McDonnell died on 8 July), he was ready to toe the orthodox line. "They were saying to me," he says, " 'If you maintain your attitude when you go up to the prison hospital and you say one thing that you've said here to us, you're going to collapse the whole hunger strike.' So I had to give a commitment—I wouldn't state my views to anyone outside my OC." In hindsight, he regrets his decision. He should, he says, have "pushed harder at Bik to make a decision. I think that Bik wasn't the person who was ever going to make the decision because he felt the commitment, he felt that he couldn't pull back." The problem with the second hunger strike "was that everybody felt powerless to make a decision at the end of the day." While the outside leadership had taken a decision, "they may as well have been talking to the wall." McFarlane wouldn't make a decision, and the hunger strikers themselves "would be the last ones to make a decision to come off it."

The absence of a strategy did not, of course, mean that decisions went unmade. But they were decisions that reflected the entrapment of both the hunger strikers and the strike's planners, especially McFarlane. There was an important shift in the nature of the hunger strikers' involvement as their degree of commitment escalated. In the beginning, there were, at least, clear-cut reasons for the hunger strike, and clear-cut decisions were made. But as their level of commitment deepened, the planners and the hunger strikers were less motivated by these "rational" reasons. Rather, there was a far greater degree of "emotional" involvement: decisions to continue the hunger strikes were made either for the psychological sake of achievement, or to justify the enormous costs already incurred, or to appear to be strong-willed and not easily deterred, or because other extraneous considerations had begun to take precedence. In short, motives shifted over time from the rational to the rationalizing. "I know we are speaking here of a terrible cost in terms of men's lives,"

McFarlane wrote Adams in late April, "but high stakes will demand a high price."

By the end of June, the high price had been exacted: four hunger strikers were dead, and a fifth, Joe McDonnell, was about to die. "I now realize," McFarlane wrote, "that as long as our resolve holds fast that the Brits are always the losers. However, if they are prepared to continue to be losers without conceding any demands, then we can go only so far." But McDonnell's death hardened McFarlane's resolve. By the third week in July, he had set aside whatever earlier questions he might have entertained.

The hardening of his attitude coincided with the reopening of the contact between the IRA and the Foreign Office in early July, through the Mountain Climber contact. (Mountain Climber was the IRA's code name for the middleman who carried messages between British government officials and the Republican movement.) The movement, Gerry Adams says, was satisfied with Mountain Climber's credentials, sure that he was dealing on the British side with someone who was "a conduit for the British government with a status above the Northern Ireland secretary of state level." The British official had provided "authoritative proof" of his standing. Adams does not say that Mrs. Thatcher herself was actually involved but he is quite certain that she was aware of what was going on, that the contact "had been authorized at the very highest level," and that Republicans were dealing "with people who could make decisions and implement them, people who were speaking with the authority of the British government including Mrs. Thatcher."

"The Brits were broke," says Jake Jackson, one of the key figures in McFarlane's leadership circle. "Instead of criminalizing the hunger strikes, they had only internationalized the struggle. Instead of marginalizing the protest, they had gained it worldwide publicity. They had tested the hunger strike for evidence of brinkmanship and found only resolve. The Brits were broke [because] they had opened the lines of negotiations of their own initiative." That was "a serious move, something they had only done twice previously in the campaign"—in July 1972 and again in December 1974[2].

Gone were McFarlane's doubts about "public opinion hammering us into the ground and forcing us to end the hunger strike," the thoughts of "giving consideration to terminating the hunger strike and salvaging something from Brit concessions," the opposition to protracted hunger striking, and the belief that "if Raymond [Mc-

Creesh] and Patsy [O'Hara] died and there was still no movement they would be forced to re-assess and call a halt."[3] "After careful consideration of the over-all situation," he wrote Adams on 22 July,

I believe it would be wrong to capitulate. We took a decision and committed ourselves to hunger strike action. Our losses have been heavy—that I realize only too well. Yet I feel the part we have played in forwarding the liberation struggle has been great. Terrific gains have been made and the Brits are losing by the day. The sacrifice called for is the ultimate one and the men have made it heroically. Many others are, I believe, committed to hunger strike action to achieve a final settlement. I realize the stakes are very high—the Brits also know what capitulation means for them. Hence their entrenched position. Anyway, the way I see it is that we are fighting a war and by choice, we have placed ourselves in the front line. I still feel we should maintain this position and fight on in current fashion. It is we who are on top of the situation and we who are stronger. Therefore, we maintain. I feel we must continue until we reach a settlement or where circumstances force us into a position where no choice would be left but to capitulate. I don't believe the latter would arise. I do feel we can break the Brits. What is the price to be? I think it's a matter of setting our sights firmly on target and shooting straight ahead. It's rough, brutal and ruthless, and a lot of other things as well, but we are fighting a war and we must accept that front line troops are more susceptible to casualties than anyone. We will just have to steel ourselves to bear the worst. I will impress upon anyone who forwards his name for hunger strike that he will only have two months to live.

A week later, with the deaths of Kieran Doherty and Kevin Lynch imminent, he had become even more insistent. "I told them [the hunger strikers]," he advised Adams on 26 July, "that we had two options—(1) pursue our course for five demands or (2) capitulate now. I told them I could have accepted half-measures before Joe [McDonnell] died, but I didn't and wouldn't now. I told them the price of victory could be high and they might all die before we got a settlement." And he got what he wanted: "I then asked them for an opinion and they each told me they'd continue and hold the line."

But the psychological cost of always having to maintain the hard line, of being relentlessly resistant to suggestions that the hunger strikers give up, having to unreservedly convince himself that the pure tenaciousness of their will would ultimately break the British, having to fill many roles simultaneously and to appear emotionally neutral—a general figuring out the best use of his foot soldiers— finally exposed McFarlane's own guilt over not being on the hunger strike, for his ambivalence at having to send others to their deaths rather than being sent by others to die himself, for an outcome that, despite his fanatical convictions to the contrary, continued to prove both elusive and illusory.

I had to explain to them all [he wrote Adams on 26 July], that I had been an advocate of hunger strike from last year and should have been on first hunger strike, only your lot or else Bob [Sands] or Dark [Brendan Hughes] recognized me as a disaster area. I told them I wanted to be on this hunger strike but Bob wouldn't even listen to me. Anyway, they all realized I would be a propaganda liability. If it makes any difference, *cara,* I don't believe I would be, not now anyhow. I no longer accept the argument that tore lumps out of me last year. I've had more publicity lately than Prince Charles and not a word about it [the Bayardo bombing]. Propaganda-wise (good or bad) I'm burned out. I've always wanted to be on that front line and I haven't changed one iota. I should have been there *sin e* [that's it] and I still want to be there. I've no need to tell you what degree of commitment I have or how much understanding of the situation I have. You know I'd do my best and I know I'd die. Please don't think my request for place on hunger strike has only come [now].

The outside leadership, of course, turned down his request.

Gerry Adams met with six of the hunger strikers on 29 July—Kevin Lynch and Kieran Doherty were too weak to attend—to explain what was available as a result of the talks the IRA had had through its contact with the Foreign Office. Prison uniforms would be abolished, and prisoners would be able to wear their own clothes; there would be effective though unofficial segregation, with free association during the weekends and for three hours every day; work would include educational courses and handicrafts; the strikers' demands on visits and parcels would be met in full. In short, it was a package of substantial concessions if not quite the full substance of the five demands. Adams reiterated that the movement would not only welcome but support their decision to end the hunger strike and that the government would not make a better offer, but the hunger strikers balked. They learned that ending the hunger strike would not save the lives of Lynch and Doherty, who were both deteriorating rapidly. They would not give up: in the circumstances, says Pat McGeown, they felt that it would be cowardly. "When Gerry was in I didn't say anything to him," he says.

Bik had already said to me, "Don't make your opinions known," to which I had given my commitment. I just accepted [the situation]. One reason was that to come to terms with the whole thing, I'd had to accept in my own mind that as far as I was concerned I was just going to drift out of here. After Gerry left I came under a fair amount of pressure from the lads who were in the hospital and you had people like Tom McElwee saying to me, "Are we really against a brick wall?"—to which my answer should have been yes, but what I had to do instead was say, "Well, there's an angle here, there's an angle there, we might be able to work it out." I had been in a cell for a long time with Tom and he probably knew me better than most and he was saying to me, "Look, I don't think that's your opinion," and I was saying my opinion doesn't count. It's the opinion of the people we're here representing. And he was saying, "Look, as long as there's a possibility I'm prepared to die," and I was saying to him, "As long as there's a possibility of us getting something out of this, we're all prepared to die."

The next day, 8 August, Tom McElwee, his doubts unresolved, died suddenly, and to this day Pat McGeown regrets that he wasn't more honest with him, that he didn't tell him what he really thought.

Micky Devine had also come to the conclusion that the hunger strike should be called off. "We were sitting talking," says McGeown,

about a week before Devine died. His voice was beginning to slur and I was saying to him, "What's your opinion?"—just making conversation—and he was saying to me, "Look, I think that we need to call an end to this. Somebody has to take a decision very shortly to call an end to it," and he says "the decision has to come from us, the hunger strikers, because nobody else can take it for us." And I said, "Right, no problem." I said, "Are you saying to me now that you think you should come off the hunger strike?" He said, "No, I'm not saying that." He says, "After I die someone has to make the decision." I said "That's crazy because if you think now that that decision has to be taken, then why not take it now before you die," and he said, "No." What he didn't say but what it boiled down to was that he didn't want to be the one who took the decision. He didn't want to be the one who appeared to save his own life.

So I said to him, "Look, I arrived at that conclusion quite a while ago that sooner or later it needs to end, and it's a wee bit crazy me sitting here going to die on it [the hunger strike] but I know how you feel, and I know whenever it comes my turn I'll probably be saying, I don't want to be the one either to break the whole thing."

What we agreed, since the doctors reckoned Micky had about ten days or so left, and ten days would have just taken us over the Owen Carron election [Carron was the Sinn Fein candidate in the election held to replace Sands], so I said to him, "Hold out for the ten days. After the Fermanagh–South Tyrone by-election I don't see any political point in us continuing the hunger strike and I'll be saying that quite openly." To say to him to come off it before it [the by-election], politically I did think we needed to stay until the whole process had been completed with Owen Carron. [Carron won the seat, beating the Official Unionist candidate Ken Maginnis.]

But it was not to be. On the day of the by-election, 20 August, Micky Devine died. On the same day Pat McGeown lapsed into a coma and his wife, Pauline, intervened to save his life.

In the end the hunger strikers were more concerned with not letting down their dying and dead comrades—"Tell outside I won't be letting anybody down" had been Francis Hughes's last message to the Re-

publican leadership, and Pat McGeown would have died had not his
wife intervened—than with the nuts and bolts of a settlement. And
thus their entrapment: what Robert Jay Lifton calls in *Life and Death:
Survivors & Hiroshima* "the inseparability of death and guilt,"[4] the
propensity for the living hunger strikers to nurture within themselves
an image of the dead hunger strikers and to act as they imagined the
dead hunger strikers did or would. "You saw yourself as the front
line in the fight against the Brits and everything sort of weighed in
on you and you were saying it's a question of you going through
with it or else you could do immense damage," says McGeown.

> You wouldn't in reality have done immense damage but you felt that you would
> and each hunger striker had to go through that to take him over the brink. They
> had to feel that so much weighed on their shoulders as individuals, and that's
> what gave you the capacity to go over. To back down would have cost so much
> that there was no other way out, just to go forward. Whenever [Mrs. Thatcher]
> used the term "This is the IRA's last card," then we actually saw ourselves on
> the front line. We felt this air of importance that we were the front line in the
> struggle and that if we were to take one step back, it would be a defeat for the
> whole movement. You'd all those things but in the end it was the case of saying
> "Right, we've come this far and we're not going back, so we will continue."

Liam McCloskey, who came off his hunger strike on 26 September,
fifty-five days after he had begun it, expresses a similar predicament:
how his intense commitment to his fellow prisoners, especially the
other hunger strikers, dead or alive, overwhelmed all other considerations. "Once you were on hunger strike," he says, "it would have
taken more courage to actually stop of your own accord than to keep
going on because it seemed so much like losing face and backing
down when other men died. . . . We were caught in our own trap
where there were ten men dead and we felt we had to keep going on
and look for a way out of it."[5]

Entrapment, say psychologists Dean Pruitt and Jeffrey Rubin, is
"self-perpetuating, engendering increasing degrees of commitment."[6]
The decision to replace the first four hunger strikers on an individual
basis when they died was followed by a further escalation in early
June, which called for adding one prisoner per week to the hunger
strike, beginning with Tom McElwee on 8 June. The rationale for
this particular decision was that it would maintain pressure on the
government, give it no breathing spaces between deaths, and thus
make it more likely to negotiate a resolution. However, it also gave
the hunger strikers no breathing space, and when the interval between

deaths began to grow smaller, the cumulative impact created a momentum of its own that was impossible to break. On the one hand, it would have seemed inappropriate to call off the hunger strike just after a hunger striker had died, since the same decision to do so days earlier might have saved his life; on the other hand, since there was increasingly less time between deaths, a decision to wait before taking action to end the hunger strike would ensure that it was too late to save the life of at least one more hunger striker. Caught between giving due respect to the dead and due regard to the living, the hunger strikers' loyalty to the dead prevailed.

McFarlane's attitude toward the attempts of outside mediators to resolve the problem was one of ambivalence and high suspicion. His energy was concentrated on trying to contain the hunger strike, on trying to control outside events. Increasingly, his paranoia surfaced. The British could not be trusted; they were using the hunger strike to try to break the IRA; the Church and others on the outside were working to undermine the hunger strikers' families; the SDLP and the Irish government had their own agendas and would ultimately sell them short; even the prison chaplains were working to break the strike.

Every prospect of mediation was an occasion for extreme anxiety, for trying to manipulate the process to the prisoners' advantage, for having to straddle the fine line between being open to reasonable compromise and not being willing to concede the substance of the prisoners' demands. While the prisoners could not appear to be inflexible, since anything that made them appear more inflexible made the government appear less inflexible, nevertheless, all intermediaries were to be treated as Trojan horses, since their intent was obviously to undermine the hunger strikers' solidarity, drive a wedge between them and their families, weaken morale, and hold out a hope that would ultimately prove to be unfounded and, therefore, dangerous to the hunger strikers' psychic well-being.

Moreover, since the strikers were convinced that Britain wanted above all to win, to turn public opinion against them, to defeat the hunger strike and hence the movement, all the government's responses or appearances of being responsive had to be discounted. Not to discount them would introduce an element of uncertainty, of doubt, and uncertainty and doubt would undermine the prisoners' psychological unity. Any suggestion that a good-faith bargaining process was possible was too threatening and posed almost insuperable problems of coping. Only in the face of the absolute conviction that Britain would remain intransigent could the hunger strikers maintain their own intransigence. The vicious circle of entrapment was complete.

6   **The** most serious public attempt at resolving the prison crisis came with the intervention of the Irish Commission for Justice and Peace (ICJP). The major function of the Commission was to monitor the Irish government's contributions to Third World countries, although it also concerned itself with a wide range of civil liberties issues, and operated a comprehensive education program in conjunction with the Irish Council for Churches. In May, following the deaths of Raymond McCreesh and Patsy O'Hara, the Commission formulated a statement which called for a resolution to the crisis that would involve no concession of principle on either side. The hierarchy approved the statement and it was published on 3 June. The Commission then met with the families of the hunger strikers and were encouraged by them to try and work for a solution, albeit an honorable one. The Commission undertook to do so, realizing that the families could become a pressure group in their own right, with the potential to force a settlement over the heads of the Republican movement.

Public hope for the Irish Commission's efforts was high. The five members of the Commission's executive committee—Father Oliver Crilly, Dermot O'Mahony, auxiliary bishop of Dublin and Commission president, Brian Gallagher, a Dublin solicitor and Commission chairman, Jerome Connolly, secretary of the Commission, and Hugh Logue, the SDLP's spokesperson on economics—had a series of intense discussions with Michael Alison, Humphrey Atkins's second-in-command and the minister in charge of the prisons, on four occasions—between 23 June and 4 July—that lasted for a total of almost seventeen hours.

From the beginning the Commission was in an awkward position, since the meetings with Alison were held on the strict understanding that the Commission was in no sense negotiating but rather "clarifying" the attitude of the British government to some proposals the Commission had put forward. In time the commissioners would describe themselves as either "catalysts of listening," "facilitators," or "mediators." But it is clear that they felt they were in some sense negotiating, even though they could not really think of themselves strictly in these terms, especially when the meetings with Alison were followed by meetings with the hunger strikers. This dichotomy, however, gave them a somewhat confused idea of their own role—not quite negotiators but more than facilitators, exploring options but not authorized to develop concrete proposals—that contributed to the disappointment and recriminations that accompanied the collapse of their efforts.

Throughout the Irish Commission's intervention, the prison leadership adopted a public posture of cautious support. But that support did not extend to their own deliberations. "We were attempting by all means to get rid of the ICJP," says Jackson, "but it wasn't a case of when to get rid of them but how to get rid of them." It wasn't all that simple. The ICJP might have been "the vehicle that the Brits wanted to use for a settlement," in which case the question became one of finding a way of "putting them on the long finger." If they weren't the means the British intended to utilize for a settlement, then they were only "a distraction, a hindrance, because the Brits were not going to arrive at their base line as long as they had a second iron in the fire, so we needed to get rid of the second iron." It was a question of equivocal surmise, at best, whether the British genuinely wanted to use the Commission to reach a solution or whether they were simply using it for a fallback position. "Bik and I," says Jackson, "both agreed they [the Commission] were a fallback position and that they were being used and we tried to tell them that from the onset." Tom McElwee, Father Oliver Crilly's second cousin, was told to "unload" Crilly—but either McElwee wouldn't or wasn't sufficiently forceful, and the Commission set out on its largely undefined mission.

The first meeting took place on 23 June at Stormont. The Commission's terms of reference were discussed but the main emphasis was on clothing; the issue of the prisoners wearing their own clothing, it appeared, would not be a problem. Over the next few days the Commission met with relatives of the hunger strikers and with members of the H-block Committee who emphasized that only the hunger strikers themselves could decide what would settle the crisis; hence the absolute importance of the Commission talking with the hunger strikers.

The second meeting with Alison took place on Friday, 24 June, at

Hillsborough Castle. The main topic of discussion was association, and at one point Alison, his aides, and the Commission members got down on their hands and knees on the floor, poring over maps of the prison trying to work out how association between blocks might be facilitated.

When Humphrey Atkins issued a statement on 29 June that the ICJP found encouraging, McFarlane simply dismissed it, in a comm to Adams, as containing "nothing we haven't heard before." But he was keenly aware of the document's propaganda value, since "the impression can be created that they [the British] are contemplating a settlement of sorts." It could, therefore, "mislead people into believing the Brits are genuine." The Commission's favorable response to Atkins's statement would, McFarlane believed, "increase the hope and expectations of the families and subsequently their distress would be all the greater." Atkins's maneuvers were "a trick to create [the] impression of movement."

On 30 June, Michael Alison wrote to Bishop O'Mahony spelling out in great detail precisely where the government stood. "At our meetings," his letter said, "we had a constructive discussion of the changes which you [the Irish Commission] suggested might be reasonably made to the regime at the Maze Prison for prisoners who were prepared to accept the authority of the Prisoner Governor." In other words, Alison was assuming that their discussions were taking place in the context of what changes in the prison regime might be considered once the hunger strike ended. There would be no question whatsoever of granting "any group of prisoners a special privileged status on the basis of the motives they claim for the acts that brought them to the prison in the first place." Furthermore, in the government's view, "the so-called five demands [were] intended to secure precisely what we [the government] cannot give. It is therefore of vital importance," the letter went on, "that there should be no ambiguity in the government's position. . . . The government believes it would be wrong to make moves in advance of the ending of the hunger strike and simply hope they would have the [desired] effect. In other words the government is not prepared to give the protesters something on account in the hope that they would not present the rest of the bill later."

The Commission was undaunted, unheeding the implicit warning in Alison's letter that the government was not prepared to concede much, and then only if the hunger strikes were called off, that compromise was not part of the lexicon. The third meeting, on 3 July, also took place at Hillsborough. It began at 2:30 P.M. and went on without interruption until 10:30 P.M. The two sides discussed a range of issues: joining up exercise yards to facilitate association during the day; the question of choice with regard to work, one suggestion being that if a prisoner didn't choose one of the forms of work on offer, work would be arbitrarily allocated to him; segregation was conceded in practice but not in principle. The sticking point, however, was clothing. The Commission's suggestion that the ending of the hunger strike be simultaneous with the availability of the prisoners' own clothing was more than simply unacceptable; in the light of Alison's obdurate insistence that prisoners would not be given the right to wear their own clothes at all times, it was peremptorily nonnegotiable. There was, Alison bluntly told the Commission, "a lady behind the veil"—a remark which the Commission took to be a direct reference to Mrs. Thatcher. (Alison does not dispute having said this. It was, he says, a symbolic way of telling the Commission that he was not the ultimate authority. He insists, however, that he had not discussed the clothing issue with Mrs. Thatcher and that he had received no instructions whatsoever from her.) The commissioners came out of their meeting with Alison feeling that their efforts had failed and that not much could be gained from further discussions in view of the British position on clothing. Furthermore, they had not received any indication that they would be given access to the hunger strikers, although, in fact, they themselves would not at that point have considered a meeting with the hunger strikers worthwhile or even desirable, given the impasse they had apparently reached with Alison.

"We now believe that the Commission has absolutely nothing in their so-called clarifications," McFarlane relayed to Adams that evening. "The lads don't expect much to come of their [ICJP's] efforts and proposals so perhaps we'll get some sort of condemnatory statement from them against the Brits which would help us." In the propaganda war, a statement that did not include an explicit attack on your antagonists was a statement of implicit support for them.

Both sides met again on 4 July for what Commission members felt was a pro-forma exercise. Within minutes of the meeting's beginning, however, Alison did a complete about-face. If the hunger strikes were to end, he told the Commission, the government would not appear to be acting under duress, in which case all prisoners would be allowed to wear their own clothes. Own clothing as a right, not a privilege? Hugh Logue asked. Own clothing as a right, Alison replied. (Alison doesn't recall this specific exchange but doesn't dispute that it occurred. Clothing, he says, was never a nonnegotiable issue.)

After the meeting with Alison the Commission was given permission to go immediately to the Maze/Long Kesh Prison. When they arrived, they were brought to the hospital wing and into a small, cream-colored room, with windows on one side, thick concrete bars built across the windows on the outside, and a small rectangular observation window at one end. The prisoners came in, dressed in either pajamas or clothing depending how long they'd been on hunger strike. Joe McDonnell, now in the fifty-seventh day of his fast and obviously in very poor shape—"looking sunken but not emaciated, in the same way as someone who had spent six months on very little rations" is how Jerome Connolly remembers him—was wheeled into the room in a wheelchair. The eight hunger strikers sat on one side of a table on which jugs of water had been placed; the five commissioners sat opposite them. The jugs of water stick in the commissioners' minds: images of the hunger strikers constantly reaching for water—not that the strikers were gulping the water down or even filling their glasses; rather it was the continual, monotonous sipping, a methodical savoring—water, itself the essence of life, became a point of reference, a symbol of what the hunger strikes entailed. The commissioners made the hunger strikers a gift of a newly published Gaelic edition of the Bible they had purchased on their way to Belfast—a gift that was intended to establish the commissioners' good will, to intimate to the hunger strikers that the Commission was, to the extent that it could be, on their side.

For the next two hours the two sides went over the proposals the Commission had hammered out with Alison and which it now thought were on offer. Prisoners would be allowed to wear their own clothes at all times as a matter of right, not privilege; association would be improved by allowing movement by all prisoners during daily exercise time between the yard blocks of every two adjacent wings within each block and between the recreation rooms of the two adjacent wings in each block during the daily recreational period; the definition of work would be expanded to ensure every prisoner the widest choice of activities—for example, prisoners with levels of expertise in crafts or the arts could teach these skills to other prisoners as part of their work schedules, prisoners would be allowed to perform work for a range of charitable or voluntary bodies, and such work could even include the building of a church "or equivalent facilities for religious worship within the prison."

The hunger strikers were suspicious—it took time to establish trust—but they were also attentive. They wanted detail, what Hugh Logue called the footnotes of the proposals. At the end of the meeting they said they had, to use their own phrase, "the skeleton of an agreement"—it was a phrase the commissioners remembered, delivered in all seriousness by the hunger strikers with no thought to its macabre appropriateness to their own situation.

The commissioners left the meeting feeling optimistic. They had, they felt, made considerable progress. While the hunger strikers had by no means bought the whole deal, they had not rejected it out of hand. Later that same evening the prisoners, increasingly sensitive to the heightening public expectations that a settlement might be at hand and fearful of being seen as outwitted by the government, moved to seize the propaganda initiative. They issued an exceptionally conciliatory statement, which had been composed before the Commission's visit: they were not looking for "differential treatment from other prisoners. . . . On this major point of British policy . . . no sacrifice of principle" was being called for. They would welcome "the introduction of the five demands for all prisoners."

On Sunday, 5 July, Bishop O'Mahony, Hugh Logue, and Father Crilly went back to the Maze/Long Kesh to talk with McFarlane. They spent about four hours with him. This was not the McFarlane of the genial disposition, the man for whom few had a bad word. The Commission found him cold, distant, hostile, emotionally detached, a man who appeared to have little concern for the lives of the prisoners—a "bad man" in the words of one commissioner—who played his cards close to his chest and made the Commission feel it was intruding. "We didn't like McFarlane at all," says Brian Gallagher. "He wasn't concerned with the lives or feelings of the people who were on hunger strike." "Bik McFarlane," says another commissioner, "was a very cold person, a steely person—obviously he had nerves of steel—who didn't seem to have become very emotionally involved. He didn't come across as being in any way greatly concerned." Father Crilly found him "tough. . . . He didn't give us any indication at any stage that he was going to listen and act. He was quite cynical in his interpretation of the British. He made it quite clear that he didn't think the British would deliver anything of what

they were saying to us. He was really coldly dismissive of any possibility that the British really meant what they were saying to us."

That evening the commissioners met with the prisoners again for
about two and a half hours. This time the conversation centered on
the question of guarantees—although the hunger strikers had not
indicated that they regarded what was being proposed as being fully
acceptable. They would, they said, have to consult their colleagues.
But they simply would not give up the hunger strike on the basis of
some goodwill understanding that reforms would be introduced; the
fallout from the first hunger strike made the question of public guarantees a sine qua non for any settlement. They wanted a senior official
from the NIO to come into the prison and spell out to them what
was on offer—they would have to hear it from the British themselves
rather than take the Commission's word for it. Nevertheless, the
focus on the question of guarantees led the commissioners to believe
that what had been put on offer the day before had not been repudiated, even after overnight consideration. They were, they believed,
beginning to put some flesh on the skeleton.

There was, however, at least one moment of anxiety when the
hunger strikers thought that Bishop O'Mahony was trying to raise
religious reasons why they should abandon their fasts. "I remember
at one stage," says Logue, "the Bishop and I trying to persuade them
that what they had was worthwhile and going beyond the facts and
asking them what were they thinking of and the Bishop trying to
raise [the moral arguments] and Kevin Lynch and one of the other
prisoners put their hands to their ears and started to wave their hands
violently saying that they couldn't take it, that this was the moral
argument against dying, that if we were going to start that kind of
talk we were to be thrown out."

But things settled down. Once again McFarlane was the person
put on the spot. "On the last night," says Logue, "they [the hunger
strikers] were all saying that we had to square any settlement we had,
even if it was acceptable to them, with Bik." In short, what the
prisoners appeared to be saying was that if the terms were acceptable
to McFarlane, they were acceptable to them. McFarlane was down
the corridor in his bed—he had been brought into the hospital wing
that evening and provided with a bed there so that he could stay over
and be available for consultation with the commissioners if the need
arose. O'Mahony and Logue went down to talk with him. "He listened to us for about two minutes," says Logue, "and turned around

and went back to sleep and Joe McDonnell was going to be dead within thirty-six hours and I never forgave him for that. He was not in the business of trying to get a solution." Nevertheless, the commissioners left the prison in a hopeful state. Before they left, Kieran Doherty spoke briefly in Gaelic to Oliver Crilly. Doherty, Crilly told Logue, had told him that if somebody came in and read the terms out to the hunger strikers, they would accept them.

Sinn Fein didn't want the Commission involved, and didn't bother to conceal its antipathy for what it considered to be a Catholic Church–SDLP–Irish establishment intervention aimed more at ending the hunger strikes than at addressing the full range of the prisoners' demands. "It was a disgraceful episode that they [the Commission] were involved in," says Gerry Adams. "An SDLP politician, a bishop and a couple of other people were involved in a disgraceful episode of raising families' expectations, of playing on the prisoners' emotions. . . . The ICJP were a diversion and not only because of their political antagonism to Republicanism. There was, one, the actual substance of what was being talked about; two, the wrong signal was being given to the British by the ICJP; three, the ICJP's own selfish political concerns overrode the issue, and then finally there was the whole time problem."

The Commission took things out of Sinn Fein's orbit of control, especially with regard to the families. Jimmy Drumm, a senior Sinn Fein official (his wife, Maire, was assassinated by Protestant paramilitaries in March 1976), had specific responsibility for the families of the hunger strikers. Often he would be the one who broke the news to a family that their son was going on hunger strike. He traveled with the families all over Ireland, would see them after they visited their sons, was always on hand for advice and comfort. He was in charge of organizing regular meetings of the relatives to keep them abreast of what was happening. When a hunger striker died, he always went to the morgue with a family to collect the remains, and he was in charge of the funeral arrangements. Drumm was both counselor and companion to the families. It was he, some say, who took Bobby Sands's mother aside when she threatened to go on television to say that she disapproved of the hunger strikes and reminded her of Bobby's wishes in the matter and where her obligations lay. He was, says Drumm, "almost one hundred percent involved with the families. I stayed with them for days." During the ICJP intervention Sinn Fein brought the families together. "We told them," says Drumm, "not to get their hopes up, not to put too much trust in what the Commission was doing, that the Republican movement had made certain contacts that looked like they might lead somewhere." The Commission, he says, "hadn't anything more than was offered weeks before. Alison was merely stringing them along."

The families were warm and receptive to the Commission, however, and the Commission regularly briefed them on what was going on. The Commission believed that the outside leadership, especially Adams and Morrison, was exerting great influence on the hunger strikers, that the IRA could order an end to the hunger strikes, that within the prison nothing could be done unless it passed muster with McFarlane, and that the Republican movement on the outside was closely monitoring the families.

Hugh Logue, one of the key Commission players, saw the tension between the Republican movement and the Commission as a struggle for the hearts and minds of the families, the Commission's threat coming not so much from what it might achieve on its own but from its imparting to the families a sense of their collective strength, the knowledge that their predicaments, taken together, were greater than the sum of their individual parts. The more the families discussed the options open to the hunger strikers, the more aware they became of the possibilities open to them and the less their sense of powerlessness. "Many of the parents, many of the mothers in particular, were simply saying, 'We want our sons off the hunger strike,' " says Logue, "but the parents were the people who were the Provos' buffer and the stronger they got the weaker the Provos would have gotten."

On Monday, 6 July, the Commission spent the better part of the day preparing a statement setting out its understanding of what it and the British had agreed to. While it was doing so, Logue and Crilly were called out to see Gerry Adams. Adams says he told them that the ICJP was undermining the prisoners' position, that the prisoners actually had on offer a better deal than the one the ICJP thought they were putting together. He did not, he says, suggest that the British had been in touch with the Republican movement, although it was implicit in what he was saying. (Crilly and Logue have differing recollections of the meeting. Crilly remembers Adams telling them there had been a contact from someone in England working on behalf of the British government and that he spelled out "what this other gentleman was offering them." Logue, on the other hand, says that

Adams "had in minute detail all of the concessions we were being offered and we didn't doubt that he was having contact with them [the British]." He is insistent, however, that Adams never used the word *negotiations*. "My impression was that he was saying 'Thank you very much but get out of the way.' I had no sense," he says, "of Adams saying that they were doing better. All I had was the sense that the British had established contact.")

This second line of contact upset the Commission. Members saw it simply as one more manifestation of an inveterate British capacity for duplicity, a betrayal of the trust the two sides had endeavored to establish with each other. And some believed that the British had opened a second line to confirm with the IRA that the terms on offer were acceptable to the IRA, that it was a kind of "authentication and verification" process to establish whether the IRA would allow or order the men to come off the hunger strike if the terms were acceptable to the hunger strikers. There was disappointment and frustration among the commissioners, and especially anger at Alison, who, they believed, had willfully misled them. Later they confronted him on the issue but his reactions—he looked "blank," was "totally non-plussed," "looked astonished," "was at a loss for words," "got up from his chair, walked back and sat down again like an involuntary act"—convinced them that he didn't know the second line of contact had been opened, that he was as much in the dark about what was going on as they were. (Alison may not have been the only one not in the know. According to Jake Jackson, the only people he could say knew for sure about the Mountain Climber initiative at that point were himself, McFarlane, block OCs Pat McGeown and Sid Walsh and the PRO Richard O'Rawe, and the hunger striker Joe McDonnell. As for the rest, he says, it would have been on "a need-to-know basis": the closer a hunger striker was to dying the more likely he was to know. Micky Devine and Kevin Lynch, the INLA members, wouldn't have been informed, one way or the other, nor would the hunger strikers who were still on the blocks. Gerry Adams, however, insists that "any communication which came from the British went to the prisoners. Not a scrap of paper, not a line, not one iota was held from them." Moreover, Danny Morrison was allowed into the Maze/Long Kesh to see the hunger strikers on the morning of 5 July— before the ICJP's second meeting with them—to apprise them of what was going on although he did not go into detail. Morrison says that he relayed the information about the contact and impressed on them the fact the ICJP could "make a mess of it, that they could be settling for less than what they had the potential for achieving.")

For Logue, the second line of contact once again marginalized the families. "The families," he says,

had moved from [the position of] being weak and timid towards the Provos to a point where the previous Sunday [5 July] they had thrown the Provos out [of a meeting] and said they only wanted to talk with us. The families had got very tough with Morrison and with Adams and Jimmy Drumm. . . . Our sense of betrayal by the British was much more a sense of the families being marginalized. . . . We had gotten the Provos to an extent sidelined and gotten the families [to the point of] demanding that the hunger strike be ended and they were putting pressure on the youngsters in the prison. We were well on the way there and they [the hunger strikers] were ready to accept what was on offer. . . . We had shaken the families free of the tentacles [of the Provos]. They were still grappling with them but they had by now said they were going to run the thing. We were in the driver's seat at that stage and our primary concern was that having taken the families that far with us and having got to a stage of the Brits making a proposal, the families were being forced back into the Provos' arms by what the British were doing.

The commissioners, having had it out with Alison over the second line of contact, now presented him with a document setting out their understanding of the agreement. Alison, they say, made only two inconsequential changes in the document. They pressed him to send an NIO official into the prison that evening to go over the document with the hunger strikers. He said he would do it the following morning. On the commissioners' instructions, the chaplain at the Maze/Long Kesh told the hunger strikers that they would not be coming in that evening but that an NIO official would be there the following morning. The following morning became the following afternoon and then the following evening, and still no official had been sent in. At one point David Wyatt, a senior NIO official who had sat in on most of the discussions, rang to explain the delay: a lot of redrafting was going on and it had to be cleared with London.

At 6:00 P.M. the British still had not sent anybody in. The Dublin government tried to put pressure on London to do so, without effect. At 10:00 P.M. Alison rang the Commission and asked for Logue and O'Mahony to come up to Stormont to see him. The Commission's document, he told them, explained what was to the prisoners' benefit but it didn't sufficiently spell out the deal's negative aspects. Asked by Logue why no representative had been sent into the prison that morning, Logue says that Alison replied, "Frankly, I was not a sufficient plenipotentiary." Alison assured them, however, that the medical reports indicated that McDonnell would not die that night or not even perhaps for forty-eight hours. He said an official would be going into the prison between 7:00 and 8:00 the following morning, Wednesday, 8 July. At 5:40 A.M., Joe McDonnell died. At 7:30 A.M. a relatively junior NIO official, Carl Jackson, went into the prison and was present when the governor, Stanley Hilditch, made a statement to the prisoners that bore little resemblance to the document the Irish Commission had drawn up. It simply stated once again that the hunger strike had to end, that there would be no change in the administration of the prison until the prisoners gave up their protest, and restated for the umpteenth time what privileges were already available to conforming prisoners.

The Commission held a press conference releasing the document it had presented to Alison and the details of their meetings with him and the hunger strikers. It blamed the British government for the breakdown, although it conceded that throughout Alison had acted in good faith. Bishop O'Mahony said there had been "a definite clawing back of the governments' position between Monday, July 6th, and Wednesday, July 8th."

Speaking to reporters in Washington, D.C., a few days later, Alison pinned the blame for the breakdown in the talks on the Commission's "overeagerness." The Commission had "exaggerated" and "misrepresented" what he had said during the talks, it had inflated his "privately expressed sentiments" to suggest "inaccurately" that a solution was near, it had come up with a document "which was wildly euphoric and wildly out of perspective." He compared talking to hunger strikers to talking to hijackers—in both cases "you continued talking while you figured out a way to defeat them, while allowing them to save face."

It was over. When the ICJP intervention collapsed with Joe McDonnell's death on 8 July, McFarlane cut its lifeline. "No one will be talking to them [ICJP] unless I am present," he wrote Adams, "and then it will only be to tell them to skite. OK? If we can render them [ICJP] ineffective now, then we leave the way clear for a direct approach without all the ballsing about. The reason we didn't skite them in the first place was because I was afraid of coming across as inflexible or even intransigent. Our softly, softly approach with them has left the impression that we are taking their proposals as a settlement. I'm sorry now I didn't tell them to go and get stuffed."

When, weeks later, on 16 July, the International Red Cross delegation arrived, McFarlane was equally blunt. "I told them," he wrote Adams, "that Brits [were] only using them to create the illusion of movement and trying to sink us simultaneously." If they wanted to help they should tell the British to "talk directly [to us] about a settlement based on our five demands."

Meanwhile, the Mountain Climber contact with the outside leadership of the IRA in the wake of the hunger strikers' statement of 4 July did not yield the anticipated dividends. According to the Republican movement, the Foreign Office intermediary said the government would issue a statement setting out concessions, including the right of prisoners to wear their own clothes, provided the hunger strikers first ended their hunger strike; the sticking points continued to be association, segregation, restoration of lost remission, and work. (This offer could hardly be described as significantly better than the proposals the Irish Commission believed it had worked out with Alison.) The IRA passed on details of its negotiations to the Republican leadership on the outside who, in turn, passed it on to the Republican leadership on the inside through a network of priests who visited the prison.

From the start both the prison leadership and those negotiating on behalf of the hunger strikers wanted public guarantees to underwrite a settlement, and public guarantees were the one thing the British, whether through the Irish Commission or the Mountain Climber conduit, would not agree to.

The Republican movement maintains that the essentials of a settlement had been worked out in late July. Prisoners would get to wear their own clothes, their visiting and letter privileges and one-fifth of lost remission would be restored, but no new breakthroughs had been made on work (the issue would be fudged), association, or segregation. Concessions, of course, would only be forthcoming after the hunger strike ended. At one point, says a senior Republican source, the contact informed the movement that Mrs. Thatcher wanted the hunger strikes out of the way before a summit of Western leaders in Ottawa scheduled to take place on 19 July. The text of what Mrs. Thatcher would say in Ottawa, if the hunger strike ended, was passed on to the Republican movement, according to the source, and the movement in turn passed the text on to the hunger strikers. (On occasion senior Sinn Fein officials said that they did not want to be identified by name because "the British are going to come back to us for some contact in the future and if they're reading your book and it's us blah, blah blahing all over the place. . . .")

But the prison leadership had not forgotten the debacle of December, when secret documents were shuttled over from London at the last moment and what appeared to them to be the government's about-face once the hunger strike was over. It wanted public guarantees: face-to-face negotiations between the hunger strikers, their outside representatives, and the NIO in the presence of to-be-named guarantors before they would consider calling off the hunger strike.

"The fact is," says Adams, "that the British government in their general demeanor and general public position were telling lies because on the one hand while Margaret Thatcher was saying the hunger strikers were the IRA playing its last card, on the other hand [a government official] was relaying to the IRA prisoners involved exactly what Mrs. Thatcher's position was. . . . The private position was a considerable bit apart from their public position in terms of the contact as well as in the substance of what they were saying."

But nothing had really changed. The government, whether talking through the NIO or the Foreign Office agent or whomever, was reinforcing the same message: concessions, substantial concessions perhaps, were possible provided the protesting prisoners called off the hunger strike. Someone had to lose face and the government wasn't about to; to the end it would maintain its position that it would not negotiate under duress. "The whole way through the second hunger strike," says McGeown, "what Mountain Climber said to us was that the position is remaining the same as in that initial document [the thirty-four-page document plus the clarifications that had been received from London the previous December]: being the one where they publicly said no flexibility, privately they said we can afford to be flexible. What Mountain Climber's [Foreign Office contact] continuously said was, 'That's the position, that's as far as we are going.' " The thrust of the hunger strikers' demands began to change, therefore, from an emphasis on the five demands themselves to the manner whereby concessions on offer would be implemented— not, of course, that they were about to abandon the essential substance of their demands.

The strategy, therefore, became terrifyingly simple: maintain the hunger strike at all costs, and the British, having already been forced to the negotiating table, would find their way back once they realized that nothing could break the hunger strikers' resolve—not even defections due to family interventions. "What we were saying to them," says Jackson, "was there had to be an agreement that was stood over by guarantors. One of our strongest lines of argument to the Brits was 'We're not doubting you're genuine but you people have to try to implement a prison administration which is Orange to the core, which is full of people who hate our guts, who don't understand where you people are at, they simply want to put their boot into us,' and we're saying that the only way you can ensure a solution is if you have guarantors who will oversee the implementation of that solution, because these people [the prison administration] are not going to do it of their own accord."

Thus the hunger strike strategy: "to clear out all the middle men and wait for the Brits." Each side settled in to outwait the other: the British, seeing for the first time, in late July, signs of disunity in the ranks of the hunger strikers' families (a harbinger of bitter divisions to come), unmindful, perhaps even unconcerned, that for the Republican movement their public words counted for naught, that their penchant for clandestine activities, authorized or unauthorized, was keeping the hunger strikers' hopes alive; the prison leadership—and the hunger strikers—confident or perhaps desperate in the belief that the pressure that had led the British to open the Mountain Climber contact in the first place would again force them to do so.

Elements of the prison leadership had respect for Lord Peter Carrington, the British secretary of state for foreign and commonwealth affairs, the man they believed was behind the Foreign Office initiative. They remembered his role in Zimbabwe when he brought all the parties together and transformed Robert Mugabe, once at the top of Mrs. Thatcher's list of most despised terrorists, into a statesman. The Carringtons of the world were, they believed, pillars of the establishment, pragmatists, open to the long view. Cognizant of the damage the hunger strikes were doing to Anglo-Irish relations in general and to the British image abroad in particular, they were men of the world, not hostages to the ideological hardliners around Mrs. Thatcher who played to a home audience; they were men who had a world view, who would do business, strike a bargain.

"Carrington," says Jackson, "would have had the long view. I wouldn't call him a honest broker. He would have been a more subtle Brit—you only have to look at his whole dealings with the Rhodesian effort and the Lancaster House negotiations. I mean this is his style. He would have taken a longer view than Thatcher. I can't think myself into a position where Mountain Climber didn't exist. Because that's how their system operates, that's how it's always operated, and that's how they'll eventually do it in this struggle." Lord Carrington had a far less benevolent characterization of the hunger strikers. "The IRA," he said, days before Bobby Sands died, "does not represent anyone. Don't tell me that the IRA represents people in Northern Ireland or people in the Republic of Ireland. They have no status. They are not accepted by anyone. They are terrorists, pure and simple."

The hunger strikers would not budge: for them, at the end of July, with six dead and two rapidly approaching death and beyond saving, the issue of loyalty superseded the lure of compromise. Their immutability increased with the number of their dead. When others called for more flexibility, they became less flexible, adding one more demand: the government had to talk directly to them.

7 **They** were ordinary young men who came, for the most part, from large families—five came from families with eight or more children—with working-class parents. Five were from the city: Patsy O'Hara and Micky Devine came from the Catholic ghettos of Derry, Joe McDonnell and Kieran Doherty from West Belfast, the cockpit of Republicanism, Bobby Sands from Twinbrook; and five from rural communities: Francis Hughes and Thomas McElwee from Tamlaghtduff, County Derry, Raymond McCreesh from Camlough, County Armagh, Martin Hurson from Cappagh, County Tyrone, Kevin Lynch from Park, County Derry—small villages of little bigotries and easy whispers where the character of a family was often measured by the purity of its Republican pedigree. Only three had finished high school, most had left school at fifteen or sixteen, and none had gone on to college. Two, McCreesh and Hurson, were very religious; two, Hurson and Devine, had lost parents—Hurson his mother and Devine both his mother and father—when they were in their midteens, and both had suffered traumatic aftereffects. Only one, Hughes, was serving a life sentence; seven had terms of fourteen years or less—sentences that would have been commuted to seven years, under current remission practices, had they put on prison uniforms and conformed to prison regulations when their sentences began.

All of them, except Hughes and Doherty, who were on the run at the time of their arrests, lived at home. They either worked at commonplace jobs (McCreesh was a milkman, McDonnell an upholsterer, Hurson a welder, Lynch a builder's assistant, McElwee a garage mechanic) or were unemployed. They did the normal things young people their ages do: they played sports, attended football games, went dancing, enjoyed the outdoors, hung out with their friends, spent time with their families. They were part of their communities, connected to the ebb and flow of life around them.

Seven came from either staunchly Republican families—families with ties to militant Republicanism that looked on Northern Ireland as an illegitimate statelet held through force by an occupying power— or from staunchly Republican areas with a history of resistance to Stormont rule, where one generation handed down to the next the tradition of resistance, often more honored in the telling than in the practice. The three who didn't—Sands, Lynch and Devine—compensated for their lack of Republican credentials with a commitment that even the ardent might at times have found excessive. Three— O'Hara, McDonnell, and McElwee—had brothers who had done time on the blanket, and two others—Hughes and Doherty—had brothers who had been interned. All came of age during the civil rights movement of the late 1960s, and all had, at one time or another, been arrested, held, interned, detained, interrogated, or physically maltreated by the security forces. Two, Hughes and Lynch, were beaten—Hughes severely so—by British soldiers.

None was brought up in circumstances of physical deprivation or in poverty except, perhaps, for Micky Devine. The oppression they had experienced was more psychic than physical—the collective sense Catholics had of living in an alien, unnatural state that denied them the expression of their Irishness. Their expectations, like those of their Catholic neighbors, were also psychic: that one day the unfinished business of national unity would be accomplished. Their affinity was with the idea of a united Ireland, rather than with the trappings of the twenty-six-county state. Indeed, in their eyes, it, too, was a puppet state: the illegally conceived Irish Free State that had turned its back on true Republican orthodoxy.

The hunger strikers all shared one characteristic: a fierce, almost fanatical determination to pursue a course of action once it was chosen. Nor was this especially surprising. Among those who had proven their determination to resist, they had shown the most determination. Francis Hughes refused to eat anything for the seven days his post-arrest interrogation lasted, fearing that his food might be drugged. Neither Raymond McCreesh nor Joe McDonnell would wear the prison uniform, even to avail themselves of the once-monthly statutory visit to which they were entitled. McCreesh did not see his family for four years and McDonnell did not see his wife and children for five years, and when they finally did see their families it was only to tell them of their decisions to go on hunger strike. Patsy O'Hara lived in conditions of chaos from the age of twelve: his father's small pub and grocery store were blown up, he was shot in the leg by the army, interned for six months, and arrested four times on charges for which he was not tried but for which he spent lengthy periods on remand. Martin Hurson's confession to the charges for which he was convicted was beaten out of him, and later, when he was on the blanket, he spent a month in hospital after he was badly beaten by warders for resisting being force-washed. Both Doherty and McElwee carried their defiance of the prison system into their day-to-day dealings with the warders: Doherty always refused the anal search over mirrors before and after visits, and for this he was consistently beaten (he had a court action against the prison authorities pending at the time of his death). McElwee invariably refused to obey the warders' orders, and on one occasion he spent fourteen days on the punishment block for refusing to call a prison warder "sir." They were the elite of the elite, the chosen few whom their generation had picked to sacrifice themselves to once again redeem the honor of their people, to inform the world that Ireland had not acquiesced in her serfdom.

Many of them shared special kinds of camaraderie. Bobby Sands was directly connected to Joe McDonnell, who took his place on the hunger strike when he died. They were friends; McDonnell's active service unit from Andersonstown provided backup for Sands's newly formed active service unit in Twinbrook; both were arrested in connection with the Balmoral furniture factory bomb attack; and both were charged and sentenced for the same offense. Kevin Lynch was on the same wing in the H-blocks as Sands, and apparently his respect for Sands was such that he would defer to Sands, the IRA OC during the first hunger strike, when there was tactical disagreement between the IRA and INLA. Francis Hughes and Thomas McElwee were first cousins, boyhood friends, and McElwee was a member of Hughes's independent Republican unit which operated in South Down before it was recruited en bloc into the IRA. Hughes and Raymond Mc-Creesh shared the same cell. McCreesh and Paddy Quinn were members of the same active service unit and were captured together after a shootout with the army. Kieran Doherty met Hughes when he was being held on remand in Crumlin Road Jail and developed a great admiration for him. Doherty had also been on active service with Joe McDonnell in Andersonstown in the mid-1970s. Patsy O'Hara's brother, Tony, shared a cell with Sands from late 1977 through the early part of 1978. Patsy O'Hara and Mickey Devine were "friends and comrades" and O'Hara was also involved in the operation that led to Devine's arrest. Kevin Lynch and Martin Hurson were incarcerated for overlapping periods in Crumlin Road Jail. Liam Mc-Closkey, who took Lynch's place on the hunger strike when Lynch died, was a boyhood friend. He was arrested with Lynch and the two had shared a cell. Pat McGeown had shared cells with both Brendan McFarlane and Tom McElwee. And there were also special bonds between the outside and inside leaderships. Two of the prisoners' spokesmen, Gerry Adams and Brendan McFarlane, had served time with Sands in Cage 11 in the compounds. Sands and McFarlane were in adjoining cells in H-3. Danny Morrison, a third spokesman, was editor of *An Phoblacht/Republican News* when Sands wrote an occasional column for it, and the two developed a close friendship.

There was nothing, however, to distinguish the hunger strikers from their peers, nothing that presaged their involvement in militant Republicanism, except perhaps for the history of their own families or the communities they came from. Undoubtedly, the arrival of the British army in August 1969 was the external catalyst. It changed the dynamics of the conflict. The army's pervasive presence became a symbol of old hatreds, a symbol that provided a renascent IRA with an opportunity it couldn't ignore: there were old enemies to be vanquished. Although the army had been made welcome in the Catholic ghettos when it first arrived (the burning of Bombay Street in Belfast and the Battle of the Bogside in Derry convinced Catholics that marauding loyalist mobs, with the implicit encouragement of a malevolently indifferent police force, would burn them out of their homes) the welcome quickly exhausted itself. Secure in their sanctuaries in the no-go areas, the IRA waged a campaign of harassment against the army, and the army, reluctantly at first, and then with increasing determination once it had convinced itself that it could weed out the militant malcontents, began to retaliate. The Falls curfew in June 1970, during which the army conducted house-to-house searches for arms, left five civilians dead and fifteen soldiers and sixty civilians injured. Internment without trial in August 1971 led to hundreds of Catholics, many of them with no connections whatsoever to the IRA, being arrested under circumstances of appalling intimidation when whole areas were sealed off while paratroopers smashed down doors and literally dragged men from their homes in front of hysterical wives and terrified mothers and children. The civil rights march in Derry on 30 January 1972 became an occasion of slaughter—fourteen Catholics, half of them under fourteen years of age, were gunned down by army paratroopers—an action for which the army was subsequently exonerated. Alienation turned to hostility, hostility to violence.

The number of house searches alone conveys the breadth of the security forces' activities: more than 36,000 in 1972, double that again in 1973 and 1974, 30,000 in 1975, 34,000 in 1976. There are only 150,000 Catholic households in Northern Ireland, and house searches were conducted mainly in nationalist areas. This meant that almost every Catholic household, especially those in the hard-core Republican enclaves, had its sense of privacy and security violated by the arbitrary intrusions of an alien army, which added to the insult by presuming itself to be protecting those whose homes it invaded.

It was hardly surprising that the Catholic ghettos were, as political psychologist Jeanne Knutson puts it, increasingly "driven by the semi-conscious knowledge that passivity assumes victimization."[1] The army's "screening"—that is, the use of the emergency powers of arrest for security purposes, which took the form of arbitrary arrests, petty harassments, and random brutality—created the pervasive feeling of being invaded, of being spied upon, not just by an alien force but by the ancient enemy with his paraphernalia of occupation. This gave rise to a collective consciousness in the nationalist community in general and the Republican enclaves in particular that made resistance inevitable. Years of having been treated as the enemy made Catholics think of themselves as just that: the enemy.

There was, however, an ironic paradox that made the work of the security forces impossible to achieve, for the more successful they were in apprehending and prosecuting suspected members of the IRA, the more the prison population swelled. And the more the prison population swelled, the more pervasive was the impact of the prison culture, its ethos of solidarity and camaraderie, of isolation and deprivation breeding a separate community more committed, more tested, and more cohesive; hence the more viselike was the grip of the IRA. For every prisoner there were mothers, fathers, brothers, sisters, wives, children, girlfriends, networks of friends and relatives who fed off the prison culture, adopting its values, cultivating its resentments, their perceptions of reality mirroring and often magnifying the perceptions of the prisoners themselves.

The state had no legitimacy in the communities from which the IRA sprang. They saw themselves as victims of state violence, the army's incursions as forms of assault, the security forces as the armed technicians of repression and injustice, "symbols of uniformed and armed lawlessness"[2] rather than of law and order. In this void of legitimacy, the IRA was given a measure of moral as well as political acceptance, especially when it assumed its primary role as defender of the Catholic community. The more aggressive and offensive the presence of the security forces, the more likely was the community to give allegiance to the IRA.

From 1916 onward every generation of Catholics had been exposed to the activities of the IRA and the injustice of internment without trial. Between July 1920 and July 1922, 453 people were killed in Belfast—nearly two-thirds of them Catholic. One quarter of the city's 93,000 Catholics lost their jobs and 23,000 were driven from their homes. Outside Belfast 104 people, including 61 civilians, of whom 46 were Catholics, were killed. Savage altercations took place all over the North following the Anglo-Irish Treaty in 1921. In the first six months—December 1921 to May 1922—236 people died, of whom 147 were Catholics and 73 Protestant. (The others were members of the security forces.) Some 718 people, all of them Catholic, were interned between 1922 and 1924 following the passage of the draconian Special Powers Act. By 1922, nearly one in five of the adult male Protestant population was in its B-Specials. In the 1930s, rioting left eleven people dead, scores injured, five hundred homes—mostly Catholic—were abandoned, and only the IRA stood between militant Protestant mobs and the hard-pressed Catholics of Belfast. In the 1950s and early 1960s, the Border Campaign resulted in five hundred incidents, including the deaths of eight IRA volunteers, four supporters, six members of the RUC, and thirty-two members of the British security forces, before it was called off in the face of Catholic indifference. Militant Republicanism was a living tradition, its heritage deeply rooted in the consciousness of the Catholic community, each generation replicating, in one way or another, the experience of a previous generation.

Joining the IRA, especially for young people whose families had a history of involvement (itself a badge of status within the minority community) was something one just did. It was the carrying on of tradition, but now in circumstances often denied to parents, uncles, or cousins; for the enemy once again was visible in their midst, patrolling their streets, invading their homes, trespassing on their lands, treating them all as potential subversives and making actual subversives of many. The social order was collapsing, the political order had imploded, and young people—caught between ignorance and innocence, meager knowledge of the world and entrenched ideas of their own past, outer perceptions of reality and their own inner terrors, the precepts of their religion and their aversion to ambiguity, feelings of helplessness and feelings of rage—turned to the IRA because it was there, because it was the one instrument that could give expression to their anger. "This need for assertive activity as a protection against fears of ultimate annihilation," writes Jeanne Knutson, "is the unifying and dynamic ingredient for the violent acts of all who experience themselves as victims. Once the first act of defiance occurs, there simultaneously emerges a full, direct, emotional awareness of intense rage, as well as unbearable anxiety stemming from the possibility of the loss of even life itself for having dared to defy the aggressor." It is the pressure of this knowledge that constitutes "the point of no return for those who engage in continuing campaigns of political violence."[3]

To defend one's community was a matter of duty rather than honor. Five of the ten hunger strikers—Hughes, McDonnell, O'Hara, McElwee, and Doherty—joined militant Republican youth organizations when they were fifteen or younger. Three—O'Hara, Hughes, and Doherty—witnessed other family members being interned without trial. Four—Sands, McDonnell, O'Hara, and Doherty—had themselves been interned. Three—O'Hara, McDonnell, and McElwee—had brothers in the Maze/Long Kesh at the time of their deaths. Five—Sands, Hughes, O'Hara, McElwee, and Devine—were insistent on being among the first group who would fast—Hughes not hearing otherwise and McElwee going to McFarlane and asking for a place further up on the list.

The hunger strikes pulled together disparate strands in the Catholic national consciousness. The strikes were encumbered with the accessories of victimhood, being both a surrender to it and an escape from it, a reaching back to tribal allegiances and a reinforcement of the myths of sacrifice and redemption. Hunger striking was a metaphor for the victim as endurer, for what Terence Des Pres calls "the allusion of grace."[4] Its associations with asceticism, penitential fasting, atonement for wrongdoing, asking of forgiveness for transgressions against others, altruistic intercession on behalf of the community, and the abnegation of self conferred on the hunger strikers a moral stature, a refinement of sensibility, an inner disposition of spiritual depth. "[They] were almost akin to Christ-like," says Father Matt Wallace, a curate in Joe McDonnell's parish, who frequently visited McDonnell during his hunger strike. "You could argue that Christ didn't have to die on the cross, he could have created a miracle, but for the good of his people he saw through to the supreme sacrifice of death. I think each individual man attempted that. . . . You felt you were in the presence of someone great, someone powerful, someone spiritual, someone close to God. They were so clear in their own minds, in their conscience that they were able to face their Maker with a serenity and with a peace and dignity that can only come from a pure conscience."

Their willingness to lay down their own lives on behalf of their beliefs provided a more human context for the hundreds of brutal killings their cause had sanctioned in the name of holy nationalism. Hunger striking was equated with suffering, with the leitmotiv of self-sacrifice going back to the legendary folk hero Cuchulain; to Patrick Pearse's appropriation and reinvention of the myth in 1916, when the chosen few would redeem their people by their deaths; to the tradition of ennobling failure linking the present to the heroic past; to the sacrificial themes of Irish Catholicism in which the mass was the ritual reenactment of Christ's sacrifice on Calvary to redeem the world (Christ's words, "What greater love hath a man than to lay down his life for the life of his friends," which every Catholic child learns in catechism school, were invoked by Sands to rebuke Father Denis Faul when Faul tried to argue Sands out of his hunger strike on moral grounds); to the enormous sacrifices the Irish people made in the eighteenth century when the penal laws forced them to give up everything—their lands, livelihoods, education, and even their lives rather than turn their backs on their religion. They had accepted deprivation, subjugation, starvation, emigration, and discrimination rather than renounce the religion of their forefathers. Their lands were confiscated, their churches closed, their priests hunted down, their schools abolished; they had been displaced by Protestant colonizers, forced to eke out an existence in the barren foothills at the edges of the rich pasture lands that had once been theirs, oppressed by a Protestant ascendancy, subdued by the English crown, abandoned by the Catholic majority in the South, policed by the Protestant majority in the North, and yet they had persevered. Perseverance had refined their capacity to suffer, and, their mythology told them, it was those who suffered the most who would eventually conquer. They had known their Calvary, and if they remained steadfast, they knew that they would, in time, enjoy their Easter. ("The cells in H-block, Long Kesh are like caves," Fathers Denis Faul and Raymond Murray wrote in an article advocating prison reform before the strikes. "The heavy door opens. A dark hole appears before one's eyes. Dirty floor. Filthy walls. A dark and dreary atmosphere. Figures squat on damp and foul gray mattresses. Blankets draped around their waists and towels over their shoulders. They remind one of the cave at Bethlehem which was the only place men would allow Our Lord and Saviour to come into the world. There is no room for 363 young Irishmen and 33 young women at the Inn of Decency and Human Rights.")[5]

The validity of each death depended upon its being followed by another, the solidarity that counted was with those who had died rather than with the living. It was clear, following Joe McDonnell's death and the collapse of the Foreign Office contact, that the hunger strikes were a failure as a tool of coercion; thus the decisions of other prisoners to either participate or continue were made with the certainty that their deaths would achieve nothing. They were left with nothing to live for and nothing to die for except their dignity. Their acts of self-abnegation were an assertion in death of what life had denied them: a moment of self-realization and freedom transcending the strictures of cause, a reaffirmation of their own sense of worth. In death they became whole. Ultimately, what was at stake was not so much their belief in the justice of their cause but their belief in their own dignity as human beings. When all means of asserting it were appropriated, they used what they were left with—their own lives. The prisoners' worlds had somehow deconstructed during the years of being on the blanket and the dirty protest, of having endured physical deprivation to the point where their reaction to it had become existential: the physical self was something that existed outside the real self, and thus was something that could be discarded.

Protest itself and the maintenance of protest, rather than the purpose of protest, became the focus around which daily life was organized. The limitations and deprivations of their physical circumstances opened to them a new world in which the organization of their own deaths became the object of their survival. Endurance became more important than the end for which it was employed, bearing witness more exigent than success; to refuse the help, always at hand, a more pivotal concern than the other-world of ordinary commerce and discourse. Familiar things receded; with death came the final act of solidarity that brought rebirth, fulfillment, and fusion.

Hence the absolute finality of their protest. What began as a protest for five demands became a struggle for self-worth. The years on the blanket and the dirty protest fostered among the prisoners a sense of camaraderie, of shared values that changed their sense of deprivation. They did not choose to die in the face of indeterminate sentences or the grim prospect of life behind bars. Rather, a metamorphosis occurred. They stumbled, unwittingly, or perhaps out of necessity, into a belief that the freedom to which they would return was no freedom at all, to an understanding, however tentative, that their collective acts, like a leap of faith or a creative impulse, were what artist Patrick Graham calls "a leap from the mortal chains of delusion—a kind of impermanent presence."[6]

For the hunger strikers, the parameters of physical reality became smaller, mirroring their progressive deterioration. From their prison cells, connected to the rest of the prison population and reinforced and sustained by the physical proximity of their fellow prisoners, they went to the hospital, the bays of ten beds centered along one corridor with a few attendants in charge but closed off to the prison and the sustenance of protest. Here they were supported only by one another, each bonded to the others beyond family and loved ones until the inevitable outcome. Finally, they went to their rooms, part hospital, part prison, to die. "If you were to call back all the hunger strikers and ask them what took them over the brink," says Pat McGeown, "it would have been their commitment to the people around them. That in reality is what it boiled down to. You were in a situation of saying while you wanted a solution, what's more important here is that we all stick together. The conscious thing that you took over the brink was [the knowledge] that the alternative to this is that we collapse everything, everything just falls down around us. So if it requires us to keep it going, then we do it."

The hope of the first group of hunger strikers (Sands, Hughes, McCreesh, and O'Hara) that something might happen—especially if Sands was elected to the Westminster Parliament, for even the hunger strikers had some difficulty believing that Mrs. Thatcher would allow an elected M.P. to die from fasting in a government prison—slowly receded. One death followed the next, with the din of public protest, perhaps having exhausted itself over Sands's death, or at least unable to sustain the fever-edge of its intensity, growing thinner, like their bodies. The hope of the hunger strikers who took their places, wishful as it may have been and necessary for their psychological well-being, receded too, so that when others joined the hunger strike in late July and thereafter, they had no hope of saving their own lives, of achieving a resolution within the time span of their fasts. But they held on to the ultimate belief: that they would prevail, that they would "break the Brits," providing they were willing to pay the enormous and terrible price it would entail. They joined the hunger strike in the full knowledge that they would die unless they abandoned their fasts, "their own self-aggression increasingly justified by their own profound sense of victimhood."[7]

And thus the fierceness of their determination to resist. Patsy O'Hara, in his most extreme moment, would not allow his sister to apply moistened swabs of cotton wool to his parched lips in case it was an attempt to revive him; Kevin Lynch, close to death, refused to take a mouthwash that would relieve his ulcerated mouth, and Kieran Doherty, four days before he died, extracted yet again from his father a promise that he wouldn't, under any circumstances, intervene. And thus, too, their increasing passivity. For in moments of extreme anxiety the organism adjusts itself to what appears to be inevitable. They had, Tom McElwee wrote in a comm, "placed it all in the hands of God." They had won what McFarlane called "the inner battle." "Every man," he wrote, "must overcome inner conflicts." It was either the five demands or death. "Thatcher can't break us. I am not a criminal," were Doherty's last words to Gerry Adams when Adams, visiting him days before his death, said, "I can go out now, Doc, and announce it's over."

In one sense, the prisoners' predilection for a hunger strike was not surprising. When the British government continued to deny them the status to which they aspired, they simply conferred it on themselves by appropriating the paraphernalia of the past. When all options closed, they took refuge in romantic stereotype. By acting heroically, they would become heroic, their legitimacy a product of their actions within the prison rather than their actions without. Like the Fenians of an earlier time, they also stood condemned in the public eye, but they too would show a capacity for sacrifice that would compensate for the opportunities they had been denied to show heroism on the battlefield. "Such," Patrick Pearse had written, "is the high and solitary destiny of heroes: to turn their backs on the pleasant paths and their faces to the hard paths, to blind their eyes to the fair things of life . . . and to follow the far, faint call that heads them into battle or to the harder death at the foot of a gibbet. They too would die from 'the excess of love' [they bore] the Gael.'"[8] It was, after all, "the fools [who did] all the world's great works. Then the world calls them heroes.'"[9]

They did not work out in advance what they would settle for, perhaps because they were incapable of articulating it; nor does it appear that the question was even discussed on the blocks before the second hunger strike was undertaken. Even in the confusion attending the end of the first hunger strike, they knew only what they would not settle for. To disaggregate the five demands would somehow impugn the integrity of their protest. They were prisoners not only of the state but of their own convictions, their posture, ironically, was one of "no surrender" and "not an inch"—an absolute position that could not appear to be less than absolute, since otherwise it would be no position at all. The whole of the five demands was greater than the sum of their parts, giving them a completeness that had the stamp of historical authenticity.

Yet it was the ordinariness of the way they went about their hunger strikes and the way in which they conducted them that compelled attention. They simply waited to die, spending their time resting, or exercising when they could, watching television, reading the odd book or newspaper, listening to the radio, visiting with family and friends.

Apart from general nursing care they were prepared to accept medical monitoring only. This was carried out on a once daily basis but more often as medical conditions warranted. They also permitted medical and opthamological consultants to examine them, but adamantly refused psychiatric examinations. Some but not all agreed to provide blood specimens, and when those approaching an advanced stage of their fasts could be persuaded that a cardiac monitor was not a resuscitating machine, monitors were used.

Their physical deterioration became extraneous to their sense of being. Their bodies quickly used up the reserves of glucose essential for the brain's functioning, and began to manufacture glucose from proteins in the muscle and ketone bodies from fatty acids in the liver. Hunger pangs disappeared on the third or fourth day, although the hunger strikers had to resist the always-present temptation of food: three times a day meals, which for reasons real or imagined seemed to be far more appetizing than the standard prison fare they were used to, were wheeled into their cells or prison hospital rooms and left there—breakfast until it was replaced with lunch, lunch until it was replaced with supper, supper until it was replaced with breakfast.

To protect their vital organs and to conserve energy the hunger strikers' bodies made a number of adjustments: metabolic rates fell, pulses slowed, blood pressures dropped. They complained of coldness of the extremities from about the ninth to the thirty-second day of the fast, and once they were sent to the prison hospital, usually at the beginning of the fourth week of fasting, many of them spent a lot of time in bed under sheepskin rugs.

The breakdown of body tissue also impaired their gastric functions. With the loss of vital salts (electrolytes, especially potassium and sodium), their bodies' basic chemistry was disturbed, making it difficult for their vital organs to function effectively. This was most pronounced in the case of their hearts, where electrolytic imbalances led to arrhythmias—the irregular beating of their heart muscles.

They also had to deal with other side effects. As nutritional depletion continued and the levels of toxin in their systems rose, symptoms attributable to lesions of the brain appeared. Nystagmus, the loss of muscle control in the eyes, became a problem after forty-five days or so of fasting when their bodies tried to extract vitamins from nonessential muscle tissues; and acute vomiting debilitated them between the fortieth and fiftieth days. The vomiting, which was accompanied by constant nausea and retching, was most distressing and disabling for the hunger strikers since they could not even hold down spring water. However, after they endured seven to ten days of abject misery the vomiting would stop, the nystagmus recede, the drinking of fluids would again become tolerable, and they would undergo what appeared to be a dramatic improvement in their overall medical condition.

Other side effects included anemia, dry skin, and ulcerated mouths, and after fifty days of fasting they would experience loss of hearing, difficulty in talking, visual loss leading to blindness in some cases, and inability to walk. Between the forty-second and the seventieth day of starvation, they developed clouding of consciousness, which attending doctors described as a "global confusional state." One medical report observed it "as drowsiness, inattentiveness, disorientation, and gross misinterpretations and misidentifications." Usually it would begin to manifest itself about six days before death. The maximum weight loss of 9 lbs. 4 oz. occurred in the first week; weight loss remained constant thereafter ranging from 4 lbs. 14 oz. to 6 lbs. 3 oz. per week. After eight weeks one-third of their body masses had catabolized. In the last stages of starvation, when the hunger strikers' body fat had been depleted, their bodies drew exclusively from their protein reserves—their bodies essentially digested themselves and their vital organs simply stopped functioning.

They were oddly nonchalant, curiously indifferent to the maneuverings outside the prison. Having renounced the world, they were almost cavalier in the face of death. "Ta seans am go mbeidh me abhaile romhat, a chara"—"There is a possibility that I may be home before you, my friend," Raymond McCreesh wrote matter-of-factly to Patsy O'Hara in a smuggled communication. When Gerry Adams, Seamus Ruddy, an Irish Republican Socialist Party official, and Owen Carron, the Sinn Fein candidate for the Fermanagh–South Tyrone by-election, visited the hunger strikers at the end of July, they found them in remarkably good spirits. The atmosphere was relaxed, jovial, and there was much joking about Carron's upcoming election campaign and the quality of the spring water provided "at such great expense" by the government.

They were normal—normal in the sense of loving their families and enjoying their friends, in their everyday pursuits, and normal in the sense that they were not exceptions within the Republican movement. Since they saw themselves as the true inheritors of their traditions, their actions and responses had to be fitted into the logic sustaining those traditions. When the political present became too overwhelming, the cumulative impact of seemingly endless successions of defeat and failure too discouraging, the prisoners turned to the mythic past to alleviate their sense of oppression, to reaffirm their sense of identity and self-worth, to remind themselves that a future recapturing the mythic past would yet be theirs if only they endured. Myth, philosopher Richard Kearney writes, "is a strategic mode of consciousness whereby we seek to negate a real world that has grown intolerable in order to transform it into an imaginary world which we can tolerate. We negate the world in order to better cope with what appear to be intractable problems."[10] For the hunger strikers, the world of the prison protest had become intolerable. Their recollection of the mythic past, their sense of being in psychological union with their Republican forebears, part of the eternal cycle of sacrifice and rebirth, and the promise of the mythic future their sacrifice would bring allowed them to repress the awful circumstances of their own situations, to compensate for the inequities of the historical present, to resuscitate their morale and reaffirm their sense of self. Faced with the unacceptable realities of the present and the comforting allure of myth, they chose myth, to imagine themselves "as sacrificial heroes taken from the old mythologies of torn gods."[11]

"If I have a duty I will perform it to the full," Francis Hughes wrote, "in the unshakeable belief that we are a noble race and that chains and bonds have no part in us." Raymond McCreesh expressed similar sentiments: "My consciousness of my Irish identity," he said, "is holding me together, giving me the strength to go through with this because to me nothing is more important than the freedom of our land." Their statements, of course, are quite meaningless in a literal sense, and unconnected to the realities of modern-day Ireland. They are ritualistic, reflexive intonations of nineteenth-century Republican cant, banal, self-conscious, narcissistic assertions of a nobility of purpose that puts belief in vague abstractions above belief in life itself, fanaticism masquerading as magnificent gesture. But in the context of myth they do have meaning. They are unconscious attempts to preempt history, not just to replicate the actions of the dead generations but to appropriate their very words to ensure total identification with the mythical paradigm being reenacted, part of the imaginary process itself. The French writer Manuel de Dieguez, writing of the hunger strikes, observed that it is "frightening to think that the call to sacrifice and salvation through martyrdom is a source of motivation for a devoted population to obediently die in order to receive the rewards of their sacrifice. This mechanism appears indiscriminate: one can die in this fashion as easily for Hitler, Napoleon, Caesar or Alexander as by the side of Demosthenes for the liberty of Greece."[12]

What happened at Jonestown, Guyana, did not discriminate. There, 780 people—men, women and children, black and white, many down and out and poor, the "junk people" Shiva Naipaul so brilliantly describes in *Journey to Nowhere,* but some who were middle class and educated and full of New Age theories—died on behalf of the politics of self-loathing or the politics of self-realization, depending on your point of view. "Die with respect. Die with a degree of dignity," their guru, Jim Jones, pleaded with them as they willingly swallowed cyanide-laced Kool-Aid, nurses advising parents on how to calm their children. "Take our lives from us," he cried out at the end. "We got tired. We didn't commit suicide. We committed an act of revolutionary suicide protesting the conditions of an inhuman world." Whose justice? Which rationality? "As it had always been," Naipaul writes, "truth and falsehood were inextricably intertwined in that statement."[13] Just as they would be in the statements of the hunger strikers.

The prisoners did what they were supposed to do. Their actions, ultimately, were not the actions of autonomous individuals but rather a reflexive embrace of the way in which political prisoners throughout Irish history were presumed to have behaved. Their self-images, reinforced by the chronicles of oppression on which they had been raised and the experiences of their young lives, impaired their ability to act independently and diminished their capacity to act in their own behalf. In the end, they were the victims of our myths.

8   By the end of August the families of the hunger strikers decided they could no longer wait for the government to acquiesce to the demand for direct talks. From the start they had been put in an invidious position, unwilling accomplices in an endeavor they disapproved of, having the power of life and death, yet forbidden to use it in the service of life. They were forced to choose between the demands of the mythologies that so strongly asserted themselves in their communities and the exigencies of saving the lives of their loved ones. They had to balance their respect for the hunger strikers' wishes with their own sense of what was right, and they often had the niggling belief that the hunger strikers were acting under orders and that the IRA could end it.

Once more, mothers were to fill mythological roles. The mothers of the hunger strikers, like the mother of Patrick Pearse, would hear from their sons that "we are ready to die and we will die cheerfully and proudly. We have preserved Ireland's honour and our own," Pearse wrote, "our deeds are the most splendid things in Irish history. We shall be remembered by posterity and blessed by unborn generations. You, too, will be blessed because you are our mothers."[1]

The hunger strikers' gift to their mothers was the gift of sorrow, and the pairing of the son who sacrifices and the mother who bears silent witness evoked powerful associations in the community's unconscious mind with Christ at Calvary and his grieving mother and the belief that the sacrifice of oneself can redeem a people just as Christ's sacrifice redeemed the world. "Blessed are those who hunger for justice," the gable walls of the Catholic ghettos in Belfast and Derry cried out, and in the prison the men made handkerchiefs for their relatives that juxtaposed images of Christ and a hunger striker in imitation of Veronica's veil.

This unconscious elevation of the role of the mother went back to the abysm of history, to the connection of Ireland, according to psychoanalyst Ernest Jones, "with the ideas of woman, mother, nurse, and virgin," with words, fantasies, and "our deepest feelings about birth and death."[2] The "mother myth" which has been ineluctably imprinted on the psyche of Irish history since its beginning, has its roots in two interlocking traditions: the ancient tradition in which the land and its sovereignty are conceived in the image of a woman, and the more modern tradition, dating from the nineteenth century, of the cult of Mary, Mother of God. In the former there is a pervasive theme within the myths themselves: a goddess of sovereignty, symbol of the land, whose union with a prospective king will either ensure or legitimize his sovereignty. Without union with her, he cannot become a king acceptable to his people; strife and famine and war will bring destitution and barrenness to the land. And without union with her rightful ruler, she is lost, an old woman, disheveled, and often deranged. Once united with her rightful mate, however, she is transformed into a beautiful young woman. Yeats draws on the myths in his play *Cathleen ni Houlihan*. An old woman convinces a young man about to be married to abandon his wedding and help her recover her fields and her home, which have been invaded by strangers. She promises nothing: "If anyone would give me help he must give me himself, he must give me all." Only through suffering—"They that have red cheeks will have pale cheeks for my sake; and for all that they will think they are well paid"—will young men achieve a goal and acclaim otherwise unattainable. When the young man abandons his wife-to-be for the old woman, choosing elusive quest over pragmatic outcome, he chooses to sacrifice himself in romantic death for her sake rather than live for the mundane and the ordinary. The old woman is changed into a young queen. She leaves with a song: "They shall be remembered for ever / The people shall hear them for ever."[3]

The cult of Mary took hold after the Famine of 1846–47 when the Catholic Church institutionalized its grip on family life: attendance at Sunday mass skyrocketed to 90 percent from the pre-Famine average of 40 percent. Mary, Mother of Sorrows, "was the most appropriate model for a generation of women, the death of whose elderly husbands left them widows at a relatively young age," writes the historian Margaret MacCurtin. Irish mothers in turn became the personification of Irish sorrows. But "it . . . was specifically in the family setting of mothers and sons, that the Marian model is most clearly visible. Patrick Pearse's poem 'The Mother,' written shortly before his execution, associates the mother of an Irish nationalist with the Mother of Jesus at the foot of the Cross." In Sean O'Casey's *Juno and the Paycock*, Mrs. Tancred "is the suffering face of Republican motherhood in twentieth century Ireland north and south when she identifies her sorrow with that of the Mother of God and turns to her for solace as she sets out to her son's funeral."[4] ("Mother o' God, Mother o' God, have pity on the pair of us," she says.)

During the funeral oration for Bobby Sands, Owen Carron extolled Mrs. Sands: "Someone once said it is hard to be a hero's mother and nobody knows that better than Mrs. Sands who watched her son being daily crucified for sixty-six long days and eventually killed. Mrs. Sands epitomizes the Irish mothers who in every generation watched their children go out to fight and die for freedom." And during his funeral oration for Francis Hughes, Martin McGuiness picked up on the theme and paid a similar tribute: "The women of Ireland can be proud of Mrs. Hughes and Mrs. Sands for the way they have borne their heavy burdens. They have shown that the women of Ireland are the backbone of our struggle for freedom." The hunger strikers' mothers became the symbol of Mother Ireland, whose sorrows drive young men to give up everything and follow her call. Wall murals graphically captured this theme: the Virgin Mary stands above the head of a dead hunger striker clasping a rosary; relatives hold an emaciated body draped in a Tricolor in a pietà-like pose; over an H-block hangs Salvador Dalí's crucified Christ.

Once the hunger strikers had begun their fasts they asked their families not to intervene if they lapsed into unconsciousness or became otherwise incapacitated. The families gave in to such undertakings, albeit reluctantly and with many misgivings. If they had not, the hunger strikes would probably have ended with a couple of deaths at most, once it became apparent to the hunger strikers that they would be putting themselves through immense distress without being able to achieve the results they wanted. The hunger strikers had not sought their families' acquiescence before they embarked on their fasts. Their requests became demands only when the hunger strikes were already under way: acquiescence was co-opted—the hunger strikers acted passive-aggressively, the families passively. The families said yes because they couldn't say no. Thus the hunger strikes were a joint undertaking in which one of the principals was a silent and unwilling partner.

But the families had their own problems. Sands's mother sought reassurance from him that the IRA was not putting him up to it. She knew her son's wishes but she was not mollified. Days before he died, she considered going on television to publicly urge all the hunger strikers to abandon their fast. She had to be reminded of what Bobby's wishes were before she was dissuaded. Afterwards she would say, "If I had [intervened] and Francis [Hughes] and Patsy [O'Hara] and Raymond [McCreesh] went on to their deaths, Bobby might never have forgiven me because he asked me not to and would have continued to refuse food. My hands were completely tied. We had arguments about it."

Mrs. O'Hara intended to the very end to pull her son off the strike. Only his last words to her before he lost consciousness—words that she immediately wrote down: "Mammy, I'm sorry we didn't win. But please let the fight go on"—persuaded her to let him die. Her motivation was not so much to accede to his request as to preclude his suffering further, since she was convinced that his determination was such that if she did intervene, he would simply go back on the hunger strike as soon as he was able to. "I could never explain the torment of my mind in those last lonely hours," she would recall. "I thought, this is how Mary must have felt when Jesus told her, 'I must be about my Father's business.' I prayed for strength. I prayed for help. It was lonely."

Joe McDonnell's parents suspected that the prisoners were being used by the external leadership and wanted his wife, Goretti, to intervene. "[We] wanted him off it," says Mrs. McDonnell, "and then we had nothing to say. He had a wife but if it had been left to me and mine, all they would want was his not going to die. People will stop me and say, 'God, Eileen, how did you let your son die?' It hurts me. How did I let him die? I didn't let him die. He would never have died if it had've been me."

Martin Hurson's rapid deterioration made intervention a moot point—Hurson would have been left with permanent brain damage. Kevin Lynch's family, strong backers of the ICJP's efforts and a source of constant worry to McFarlane, almost intervened on several occasions. Both his father and his sister wanted him off, and his father even went so far, three days before Lynch's death, as to bitterly accuse Adams of being responsible for allowing his son to die. But in the end, Mrs. Lynch stood by the promise that her son had wrung from her: she would not intervene. "He puts his hands over my hands," says Mrs. Lynch, "and he says 'Mammy, I never needed you more. You never let me down and I never needed you more than I need you now. I want you please to give me your support.' My son was calling for something I could not keep from him because it's what he wanted and I said 'yes,' and he says 'if it comes to the worst you'll not let me down.' What could I do? If you love a family and one of them wants something desperately, you might see other ways but how can you turn them down? I couldn't turn him down, and I didn't turn him down."

Paddy Quinn's family begged him to come off his fast, and finally, when his mother could no longer endure his desperate cries of pain before he went into a coma, she intervened. But even then the family sought to protect Quinn himself from the consequences of his mother's action and to denounce suggestions that they were opposed to the hunger strike. "We would like to utterly condemn the media suggestion that other hunger strikers' families should have acted and should still act in the way that ours did," the family said in a statement released through the Republican Press Centre. "One must remember that had Paddy been conscious we could not have taken the decision to give him medical treatment. He was determined to go on to the end." The McElwees were in the middle of a family conference with their doctor to decide what they should do when they got word Tom had suddenly died. Kieran Doherty's girlfriend, Geraldine Scheiss, who also believed that the prisoners were being used by the movement, hoped fervently that Doherty's family would intervene; at the end she had even convinced herself that Doherty himself wanted intervention. "The strain is very bad. I'm afraid of cracking up," Laurence McKeown's mother was quoted as saying in the *Belfast Telegraph* after Mrs. Quinn had taken her son off the fast. Eventually, after McKeown had gone seventy days without food and was about to become the eleventh hunger striker to die, his family, too, would intervene to save his life.

McFarlane's concern with what the families might do became an obsession. His messages to the outside leadership reflect his increasing fears that their commitment not to intervene was soft, that they were being manipulated by outside interests—the Church, the SDLP, various well-intentioned intermediaries—opposed to the hunger strikes, that the families would, unless constantly paid court to and their doubts repeatedly assuaged, capitulate to the voices urging them to act. He could control the hunger strike within the prison, enforce the ruthless discipline the strike demanded, be intolerant of sentimentality and dismissive of the doubting, be icily detached when choosing who next would join the hunger strike and achingly heartbroken when one of them died; but the families were beyond him, and their capacity to undo all that had been done, to make the sacrifices incurred and the terrible human toll exacted irrelevant, maddened him. The families became, if not the enemy, the enemy's potential collaborators. Thus his insistent preoccupation with the families in his communications to the outside. On 7 June he wrote: "Kevin [Lynch] is coming under heavy pressure from his family to adopt [Paul] O'Dwyer's proposals. There is a very strong SDLP alliance hanging over his family [and] strong church connections with Father McIldowney [a curate in the Lynch's parish], so you can see the difficulty with the family. Now he is sound enough but family pressure may have an effect on him." On 9 June: "Big Tom [McElwee] got a letter from his family saying that the [ICJP] proposals should be accepted. . . . I explained to Tom that there was nothing in the proposals except a suit of clothes." On 16 June: "The families had a private meeting. Apparently all the families agreed [that] if the proposals were granted then they would be accepted [by the families]. I think we need to get more families on the right line of thought: I have boxed the hunger strikers to ensure they are 100% sound on our position, that they leave no one in any doubt that we make the decisions and they get the points across to their families and bring them around." On 28 June: "Families of hunger strikers appear ready to grab what comes as a feasible settlement." On 29 June: "There's no way am I happy with the situation with the families." On 8 July: "I'm worried about Kevin [Lynch]. His family as I told you got a special visit today and he is coming under pressure from them constantly." And on 31 August: "It certainly appears that the Germans [British] will sit tight to test the clans [families]. Deadly state of affairs altogether. It wrecks me to think the breaking power lies with those who haven't a clue what our struggle is all about. I'm shattered even thinking about it."

"In my own wing," says Jake Jackson,

I was going into the cells of the hunger strikers—they [the authorities] were allowing me in to brush them out and change their water and stuff like that and Bik was saying to me, "Look, this is the line you have to tell them to take with their family." You were saying to them, "You have to go out to your family and ensure that they understand you're dying. You have to be fairly clear that there's to be no interference from your family." It was one of the hardest things to do. You were dealing with somebody who was going without grub, you were dealing with somebody who had a whole internal battle going on, and you were coming in, eating grub, no matter how much you want to be on hunger strike you're not on it [Jackson had volunteered for the hunger strike but was turned down because he had only a short time left to serve], you're going in, talking to people who are on a hunger strike, saying to them, "Here's the line, you have to take it, and you have to toe it"—it put you at a psychological disadvantage.

The INLA hunger strikers, who did not come under the command of the IRA leadership, were a particular problem. Liam McCloskey was chosen as Kevin Lynch's replacement but Jackson, for one, saw him as soft from the beginning.

As soon as I went to talk with Stanley [McCloskey] when I saw him on hunger strike [I knew he was weak] and when I came out I says to Bik, "Get him off the hunger strike," and Bik says, "We've no control over it." When I went into him I was saying, "You're going to have to tell your parents you're dying," and he says, "Sure we'll need to face that when we come to it." [I said] you can't have that attitude: you're dying, if you're not dying you shouldn't be on the hunger strike, and he was going, "Sure you never know what's going to happen." I said to Bik, "Get him off." Stanley was the first visible weak link in the hunger strike and I knew he was going to fold. It wasn't his family as much as him. It was his attitude which allowed his family to intervene. [McCloskey's family intervened on 26 September, after he had completed fifty-five days on hunger strike.]

You knew when you went into a cell if somebody wasn't taking the line, and we needed to adhere rigidly to the line. We could all argue and we could all discuss any issue but once a line was decided on and a line was taken, we had to be committed to that. If anybody wavered in their commitment to that line, then there was danger straightaway, and with McCloskey, his attitude was wrong from the start.

Paddy Quinn's mother was also becoming a problem. Paddy Quinn's mother was bitterly opposed to Paddy going on the hunger strike. She even wrote a comm into Bik asking why he was letting her son die and Paddy was being told "get your Ma straightened out, there's nobody telling you to die, Paddy, if you don't want to be on hunger strike come off it, get your act together."

While Sands was alive, it was easier for the families to be silent, since they, too, had hope, and their hope extended to support for their sons and brothers and husbands. Once Sands died, however, intervention—or even a declaration by the families that they would intervene—would have slowed, perhaps even halted, the assembly line of death, invalidating Sands's death and the deaths that followed his. Thus the families' entrapment: their responsibility had become communal, no longer just to their own kith and kin but to the families of all the hunger strikers. And when the hunger strikers began to die, the families, by their actions or inactions, were responsible for ensuring that the sacrifices of those who had died, and of the families who had allowed them to, were not in vain. The bond within the prison requiring each hunger striker to validate the deaths of the prisoners who had died before him was paralleled on the outside: each family about to lose a son had to validate the losses of the families who already had.

With the end of hope, the families found their own position increasingly untenable and they were less and less convinced that the IRA could not order an end to the hunger strikes. Their promises to the hunger strikers not to intervene were given partly in the belief that the hunger strikers' solidarity, even in death, would finally force the authorities to move in the direction of accommodation, if only to appease public opinion. But when it became clear that no redress would occur; that the British government, far from becoming unnerved, had reaffirmed its determination to stay the course; that the Irish government, having weathered the worst, had become unsympathetic; that the public furor had peaked and was now waning; that the marginal impact of each new death was decreasing; that the hunger strikers were at least implicitly colluding in their own deaths to the extent that the purpose of the hunger strike ostensibly had become death without meaning, the families by default became the only source of possible action. Their anxiety became so overpowering that they had to do something to reduce it, find some outlet for its dispersion, if only, psychologist Jeanne Knutson says, to "deflect their own sense of guilt for their passive participation in acts for which they felt a shared social responsibility."[5]

When Paddy Quinn's mother intervened on 31 July, the consensus to follow the wishes of the hunger strikers began to waver. Father Denis Faul, the Dungannon priest long active on behalf of prisoners' rights and a frequent visitor to the Maze/Long Kesh, was now convinced that the IRA was allowing the prisoners to die for political benefits, and began to organize meetings of the families. He spelled out to them the reality as he saw it—the British would not yield on the five demands, thus making the decision to go on hunger strike a certain sentence of death—and increasingly he impelled the families toward a new consensus, a collective decision to seek medical intervention in the event of the hunger strikers' lapsing into comas or otherwise becoming incapable of making rational decisions on their own behalf.

At first Sinn Fein argued that the trend of families taking their sons and husbands off would be reversed at some point "by a man going back on hunger strike again." "The problem," explained Danny Morrison, "is that once the medics get their hands on a hunger striker and a family has sanctioned medical intervention, he is given a drug which creates an enormous dependence on further nourishment." (Sometimes this is called food!) But there was no going back. The psychological bond between the hunger strikers and their families had been disrupted, and the families themselves did what the British could not do: they broke the will of the hunger strikers.

Within the prison the leadership moved apprehensively to counteract the perceived threat of family interventions. The short-list was changed. People who were on the short-list were longlisted and other names were brought forward. John Pickering and Pat Sheehan were commed. "We're thinking of bringing you forward," they were told by McFarlane, according to Jackson. "The major threat to the hunger strike now [comes from intervention]. We believe the Brits are broke and that all we need to do is pull them to a position where we move them from their gentleman's agreement to a position where they're prepared to give us public guarantees. . . . We're getting feelers from the Brits through certain channels, they're telling us that they want to settle." And they were also told how they should deal with their families. They were instructed: "You need to be telling your family, 'when I come to the point of dying, if necessary I'm going to get a legal document which makes you and my family outlaws if you talk about intervening.' "

Of course it never came to that. But at one point the inside leadership had explored through a number of solicitors how they might have legal documents drawn up which would preclude a hunger striker's family from intervening should he lose consciousness and how he could designate somebody other than his immediate family to be his legal next of kin. But when it raised the matter with the outside leadership, the outside leadership balked, pre-emptorily vetoing any suggestion of the proposed maneuver. What, it wanted to know, were the prisoners trying to do? Could they not see that any move in the direction they espoused would only give support to their enemies' accusations that it was the people on the outside who were running the hunger strike, even to the extent of telling the hunger strikers how to circumvent the problems posed by their families intervening, and that here was irrefutable evidence of it?

Within the prison the necessity to "adhere to the line" became even more pressing. "A family only intervened," says Jackson, "if they knew they were going to get away with intervening and an element in that was the hunger striker [himself]. That held true right through the whole series of interventions except, perhaps, for Paddy Quinn. Paddy snapped. He had gone into a coma when the family intervened. Paddy's mother took him off and Paddy sent word up to the jail from the hospital that he wanted to go back on." Any suggestion of ambivalence became a sign of weakness, subtle evidence of complicity on the part of the hunger striker with his family's implicit intention to intervene, any behavior that didn't appear to resolutely reinforce a hunger striker's unyielding opposition to even the mention of intervention became cause for alarm.

The greater the threat of family intervention, the more the inside leadership became convinced that if only it could hold the hunger strike together, it would force the British hand. There were even some who argued that Paddy Quinn and then Pat McGeown should go back on the hunger strike. But McFarlane wouldn't agree; it would, he said, make them appear to be "squabbling over what would be done with somebody in a coma." Moreover, once a family had intervened, there was nothing that would stop it from doing so again. But these suggestions, full of a mad desperation and a disregard for their impact in the Republican community itself, never mind the larger nationalist constituency, were a measure of how removed a number of the inside leadership had become from what on the outside appeared to be increasingly immutable realities, of how oblivious they had become to the impact or even the direction of external events.

"We were seriously considering either having to cut our losses and stop it there or having to put it back together," says Jackson,

and that's why we had the moving forward of more people [who were considered capable of dealing with their families] even if we couldn't arrive at a position where we had legal guarantees. But we could arrive at a position where we were starting to phase people off. We were actively talking about taking Matt Devlin off the hunger strike [Devlin's resolve had become suspect; his family intervened on 6 September, ending his hunger strike after fifty-two days], just saying to him, "Come off" and replacing [hunger strikers like him] with people who were going to die. That in itself would have sent a clear message to the Brits: we're not folding here. We don't give a damn that a couple of people folded and their families have taken them off. We're telling you that we're bringing people on here who are saying to you they're dying, so you had better get your act together, move across that line, and let us know that you've met our position.

To the very end the inside leadership was saying "No, the Brits can be publicly broken and can be forced to resolve this issue."

"If you were strong enough with your family, your family would back you" was the leadership position, according to Jackson.

What did you say when your people came up and they're talking about your dying? We said you tell them to get lost. Sure they're wrecked, but once there was an element of "they're threatening to take me off and what do I say to them" present in a person's head, then they were weak and a family would grab that and a family would intervene if they felt there was a possibility of getting away with it. Nobody wanted their son to die on a hunger strike. And that's what Father Faul played on. That was the seed that ended the hunger strikes. The minute there was this realization that these people didn't need to die, that there was a way of stopping them dying, once that door was open, it then became a floodgate and you had a whole series of interventions and threats of interventions.

Faul would become the Republican scapegoat. *Iris,* one of the Republican movement's publications, called him, "a conniving, treacherous man . . . the tool of the Irish establishment" whose "craven acquiescence in the British partition of Ireland" was "a major contribution to the specific circumstances whereby Westminster was permitted to murder ten young Irish men in the hospital wing of the

H-block rather than make five simple concessions to them." Father Faul "had nursed, cajoled and nourished with emotional and moral exploitation, distortion of truth, vilification and downright political hostility to the hunger strike and the achievement of the prisoners' demands." The result was an "irreversible trend of family intervention."

The families kept their silence.

9   Micky Devine was the last hunger striker to die. At the time he entered the critical phase of his fast in mid-August, it was clear that the hunger strikes were collapsing—the hunger strikers themselves had begun to accept the fact that further deaths would bring no relief to the prison situation. Yet to Devine death was necessary, although he insisted that his own should be the last, and his pursuit of it was both tenacious and self-centered. Death would provide him with the means to erase the failures of his life; it would compensate for the humiliations he had been subjected to by his peers, atone for the weaknesses he had displayed following his arrest, allow him to get even with the wife who had abandoned him. Somewhere in this tangled web of motivations—for he was at once dogmatic, doctrinaire Republican, radical socialist, founding member of the Derry branch of the INLA, deprived child, inadequate adult, passive-aggressive victim who sought dignity through his own destruction, victim who became victimizer—lay the truth of his lonely odyssey.

Micky Devine may have died for the cause, for the nine hunger strikers who had preceded him, for the five demands, or for political status, but Micky Devine also died for Micky Devine, having put himself willingly, eagerly, and enthusiastically into a situation from which he could not retreat. The truncated realities of the present, which he could see only in terms of his own obituary or of his having joined the pantheon of the dead hunger strikers with whom he had shared so much, depleted the future of possibility, made it a fiction that existed only in other people's imaginations. In death he sought the control over life that had always eluded him. The hunger strike provided the certainty that the vicissitudes of his own desultory existence made him crave.

He was born in Springtown Camp, a former World War II U.S. army base on the outskirts of Derry that had been converted into public housing of a sort for Catholics. In 1960, the family—the father, Patrick, who had served in the British Merchant Navy during the war and who worked on and off afterward as a coalman; mother Elizabeth; sister Margaret, who was thirteen; and Michael, then six— moved to the Creggan, a new Catholic ghetto in the inner city, and the young Devine settled into school and a normal childhood. When he was eleven his father died of leukemia and Devine, who was especially close to his father, was deeply affected by the loss.

The first civil rights march took place in Derry in October 1968. Police attacked the marchers and the scenes of the police, without any ostensible provocation, brutally clubbing the people they were supposedly protecting, were brought into every Derry home on the evening television news. That night, Devine, along with hundreds of other young people, was downtown smashing shop windows and stoning the police. He was fourteen years old and his politicization had begun. He joined the Young Socialists, and then the Young Socialist Group, a Trotskyite youth wing of the Northern Ireland Labour Party. He left school in the summer of 1969, having just turned fifteen, and took a job as a shop assistant. He manned the barricades protecting "Free Derry" after the Battle of the Bogside in 1969, joined the Official IRA when he was seventeen, and took part in the march on Bloody Sunday. From that point on, his hatred of the British army was palpable. The Officials' cease-fire in May 1972 left him at loose ends, a revolutionary who had been ordered to the sidelines while all around him the Provisional IRA's revolution ignited. There is some suggestion that he and others who were unhappy with the restraints the Official IRA put on their activities free-lanced, planting the odd bomb or lending the Provisionals the occasional helping hand.

Sometime in 1972, Devine got into trouble with the Officials when a local shopkeeper accused him of having broken into his shop and stolen some money. Rather than kneecap Devine, which was the favored punishment for such an offense, the Officials humiliated him, making him clean the streets for a couple of hours wearing a sign that said "I am a thief." Months later, he faced heartbreak yet again when he came home one evening in September 1972 to find his mother dead on the living room sofa. She was only forty-three. The death devastated him, since he had turned to her after his father's death for the comfort and love that helped him to bear the loss. Now he had no one to turn to. He was on his own in a city that had become a household word around the world for mayhem, indiscriminate violence, and sudden death. He went to live with his sister, Margaret, and her husband, Frank, but he moved out after a row with her. He rented a room from an old Republican family, the Walmsleys, and began dating their daughter, Margaret.

"I felt very secure when I was with him," says Margaret, "because everybody knew he was in the IRA and he used to act as Billy the Kid and he'd come down the street and he'd be showing off with two guns in his pockets and he'd pull them out and everybody used to call him Billy the Kid because he wanted to act as a big hero. We used to sit in the swing park and he used to sit and say to me 'I'll die as a hero' and I used to say, 'No wonder. If you're going to act as Billy the Kid, you will die a hero.' I used to enjoy him doing things like that. I felt secure when I was with him because everybody knew he was crazy."

Margaret got pregnant, and that led to a quick and volatile marriage. He was nineteen, she seventeen. He drank, they fought. He left his job to become a full-time activist with the newly formed Irish Republican Socialist Party (IRSP) and then with the fledgling INLA. The fighting at home, often physical when he hit her and she tried to hit him back, continued. He was rarely at home, gone most days and often during the night. Margaret would wake to find he wasn't there. "He was away," as Margaret puts it, "with his friends." Margaret wanted him out of the movement—they were expecting their first child. Micky wanted to stay in, and Micky, of course, had his way. Margaret, after all, had been raised in the tradition; it was what she was used to—and Micky was only following in her father's footsteps. He stored guns and other weapons in the house, seemingly oblivious to the dangers of being raided, or simply not caring. Everything he did was out in the open.

He was arrested in September 1976, following an INLA arms raid on a private weaponry in Lifford, County Donegal. He talked, signing a thousand-word voluntary statement telling the full story of the robbery, after only three hours of interrogation. "When he went into jail first," says Margaret, "nobody would claim him. [They] said he wasn't involved in our movement. They didn't want to take any responsibility for him." That, of course, would later change. Sentenced to twelve years in 1977 for the possession of nine rifles, three shotguns, and ammunition, he went on the blanket, and from that on to the dirty protest. He kept to himself, a loner who would not share much about himself with his fellow prisoners—many of whom did not know he was married—but who was always eager to join in their protests.

In prison, his relationship with Margaret deteriorated. Left alone with their two children—Michael, their first-born, and Louise, who was only six months old when Micky was arrested—Margaret could hardly cope. She was, she says, a child trying to raise children. When the blanket protest turned to the dirty protest she couldn't take it any longer. "He was an awful sight," she says. "The children would have to sit on his knee and he would be all human dirt up his arms and human dirt on his whole body. It was an awful sight to see and my stomach used to turn. And then I said 'That's it. The children are not coming up any more.' I couldn't put them through this hell. I said, 'The children have to go to school, it's not right for them.' And I said, 'I'm not coming up any more.' " She stopped going to see him, but she kept contact, writing letters, sending him Christmas cards.

But she was lonely, eventually turning to Seamus McBride, a local ice-cream vendor. He became a friend, gave her money, helped her out, and in time the relationship turned into something more. She remained unmoved in the face of Micky's declaration of love and his pleas for her to visit him and bring their two children. His anguish turned to anger, and then the INLA took a hand. A couple of its enforcers visited Margaret and Seamus and roughed them up a bit, chopping off Margaret's luxurious braids that went almost halfway down her back, branding her a slut, and making her disgrace public in the small, tight community already shocked by her defiant flaunting of its standards. In late 1979 Margaret had McBride's child. A year later, Devine volunteered for the first hunger strike, and when that collapsed he immediately volunteered for the second and started divorce proceedings.

Once he was on hunger strike, Margaret had a change of heart. Now she wanted to see him but he would not have it. Now it was her turn to beg and his to spurn her pleas. Not only would he not allow her to share in his death, he moved to exclude her totally, giving his sister the legal authority to make his funeral arrangements and demanding specific action to ensure that Margaret would not be allowed to attend. An IRSP representative was sent to inform Margaret of his plans and to tell her to get the children ready for a farewell visit to their father. The news that she would have no part in his funeral whatsoever, even to the point of being barred from seeing his body, devastated her. The honor bestowed on him in death by their community would not reflect on her—his becoming a somebody

would not make her a somebody too. Micky would not have her
publicly recognized as Mrs. Michael Devine, wife of the dead hunger
striker.

He died at 7:50 A.M. on Thursday, 20 August, having returned to
the fold of the Church, duly anointed. He made his peace with God,
but not with Margaret. To the end, he held his resolve: he would
not see her, she could not view his dead body, she could not attend
his funeral. He would damn her with the ferocity of his rejection.
And damn her he did. For although she would have two more children
by McBride, she would not marry him. All five children carry the
dead Devine's surname, but for Margaret there was no peace.

On the day of his funeral she hid in bed, almost an outcast in the
city that was honoring her dead husband. She would not accept that
Micky was dead. A priest had come from the prison to tell her that
he had forgiven her, but his forgiveness taunted her; it was an ac-
cusation that cut her like a knife, a sharp clean thrust that belied the
deadliness of the silent aggression, begging the question she could
not face or answer. For what was she being forgiven? For not being
a good wife? For abandoning him? For making him go on the hunger
strike? For his death? And so she blamed herself for his death, surrounding herself with memorabilia of their past, evoking their lost
love, shutting out the bad times and the troubles they had had, talking
to his picture, begging him to come back, dreaming of him walking
through the front door, visiting his grave every day, often spending
the whole day there, trying to expiate her own guilt, yet not quite
sure just what it was she should be guilty about, fantasizing about
their togetherness, even to the extent that when she had another child
by McBride she called it a miracle—it was, she said, Micky's child.
She cried all the time, despaired, wouldn't let go of a past that probably had not existed, compelling herself to prove her love for Micky
by refusing to give up her grief, holding onto her feelings of loss to
reassure herself that she had truly loved him, blaming the INLA for
coming between them, spending periods of time in the hospital. In
death Micky possessed her as he never had in life.

The attention that had eluded Devine in life almost eluded him in
death. On the day of his death, voters in Fermanagh–South Tyrone
once again went to the polls, and once again they voted along tribal
lines. Owen Carron's election to Westminster overshadowed Devine's death, and when Pat McGeown's wife intervened to end his
strike the same day, after he had unexpectedly lost consciousness on
the forty-second day of his fast, it somehow robbed Devine's death

of significance. It was a statement of futility and meaninglessness rather than of purpose. Nor did his death excite much interest. Media coverage was cursory. There was little violence in either Derry or Belfast, and there were few protesters on the streets. Apathy had begun to take the place of anger; the anger had exhausted itself, leaving only a cynical indifference. In Dublin, Garret FitzGerald, departing from previous government practice, issued no message of sympathy to the family of the dead hunger striker. But in Derry, at least, they did him proud. Devine got the funeral he wanted, and, finally, the respect he yearned for.

Devine's life and death, with their overlays of loss and abandonment, of anger and anguish, of the struggle for certainty in the face of a capricious and seemingly frivolous fate, of the need to mourn and the search for reassurance in a hostile and unfeeling world, of principle upheld and commitment gone awry, of compassion reduced to bathos and hope to escape, reflect the essential condition of the Catholic community itself. The sediments of loss and abandonment are so deeply embedded in the sand grains of time itself that they have become a permanent, indispensable, defining part of the national psyche, integral to the culture's conception of itself, an indelible legacy of the literature of dispossession and defeat that the Gaelic poets created in the eighteenth century—a legacy refined and reinvented by events in the twentieth century.

Ultimately, there is something ineffably sad in the image of Margaret expectant and anxious and sure, when the IRSP representative came to her door, that Micky had sent for her, that her betrayal had been forgiven; of Margaret being told in terms so final that there was no hope for a reprieve, that she was out, out of everything—the wake, the church services, the funeral procession, the graveyard ceremonies. In Micky's eyes, she had died before he had, and if not, he would humiliate her even from beyond the grave.

Margaret was the victim's victim, and the two of them, locked into each other and the circumscribed possibilities of the ghetto in which they lived, could have been any two young people in Derry, any couple in a generation of young people at the bottom of the economic and social ladder, among the first to be harassed by the security forces and the last to be released from their interrogation centers, familiar with the vagaries of discrimination and the arbitrary inequality of the law, for whom there loomed a future more bereft of promise than the present.

2 REACTIONS

. . . their minds are but a pool
Where even longing dies under its own excess.

William Butler Yeats
"Meditations in Time of Civil War"

10   The hunger strikes exposed the contradiction at the core of the Catholic nationalist psyche. The revolutionaries won the War of Independence in 1921 but the pragmatists inherited it. The new Irish state was nonrevolutionary. It changed none of the institutions it had inherited—98 percent of the twenty-one thousand civil servants in some forty-seven government departments, offices, and boards were simply transferred from the service of the United Kingdom to the service of the new Irish government. The new government wanted to show that it could govern; continuity rather than change, especially in the formative circumstances of the Civil War, preoccupied it. Moreover, because of the Civil War the government was put in the position of being the defender of the status quo. Accordingly, the tradition of physical force, of an elite minority whose actions had the imprimatur of history and the sanction of dead generations, triumphed but did not prevail.

The myth of nationhood that emerged after the Civil War was the product of historical fallacy. All of history was viewed through the prism of 1916. It was refracted—what did not fit the condition of the myth was discarded. To perpetuate the 1916 Uprising as the apogee of an eight-hundred-year struggle against foreign oppression, nationalists had to invent a past that conformed to the legend of heroic struggle against a hated oppressor. Martyrdom forged an organic connection between succeeding generations of heroes; separatism was apotheosized as the national aspiration. National identity was endowed with transcendent attributes. It was not something utilitarian that could be traded in the marketplace of politics, it was "a spiritual thing," the nation "a thing inviolate and inviolable, a thing that a man dare not see or dishonor on pain of eternal perdition."[1]

There is "good" violence—the tradition represented by Wolfe Tone, Robert Emmett, Thomas Mitchell, the Fenians, the Uprising of 1916, the War of Independence; there is the violence not spoken of—the abominations of the Civil War, which are neither condoned nor condemned; and there is "bad" violence—the violence of the IRA today. But in fact, the "good" violence was condemned in its time for being "bad" violence, and every argument brought up today to condemn the IRA was also brought up in 1918. Only the Treaty in

1921, historian Margaret O'Callaghan writes, "retrospectively sanctioned actions which had previously been semantically categorized as immoral in condemnations that labelled them terrorist or criminal. British recognition of the Dail's claim to represent the people transformed these actions into acts of war. Their perpetrators, who had always viewed themselves as soldiers of the Irish Republican Army, were now recognized as such."[2]

Central to the myth on which the Irish state is built and to the prehistoric gestations of the Celtic ethos is the idea of heroic sacrifice. The crisis for nationalist Ireland came in trying to deny that the actions of the hunger strikers were a substantiation of this myth, and, therefore, legitimate in terms of their connection to a historical past, and in trying to assert, at the same time, that the prisoners were somehow different. They were not criminals, even if they were not political prisoners; not terrorists, even if they were not freedom fighters.

Opinion surveys reflected the public's ambivalence. In late October 1980, shortly after the first hunger strike began, most respondents in a poll conducted on behalf of Radio-Telefis Eireann (RTE) felt that the British government was right in principle to make no concessions to the hunger strikers. Nevertheless, 45 percent felt that for practical reasons political status should be granted, and only 30 percent were unequivocally opposed to the granting of political status. Charles Haughey, leader of Fianna Fail and Taoiseach (prime minister) at the time, chose his position evasively: some adjustments could be made in the prison rules; political status should not be an issue. Fine Gael leader Garret FitzGerald was more forthright: the Irish state had always rejected the IRA's demands for political status; it could not urge another government to do what the Irish government itself would not do. However, when FitzGerald became prime minister in June 1981, four hunger strikers were dead. In July, following Joe McDonnell's death and the collapse of the ICJP's talks with the NIO, FitzGerald accused the British government of making a "complete mess" of the prison situation and called for direct talks between the British government and the hunger strikers.

The first hunger strike was quickly forgotten in the relief following its abrupt ending—relief not only that the hunger strikers' lives had been spared but that the country did not have to declare itself. The troubling issues the hunger strikers posed were simply swallowed up in the last-minute binge of Christmas shopping, and the country settled down to tantalize itself with the question that appeared to

preoccupy everyone: Would Prince Charles propose to his Lady Di?
Nor did Sands's hunger strike initially arouse much emotion other
than a somewhat jaded sense of déja vu.

However, the crisis in nationalism became acute when Sands was
put forward as a candidate in the Fermanagh–South Tyrone by-
election. For to endorse Sands's candidacy was to concede the continuing legitimacy of the tradition he represented and, therefore, the
legitimacy of his cause. Sands represented the historic symbiosis of
the constitutional and the unconstitutional. Myths can be comfortably
sustained when we are not called on to reaffirm their continuing
validity. Indeed, the disjunction between myth and reality provides
the psychic breathing space that allows us to subscribe to the shib-
boleths of national identity without requiring us to champion the
myths that underpin it in a way that is overpowering or too ritually
self-limiting.

During the 1919–21 War of Independence no one gave the IRA a
mandate to pursue a campaign of violence. They simply assumed it.
"The one thing they [the electorate] were certainly not voting for,"
writes historian Robert Kee in *The Green Flag: Ourselves Alone,*

was an attempt to win sovereign independence by force of arms or a campaign
of terrorism. This was a goal believed in by only a minority of Volunteer activists
who in the long run saw violence rather than democratic politics as the final
arbitrator; though they would have maintained that they were thereby expressing
the national will. At all elections up to and including the General Election of
1918 it had been constantly repeated, even by former rebels of Easter Week, that
further resort to rebellion was unnecessary. . . .

[The] question of taking offensive actions against police and soldiers in Ireland
in order to establish an Irish Republic had never been put before the Irish people
and if it had been at the General Election of 1918 it would have been decidedly
rejected. The only specific methods proposed by Sinn Fein to establishing the
Irish Republic had been an appeal to the Peace Conference [i.e., the Versailles
Conference that took place at the end of World War I] combined with the passive
resistance involved in abstention from Westminster and the creation of a National
Assembly in Ireland.

However, the vast majority of moderate Sinn Fein support was simply
swept aside by extremists within the movement who were "determined to force a revolution at all costs." Increasingly the Volunteers
(i.e., the IRA), who did not come under the jurisdiction of Sinn Fein
but rather were an autonomous body operating in their own right,
took matters into their own hands: "the sooner fighting was forced
and a general state of disorder created the better it would be for the

country," Michael Collins is reported to have said. Their cold-blooded attacks on individual policemen—more than twenty, all of them fellow Irishmen, were killed between January 1919 and March 1920—provoked a predictable government response: repression.

"Throughout 1919," Kee writes,

members of popularly elected bodies, such as urban and rural district councils, often supporters of Sinn Fein, were to express condemnation or at least dislike of what was being done by the Volunteers [IRA]. It was only when condemnation and dislike for what the British government were to do by way of retaliation began to exceed this, that popular acquiesence in what was in reality the rebellion of a small minority materialized. . . . In the absence of any realistic policy but repression from the government, [the Irish people] were bound to come down for all their early misgivings on the side of the Volunteers. In this the policy of Collins and the other extremists in Sinn Fein succeeded brilliantly. They [the extremist elements in Sinn Fein] won their battle against the moderates in Sinn Fein by making moderation irrelevant.[3]

The fact that the adherents of physical force—the unconstitutional—triumphed in 1921 necessitated that history be rewritten to reflect the primacy of the myths of insurrection. The War of Independence had to be connected to the struggle of other generations. Validation came through historical continuity. History was linear when extrapolated backwards. Lip service to the idea of heroic sacrifice was rhetorical; the ideals of the Proclamation of Independence were invoked with the understanding that they would remain just that.

Continuity, however, no matter how skewed, works in both directions. The IRA does represent something. It is the embodiment of a concept of Irish nationalism that is largely the creation of the Irish state itself. It symbolizes the holy writ of indivisible nationhood. It takes its purpose and tradition from Wolfe Tone's call two hundred years ago "to break the connection with England to assert the independence of the country and to unite the whole people of Ireland." It has pursued this aspiration relentlessly and ruthlessly. It can summon eight hundred years of what the state itself propagates as history and seventy years of its own enduring tradition to bear witness to its purpose.

Accordingly, Sands's hunger strike, forced into the national consciousness by the Fermanagh–South Tyrone by-election, created an awful tension between traditional beliefs, submerged in the national psyche and serving as a reference point for national identity, and present realities. The efforts to relieve this tension, to somehow balance the conflicting demands of adherence to the imperatives of myth, to distinguish between the legitimate Republicanism of yesteryear (which was condemned in its time for being elitist and violent and to which homage was now paid) and the illegitimate Republicanism of the present (which was condemned for the same reasons) and to synchronize the sociopolitical realities of the Irish state with the precepts of Irish nationhood created an almost unbearable anguish.

In time, the contradictions inherent in these efforts to uncouple the past and the present produced their own distortions. The distinguished critic Denis Donoghue, writing in the *Listener,* referred to the "leaders of the IRA . . . maintaining a carefully devised campaign to take possession of the entire tradition of Irish Republicanism, from the rising of 1798 to the Fenians and the Men of Easter Week, 1916"; the IRA wanted political status "so that they could represent themselves as the legitimate heirs to the great Republican tradition"; the IRA leaders in the Maze/Long Kesh had carefully planned a campaign "to have themselves accepted as the only legitimate heirs to the true Republican tradition" so they would be "accepted as soldiers, heroes rather than terrorists"; the conflict with the British government was nominal, the real conflict was "with those Irish people who regarded the IRA as perverts, corruptors of a great tradition"; the Provisionals had only one aim: "to compel the Irish people to acknowledge them as their true legitimate sons."[4]

Yet the "true Republican tradition" of which Donoghue spoke never had the support of the Irish people. It denounced as anti-Irish those who did not subscribe to its extreme nationalist views, and the swing in public opinion that came in the wake of the 1916 Uprising was due to public revulsion at the number and manner of the executions that followed, not public support for the ideas of the dead leaders. Irish Republicanism as articulated and practiced by the few had little appeal to, or support among, the many. The few simply took it upon themselves to know what was best for the many; the inflexible few simply pressed ahead, intent on leading the reluctant many into the hallowed land of "ourselves alone."

The South's need to deny the legitimacy of the hunger strikers' actions, to show that there was no historical continuity between 1916 and the IRA today, produced convolutions in the national psyche that could not be resolved. For if Sands—and by extension the IRA— were not a part of the "true Republican tradition," it followed that the true Republican tradition had represented the aspirations of the people. But, of course, it had not in 1916, and the IRA does not today. Statements denouncing the IRA—such as the assertion of bishop of Down and Conor, Cahal Daly, in November 1974 that "there is no historical continuity whatsoever between the present, largely faceless leaders of the self-styled 'Republican movement' and their honorable forebears"[5] or the April 1976 declaration of Sean McEntee (who played a prominent part in both the War of Independence and the Civil War, as well as subsequent Fianna Fail governments) that "it is blasphemous to mention the name of Pearse and the Provos together. They have disgraced everything that the army of the Irish Republic stood for"[6]—overlook the fact that those "honorable forebears" were engaged in what Robert Kee describes as "a vile and squalid war"[7] using the same tactics—the clandestine bomb, assassination on the street, murder from a ditch, savage reprisals, random terror, destruction of property—that the IRA uses today.

McEntee's remarks were especially self-serving and hypocritical. During the Civil War, writes Margaret O'Callaghan, the hierarchy had summarily excommunicated members of the IRA who "carry on what they call a war but which in the absence of any legitimate authority to justify it, is morally only a system of murder and assassination of the National forces—for it must not be forgotten that killing in an unjust war is as much murder before God as if there were no war."[8] The IRA—that is, McEntee's colleagues—were not impressed with the hierarchy's stance. They simply released a resolution passed by their own alternative parliament in 1922 which called on their president, Eamon De Valera,

to make representations to the Vatican formally and emphatically protesting as Head of State against the unwarranted action of the Irish hierarchy in presuming and pretending to announce an authoritative judgment upon the question of the constitutional and political fact now at issue in Ireland—viz. whether the so-called Provisional (Partition) Parliament, set up under threat of unjust war and by coup d'etat, was the rightful legislature of the country or not—and in using the sanction of religion to enforce their own political views and compel acquiescence by Irish Republicans in a usurpation that contains no less consequences than the partition of the ancient territory of our nation, the loss of its sovereignty and declared independence, and the imposition of a test oath that amount to the disenfranchisement of Republicans who, having regard for the sacred bond of an oath, will not take it without meaning to keep it.[9]

(These contradictions in the way constitutional nationalism views good and bad violence continue to bedevil it. On 22 August 1984, for example, Michael Noonan, minister for justice, went to Beal na mBlath, County Cork, where Michael Collins was killed sixty-two years earlier, to memorialize him. "Collins was the man," he said, "whose matchless and indominatable will carried Ireland through the terrible crisis. He was the man who fought the Black and Tan terror until England was forced to offer terms." A week later, in *An Phoblacht/Republican News,* Mick Timothy, an old-time Republican, had a question for Noonan. How, he asked, did Collins achieve his success? "Collins," he wrote, "identified those who were the tools of British rule in Ireland and directed his men against them. And in particular he targeted members of the Royal Irish Constabulary (RIC), those 'fellow Irishmen,' often 'fellow Catholics,' those 'policemen doing their duty.' . . . [Collins] had his men shoot them down without mercy; a bullet in the back, in the dark, on their way to or from Mass, when they were unarmed, or with their families—it mattered not to Collins. Many more native RIC men were killed than Black and Tan Brits.")

Condemnations of the IRA by the Catholic Church were frequent and vociferous throughout the War of Independence from 1919 to 1921. "Cardinal Logue himself, the three archbishops, and the entire hierarchy," writes Robert Kee, "together with the vast majority of parish priests, condemned bloodshed by the Volunteers [IRA] as crimes and offenses against the law of God."[10] However, to acknowledge this would somehow legitimize the hunger strikers, and to legitimize the hunger strike would be to delegitimize the myths of the state.

Bishop Daly uses the concept of "the balance of moral probability" to make the distinction between the violence of 1919–21 and the violence practiced by the IRA today. "This balance," he says, "rested with those who felt there was no way forward between 1916 and 1922 other than the way of violence to secure even a minimum degree of freedom for the Irish people—the campaign of violence at that time was just." For violence to be justified, he argues, it must be shown "that there is no other peaceful way forward in which justice can be secured, that there is a reasonable prospect of success, that the amount of death and suffering caused by the rebellion or war does not outweigh the good which was hoped to be attained by it and that the operations carried on in the conduct of the war are themselves in conformity with the moral law." In other words, "a war can be justified, yet many of the things done in its name can be quite immoral." Bishop Daly would hold, therefore, that while "many of the things done by the Irish Freedom Fighters [in 1919–21] were immoral at the time, overall the thrust of the war was justified."

Father James Healy, S.J., a teacher of moral theology at the Milltown Institute, Dublin, disagrees with the bishop's analysis. "The 1916 uprising," he argues, "was an unjust rebellion. I'm quite willing to say 1919–21 was an unjust war and that doesn't make me a Unionist. You can have results you rejoice in after an evil."

The 1981 hunger strikers forced the wider nationalist culture to face the contradictions in the history it had created for itself. It was not up to the task, and it resented the hunger strikers for putting it into the position of having to look at itself. And so it changed the issue: the IRA was to blame for prolonging the hunger strikes, the IRA wanted to destabilize the state, the IRA was taking a ghoulish satisfaction in the upheavals the hunger strikes were causing. The logic was simple enough: since the prisoners represented themselves as belonging to an army, and soldiers followed orders, the IRA leadership could simply order them to end their protest.

Moreover, the British government's response—its unwillingness to heed the urgent pleas of the most respected Church leaders, the most middle-of-the-road politicians, the prime ministers of successive governments, in fact, to heed anyone who counseled some attempt to mediate a resolution—rubbed the raw nerve of the country's sense of powerlessness to influence, and with the sense of powerlessness came anger at Britain for its obstinacy. In July alone, twenty-three messages passed between the two governments in thirty-one days. (Garret FitzGerald, who became Taoiseach on 30 June 1981, suspects the continual barrage of messages may have irritated Mrs. Thatcher. He now believes his own reactions were possibly excessive. "The amount of time I gave to it," he told me, "was regarded by my colleagues as being disproportionate and [they thought] that I was far too emotionally involved. I think in retrospect I did give too much attention to it and became too emotionally involved in something which was unlikely to yield any results.")

The sense of powerlessness among Catholics was pervasive. It tapped into the folk memories of the past, of an unheeding imperial power dismissive of Irish opinion. "Restraint has been shown on this side of the Irish sea," the *Irish Press* said on 5 May 1981, "but that restraint has not been met by magnanimity or flexibility in London. Restraint cannot be maintained indefinitely when the political climate in Ireland is worsening hourly because of decisions made in London over which Dublin has no control, but is nevertheless placed in the position of having to deal with their effects." Not only did Irish opinion not count, but the fact that it could be so urgently expressed and so insistently dismissed only reinforced the perception that the British regarded it as being worthless. "The Irish government seemed to have so little that they could do," Hugh Logue of the ICJP recalls, "and that shocked me, to get so close to the Irish government and find it so helpless. That disturbed me later, looking back on it." Whether they liked it or not, most Catholics were being forced to side again with a bankrupt ideology that had become alien to most and irrelevant to many. "First Sands. Hughes may be next. And how many to follow?" the *Irish Times* asked despairingly. "Does no one in Westminster read Irish history? Does not even Michael Foot [leader of the opposition Labour Party] remember what the 1916 execution did to Ireland—and to England? One by one . . . thousands of ordinary Irish people who never had a nationalist thought in their lives were into the separatist movement and into the Volunteers." And, two weeks later, on 19 May, two days before Patsy O'Hara and Raymond McCreesh died, it warned that "no matter what these men have done, no matter how people despise the Provisionals and their methods, if more and more coffins come out of that prison, an ugly metamorphosis could come over the whole island, North and South."

The hunger strikes caught the South in the middle of a social transformation. A new order was emerging as the country changed from a producer to a consumer society, freeing itself from the constraints of scarcity, adjusting, with overhaste, perhaps, to the new values of abundance. The older visions of self that sustained the producer society—hard work, thrift, "sacrifice in the name of a higher law, ideals of duty, honor, integrity," the "sublimination of self-needs"—were being pushed aside for the newer vision of personality with its emphasis on "self-fulfillment, self-expression, self-gratification."[11] But the old order did not yield willingly, and the hunger strikes became a powerful symbol of the old values, the hunger strikers silent accusers, adding to the sense of dislocation, compounding the stirrings of latent guilt.

The unease these predicaments brought was a harbinger of a greater unease: that things were out of control, that the economic boom that had been enjoyed throughout the 1970s was an illusion, less the product of native effort than a case of rising tides lifting all boats, that the new myths of money, mobility, and me-too-ism were as empty as the old myths. The 1960s and 1970s, with their dogmas of economic growth and industrialization and the opening to Europe, had brought the South to believe that it was equal, a nation standing on its own feet, no longer in the shadow of another nation. By 1981, however, the economy had run out of steam; per capita income was falling, the growth in population outstripped the growth in output, foreign borrowing accounted for 15 percent of GNP. When Garret FitzGerald took over as Taioseach, he found himself faced with an economic crisis he had not been aware existed, despite his own misgivings, until he had been told the extent of the problem immediately after his appointment: either he had to cut spending dramatically and immediately, he says, or the economy would have been in danger of a general collapse.

The hunger strikes were a distraction, albeit a major and important one. But in the country at large they had disrupted the newly discovered sense of equality. Mrs. Thatcher's repeated disparagements of the Irish government's representations in the matter were a clear reminder that, in the English view, at least, the fundamentals had not changed. Thus the demonstrations and marches and sloganeering—the destruction of a Dublin landmark (a monument commemorating Queen Victoria's visit to Dublin); student occupations of British Airways offices, the Dublin Stock Exchange, and Fine Gael's offices, as well as the sit-ins in the General Post Office and at government offices; and calls on the government to expel the British ambassador—had less to do with the justice of the hunger strikers' demands than with the anger that the new sense of powerlessness had awakened. The unheroic past would not go away: the subservience of the unfree had been replaced by the pretense of the free, making the Catholic Irish again question who they were.

Once again the South was in need of a scapegoat. And once more the British provided a convenient target. "To quite an extraordinary extent," the *Irish Times* asserted, "Mrs. Thatcher personally is being blamed for the failure of the attempt to end the Long Kesh hunger strike." Mrs. Thatcher, the cold, unyielding, unfeeling prime minister who deflected every question about the hunger strikers with one about their victims, became the rallying point for Irish anger. To her the hunger strikers were no longer human beings, no longer, for that matter, British subjects for whom the British government was responsible. She reduced them to terrorists, criminals, murderers, convicting them of offenses for which they had not been tried, making them collectively responsible for 2,400 deaths. They were "evil men" manipulated by the godfathers of violence. She dehumanized them in the name of humanity, referred to them contemptuously and dismissively as "men of violence" who had "chosen to play what would be their last card." She taunted them: "It would seem," she said during a one-day visit to Belfast at the end of May, "that dead hunger strikers who have extinguished their lives are of more use to the IRA than living members. Such is their calculated cynicism." Refusing to see the hunger strikers as ordinary human beings caught in a situation as much her own government's making as their own, she degraded them in the name of compassion for others, and in diminishing them she diminished herself, divesting herself of responsibility for their deaths. They were suicides, self-imposed or under orders of their superiors; their deaths were a matter of choice, something denied to their victims. Mrs. Thatcher's policies "are correct," the *Guardian* noted, "but her posture has been disdainful."

Because Irish Catholics could not understand the depth of her stubborn refusal to concede anything, they sought to rationalize it, seeing her actions as a response to the death of Airey Neave, her closest political confidant, who had been assassinated in 1979 when a bomb planted by the INLA exploded in his car in the basement garage of the House of Commons. Even Garret FitzGerald finds ways to excuse her behavior: she did not fully understand the psychology of the situation; she could see only the direct effects of actions, not their indirect impact; she was still smarting over Haughey's behavior—and by extension irritated with the Irish in general—for having blatantly misrepresented, in her view, the character of their meeting at the Anglo-Irish summit in December 1980. (The first Anglo-Irish summit between Thatcher and Haughey took place on 8 December 1980 at Dublin Castle. Afterwards the statements made by Haughey and other members of his government seemed to suggest that some change in the constitutional status of Northern Ireland was in the cards. Thatcher, reportedly, was livid and hotly denied that any change in the status of Northern Ireland was being contemplated. Her reassurances, however, failed to mollify the Unionists, who were, as always, prepared to believe that the worst was about to happen.) This had made it difficult for FitzGerald to establish a relationship with her even though they had known each other since 1975 and gotten on well together.[12] The conventional wisdom was that the prison issue was not a political issue for her but a personal one, that she was motivated by considerations of revenge rather than policy, and that in the battle of wills, the eyeball-to-eyeball contest, she would not be bested; that she would settle not just for the prisoners' defeat, but for their humiliation.

The Irish public drew a distinction between Mrs. Thatcher and the British government. Actions that reflected or reiterated the hard line—no flexibility, no negotiations, and no giving in to the five demands—were attributed to her imperiousness, while actions that reflected a more flexible approach were attributed to the government, to the prodding of the more politically attuned, moderate elements in her Cabinet. When the government appeared to do an abrupt about-face on the issue of civilian clothing in October 1980 (at one point it seemed that it would allow all prisoners in Northern Ireland to wear their own clothes, a move both Cardinal Tomas O'Fiaich and Edward Daly, bishop of Derry, who had pressed the concession in a series of meetings with Atkins, were convinced would forestall a hunger strike) the apparent change of heart was attributed to Mrs. Thatcher over-ruling Atkins during a Cabinet meeting. And again, when Michael Alison insinuated to the ICJP that the NIO would like to be more concessionary but that there was always "the lady behind the veil," the ICJP mediators immediately took this to be a reference to Mrs. Thatcher. So, when Michael O'Leary, the Irish deputy prime minister, declared in early August 1981 that the hunger strikes would have been settled by then "had there been any Prime Minister in Britain other than Mrs. Thatcher," few disagreed. But few chose to point out that Mrs. Thatcher's hard-line stand had the unqualified backing of Michael Foot, leader of the Labour Party, David Steel, leader of the Liberal Party, and Roy Jenkins, leader of the Social Democratic Party, as well as the support of all the European communities, foreign ministers, and U.S. presidents Carter and Reagan.

At the official level, however, criticism of Mrs. Thatcher was oblique, for the most part, and implied rather that stated. Given her obduracy and penchant for the imperious gesture, the Irish government went to great lengths not to further stiffen her hard-line attitude by appearing to criticize her personally. But more important, the relative absence of criticism reflected the quandary in which the government found itself. It could not be seen to be on the side of the IRA. It was sensitive to being manipulated into using its authority to argue the prisoners' case, to appearing to countenance more for the prisoners at Long Kesh than it had itself been prepared to give to Republican prisoners at Port Laoise. Excessive criticism of Mrs. Thatcher would have made it part of H-block propaganda—a perception the government would not permit.

The predominant sense in the South was one of being pulled simultaneously in several directions. On the one hand, the hunger strikers were embraced, on the other, repudiated. Feelings oscillated between concern over the slow, inexorable progress of their death-fasts and fear of what might happen should their deaths set off a frenzy of killing that would spill over into the comfortable life of the South. The public empathized with the hunger strikers to the extent of believing that they were somehow special; its reluctance to condemn and silent empathy implied a benign benediction of their cause.

There was more than one kind of silence, however. On one sensitive issue, not only did the Irish government eschew confrontation with Mrs. Thatcher, it ignored the matter altogether. FitzGerald chose not to respond, on either a government-to-government level or on a private one-on-one basis with Mrs. Thatcher herself, after Hugh Logue had informed him, in the course of a briefing on the progress of the ICJP's efforts, that the British had established direct contact with the IRA. FitzGerald, Logue recalls, was angered but did not appear to be at all surprised. Although FitzGerald himself has no clear recollection of the meeting, he believes that had the information not been hearsay, he would not have been as reluctant as he was to face down the British on the issue. "I remember being totally frustrated," FitzGerald says, "knowing this had happened but not having the degree of certainty that would enable me to use it. Because if I had alleged this to the prime minister, that she or somebody under her authority was doing it, and she denied it, and I couldn't produce any evidence for it or had no clear authority [for the statement], that would really have damaged our relationship and made it very hard to achieve any objective [relating to] the hunger strike or anything else. You don't do that politically unless you're sure of your ground." As a result the Irish government never did confront the British government on the question of Britain's direct or indirect, authorized or unauthorized, lines of contact with the IRA; had no sure knowledge of the concessions that were allegedly made in the course of these contacts, and which were, therefore, open to being denied, no matter how unconvincingly. While knowing that the British government's public rhetoric—a rhetoric that contributed so much to the precarious state of relations between the two countries and to the general malaise of Irish anger and frustration—may have been at considerable variance with its private actions, it never learned whether the British prime minister, who had vowed never, never, to negotiate with terrorists, knew that her minions were busily engaged in just such clandestine practices, with or without her knowledge. "I'd no illusions on that score given the British record in dealing with the IRA right back to 1971," says FitzGerald. "I had no illusions at all, although I wondered at the time whether this was being done with or without Margaret Thatcher's consent. I suspected she might not have known about it. And knowing the British administrative system, its complexity and scale and the muddle and confusion and stupidity that characterizes it very often, it seemed likely that she didn't know about it. Within that system I don't think she did. I would have been surprised had she authorized direct contact with the IRA."

FitzGerald's concern was with establishing a good working relationship with Thatcher, to repair the damage done to Anglo-Irish relations following the summit of December 1980, an issue which was still a matter of some anger to Mrs. Thatcher. The hunger strikes were an irritant, important and pressing and calling for immediate resolution, yes, but an irritant nevertheless, an unfortunate detour on the road to a wider Anglo-Irish understanding.

The IRA, of course, sought to exploit the situation to its own advantage. In mid-July a priest—an emissary of the IRA—turned up at the Department of Foreign Affairs in Dublin with a warning: both the H-block candidates—Paddy Agnew and Kieran Doherty—who had been elected to the Dail in the general election that brought FitzGerald to power, would resign their seats and force two crucial by-elections (FitzGerald's coalition with Labour had a tentative majority of one or, at best, two votes) unless the government came out in favor of the five demands. The emissary was quickly made less than welcome.

On at least two occasions the *Irish Times* pleaded the case for some kind of special designation. "Sands should be rescued," its lead editorial said on 23 April, the week after he had been elected to the Westminster Parliament. "And the British government should be rescued from a stance which is not based on principle and which is not based on any logical approach to penology or politics. The fact that in the same prison are men who enjoy a special category, merely because they were convicted of crimes committed before 1976, says it all." And in August, two weeks before Micky Devine died, it pressed the argument again: "The British Government sometimes claims," it wrote, "that the issue is a matter of principle, there must be no special category. Yet everything is special about the prisoners in Long Kesh, be they Provisionals, INLA, or UDA. The whole state of Northern Ireland is special and was set up to be special."

The prisoners' demands became, if not just, at least reasonable, when the possible consequences of their demands not being met became threatening. The public disavowed the hunger strikers to the extent of being against the IRA, of being opposed to the IRA's campaign of violence in Northern Ireland, if only because it felt that the violence would ultimately rebound on the South. The scenes of violence in Dublin on 18 July when seventeen Gardai (police) and fifty protesters were injured during an H-block demonstration outside the British embassy left the country shaken. "[The] so-called peaceful demonstrators were infiltrated by vicious savages . . . the skill acquired by the violence-makers in the North was imported for the day," the *Irish Independent* declared in an unprecedented front-page editorial. The police, it said, "responded in a manner used by all police forces all over the world—if you are caught among a mass of trouble makers then it is your look-out if you are hit by a truncheon." The *Irish Times* called the riot "abominable thuggery . . . planned and organized in advance. . . . In the background [could be] discerned the godfathers of the Provisional IRA manipulating [the rioters] for their own sinister ends," ends which included "nothing less than the destruction of Irish democracy." The violence, said the *Irish Press,* was "unparalleled in its ferocity, premeditated [and] probably succeeded in alienating the groundswell of moderate opinion which had shifted noticeably in the wake of the British sabotage of the H-block settlement formula produced by the Commission for Peace and Justice." (The *Church of Ireland Gazette* had a somewhat different perspective. "To the more seasoned observer," it noted wryly, "it was obvious from television news clips that the [Gardai] did mete out retribution on a scale which would not now generally be acceptable from the police service in Northern Ireland. . . . Demands would have been made from civil and human rights associations, politicians at home and abroad, especially in the USA, and the Dublin press for a total and impartial inquiry into the behavior of the police.")

The H-block movement saw matters differently, of course. "I don't think that the H-block campaign has ever been given any credit for the amount of discipline it was able, not to enforce, but to encourage within the campaign," says leading H-block activist Bernadette Devlin McAliskey. "The bitterness towards the Southern administration was actually much deeper than towards the British because in some ways the British actually behaved as you expected them to. To be confronted by a Southern administration seemingly unwilling or incapable of making the most basic gesture, to call in the Ambassador or to send him home engendered a great deal of bitterness."

The Irish public was angry with Britain, believing that Britain could do something to meet the prisoners' demands at an acceptable halfway point. Once again the *Irish Times* captured the national mood when it declared that "Mrs. Thatcher must face what has to be done and find the flexibility once and for all for a solution." When she would not, her unwillingness to do so was put down to the prisoners' being Irish. And when, in early July, the British government ruled out the use of plastic bullets, on the grounds that they were lethal, in English cities in which severe rioting had broken out, there was a visceral reaction in Catholic Ireland: it was all right to shoot Irish rioters in Belfast but not English rioters in Liverpool.

The result was a pervasive disorientation, a collective nervous breakdown that manifested itself not so much in sudden and unpredictable shifts in opinion as in the simultaneous advocacy of what would be, under normal circumstances, opposing viewpoints. Editorials in the *Irish Times,* hardly a repository of anti-British sentiment, railed at Britain for its pertinacity and at the IRA for its inflexibility. They opposed political status yet argued that the prisoners were indeed special; they harshly criticized the British government for its dilatory tactics in mediation efforts and lambasted the IRA for appearing to want more hunger strikers to die. In government, Charles Haughey would not endorse the five demands; in opposition he did. In opposition, Garrett FitzGerald urged the British government to make no concessions to the hunger strikers; in government, he called for flexibility and direct negotiations between the British government and the hunger strikers, even though he himself refused to meet with Owen Carron after he became Sands's successor as Sinn Fein M.P. for Fermanagh–South Tyrone. He called in the British ambassador to protest Mrs. Thatcher's misrepresentation of his position on the hunger strikes in a letter she sent to leading U.S. politicians, and he condemned the IRA for exploiting the prisoners, convinced of its power to order a stop to the fasting. The hunger strikers' families denounced FitzGerald for not doing enough to save the lives of Kevin Lynch and Kieran Doherty, and FitzGerald met with relatives on one occasion and refused to meet with them on another. The Irish state, which had praised its own mettle in 1977 for refusing to negotiate with Republican prisoners at Port Laoise who had gone on hunger strike for political status, now urged the British state to display its mettle by negotiating with the Republican hunger strikers at the Maze/Long Kesh.

11   In the North, geography and proximity resulted in a sense of powerlessness different from that in the South. In the Catholic ghettos, among those who believed they were unempowered and who attributed their condition to Britain, the authorities' unwillingness to consider any concession to the hunger strikers simply reinforced what they already knew—they were neither confused nor surprised. Indeed, if anything, they were somewhat smugly righteous that they had been proven correct, because if their analysis was accurate, the rightness of their cause had to be conceded.

For others in the broader nationalist community, their sense of powerlessness came from not being able to disengage, of having to heed the tribal call to solidarity. Not to be on the side of the hunger strikers was to be against them; not to share in the opprobrium directed at Mrs. Thatcher was to condone her actions; not to accept that the hunger strikers were being reasonable was to imply that the authorities were; not to accept the justice of their demands was to want the strikers to die. It was not sufficient that they accept what the hunger strikers were doing, they had to approve their actions.

Thus, their predicament: to appear both supportive of the tribe's folk values as it closed in on itself, and not to appear supportive of the violence the folk cause invoked in its name. For most, the distinctions were too fine, and since there were no dispensations, they would not be found wanting. Not too many people in the North might have been able to recite the five demands, but it did not matter: support for what the hunger strikers were doing didn't require knowledge of what they wanted. The vote in Fermanagh–South Tyrone for Bobby Sands was not so much a vote in support of the prisoners' five demands as a vote against Mrs. Thatcher and what she stood for: the arrogant, tyrannical oppressor whose hubris invites retaliatory aggression, the unheeding imperial power. When the tribe summoned the ghosts of heroic failure to bear witness on its behalf, the tribe responded. It was a vote about symbols.

The tribe responded in other ways, too, sometimes enthusiastically, often reluctantly, and, on occasion, because it was compelled to. Nor was its anger reserved only for Mrs. Thatcher or the British government. It was angry, too, at the IRA, since it believed that the IRA could order an end to the hunger strikes, that the deaths of the hunger strikers were in a sense as much due to the IRA's need for coffins in the street to bolster its tarnished image as they were to Mrs. Thatcher's willingness to allow them to die.

"One of the most horrible things that I saw was a couple of days before Bobby Sands died," says Father Rogan, a curate at the Twinbrook Church from which Sands was buried. "On the playing field just as you come into Twinbrook, facing below the church, they built a thing like an altar [to Sands]. Whoever put that up there wanted a body: we need a body; Sands, give us your body, we are ready and we are prepared. They almost demanded that he die, and if he hadn't died, the impression I got from that was that there would have been a very big disappointment."

Even among many who supported the hunger strikers there was also, especially in Belfast, anger with H-block supporters and their hangers-on who tried to ensure support through intimidation. In the ghettos, not to display a picture of a hunger striker or fly a black flag was to draw suspicion on yourself; not to respond in the middle of the night by turning on your lights to the rattling of dustbins and the blowing of whistles that announced the death of a hunger striker was to invite a brick through the window; not to heed the demand of the placards held up by activists manning the white line pickets to toot your horn in support of the hunger strikers put you in danger of having your car window smashed.

"Everyone was very lonely," says Paddy Devlin, a longtime Catholic community leader.

People came out onto the streets and they lined themselves up along the white lines [the white stripes that run down the center of the major streets] and as you were coming up you were forced to blow your horn as you were going past them. In all the Catholic areas—up in the Whiterock in Andersonstown—on all the roads, you had the white line protests and the people there would whack you with a bottle as you went past if you didn't blow your horn. Then they lifted money for the hunger strikers—they wanted the money to buy them food or something? With the money they would buy petrol—or personal things.

Decent people in the community were frightened and they stayed in and kept their doors locked; the other crowd paraded around the ghetto. You had people coming out onto the streets to whitewash the gable walls, to throw petrol bombs every night at the transport or traffic that they felt was hostile. Being angry at the people who intimidated you is one you couldn't win. People cleared off, got into their homes, and closed their doors. It was down to work in the morning, come home, and then hide inside. People at the time were horrified mainly at the excesses of the supporters of the hunger strikers.

Moderation fell silent, sullenness became a substitute for passiveness.

The ghetto turned in on itself: shops were looted, cars and trucks hijacked, barricades erected, factories fire bombed, streets strewn with tangled debris, smashed bottles, burnt-out stores, smoldering cars, mangled machinery, whole areas turned into wastelands of violence. "You've no idea how terrifying it was," one woman who lived in the Catholic ghetto of Shantallow in Derry told the *Newsletter*. "Midnight they come out. It's pitch dark outside—they've smashed out the street lights. All you can hear is the smashing of bottles and the thudding of stones. They wreck and shout and fire anything they lay their hands on. They don't give a damn about old people. When you look out the windows all you see is scores of them in masks. Most of them are kids"—kids terrorizing their own people, destroying their own community, with no other outlet to vent their rage and frustration. Sealed by the security forces into their own estates, they destroyed them. Youths, frequently the targets of British oppressiveness, imposed their own oppression with a ruthlessness that matched the ruthlessness they themselves were often subjected to.

Even the tribe would intimidate its own to secure their loyalty. Having seen repression at first hand and often having been the victim of it, it had learned its ways and practiced it just as efficiently on its own. In the days after Sands's funeral it commanded the community to stop and the community stopped; it commanded allegiance and received it. Oppressed and oppressor became one, the victims of one kind of oppression often the perpetrators of another kind.

"My most vivid memory," says Devlin,

is of being up all night, all the family up and water all over the house, in basins and buckets and the bath, while they made petrol bombs outside your window and threw them from forty or fifty yards down the road or from ten yards under my front window. Then they'd blow the whistle and go, and then they'd blow the whistle again in the middle of the night, maybe about four o'clock, and come dashing around with hurleys and beating the doors shouting, "Paddy, come out, you bastard." They'd keep that going for half an hour and away they'd go again and then another whistle went. Once the whistle blew again you knew they were going away.

All because Devlin had challenged in the press statements that the hunger strikers were all members of the Amalgamated and General Workers' Union (AGWU), his union, because some people in his neighborhood felt that his support for the hunger strikers was less than a full-blooded endorsement of their actions. Devlin, a longtime socialist, a Republican activist in the 1940s and 1950s, an internee in the 1950s, a founding member of the SDLP, was now intimidated out of his home by members of his own Republican community. Would Bobby Sands have sympathized with Devlin? Would he have recalled the terror of waiting, petrified in the total darkness, for the first brick to shatter the glass, for the first fire bomb that had to be quickly doused with the waiting water? Would he have remembered the minute preparations you made to save your "humble" home from "the rampaging mob"? Would he have recognized that oppression in the name of ideological correctness is as heinous as oppression in the name of imperialism or sectarianism or Orangeism? Would he have grieved with the Devlins for their lost home?

There was also, of course, the enemy from without, the old enemy waiting to invade their sorrow and their territory. Handbills were pushed through letter boxes in Republican areas. "Already the Orange Order, the UDA, UVF etc. have bonfires built to celebrate his [Sands's] dying," they read. "The Paisleys and McCuskers who have a hatred of anyone Irish have already set in force plans to put an embargo on any foodstuffs, heating fuel and medical equipment reaching Catholic areas. Outlying Catholic ghettos will be overrun by loyalist paramilitaries, led by the UDR and RUC." In West Belfast stores were stripped of goods as the local people stocked up for what they felt would be the "inevitable" holocaust that would follow Sands's death. In the ghettos they were warned that they must prepare for "the loyalist attack." One leaflet told people that "defence and street communities will be set up to organize communication and the control and distribution of food etc. in the event of a possible attack from loyalist paramilitaries." "People were thinking in terms of us versus them," says Ray Mullan, a teacher at St. Louise's Comprehensive School for Girls, located in the middle of the Falls, "and all my work in this school had been trying to get students away from this us/them attitude. I found all my good work over the years had just been destroyed in a couple of weeks." Uncertainty fed fear, rumors had the currency of fact and proliferated wildly, and through-out it all the community itself waited for Sands to die—for the un-known to reveal itself.

As Sands lay dying he became theirs, one of their own, a neighbor's son, the boy next door pitting his frail mortality against the might of the British government, and the unequal contest—the struggle of one isolated, powerless, pitiful individual confined in circumstances of extreme deprivation, devoid of comfort or resources other than the sheer tenacity of his own willpower against the anonymous, im-personal machinery of the bureaucratic state—stirred in Catholics the emotional wellsprings of their ancient grievances, of their own sense of having been wronged.

The extended death watch engulfed them, making them partici-pants in rather than observers of Sands's ordeal, connecting them to him and him to the past generations who had suffered, and in this psychological and symbolic union Sands came to stand for the ac-cumulated wrongs done to Catholics: for the discrimination that de-nied them jobs and housing; for their humiliation at being policed by their Protestant neighbors; for being made to endure subserviently; for the triumphalism of the Orange state that used every opportunity to drive home the relentless message of raw power—that Northern Ireland was a Protestant state for a Protestant people; for being made to feel less than equal; for having their Irishness and Catholicism reduced to labels of inferiority; for the harassment of the police, the indignities of body searches, the outrage of home searches; for being made to feel that they did not belong. And when Sands died, they responded. Seventy thousand marched the funeral route from Twinbrook to Milltown Cemetery, standing for hours in the con-tinuous downpour of rain, somber and silent, and, in their hearts, unforgiving.

The hunger strikers' funerals became the centerpiece of Republican liturgy. The ceremony followed the same elaborate, stylized ritual: the funeral mass, the draping of the Irish Tricolor over the coffin, the funeral procession to the cemetery, the last volley, Lastpost, orders to pallbearers, orders to firing party, the flag on the coffin, gloves instead of army cap, the lone piper leading the procession, the funeral oration at the graveside—all of it awakened a deeper Catholic aware-ness of their own inner sense of historic victimization.

The funerals, somber rituals of death and burial, atavistic exercises in renewal and repentance, compelled the participation of the nationalist community, inviting it to empathize with the families in their grief, an empathy which in turn was transmuted into expressions of solidarity with the dead hunger strikers. The mobilization of people around the hunger strikers' funerals, in which the act of mourning itself could be converted into support for the armed struggle, and, through the medium of television, the vehicle for conveying powerful images of oppression, became an essential element of armed propaganda.

The funerals dissociated the IRA from the violence it inflicted, sanctioned martyrdom, invoked memories of personal and collective suffering. The funerals bonded the IRA to its community; each death eliciting forgiveness for the mistaken operations that had resulted in the deaths of innocent Catholics; pardon for the brutalities it inflicted on its own, for making the community hostage to its aspirations. The funerals purified, cleansed actions of their heinous intent, gave definition to atrocity, context to violent aberration. They solidified the complicated nature of the relationship between the IRA and its community, a love-hate relationship that would always resolve itself on the side of love, especially in the matter of death, where the quarrels are always internal—almost like family rows—and always misunderstood by outsiders who mistook occasional disapproval for disavowal. The funerals exalted the dead, glorified their deeds, reaffirmed the cause for which they died, reburnished the glow of idealism, removed the tawdry and tarnished, gave existential affirmation to the permanence of the past. "Nationalisms are not merely 'like' religions," writes Frank Wright, "they are religions."[1]

The strikers were eulogized as "symbols of the struggle for freedom," "symbols of Irish resistance to British rule in Ireland," "symbols of the true Irish nation which never had surrendered and never would." They had, we were told, "epitomized the history of our country: suffering and hardship and sacrifice." The world "stood in admiration." Their graves "would be places of pilgrimage to which the young of Ireland would come to renew their Republican faith." Their deaths would "lead us all to greater things in striving for the cause for which they died." They had given their lives for a cause "that was greater than man." "Refusing to be separated from their principles in life, they could not be separated from them in death." They had served their country "in a way that had been honored by generations of resistance fighters in Ireland and would be remembered

for all time in the annals of our country's history." They had placed
their bodies "before the juggernaut of imperialism, placing their frail
bodies there to be crushed." "A new generation in Irish history had
been carved out by the men of this generation, the most heroic generation yet to resist foreign resistance." "These hungry and starving
men on their beds of pain, by superior moral strength, had pushed
the British government to the walls and had shamed them in the eyes
of the world." They had "died for human dignity, for the dignity of
all mankind at its highest stature." "There could never be a moral
wrong in any oppressed people anywhere using force against their
oppressor, and there could especially be no wrong in an Irish man
or woman destroying British rule in Ireland." "The hunger strikers
were not dead."

The legacy of that sense of historic vulnerability informed Catholic
reactions from the beginning. When the prisoners insisted at the end
of the first hunger strike that the government had made a deal with
them that would have given them the substance of their demands,
their statements were largely accepted by Catholics, North and South,
despite the fact that no evidence of a deal was ever forthcoming.
None would question the hunger strikers' assertions. While some
might have believed that the hunger strikers misunderstood what was
on offer because they were in diminished states, most conceded, if
only defensively, that the British were indeed capable of reneging on
the promises they had given. The hunger strikers' cry of foul accorded
with folk memory and could be accepted in the light of universally
accepted, if factually flawed, historical precedent.

Indeed, so deeply enshrined is the memory of a perfidious Albion
that the circumstances of the prison protest were buried under the
weight of the past. Had not the English broken faith with the earls
of O'Neill and O'Donnell when "the flight of the earls was taken as
evidence of their treason, their estates were forfeited to the Crown
and the King reversed his earlier policy by assessing a claim to con-
fiscate the whole area over which the earls had earlier wielded authority"?[2] Had they not repudiated the provisions of the Treaty of
Limerick safeguarding Catholic rights, after the defeat of James II,
when they sanctioned passage of the penal laws in 1695; abjured
promises that Catholic emancipation would immediately follow en-
actment of the Act of Union in 1800; reversed themselves on the
promise that Home Rule would be enacted at the end of World War

I; flip-flopped on the promise that the Boundary Commission would substantially redraw the line of partition making a Northern Ireland statelet nonviable; and backslid on the promise to implement the Sunningdale Agreement of 1973 even in the face of violent opposition from loyalist extremists? The past built one betrayal on the next, and besotted itself with imagery of honorable Gaels, outnumbered but not outfought, willing for the greater good to negotiate but not to give in, lured to the bargaining table by a cynical and unscrupulous England that entered into agreements with no intention of keeping them. Even if history was not repeating itself, Catholics were prepared to believe that it might. When the past was collapsed in time, the lesson was one of betrayal. What was believed to have been far outweighed what might now be: no one was willing to dispute what had been so successfully internalized. Because the prisoners' claims fitted the Catholic perception of us versus them, of the Gael versus the foreign occupier, with such a comforting sense of familiarity, the real circumstances of how the first hunger strike ended were reshaped to conform to the requirements of the past.

12   **After** Father John Magee, the pope's emissary, saw Sands and the other three hunger strikers, he met with some of the families of their organizations' victims, praying at the coffin of UDR Lance Corporal Richard McKee, killed in an IRA ambush the day Father Magee arrived in Northern Ireland, and meeting with relations of a Catholic member of the Territorial Army, Hugh McGinn, shot dead by an INLA gunman near his home in Armagh late the previous year. But Mrs. Jennifer Acheson, a Protestant, whose husband, Constable Kenneth Acheson, was murdered when an IRA booby trap exploded under his car as he drove home from Bessbrook RUC station in Armagh three weeks before Father Magee's intervention in the hunger strikes, refused to meet with Magee. "I have nothing to say to him," she told the *Newsletter*, "and I don't think he has anything worthwhile to say to me." She was, she said, only being used. "They [the Catholic clergy] did not come to see me when Kenny was killed and the only reason for the envoy's visit to Ulster is because of Bobby Sands and the hunger strikes." Magee's meeting with the hunger strikers was a "stunt for publicity." She was sick of it all, sick of the coverage given to the hunger strike. Were the hunger strikers' lives more important than her husband's? Her Kenny had been forgotten by most people while Sands and the other hunger strikers were on TV and in the papers every day. "Before Kenny was killed," she said, "I really didn't have any strong feelings about the H-blocks, but now I don't care if Bobby Sands dies. At least he has a choice. Kenny didn't."

Northern Protestants were caught in their own social entrapment. They, too, selectively interpreted events, developing a subjective social reality around the hunger strikes that confirmed their perception of the wider conflict and sustained their historical self-vision of being engaged in what historian Terence Brown calls the "endless repetition of repelled assaults."[1]

The hunger strikes, with their attendant rituals—the fasting, the ministrations of priests, the visit of the pope's personal emissary and the prominent display of the crucifixes for the hunger strikers the pope sent with him, the benediction of the last rites, the comings and goings of the prison chaplains, the pronouncements of clerics, the public intervention of the ICJP, the political role of the bishops, the elaborate liturgy of Catholic funerals—became the embodiment of Protestant fears of the Catholic Church. Because their belief in the absolute power of Catholic priests to impose their own views on Church members was so deeply embedded, Protestants could not believe that neither the hunger strikers nor their families would defer to the Church's view that the hunger strikes were immoral, put the souls of the strikers in jeopardy, and had to be terminated. The failure of the Church to be that explicit, to articulate the Protestant interpretation of what Catholic teaching on suicide should be, and of the families to listen to their priests, confirmed Protestants in their belief that the Catholic Church and the IRA were in collusion. When the Orange Order condemned the violence of the IRA "as an indictment of the false religion of many of the people of the province," deploring "the Roman Catholic Church funerals and terrorist burials," calling attention to the hypocrisy that sanctioned "the singing of hymns and the banging of dustbin lids; the reciting of prayers and the throwing of petrol and acid bombs; the anguish of suffering and the adulation of murderers," it spoke for the overwhelming body of Protestant opinion.

The hunger strikes also reinforced deeper, more primitive fears, which manifested themselves in a "vague, almost pristine uneasiness" Protestants had with a body which to them was "full of mysticism, symbolism, clandestine activity."[2] (On 21 March 1981, the *Anderstown News,* one of the major Catholic newspapers in West Belfast, carried the following item. A rosary procession, it announced, would be held in the Newington area [Holy Family Parish] the following day. "A statue of Our Lady of Fatima," it said, "will be carried in the procession. This particular statue was blessed at the Chapel of Apparitions near Fatima. It was brought to Ireland from Fatima by a Dominican priest. A lady doctor in Dublin brought it before last Christmas to Belfast and left it in the care of a priest in a monastery in the city. She realized later that day that by a strange coincidence, the hunger strike at Long Kesh prison camp ended just about the time she passed it [Long Kesh], on her way to Belfast. The priest in Belfast who received the statue also told the present custodian that the hunger strike ended on the day the statue arrived in Belfast.") Protestants' feelings that hunger striking was somehow unnatural and unwholesome reinforced their feelings that "for young men to enter holy orders and subject themselves to such sacrifices as chastity, is somehow unwholesome."[3]

The actions of the hunger strikers were beyond Protestant comprehension, so they were disassembled and then reconstructed to justify preconceived Protestant attitudes regarding the inadequacy of Catholics: their inherent second-class status, which was perceived to be self-imposed; their high unemployment, which was attributed to their unwillingness to work; their less favored status in the state, which was credited to their own political actions. The deprivation the hunger strikers wallowed in was self-imposed and in keeping with other self-imposed Catholic deprivations, and should, therefore, be treated with the disdain reserved for other Catholic displays of self-inflicted indignities, since they were, ultimately, a pretext for the same thing: bringing about a united Ireland. Once again, Protestants took refuge in their own sense of supremacy and the triumphalism it inspired: they would find ways to live for their country; Catholics could only find ways to die for theirs. "It disgusts us at the way these people are throwing their lives away. We are only sorry we didn't have the choice the mother of Bobby Sands had. We certainly would not have stood back and not allowed the medical staff to help him," said Mrs. Joan Baggley. Mrs. Baggley's husband, William, a member of the police reserve, was shot dead by the IRA in January 1974, and her daughter, Linda, also a member of the reserve, was shot dead in March 1976. "They [Protestants] couldn't really understand the mothers going to the jail, the wives, the girlfriends, the families. They couldn't quite understand this," Dr. Robin Eames, the Church of Ireland Primate of All-Ireland, told me. "It was playing out, looking for world sympathy. Here they're at it again [Protestants were saying]. They're getting America on their side. They're getting the civil rights thing all stirred up again. . . . The fear you had at the time was basically a fear of the unknown."

Protestant attitudes were shaped during the dirty protest. The protesters' willingness to live in their own excrement, to forgo washing, to inflict on themselves the most dehumanizing assaults, and the almost universal association of excrement with "imagery of corruption and decay, of dirt and contagion, of things contaminated, rotting or spoiled"[4]—images which embody perceptions of evil—aroused their deepest disgust, and their disgust at the actions of the protesters became disgust at the protesters themselves. "If cleanliness is next to godliness," asked Peter Robinson, M.P., deputy leader of the Democratic Unionist Party, "then to whom are these men close?" The answer came in verse:

> Those men who set the bomb,
> Caused you to die.
> Like animals they live,
> But that's their way,
> Existing in their filthy degradation day by day.

Since they could not believe that anyone would voluntarily live in such circumstances, Protestants attributed the actions of the prisoners to the orders of the IRA, thus reinforcing their perception of the IRA as an evil organization. "It is quite clear that the prisoners who have refused food have been doing so under the direct orders of the Provisional IRA leaders in Dublin," the *Newsletter* informed its readers. "These arch thugs could call off the fatal protest . . . at any time, but the reason they have not done so is that to abandon the hunger strike 'card' would be a confession of failure that they don't want to make, and would mean a loss of prestige for the whole murder mafia." There were few who would disagree with its assessment of the situation. "I saw this sharp contrast, perhaps for the first time in my Irish experience between the two traditional outlooks," says Archbishop Robin Eames.

On the one side it was leading to martyrdom, it was gradually building up a community support, the black flags on the lamp posts, the protest riots, the protest marches. On the other side it was the downward graph which was saying

"This is choosing death, this is committing suicide and no one asked them to
do it." . . . In one case you had the fatalistic-Celtic misty attitude towards death
and on the other you had the Protestant work ethic, the ethic that you get what
you deserve, the ethic that you get your just deserts, and the result of it was that
you had a conflict situation in practical terms [that reflected] something that lies
deep in the two cultures.

Protestants followed the countdowns to the hunger strikers' deaths
with the expectant titillation of the voyeur, balancing dread anticipation of the consequences with an unquenchable desire for revenge.
"The best news recently heard by the law-abiding Ulster majority,"
independent Unionist M.P. James Kilfedder told the Commons, "was
the statement that the evil bunch of murderers and thugs of the Provisional IRA in the H-block had decided to go on hunger strike."
The strikers were all murderers, the worst actions of one the work
of all, forced into their death rituals by a perfidious and murderous
IRA. They deserved to die, the sooner the better, the more the mer-
rier—"Let Bobby Sands die," their gable walls demanded.

However, uproarious hilarity at "slimmer-of-the-year" jokes
masked the fear of what loyalists could not understand. The hunger
strikes were "only a stunt," Tom Passmore, the Belfast Orange
grandmaster, told the media. "Like most people I am convinced,"
he added "[that] the protesters have no intention of going through
with it." It seemed incongruous to them that those they despised so
vehemently and whose deaths they so ardently desired could face
death with such equanimity. That others would slowly and willfully
be instruments of their own deaths for their beliefs made them un-
certain of their own beliefs and of their will to resist, without which
their fortress mentality was a facade, an empty threat drawing on the
exhausted legacy of the past as a harbinger of future action. The
hunger strikers became grotesque figures, the vanguard of militant
Catholicism bent on Protestant genocide, a lightning rod for Protestant rage, for Protestant impotence to control events in the face of
what appeared to them to be the feckless behavior of the authorities.

Their rage was threefold. Its most obvious target was the hunger
strikers themselves, who represented the collective past that had imprisoned them in their imagined fears and who made them question,
if only subconsciously, their commitment to their own cause. The
hunger strikers impugned the integrity of Protestants' own most cherished myth: the siege of Derry in 1689, which provided Protestantism
with its "enduring watchword." Once upon a time, in their fabled

mythology, their enemies had attempted to starve the Protestant people into submission. Now, almost three hundred years later, they were faced with a perverse changing of roles: the most visible and determined of their enemies were starving themselves in order to force them, the Protestant descendants of the heroic defenders of Derry, into submission. Not only had the hunger strikers asserted claims to their physical territory, they were appropriating their psychic space.

It was what historian A.T.Q. Stewart calls a "nightmarish" juxtaposition "of the folk memory of Jungian psychology" unleashing "the monsters which inhabited the depths of the community's unconscious mind," a "storm at sea" bringing to the surface "creatures thought to have been long extinct."[5] Hence their rage at their mentor, the British government and its proconsuls in Northern Ireland, for making them dependent on its actions for their vindication, for leaving them with a sense of powerlessness, and at the Catholic community for having somehow unempowered them. Sands's election to Westminster simply reaffirmed their conviction that there were no moderate Catholics, that the so-called constitutional politics of the SDLP and its repeated denunciations of violence and the IRA were a charade concealing the murderous intent behind the conciliatory words of Catholics. All Catholics were Republicans, enemies of the state.

How can we, Protestants asked, trust neighbors who side with the murderers of our kith and kin? Armagh Official Unionist M.P. Harold McCusker warned that attitudes would harden. "The result [of the Fermanagh–South Tyrone election] is like thirty thousand standing over the grave of census enumerator Joanne Mathers [Mrs. Mathers, a Protestant, was shot dead by a masked gunman as she collected census forms in a housing estate in the Waterside in Derry days before the election] and shouting three cheers for her killers." The Democratic Unionist Party said the vote "explodes for all time the SDLP–Roman Catholic perpetuated myth that they have no sympathy for the IRA and its campaign of genocide against the Protestants of County Fermanagh." The *Church of Ireland Gazette* was even more damnatory: "The people of Fermanagh–South Tyrone certainly chose Barabbas and they well and truly recrucified Christ." When, it asked, is the Roman Catholic hierarchy likely to put its case before "these people" (the thirty thousand nationalists who voted for Sands)? "It is time for questions as blunt and Christian as 'why did you vote for a man whose organization will murder your neighbor? Why did you vote for a man who disobeyed the commands of our Savior Jesus? Why are you persisting in supporting evil?' " In contrast, they saw themselves as law-abiding, preening themselves on their belief that Protestants refused to support men of violence. "The vast majority of Protestants in Northern Ireland regardless of their political loyalties refused to support the paramilitary men who sought in the early years of the present troubles to gain control of Protestant areas," Dr. Gordon McMullan, bishop of Clogher, told his Diocesan Synod. "They have continued to refuse such people and organizations any political mandate or ballot-box support. It is, therefore, very difficult for such a community to understand how any other community could either directly or indirectly give their vote to those who belong or support violent men or violent organizations." And when a part-time UDR man, Jack Donnelly from Moy, County Fermanagh, was murdered by the IRA a week after Sands's election, Unionist fury exploded. It was, McCusker said, the conversion of votes into bullets. "The Roman Catholic community of Moy know who killed Mr. Donnelly," he angrily asserted, "[but] it is probably just as futile as it has been in the past to appeal to them to give up their executioner."

The attention focused on Bobby Sands, especially in the weeks leading up to his death, demeaned the Protestant sense of grievance. Dr. John Armstrong, the then Church of Ireland primate, officiating at the funeral of a former UDR man, John Robinson, shot dead in Armagh as he drove to work during the height of the media extravaganza over Sands, decried the media's "wicked inversion of priorities": the countless columns of newspaper print and hours of radio and television devoted to "the slow, calculated suicide of Mr. Bobby Sands" and the meager reporting of Robinson's death. Sands had a choice. John Robinson had none. "Mr. Sands was a member of an illegal organization using murder as a political tool. Mr. Robinson was yet another law-abiding victim of such a group." Even the *Belfast Telegraph,* which prided itself on the evenhandedness of its news coverage despite its progovernment position during the prison dispute, could not restrain itself. "The concentration on the physical and mental condition of Mr. Robert Sands M.P. starving himself in a well-appointed prison cell contrasts painfully with the lack of concern for the latest victim of the violence, Mr. John Robinson, bus driver of Aughnacloy."

But it was McCusker who once again spoke for the silent majority. "I have watched the television channels of this province," he said, "given up to politicians and clerics apparently so concerned about the civil rights of Sands that they forget the ongoing murder campaign being waged against the rest of the community." The death of Mr. Robinson, he added, "would be reported in the media. His funeral will be given a few fleeting moments of television and then we'll be back to the endless crocodile tears streaming from the Maze Prison."

Within days of Robinson's death, two more members of the security forces, Constable Gary Martin and UDR Lance Corporal Richard McKee, were killed, Martin when an INLA booby trap bomb exploded in West Belfast and McKee in an IRA ambush near Castlewellan, County Down, and their deaths received the perfunctory media coverage their anonymity guaranteed. They were a backdrop to the main event, consigned to supporting roles in a larger and more compelling saga of death. The media's single-minded and overwhelming preoccupation with Sands reinforced the Protestant sense of isolation, of an outside world hostile to the Protestant cause and sympathetic to Republican propaganda. Once again, Catholics were more adept at projecting themselves as victims, which they could not be, in Protestant eyes, since it was not a question of what others were doing to the hunger strikers but of what the hunger strikers were doing to themselves. Victimhood could not be self-inflicted. These men, after all, said Dr. Armstrong, "had a choice about their deaths, their victims did not."

As Sands's death approached, Northern Ireland was caught in what anthropologist Vincent Crapanzano calls "a deadened time of waiting."[6] For many Protestants, especially in the ghettos and the border areas of Fermanagh and South Tyrone, the waiting was compounded by fear, resulting in a kind of psychological dualism in which Sands became at once "a menial object to be derided and a mystic object to be feared."[7] There are, said the Reverend Derek G. McMeekin, minister of the Epworth Methodist Church in Portadown, "subtle and sinister forces at work in the land which are implacably bent on the destruction of all that is morally good, politically right and spiritually helpful. The fiery furnace is being heated with fury and ferocity and our faith is under trial." The Most Reverend Robin Eames, at that time the Church of Ireland bishop of Down and Dromore, articulated the feelings of those he called "ordinary, decent people":

"Anger, frustration, resentment and bewilderment—these are not the feelings of extremists or people who constantly take a decision of life and death into their own hands. These are the continual, deeply personal, intensely felt reactions of those who have watched attempts to turn upside down the community's sense of values."

The UDA mobilized, determined to defend Protestant enclaves in the predominantly Catholic areas of Belfast and Derry; both communities mimicked each other's actions, reports of defense associations being formed and the stockpiling of food in one community immediately triggering similar rushes of activity in the other; and the Reverend Ian Paisley, once again the personification of political Protestantism, claimed to have evidence that the IRA would unleash "a savage war" if Sands died, and warned Protestants to be ready to take matters into their own hands ("We'll have to kill the killers") if the government would not protect them. Sands's death would trigger a Catholic uprising: 1641 would come again, the state would fail to live up to its contractual obligations, the Protestant people of Ulster would be betrayed but their vigilance would ensure that they would endure and triumph.

Fourteen people died during the sixty-six days of Sands's hunger strike, including three part-time members of the UDR, one former member, one policeman, and two other Protestants killed either deliberately or mistakenly. And when Sands finally died, the Protestant community remembered its own dead, the "Protestant after Protestant . . . the Sands's organization has relentlessly killed . . . who had no choice but to accept summary death during this entirely self-inflicted publicity-seeking death wish," as the *Church of Ireland Gazette* put it. "I remember today," said an embittered Harold McCusker, "the two hundred of my constituents who, since I was elected an M.P. just seven years ago, have been killed by the associates of Mr. Sands. No President, Prime Minister or Pontiff shed tears for them." On the day that Sands was buried, the Protestant community held its own memorial service at Belfast City Hall for the victims of Republican violence. About three thousand people gathered to sing psalms, pray for their dead, and lay wreaths at the cenotaph. Before the end of the hunger strikes, sixty-four people, more than half of them civilian, would die in addition to the ten hunger strikers. The toll would include twenty-two members of the indigenous security forces (twelve policemen, seven UDR members, three RUC reservists), eight British soldiers, and thirty-four civilians.

The UDR and RUC men who were killed became symbols reaffirming the Protestant sense of siege. They were public servants murdered because they were preserving the peace, protecting their communities from the threat their forebears, and their forebears' forebears, had met and mastered, and they were eulogized for their dedication to saving the lives of others, for their adherence to life-enhancing values, in contrast to the hunger strikers, whose deaths led to "further wanton and destructive violence." Officiating at the funeral of Mervyn Robinson, a well-liked RUC constable from South Armagh, shot dead by the IRA at the end of May outside a pub about three hundred yards from his home, the Church of Ireland primate, Archbishop John Armstrong, told mourners "[this] attack on a defender of peace and safety was an attack on the whole community. For he has been our shield," he said, "appointed by the proper authority to preserve the peace. If this shield is broken we are all threatened."

Once again Britain needed Protestants, the Protestant community believed, to protect the state from subversion from within, and once again Protestants were prepared to put their lives on the line to safeguard Britain's interests. They deeply resented what they saw as Britain's lack of commitment to upholding the quid pro quo: the maintenance of their privileged status within the state, which they saw as the right of the elect, not a handout to dependents—although they would never admit that their status was in any way privileged.

The government's determination to stand up to the hunger strikes became the litmus test of its larger intentions. Bitter memories of past sellouts—of the imposition of the penal laws that severely constricted the civil liberties of Presbyterians in the eighteenth century, despite their support of the Protestant king William of Orange during the Glorious Revolution; the granting of emancipation to Catholics in 1829; the prolonged Home Rule crisis after the 1880s; the government's willingness to legislate them into an all-Ireland Catholic state in 1912; the intentions of the Government of Ireland Act of 1920, with its provision for a Council of Ireland, and of the Boundary Commission with its potential to dismember the Northern Ireland state; the abolition of their Parliament at Stormont in 1972; the power-sharing imposed on them in 1973; the Council of Ireland proposed in the Sunningdale Agreement in 1973; the Anglo-Irish summit between Thatcher and Haughey in December 1980, with the latter's claim that their discussions did not exclude anything—fueled their historic distrust of their patron. (In Dublin, Haughey did his bit to stoke their fears. Referring to his talks the previous December with Mrs. Thatcher, he told the Fianna Fail Ard Fheis [annual party convention], which was held shortly after Sands's election to Westminster, that in Northern Ireland they would "in a year . . . begin to see a clearer light at the end of the road on which we have set out.")

When the BBC reported, days before the first hunger strike was due to start, that the government had agreed to let the prisoners wear their own clothes, Unionists were furious: the proposed concession was "a back-door means of capitulating to Republican murderers," and even the fact that there was nothing to the report, that all that was on offer was civilian-type clothing, did not defuse their anger. "The surrender of the Government to IRA blackmail on the civilian clothes issue bodes ill for the future of Ulster. A Government that is prepared to do a deal with the murdering thugs of the IRA is a government which is prepared to grant an amnesty and is a government willing to betray the Loyalists of Ulster," thundered the *Protestant Telegraph*.

The idea that concessions were under consideration was more important than the details. When the first hunger strike ended, Enoch Powell, Official Unionist M.P. for South Down, accused the government of allowing the hunger strikers to end their protest "if not with a victory, at least with a draw." Almost reflexively they took their stand: they would resist any attempt on the part of the government to "do a shabby deal with the IRA." Every government statement on the hunger strikes was dissected for evidence of an imminent collapse of will on the government's part, for the between-the-line nuances signaling the compromise in the making that would undermine the basis of Protestant loyalty. Their premonition of incipient betrayal aggravated their collective sense of insecurity, of being dispensable. Since every action had to be judged in the context of only one criterion—whether it upheld the constitutional settlement of 1689 and the perpetuation of Protestant hegemony—their reactions to the hunger strikes exposed their limited understanding of themselves and their own possibilities.

In late 1978, loyalist prisoners began a prison protest of their own when they too went "on the blanket," refusing to wear prison clothing or do prison work. They wanted segregation from Republican prisoners. "Young Protestants," according to *Ulster*, the mouthpiece of the Ulster Defence Association, "are forced by the state into a situation where they were expected to live alongside and associate with their mortal enemy—the IRA." They wanted segregation so that loyalist prisoners would "not have to come into contact with Republican terrorists" or "have to endure the stink of the adjoining 'dirty cells' " or have their "stomachs turned over as they looked at the knives and forks they were about to eat with, wondering if some Provo had used them to spread his own filth on the wall of a cell." (Loyalist prisoners shared a special revulsion for the dirty protest; *Ulster* never tired of pointing out that loyalist prisoners, unlike Republicans, "would not lower their dignity and self-respect by fouling their own nests.") Their protest inevitably got absorbed into the Republican protest, and when six loyalist prisoners began a hunger strike of their own to draw attention to what *Ulster* called "their clean, dignified and unnoticed protest for segregation," and to emphasize their demands "to be distinct and separate from those of the IRA" in the middle of the Republicans' first hunger strike, it was a cry for attention, for notice, for an affirmation of their own identity, which, once again, was in danger of being submerged in the vortex of Republican protest. But the loyalist community outside the prison could not handle the dichotomy.

In the end, loyalist prisoners had to abandon all protest, since their actions appeared to put them on the side of Republicans. The Ulster Defence Association's position on special status reflected its confusion. Since there were special courts and special legislation, it argued that there should be special prisoners. And since loyalist prisoners were in jail for their actions in defense of the state ("Young men from the beleaguered Protestant community, fearful of a British sell-out, took up arms to defend the Ulster state from the forces of Republicanism," is how *Ulster* put it), they should be more special than Republican prisoners, who were in jail for actions to destroy the state, and besides, since Republican prisoners were under IRA orders to starve themselves and dared not disobey, the IRA was guilty of murder.

13   In July 1978, Cardinal Tomas O'Fiaich visited the Maze/ Long Kesh. The stench of the dry human excrement caked on the cell walls, the sight of the protesting prisoners—unkempt and half-naked, long-haired and swollen-eyed, bone-thin and malnourished, confined, animal-like, to their empty, filthy cells—and their tales of the beatings, routine humiliations, and degrading searches to which they were subjected made him furious.

Following the visit the cardinal issued a statement. He was, he said, "shocked by the inhuman conditions prevailing in the H-blocks." One "would hardly allow an animal to remain in such conditions, let alone a human being"; they reminded him of "the spectacle of hundreds of homeless people living in sewer pipes in the slums of Calcutta." The prisoners' cells were without beds, chairs, or tables. The prisoners slept on mattresses on the floor, and had "no covering except a towel or blanket, no books, newspapers or reading materials, no pens or writing materials, no TV or radio, no hobbies or handicrafts, no exercise or recreation." They were locked in their cells for "almost the whole of every day." Some of them "had been in these conditions for almost a year and a half."

"The fact," the cardinal went on, "that a man refuses to wear prison uniform or to do prison work should not entail the loss of physical exercise, association with his fellow prisoners, or contact with the outside world." These were, he said, "basic human needs for physical and mental health, not privileges to be granted or with-held as rewards or punishments." To deprive anyone of them, there-fore, over a long period, was "a grave injustice that could not be justified under any circumstances." In his view, the prisoners would "continue their protest indefinitely" and would "prefer to face death rather than submit to being classed as criminals." Anyone "with the least knowledge of Irish history knew how deeply-rooted the pris-oners' attitudes were in their country's past. In isolation and perpetual boredom," he continued, "they maintain their sanity by studying Irish. It was an indication of the triumph of the human spirit over adverse material surroundings to notice Irish words, phrases and songs being shouted down from cell to cell and then written on each cell with the remnants of toothpaste tubes."

His conclusion was pointed: "The authorities refuse to admit that these prisoners are in a different category from the ordinary, yet everything about their trials and family background indicates that they are different. They were sentenced by special courts without juries. The vast majority were convicted on allegedly voluntary confessions which are now placed under grave suspicion by the recent report of Amnesty International. Many were very youthful and came from families which had never been in trouble with the law." The jump in the prison population of Northern Ireland from five hundred to three thousand could not be explained "unless a new type of prisoner had emerged."

The cardinal's statement created an uproar, drawing a furious, ill-tempered response from the NIO and hostile reactions from the Protestant churches, putting them both firmly on the same side of the prison issue, and the Catholic Church, if only because of its unwillingness to dissociate itself from the cardinal's remarks, on a different side. For the larger Protestant community, of course, there was no different side—its position, as in everything it could reduce to ultimatums on the constitutional question, was starkly straightforward: unless you were wholeheartedly against the prisoners' protest and everything it stood for, you were for it; there was no middle ground. The Presbyterian Church accused O'Fiaich of "grave moral confusion in obscuring the primary responsibility of the prisoners themselves for the situation," for it was the prisoners, it argued, who had reduced "some of the most modern and best equipped prison accommodations in the British Isles to the most deplorable and degrading conditions possible," while the *Church of Ireland Gazette* said that O'Fiaich's statement "left the rest of us in little doubt about where his loyalties lay."

The *Gazette*'s comment was an indirect and not too subtle reference to O'Fiaich's background. He was born in Crossmaglen, the heartland of militant Republicanism. He called himself a Republican, although he strongly opposed the violence of the IRA, and had repeatedly and in the most trenchant terms denounced the murder of "brother Irishmen, Catholic or Protestant." Protestants, however, were of the view that while "you could take the cardinal out of Crossmaglen, you could not take Crossmaglen out of the cardinal," an opinion that hardened when O'Fiaich made it clear in a 1978 interview that he was in favor of a declaration of intent by Britain to withdraw from Northern Ireland. In the narrow ground of Northern Ireland, O'Fiaich was not just suspect, he was a proven fellow traveler. ("Half the opposition to what Cardinal O'Fiaich would say," says a senior Church of Ireland bishop, "is opposition not to what he says but to him.")

His statement on conditions in the prisons laid whatever doubts might have lingered to rest: the cardinal was a surrogate spokesperson for the IRA, his disclaimers on the use of physical force notwithstanding. "The Church of Rome is to blame for the hunger strike saga," Ian Paisley's *Protestant Telegraph* declaimed. "Rome has unleashed the violence on our streets once again. . . . Archbishop O'Fee [*sic*] and Bishop Daly have been agitating for political status under the guise of Prison Reform. Their so-called persistent intent in the so-called humanitarian aspects of the H-block issue has sparked off the present terror campaign that has once again slain many and wrought untold destruction. The Church of Rome today is no different from the Church of the Inquisition. The Church of Rome is a cruel institution prepared to spill the blood of thousands in Ulster in order to achieve power."

O'Fiaich's very visible and much publicized efforts on behalf of the prisoners and the absence of any opposition to his actions within the Church hierarchy had an inevitable consequence: they identified him with the protesting prisoners, added to the ambivalence mainstream Catholics were experiencing, and confirmed Protestants in their belief that the Catholic hierarchy supported the prisoners' demands and, therefore, approved of the actions for which the prisoners had been jailed—a belief that their own churches did little to discourage.

The refrains would become familiar, the Protestant churches vocal. The Irish Council of Churches—which represents all the mainstream Protestant churches, North and South—articulated "the Protestant attitude" to the H-block issue in a special report. The churches, it said, "are emphatic that there are no people in Northern Ireland prisons who are there for their political opinions or for reasons of conscience." It was not clear "whether if some of the privileges became rights . . . the prisoners would take them up as the whole basis of the protest [is] political. The prisoners believe that they should not be there at all or that they are prisoners-of-war, to be held until the 'war' ends and should be treated as such. Assumptions about reasonable behavior and the legitimacy of the prison regime are absent. The prison regime is there to be challenged . . . the protest, the prisoners, and their conditions have become . . . another part of the 'war' being waged against the Government, subject to the propaganda implicit in wars, both inside Ireland and outside." Any reintroduction of special-category status, it concluded, "would be seen as a defeat for the Government and would give recognition to the claims of the Provisional IRA and other paramilitaries." A more favored special category for "political prisoners" simply "could not be justified."

As the hunger strikes approached, the divisions between the churches became more defined. The Church of Ireland's Dr. John

Armstrong called the hunger strikes "a calculated form of moral blackmail." Government policy in both the North and the South had always been "to resist any coercion from hunger strikers" and that was "as it should be." The propaganda unleashed by "the sponsors of the hunger strikes," which would be "aimed at playing on the natural human and Christian sympathy for the imagined underdog, would ensure that truth [will] be the victim; the deeds of the hunger strikers and their colleagues—deeds that [had] shamed and blackened the name of Irishmen throughout the world"—would be forgotten; the prisoners in the Maze had "been convicted of some of the most dreadful crimes imaginable, committed without a shred of pity for the victim or his family. Their victims had no choice. The prisoners do have a choice. This is incontrovertible."

The Right Reverend Gordon McMullan, bishop of Clogher, told his Diocesan Synod "It [the H-block campaign] seems to imply that in the realm of internal political action murder or violence have no real moral or spiritual significance. The claim that imprisoned members of such organizations [as the PIRA and INLA] should be able to demand and determine the conditions of their imprisonment is again the claim that politically motivated violence is excusable or justified, that murder of people who serve the community and the destruction of other lives is not murder at all."

The other Protestant churches, whether mainstream or fundamentalist, agreed. Indeed, there was a remarkable concurrence of opinion: the hunger strikes were self-inflicted; if they were pursued to death, the deaths would be suicide and should be condemned by the Catholic Church. The hunger strikes were being carried out on the orders of the IRA; there should be no concessions to the hunger strikers' demands and little sympathy for their situation—sympathy should be reserved for their victims.

"For the Protestant, [the hunger strikers] were committing suicide. Full stop. He contrasted that with his own people being shot down. They had no choice at all," says Victor Griffin, dean of St. Patrick's Cathedral, Dublin, "and then the Protestants wondered, now the Roman Catholic Church is always talking about respect for life, reverence for life and how important it is to preserve life at all costs, why wasn't [the Catholic Church] so insistent [in saying to the hunger strikers] that you are really embarking on a mortal sin because you are destroying your own life, that's God's life not yours, God had given that life. So the Protestant found it hard to reconcile the Roman

Catholics who were more or less going along with this hunger strike as a legitimate moral option and at the same time espousing a sort of reverence for life."

On the other side of the religious divide, spokespersons such as Cardinal O'Fiaich, Bishop Edward Daly of Derry, and Father Denis Faul articulated the Catholic Church's position. They disapproved of the hunger strikes, but would not condemn them as wrong, arguing that the prisoners were indeed somehow special, if only in the manner in which they had been tried and convicted, and they felt that some concessions should be made, although they would not endorse the demand for political status.

Each church appeared to be a faction fighter for its own cause, the Catholic clerics who advocated concessions to the prisoners proof to Protestant hardliners of the collusion between the Catholic Church and militant Republicanism and cause for questions about the relationship between the two, even among moderate Protestants. "It seems astonishing—even shocking—that some priests of the Roman Catholic Church," Dr. Arthur Butler, bishop of Conor, told his Diocesan Synod, "have taken up the issue of the H-blocks with such clamor and have insisted upon it with such persistence in a vein which almost totally isolates the conditions of the prisoners from every other related circumstance, that there has emerged the clear impression that their concern is vastly more for the perpetrators of violence than for those who have been the victim of it." The *Church of Ireland Gazette* went even further: "[The] world has now come to know as never before," it wrote, "that the atrocities of the IRA have at least a suspicion of a base in Roman Catholicism, that the lead given by the Roman Catholic Church in Ireland has not been without a degree of ambivalence . . . that from now on IRA violence can be castigated, however unfairly, as 'Catholic violence.' " (Much of the criticism must have had a familiar ring to it for Cardinal O'Fiaich. A historian, he had written an article, years earlier, for *The Ecclesiastical Record* which documents the considerable support among the clergy during the 1860s for the Fenians. "I know nothing more humiliating in ecclesiastical history," he quotes one Westminster M.P. as saying in the House of Commons, "than the connection between the Fenians and the Roman Catholic clergy."[1]

This perception of Irish Catholicism as wedded to militant Republicanism was further reinforced when Cardinal Basil Hume, the Catholic archbishop of Westminster, called the hunger strikes "a form of violence, violence to the hunger strikers themselves" that "could not be condoned by the Church as being in accordance with God's will for men." Sands's death, he said, was suicide, as was "any hunger striker's death that [included] with it the intention to die." Protestants, of course, immediately fastened on to Hume's words as being the authentic and official exposition of the Catholic Church's teaching. The Irish hierarchy's refusal to endorse what Hume had said was met with knowing nods: to the Protestants it simply proved yet again what their long experience had taught them—the Irish Catholic Church put loyalty to the precepts of Irishness before obedience to the teachings of the Church. "The choice facing the Roman Catholic leadership," the *Church of Ireland Gazette* observed, "is once again between 'Roman' Catholicism and Irish Republican Nationalist Catholic sectarianism which at its best can be only sub-Christian." Increasingly, the churches, observed the *Irish Times,* were coming "perilously close to sustaining each other's mythologies."

The Catholic Church's teaching on suicide is sufficiently ambiguous to accommodate theological hair-splitting. After Bobby Sands's death the Irish bishops issued a statement: "The Church teaches that suicide is a great evil," they said. However, they added the caveat that "there is some dispute about whether or not political hunger striking is suicide, or more precisely, about the circumstances in which it is suicide."

There is suicide and willful suicide; only the latter carries with it the intention to die. (Since it is laid down in canon law that a person who commits suicide to avoid, for example, public disgrace, will be denied an ecclesiastical burial, inquest juries in the South traditionally do not return straightforward suicide verdicts. They add riders saying that the person has taken his life while the balance of his mind was disturbed, thus ensuring that the suicide's act does not come under the Church's sanction. One consequence of this practice is that Ireland has one of the lowest recorded suicide rates in Europe.) One body of ecclesiastical opinion holds that death by hunger striking is suicide even when the hunger striker is convinced he is being unjustly treated, because life is in the hands of God, and no one has the right to take his own life. A second body of opinion, however, holds that a hunger strike simply means the refusal to cooperate, even to the extent of refusing food. Death in these circumstances is not chosen as a means to an end; it is not direct or intentional, even though it could be foreseen. The Church, it was argued, does not require Catholics to bow rigidly to Church teaching. If Catholics, for reasons that seem good and sufficient to themselves, find they are at odds with the Church's position on some matter, the Church does not condemn their actions as sinful. It ultimately will give the benefit of the doubt to the conscience of the person concerned.

To abstain from food simply in order to bring about an end to one's life would be sinful, both sides agreed, since the primary intention would be death and abstinence from food the means chosen to accomplish that end. But, advocates of the more flexible interpretation pointed out, the hunger strikers were not aiming to die. Even when they followed their fasts through to their fatal conclusion, they were still not seeking death. Their object was to bring the pressure of public opinion to bear upon what they perceived to be an unjust aggressor in order to secure redress of their grievances. Their state of mind could not be compared to the mentality of a suicide whose object was to escape from a life that had grown hateful to him.

The crucial theological consideration, therefore, appeared to come down to the hunger strikers' motivation. It was that which distinguished them from the person who killed himself because he was despairing of God's love and mercy. The hunger strikers, it was maintained, were seeking a positive change in their condition of imprisonment, which was being denied to them by the civil authorities. Self-inflicted death, consciously willed, was not the fundamental purpose. The hunger strikers were in a state of "good conscience." They were not despairing. When Brendan McLaughlin had to give up his fast early on because it was clear that a medical complication would cause his immediate and premature death—and which would have been counterproductive since it would have come, according to a Sinn Fein statement explaining his action, "before the effects of a long hunger strike would have drawn in and built up the necessary pressure to break the British government's intransigence"—Father Denis Faul cited it as proof that "the hunger strikes are not suicide" but rather "a responsible protest though of a sacrificial nature."

Sands, Bishop Edward Daly of Derry said, implicitly invoking the principle of double-effect, which distinguishes between the end willed and the end foreseen but not willed, "did not intend to bring about his own death"; his death was not suicide. Cardinal O'Fiaich concurred. Other members of the hierarchy maintained silence.

Much of the differences between the Catholic Church and the mainstream Protestant churches on the hunger strikes could be traced to their differences on questions relating to the source of ecclesiastical authority. The Catholic Church adheres to a hierarchical structure of government: deacons, priests, bishops, and pope. Authority resides first with the pope and then with the pope acting in concert with the bishops. The pope has supreme authority and when he speaks *ex cathedra* on matters of faith and morals, he exercises divine, infallible authority. The Anglican Church looks to the archbishop of Canterbury not as pope or supreme ruler but as one among equals, although he occupies a position of considerable esteem. Authority resides in the whole Church, with bishops, clergy, and laity meeting and acting together in council or synod. The Presbyterian Church is governed through a series of church courts (sermon, presbytery, synod, and General Assembly). Meetings can be held only when the laity have the possibility of attending and participating in decision making.

The Protestant churches, therefore, see Catholics in terms of the individual's relationship to his or her church: there is the teaching church and the listening church, in which the teaching church has an authoritative role in interpreting God's Word to the listening church— the laity—and they see themselves in terms of the individual's relationship to God. Catholics, they believe, are bound by the teaching authority of the church embodied in the pope and bishops, whereas Protestants, they would hold, rely on private judgment. And thus their confusion: for had not the pope himself, the supreme authority, come to Ireland to say unequivocally that "murder is murder and must not be called by any other name"? Had he not called on Bobby Sands to end his hunger strike? Were not the Irish Catholic Church's seeming casuistry on the prison issue, its silence, especially when it appeared to be at odds with the English Catholic Church on the question of suicide, its failure to censure Catholics who flagrantly disregarded its teachings yet in death sought the solace of its services, somehow abrogations of its responsibilities? Was not its refuge in statements that the hunger strikers' refusal to end their strike, despite the requests of their bishop to do so, an act made in good conscience, somehow not quite Catholic, a clever circumvention of the issue, a plain cop-out? In short, the Irish Catholic Church appeared to be allowing the hunger strikers to act like good Protestants—to follow the dictates of their conscience—and Protestants found this unac-

ceptable, an inchoate and grotesque transfiguration of their understanding of how the Catholic Church worked. "Protestants would
say follow your private conscience," says Dean Victor Griffin, "but
where it's a clear-cut issue such as suicide, you've the word of God
laid down and there's no doubt about what God's mind is on this
subject, and therefore you must obey the word of God and the word
of God is that suicide is wrong, and so they [Protestants] would see
it that way and they would point to [the Roman Catholic position]
as another example of Roman Catholic casuistry, even to the extent
of using a Protestant concept such as private judgment to get away
with their ambivalence. That's the way the Protestant would look
at it."

The Protestant churches had no ambivalence about the question
of suicide, no caveats, no place for theological niceties. Commenting
on reports that the hunger strikers received Holy Communion before
commencing their fasts, the *Gazette* observed that "if this is so it
destroys the very core of Christianity, a core of attitude to participation in Holy Communion shared by Anglican and Roman Christians alike." The hunger strikes, they held, were suicide, because it
was the intention of the hunger strikers to die, since they had been
ordered to do so. The hunger strikes were unjustified because they
were self-inflicted for demands that were themselves unjustified, and
they were immoral because they had as their ultimate intention the
furtherance of murder and the destruction of the state.

"A Protestant will say, 'a life shouldn't be sacrificed, life is sacred,
a very precious gift,' " Dr. Robin Eames says, "and when he looks
at his Catholic neighbors he will see many instances of a similar
attitude. But when he is confronted with something like the hunger
strikes he will say, 'they [Catholics] are making life so cheap. They
are making life so worthless, and it's not that they're proving a point
by sacrificing their lives, it's because they have a different perception
of what the value of life is.' For the ordinary Protestant it is the reason
for which a person makes the supreme sacrifice rather than the sacrifice
itself that dictates his attitude. Protestants would tend to justify or
not justify the cause of the sacrifice itself rather than delve into the
sacrifice itself. Loyal Ulstermen going over the top at the Somme,
yes; Irish rebels holing up in the GPO [General Post Office] in Dublin
in 1916, no."

The Protestant churches saw the Irish Catholic Church's apparent
ambivalence, its propensity to balance criticism of the hunger strikers

with criticism of the regime, to equate the violence of Republicans with the violence of the state, to couple the intransigence of the hunger strikers with the intransigence of the government, to allow the funerals of the dead hunger strikers to become occasions synergizing Catholic liturgy and Republican ritual (sixty priests had attended the funeral mass for Raymond McCreesh) as political acts signifying solidarity, or at least sympathy, with the hunger strikers. "From Cardinal O'Fiaich downwards," the *Belfast Telegraph*'s church reporter wrote, "they [the Catholic clergy] have condemned violence. But those words are worth little set against front page newspaper pictures showing Catholic priests officiating at funeral services alongside masked IRA men, toting at the graveside, perhaps, the very weapons used to murder their [Protestant] fellow countrymen and women."

On hearing of Raymond McCreesh's death on 21 May, Cardinal O'Fiaich, who knew the McCreesh family well, told the media that "Ray McCreesh was born in a community which has always openly proclaimed that it is Irish, not British. I have no doubt," he went on, "that he would never have seen the inside of a jail but for the abnormal political situation. Who is entitled to pronounce him a murder or a suicide?" (The London *Daily Express* was quick to respond. "The answer we would have thought was pretty obvious," it wrote. "If he was not an actual murderer it was not for lack of trying. And if starving yourself to death isn't suicide, what is it? . . . The cardinal," it concluded, "abhors violence and then goes on to make every conceivable excuse for the men who perpetrate it.") And in July, following the deaths of Joe McDonnell and Martin Hurson, Father Denis Faul was quoted in the *Irish News* as saying, "These two young Irish men died noble deaths in defense of their human dignity and integrity and to protect the dignity and integrity of their fellow prisoners—a perfect fulfillment of the Catholic education received in Catholic schools."

The Protestant churches began to respond in kind. The funerals of the twenty-two UDR and RUC men killed by the IRA during the hunger strikes became increasingly political occasions. Presiding clergymen berated the government for its failure to provide adequate security, denounced the IRA for its campaign of genocide, criticized the Catholic community at large for its tacit support of the prisoners, comforted the bereaved Protestant community for its losses, and praised it for its restraint. Parochial pulpits became an instrument for the articulation of grievance, for the bonding that resulted from the

Protestants' increasingly keen sense of isolation. "So many members of the Church of Ireland served in the security forces and had been killed that there was a general feeling well, why should the Church of Ireland go on paying this awful price for the security of the whole community? They resented it," Archbishop Eames told me. "And they believed that they heard from nationalist politicians and [their] church leaders nothing but condemnation of the security forces rather than even grudging support or congratulations to them when they got it right. This ran very deep in the Protestant community because they believed their security forces were being made the whipping boys for the failure of the Catholic community to support the state."

It was their people who were being murdered, their neighbors or friends of neighbors. Where were the world's media, they asked, when it came to their dead? Who captured their pain? Who listened to their stories of the violence done to them? Their perception was that the IRA's killings were downplayed, that little attention was being paid to the brutal circumstances in which UDR and RUC men were murdered, that too much attention was lavished on the deaths of the hunger strikers, that Republican propaganda had orchestrated the international clamor for some accommodation with the prisoners, that Protestant losses were simply being swallowed up and devoured by the pervasive penumbra of the hunger strikes. "Today we have the right," said Dr. Eames, speaking at the funeral of RUC Constable Philip Ellis, who was shot dead on the day Sands died, "to ask the world to recognize the real agony of Northern Ireland. We have the right to ask the world to make a fair judgment: where does the real agony lie? Is it with those who use the threat of the choice of death or with those who have no choice?" But the world did not make fair judgments.

These perceptions once again reaffirmed Protestants' sense of their own victimhood and helplessness, invalidating their grievances, making meaningless the deaths of their coreligionists who gave their lives for the protection of the state, reminding them of the perilous state of their existence, exposing their limited ability to control the vicissitudes of their own lives, their tenuous capacity to deal with ambiguity and uncertainty. Their fears and anxiety stimulated their desire for action. Their emotional, often irrational responses to the hunger strikes, which on occasion degenerated into sectarian murder, were the product of their need to alleviate this fear rather than a considered appreciation of their own position. The hunger strikers aggravated the Protestants' sense of vulnerability, occasioning forebodings of being overrun and a pervasive sense of being threatened. Hence their need to distance themselves from the hunger strikes, to stereotype the hunger strikers, to vent their rage on those they perceived as being the hunger strikers' surrogates.

The difference between the Catholic Church and the Protestant churches on the issue of suicide was symptomatic of more fundamental differences. The Protestant churches saw the Irish Catholic Church's equivocation on suicide as evidence of a larger equivocation on the question of right and wrong. "The whole basis of right and wrong is on trial in Northern Ireland today," said Dr. Eames at Constable Ellis's funeral. "The whole meaning of what a society should be is in question." And in a sermon during a service opening the General Synod of the Church of Ireland, Dr. Eames again returned to the theme. "What the vast majority of ordinary people require of their church is reassurance," he told the assembled churchmen in St. Patrick's Cathedral, Dublin. "Reassurance that there is still virtue in goodness, truth and honesty. That there is a difference, and a fundamental difference between right and wrong. There are so many gray areas in Irish life today, areas in which it is so difficult to make a clear moral choice. There are too many examples of double thinking and double standards."

Catholicism is perceived by Protestants to be a religion of equivocation, where right and wrong are gradations on a theological curve, weights variously described as venial or mortal on some eschatological scale. The imposition of a church which claims a special authority to interpret and preach the written Word of God, between God and humanity, is inimical to many Protestants and smacks of perversion to others. Moreover, the Catholic Church's claim, asserted in the *Directory of Mixed Marriages,* that it alone, "as distinct from other churches has been endowed with the fullness of the means of salvation," and that this fullness implies "more than simply a greater total of truths and means of grace," that it means, in fact, "that Christ's presence to his followers and Christ's saving work in the world find their focal point and their most complete historical expression in the order, faith and worship of the Catholic Church,"[2] is perceived to be a statement of Catholic supremacy, reinforcing the fear of cultural and religious absorption, inspiring the extremism of the ultra-

Protestant sects, which, in turn, sometimes find resonances within the main Protestant churches.

(The basic problem of Ulster is not political, is not about land and counties, Ian Paisley told his party faithful in 1979, "but is spiritual and has to do with 'the faith once delivered to the saints.' " This, he said, was the land's great heritage. At great length he compared the two religious ideologies, the one, Protestant, was "basically Scriptural and should not be thought of as sectarian as it was founded on God's Holy Word"; the other, Roman Catholic, was "founded on an earthly head and hierarchy and therefore was not Scriptural and could be termed sectarian." "These two," said Paisley, "are poles apart and can never be reconciled, except by a capitulation of one side to the other.")

Catholics, in the Protestant perspective, appear to put little premium on truthfulness—dishonesty is assigned to a lesser category of sinfulness, being at best a venial offense, and, therefore, not to be taken very seriously. ("The Roman Catholic Church," says Dr. William Fleming, former moderator of the Presbyterian Church in Ireland, "divides sins into mortal and venial whereas the Protestant community doesn't see that as a legitimate division in regard to sins. Venial sins just mean a sort of untruthfulness. Deceptiveness for what's thought to be a good purpose is not a very major sin whereas the Protestant ethos has been that a man's word should be his bond and that if he says something he means it and will stand by it and will go to any lengths to be a man of his word and a man of honour.")

Northern Protestants believe that Catholics do not say what they mean, that they are profligate with words, "past masters of the art of the fine point, the innuendo and the half truth," as the Reverend Sydney Callaghan, past president of the Methodist Church in Ireland, put it. Language itself, despite the fact that it is common to both traditions, is a barrier to communication, a medium to parade the legitimacy of competing claims or to deny rival claims, especially since many Protestants take the Bible to be the literal word of God and bring a similar literal application of language to their daily lives.

"The Protestant work ethic, the Protestant use of language, is very straight up and down," says Dr. Godfrey Brown, a former moderator of the Presbyterian Church. "One of the things we reacted against at the time of the Reformation was the spiritualization of Scripture. We believed that there was a plain sense of Scripture and that in the words of Jesus our yes should mean yes and our no should mean no.

There is a literalism, sometimes an overliteralism, about Protestant-ism and about Protestant reactions to things political."

"Protestants are really puzzled by what they feel is the ambiguous attitude [on the part of the Catholic Church] and the failure to define ordinary concepts in a clear, straightforward way," says Dean Griffin. "There is much more of what would be called sophistry, casuistry in the Roman Catholic attitude to honesty. Protestants generally find that Catholic concepts of right and wrong and truth and honesty are more complicated. Honesty and truth and right and wrong have a rather simplistic, straightforward, uncomplicated meaning for Prot-estants and Protestants sometimes find it very difficult to understand the sophistry, the playing with words which we got [from the Cath-olic Church] when the hunger strike was on."

Language in the two communities has been used to develop rival systems of labeling. Particular words and phrases have become what Alasdair MacIntyre describes as a means of "naming for," instru-ments of "identification *for* those who share the same beliefs, the same justifications of legitimate authority, and so on. The institutions of nam-ing embody and express the shared viewpoint of the community, and characteristically its shared traditions of belief and enquiry. . . . There may be rival systems of naming, where there are rival communities and traditions, so that to use a name is at once to make a claim about political and social legitimacy and to deny a rival claim."[3] (A few examples: It is Londonderry to Protestants, Derry to Catholics; the Maze to Protestants, Long Kesh to Catholics; Northern Ireland to Protestants, the Six Counties or the North of Ireland to Catholics; Toombridge to Protestants, Toom to Catholics.) Although both communities share a common first language, they both need what MacIntyre calls "a second first language"—a common idiom that will allow them to articulate shared values and overlapping aspirations without having to submit them to the litmus test of mutually exclusive political legitimacies—if they are ever to explore common ground, since "finding common ground," as philosopher Donald Davidson points out, "is not subsequent to understanding but a condition of it."[4] (Even the concept of common ground means different things in the two communities in Ireland, especially in Northern Ireland. "The whole idea of society and government and the state if you look at it from the traditional Roman Catholic point of view is corporate," says Dean Griffin, "whereas the Protestant angle is much more private, more individualistic. The common good will generally be thought of by Roman Catholics as a more or less philosophical or theological concept. The Protestant will regard the concept of the common good in a very practical way—the maximization of tolerance and the minimization of suffering. [Catholics] have a different concept of it—it's to help the fabric of the state in a more or less monolithic way.") The language-in-use embodies for each community in Northern Ireland "different and incompatible catalogues and understandings of the virtues, including justice, or the different and incompatible stock of psychological descriptions of how thinking may generate action."[5]

During the hunger strike Protestants sensed that Catholics used language to equivocate, to conceal their real intentions. Thus Bishop Daly's statements that the hunger strikes were not morally justifiable but that the hunger strikers' deaths were not suicide implied to Protestants that Catholics did not regard the hunger strikes as being wrong; the statement by a number of Catholic bishops that the first hunger strike "would probably never have arisen if a more urgent and sensible attempt had been made to prevent the prison situation from deteriorating" appeared to put the blame for the hunger strikers' actions on the government; the Church's unwillingness to call Republican violence terrorism suggested that there might be some justification for it; the Church's opposition to the use of plastic bullets seemed to encourage disrespect for the security forces.

In short, Protestants were left wondering just where the Catholic Church stood, what its real agenda was. "Can the Cardinal," asked the *Church of Ireland Gazette,* "place his hand on his pectoral and swear that his church under his leadership has been flexible in the matters regarding mixed marriages and the human rights of minority religious groups within the territorial jurisdiction of his church? Can the Cardinal affirm publicly that he has encouraged the same degree of flexibility in all matters of Roman theology and ethical standards, as he has led and encouraged in the assessment of the morality of the current hunger strike?" "Perhaps," it observed wryly in another edition, "in the agonizing over 'conscience' as pertaining to the hunger strikers, our Roman brethren will gain new insights into the Protestant case for primacy of conscience in matters of marriage and family." (In a mixed marriage the Catholic partner still has to give an undertaking that she or he will do everything possible to raise the children as Catholics.) Later it would voice its concerns even more bluntly: Why was it, it asked, that a "Roman Catholic married to a divorced Protestant cannot receive Holy Communion, yet an ample supply of Catholic clergy files through prison gates to make available the same divine facility to bombers, robbers and intimidators?" In Dublin, Griffin used his Easter sermon to highlight his concern that legislation on morality in the Republic "appeared to be conforming as far as possible to the canon law of the Roman Catholic Church even if the legislation denied basic human rights. Let them [Dublin legislators] reflect that Christ was crucified by a majority decision implemented by Pilate." It was their duty, "in a true Republic," to legislate "for human rights for all even if the majority of denominational groups were prepared to deny basic human rights." People must decide, he said, "whether they wanted a Republic or a Roman Catholic Nationalist State." They cannot, he said, have both.

Even on the question of the morality of the hunger strikes, Protestants felt that the Irish Catholic Church equivocated. When Sands started his hunger strike Bishop Edward Daly took the public position that a hunger strike was not morally justified. Other members of the hierarchy were silent. When the Irish Catholic Bishops' Conference met in June, it urged the hunger strikers to endorse the ICJP's proposals as the basis for a solution but they, too, were silent on the question of the morality of the hunger strikers' actions. They did, however, issue a strongly worded statement. "We implore the hunger strikers and those who direct them," they said, "to reflect deeply on the evil of their actions and its consequences." However, it was never quite clear whether their phrase "evil of their actions" referred to the strikes themselves or their violent repercussions.

One senior Irish Catholic theologian, Father Denis O'Callaghan, professor of moral theology at Maynooth, did speak out. "A hunger strike," he wrote in the *Irish Press* on 14 November 1980—in the middle of the first hunger strike—which "aimed to promote the Republican campaign of violence," which "no morality, human or Christian [could] accept . . . would be an accessory to its crimes." However, since the motive of the hunger strike was to protest against "the intolerable conditions in which the prisoners existed and the absence of opportunities for normal forms of protest," this, he argued, was a factor "which [might] isolate their action from the general campaign of violence." The claim that the prisoners had voluntarily imposed these conditions on themselves was "unconvincing," he maintained, "both on humanitarian grounds and on grounds of expediency." In short, the morality of a suicide had to be judged in the context of the morality of the cause for which it was undertaken. Accordingly, "the granting of special status—or whatever phrase one wishes to use—to prisoners who do in fact constitute a special category, both in the motivation of their actions, terrible as they are, and in the mode of their conviction"[6] was justifiable.

In June 1981, O'Callaghan examined the concrete circumstances of the second hunger strike. "One must ask," he wrote in the *Irish Times,*

are the matters which motivate the hunger strike substantial enough to justify this extreme action and is there a real likelihood that the action will achieve its purpose? What will be the consequences for the community at large, will tension be increased and destructive forces released, will certain groups exploit the situation for their violent purposes?—if one intends that one's actions further a campaign of murder and violence it takes its moral measure from that intention, but even apart from any such explicit intention one cannot ignore the general consequences which will follow on one's action, because one is responsible for the full foreseeable consequences of what one does.

On these grounds, he concluded that the hunger strike was morally unjustifiable.[7]

To many Protestants O'Callaghan's pronouncements seemed counterintuitive. On the one hand, he suggested that the granting of special category status was justifiable, and on the other hand, that the hunger strike itself was morally not justifiable. The nuances escaped them. It was simply more of the same old stuff, the jesuitical distinctions, the sophistry, the playing about with words. Other Church actions invited censure, and some, such as Father Magee's gift to the strikers of crucifixes blessed by the pope himself, hardly suggested, especially to Protestants, that the Church was opposed to the hunger strikes on moral grounds.

The Protestant sense of the Catholic propensity to use language to conceal their real intentions was especially inflamed after the first Anglo-Irish summit was held in December 1980. Haughey's grand proclamations that "we set no limits on what institutions might be brought forward, might be considered, might be designed, might be conceived," that further meetings would give "special consideration to the totality of relationships between these islands," that "nothing was out of the question," that the framework he and Mrs. Thatcher had established "indicates bringing forward a solution through government-to-government co-operation," suggested the worst, that the Union itself was in peril. Thatcher, however, was insistent that no constitutional changes were in the offing, that the Union would not be prejudiced, that Unionists had nothing to fear. The different interpretations the two governments put on the postsummit communiqué, the triumphalist attitude in Dublin suggesting that Protestants had good reason to fear and the paternalistic attitude in London suggesting that Protestants had nothing to fear—on the one side, the hint of history in the making, on the other, the assertion of the status quo—left Protestants more than ever convinced that they were right not to believe a word of what Catholics had to say. "Once again truth is at stake," said a report by the Presbyterian Church's government committee. "Who is speaking the truth, the whole truth and nothing but the truth?"

For Northern Ireland Protestants, heavily influenced by Calvinistic puritanism, right and wrong were not only morally distinguishable, but absolutes, and they brought the same inflexible, no-compromise stance to their attitudes on every issue, and the same distrust of others, especially Catholics, who did not share their rigidity. They mistook their own rigidity for virtue, for standing for principle, for an honesty they were unwilling to impute to others who did not share their unyielding dogmatism. All things were reduced to zero-sum components. Since protesting prisoners had inflicted their conditions of degradation on themselves, their demands were blackmail, and blackmail could not countenance compromise. Since they had chosen to die, they deserved to die. Since they represented the forces of evil which were out to destroy the state, those who argued for concessions colluded in their intentions and designs. Compassion for the prisoners somehow implied a lack of compassion for the victims of their paramilitary organizations. To condemn violence with a caveat was to condone violence. To call on the hunger strikers to end their fast but not to call their deaths suicide was to concede the morality of the hunger strike. If the morality of the hunger strike was conceded, so too was the morality of the hunger strikers' actions, and hence of their cause. Papal crucifixes meant papal approval.

14   "One of the most persistent myths believed by Irish Republicans," wrote Simon Hoggart in the *Guardian*, "is that they have the mute support of the British working classes. I remember trying to tell an Irish Republican in Belfast how hopelessly untrue this was, how the pubs of Britain were full of people eagerly hoping that Bobby Sands would die . . . [that] the IRA and its many supporters and more numerous half-supporters have failed to recognize the depths of the odium felt against them [by working-class people in Britain]."

The British were bored and angered by Northern Ireland. For them it was a country "more foreign than America or West Germany," according to another *Guardian* writer. They were untouched by the complexities, indifferent to the grief of three hundred years. They disliked the fact that they, as British taxpayers, had to pay out money year after year to keep the province even marginally afloat. "And in small, scattered and individual ways they [were] bitterly resentful of the toll of English military life this benighted foreign country exact[ed] week by week." A majority wanted Britain simply to pull out.

In the spring and summer of 1981, the boredom and anger co-alesced, and the odium became a national infection that contaminated public discourse. Whetted for months by the lurid revelations at the murder trial of Peter Sutcliffe, the Yorkshire Ripper, who admitted to the gruesome murder of thirteen women, the tabloids turned their attention to the saga of Robert Sands, "The Hon. Member for Violence." The psychopath Sutcliffe and the fanatic Sands were woven into a tapestry of mad murder and self-murder in the name of madness. "It is theater," the *Daily Mail* informed its readers, "the theater of terror. 'If you don't do as I want, I'll kill myself. And if I kill myself, many others will die too!' That is the Sands ultimatum."

Hunger striking, the public was repeatedly reminded, was suicidal, "an offense against the teaching of the Roman Catholic Church," which "if persisted in to the end [was] a mortal sin." Even the *Times* indulged itself, observing after Father John Magee failed to convince Sands to give up his hunger strike that "ordinary Roman Catholics must now be shocked at Mr. Sands' determination to defy even the Pope's appeal." These sentiments reinforced the characteristics of the Irish stereotype: Sands was an Irish Catholic, and if nothing else, Irish Catholics, everyone knew, did what their bishops told them to do—they were, after all, priest-ridden. If Sands wasn't listening to the bishops, either they were being insufficiently vigorous in pointing out the mortal sinfulness of his act, thus implicitly encouraging him to persist, or Sands was a special kind of madman who would risk not just death but damnation in the pursuit of his unconscionable demands.

The British government brought to its handling of the hunger strikes all of the ambivalence it felt about things Irish. It absolved itself of responsibility in the matter, publicly casting itself in the role of the model jailkeeper who refused to submit to blackmail by hardened inmates acting under the orders of unscrupulous masters.

Early in the prison crisis the government adopted a tone of response to the issue that reflected not so much a position as an attitude, composed in equal parts of self-enhancing feelings of moderation, moral superiority, political calculation, and petulant self-righteousness. "These criminals," the NIO furiously admonished Cardinal O'Fiaich after he condemned the prison conditions in July 1978, "are totally responsible for the situation in which they find themselves. It is they who have been smearing excretion on the walls and pouring urine through cell doors. It is they who by their actions are denying themselves the excellent modern facilities of the prison. It is they and they alone who are creating bad conditions out of very good conditions." The prisoners were not political prisoners. They were members of organizations "responsible for the deaths of hundreds of innocent people, the maiming of thousands more, and the torture, by kneecappers, of more than six hundred of their own people." They had been tried "under the judicial system established in Northern Ireland by Parliament." Those found guilty, "after due process of law," served their sentences "for what they [were]—convicted criminals."

Later, in June 1980, when the European Commission on Human Rights ruled against the prisoners on each of their five demands, the government embraced the Commission's findings with a relish bordering on exuberance. The Commission's findings that conditions were "self-imposed" and could, were the prisoners "motivated to improve them, be eliminated almost immediately," were seized upon and became, in effect, part of the official response to counter every criticism of the government's no-compromise stance—which was ironic and precisely the opposite to what the Commission had intended in view of its own concern "at the ineffective approach of the state authorities which has been concerned more to punish offenders against prison discipline than to explore ways of resolving . . . [the] deadlock."

The *Times*, the publicly anointed voice of the British establishment, voiced the prevailing British view. "The Northern Ireland authorities [have] wriggled too much on the back of the hunger strike," it declared on 21 May 1981. "They have a clear conscience in the matter and should act accordingly." Protesting prisoners had been convicted for "serious crimes against the person," and had often shown "reckless disregard for the lives of others." They were being held "in a modern, well-appointed prison under a regime more relaxed than is found elsewhere in the United Kingdom or in much of the continent of Europe." It was by "their own volition that they did not have the full benefits of those conditions." "They demanded political status or the substance of it—a status unknown to the law and not acknowledged by the Government of the Irish Republic, or of West Germany, or the European Commission on Human Rights." They had been enforcing their demand "by behavior that deliberately degraded their conditions."

"In the face of this," it concluded, "the prison services in Northern Ireland and the political authorities there have acted with patience and flexibility." Changes had been made in the prison rules "that went quite a long way to give the Provisional prisoners the conditions they want[ed]." To go any further, it argued, "in order to save life inside the prison and calm agitation outside [would be] wrong." It would "give the IRA prisoners freedom to organize themselves and to dispose of their time within the perimeter." That was "a right to which they [were] not entitled, a concession they would proclaim as a defeat for their captors, a success that would embolden their comrades at large in the further destruction of life and property." Moreover, "one [could] be certain that before very long the prisoners in the Maze would have identified another grievance and be exploiting it by means shown to have been irresistible."

With self-righteousness came sanctimoniousness. "There is something about the rising Irish wrath that does not ring true," another *Times* editorial exclaimed two weeks before Sands's death, when concerns in Dublin regarding the consequences, North and South, were becoming acute—especially in the Haughey government, which could no longer postpone a general election. "Mr. Sands' approaching death," it said, "was being represented as an act of inhumanity on the part of those who hold him prisoner, a crime of British policy, an enormity as to provoke other deaths." And weeks after Sands's death the paper pursued the line of reasoning that had become secular dogma. "The words and actions of some members of the [Catholic] Church," it declared on 27 May, "have undoubtedly fed misinterpretations of what is happening in Northern Ireland." While it might be possible to explain away Cardinal O'Fiaich's remarks that the British government would face the wrath of the whole nationalist population if it did not compromise on the hunger strike, "their effect [had] been to strengthen the mistaken belief that the hunger strikes can be blamed on the British government's refusal to compromise. . . . Furthermore, although the priests at the funerals [might] not have wished to identify the Church with the hunger strikers, the consequence has been to confer an aura of martyrdom upon men who have sought by their own deaths to bring about the deaths of others."

Even after nine hunger strikers had died, the *Times* still would not let up. "It must be said with sadness," an editorial read in late August, "that the gains the Provisionals are making out of their gruesome policy of suicide would be markedly less were it not that the Irish government and the Roman Catholic hierarchy so conspicuously qualify their condemnation of this extension of terrorist violence by piling the blame on British ministers for allowing it to continue." By doing so, "they articulate[d] and reinforce[d] the feelings of many Irishmen," they also, "unintentionally but obviously, confer[red] on the hunger strikers something of the status of martyrdom and therefore of legitimacy. That above all else was what the Provisionals needed."

The pope himself was not spared the tincture of reproof. "It is a pity," a *Times* editorial opined in late May, "that the Pope has not found the words to condemn an act of self-violence calculated to incite others to further criminal and sinful acts. Had he done so any impression would have been avoided that his emissary was coming to mediate between the prisoners and the Government that regulates their imprisonment over demands for special treatment which are plainly devoid of merit in law and possess no humanitarian imperative."

And thus the government's operating assumptions: that it knew what the five demands stood for—a reversion to special-category status—and that while the prisoners wanted the whole five, it mattered less whether they got them piecemeal or in toto; the ceding of one or two of the demands would not end the hunger strike but simply encourage the hunger strikers to hold out for the balance. "What the hunger strikers are asking for," Mrs. Thatcher announced after Francis Hughes died, "is political status by easy stages. They cannot have it. They are murderers and people who use force and violence to attain their ends. They made perfectly clear what they want and they cannot and will not have it."

Today Humphrey Atkins, secretary of state for Northern Ireland during the hunger strikes, is no less certain of how strong the government's resolve had been. "It was perfectly clear to me and the prime minister and the rest of the Cabinet that there was no way in which we were going to give in to the demands of the hunger strikers," he told me. "It is said, and quite rightly, that she was quite determined that we were not going to give in to the prisoners' demands. But I was no less determined, and indeed if the government had given in, I would have left it. If I'd been overruled in the Cabinet and they said no, we'll have to give in to this, I would have resigned because I felt that strongly about it. She [Margaret Thatcher] has a reputation in all sorts of fields for being fairly tough; in this particular case I was just as tough as she was and so was everybody else."

And thus his policy with would-be mediators. "Take for instance the Irish Commission for Peace and Justice," he says. "They said, 'Can we go and see the prisoners?' and I said, 'Yes.' 'May we come and see you again afterwards?' and I said, 'Yes, you can, but what you can't do is then go back and see the prisoners again because then it will look like you're negotiating and there's nothing to negotiate about.' I tried very hard to get it into the minds of the prisoners that it wasn't any good going on trying to negotiate because there was nothing to negotiate about. They either lived or died. It was entirely up to them."

"I wouldn't have it," he says, "that anybody who saw the prisoners and saw me would see the prisoners again, simply on the grounds that we were not negotiating." This, he says, is the reason why the Irish Commission for Peace and Justice was referred to Michael Alison and why Atkins did not see its members. Alison was not empowered to make any agreements without reference to him. "It was important for me to carry my colleagues with me at all times—because it was the government, it wasn't me [who made decisions]." Every document, therefore, "had to be crawled all over" by experts in the English language; they were "terrifyingly careful about every precise word in any statement, a comma, anything, so that there wouldn't be any difference of view."

Prisoners of war. "That's what the whole thing was about from beginning to end and we wouldn't have it." Dublin wanted London "to fudge" the issues. "There was a great deal of pressure on us to try and find a way out that would have kept these people alive and which would, to use my own word 'fudge it' and we resisted it." Although the whole thing was ostensibly about what sort of clothes prisoners might wear, it was really "an attempt to reestablish in the minds of the Provisional IRA that they weren't prisoners because they had committed crimes but that they were prisoners of war and should be treated as such, different from people who'd murdered other people because they'd stolen their money or ran away with their wives or something." The British were urged to make some kind of fudge on the issue of clothing, and they did make some alterations in the clothing regulations. They were prepared to allow prisoners to wear "civilian-type clothing" but it had to be applied throughout the U.K., otherwise "we would have been giving something special to this group of people and thereby indicating that they were something different and in our view they weren't." Nevertheless, it was "constantly being urged on us 'Oh, it's not really about prisoner-of-war status, it's just a question of how people are treated and why shouldn't they wear their own clothes and you could surely make some kind of gesture to them which would satisfy everybody.' Well, we didn't believe that."

The Dublin government wanted to avoid trouble, it was "very anxious that the hunger strikes would not result in the deaths of a whole lot of Irish people. So it said, there must be ways you can fix it somehow." Dublin felt that "if the hunger strikers died there would be an awful lot of trouble in the North and that it would spill over into the South—they [the Irish] didn't want any more, they'd had enough already. They wanted to avoid trouble and they wanted to show they had a hand in the affairs of Northern Ireland."

Atkins discussed the issue with two people: Prime Minister Margaret Thatcher and Home Secretary William Whitelaw. Decisions were initially made by the three of them and then brought before the Cabinet, where they usually had their way, because "the truth of the matter [was] that most people in the Cabinet didn't know a lot about Northern Ireland." In fact, he himself didn't know a lot about it until he went there in May 1979. As regards the Irish Commission, its deliberations with Michael Alison were discussed in Cabinet "only [to indicate] what they were on about because it [the Commission]" was "a body with international renown," but he could not recollect that the Cabinet's position altered at all. (According to Michael Alison, the ICJP deliberations never actually reached the point where Atkins had to go to the Cabinet with "a clear-cut suggested deal." Had there been one, he says, Atkins "would have had to go to the prime minister and he probably would have brought it before the Cabinet—it had reached that level of significance internationally.")

And what about the Foreign Office mediation and the Mountain Climber initiative? I asked him.

I had no personal knowledge. I've never heard of Mountain Climber as such. You've just mentioned the name, it's the first time I've ever heard it. All I can tell you is that any contact with Her Majesty's Government and any of these organizations by subterranean means was not a matter under my control at all. I'm bound to say I've always assumed there were [contacts]—after all, what are the security forces about in some respects?—they're about a lot of other things but I mean that's one of them. . . . It doesn't wholly surprise me that that kind of thing was going on but what is surprising is an assertion, if such an assertion has been made, that any offer was made in different terms to the one agreed to in Cabinet. Now, whether in fact discussions took place and when people were talking backwards and forwards somebody had said "well now, if the government were to do this how would that seem?" in order to carry the information back to feed it into the government, this kind of thing might be a good idea if the government agreed to it. But I don't know, I can't tell you because I've absolutely no knowledge of it.

"Someone might have come over from London with documents" on 18 December 1980, the day the first hunger strike ended, but "he wouldn't have had anything different. He would have had the same thing [which the NIO had supplied to the hunger strikers] because it was absolutely essential that there [should be] no misunderstanding. . . . What discussions such a person [i.e., a Foreign Office contact] had, if indeed he existed, I can't possibly say," Atkins says, but one way or the other, "he had no authority to say anything different to what I had said, and indeed the prime minister for that matter in answering questions in the House and things like that." (In short, says Gerry Adams, "he [Atkins] isn't saying there could be no negotiations. He isn't saying a program of reform could not be worked out until the hunger strikes ended. He's saying all these things could happen, as in fact they did happen, that all these consultations and negotiations took place and different options were discussed but they could not be implemented until the hunger strike ended, but that the hunger strike couldn't end until they had been agreed to. There's a duplicity of language there which again shows the hypocrisy of the

British position. That they could publicly take a position that there would be no concessions until the hunger strike ended but they could privately have a position, there'll be no concessions until the hunger strike ends but let's work out the concessions now because we know you won't end the hunger strike until the concessions are worked out.")

Sir Ian Gilmour, who was Lord Privy Seal, deputy to the secretary of state for Foreign and Commonwealth Affairs and a senior member of the Cabinet at the time, is no less forthright—or cautious. There were, he admits, some policy differences—what he calls "differences in emphasis" between the NIO and the Foreign and Commonwealth Office on the question of how to handle the hunger strike. The Foreign Office wanted the hunger strikes over. Its main concern was with the impact they were having on world opinion, especially in the United States. The hunger strikes were, in his view, "a disaster . . . a great propaganda coup for the IRA." The Foreign Office pushed the Northern Ireland Office to make some concessions but without success. As regards a Foreign Office contact with the IRA through a middleman, he would regard such a contact as being unlikely but nevertheless possible; it was more likely, if a contact did exist, that M16 or even M15 (the British military intelligence services) was involved, with M16 or M15 feeding information back to the Foreign Office. Either there was a contact and he wasn't told about it—which he would regard as unlikely, or there was a contact and he couldn't remember it, which he would regard as less unlikely but improbable. He was inclined to think, therefore, that it didn't happen, or that if it did happen, he wasn't told about it. "Civil servants, after all," he observes, "are very good at not telling ministers what they don't want them to know." Moreover, "talking to terrorists" would have been "the sort of thing Mrs. Thatcher would have been very much against." And since the Northern Ireland Office was dealing with a network of priests who were in close contact with the IRA, he felt that these connections obviated the need for direct contact with the IRA itself through other channels. The Foreign Office would have been "immensely incompetent" if it had been trying to undercut the ICJP talks with the NIO and the hunger strikers. He found such a suggestion "extremely unlikely and highly improbable." He could not recall any discussions in Cabinet regarding proposals to end the hunger strike—Cabinet would of course get reports of what was going on but they did not provoke discussion.

Michael Alison does not recollect the Mountain Climber matter. He had no prior knowledge of any such talks. He did not raise the issue with Atkins. He doesn't recall it as being a significant factor in his own discussions with the ICJP. He had no sense of being shadowed by other discussions. If parallel lines of communication were open they would have been echoing his own discussions, not superseding them. If anything, he probably thought the whole thing was an attempt on the part of the IRA to undermine the talks between himself and the Commission. He would have been surprised if the IRA's account of the talks they were having could be taken at face value. It could perhaps have been a piece of disinformation. A channel, if in fact one did exist, would, however, merely have reinforced his own efforts. "I had," he says, "a pretty free hand in the province. I knew well what the government would have considered concessions of principle. I had no sense of the Foreign Office carrying on something over my head. I would have considered it inconceivable." His instructions were explicit. "The whole basis to my discussions with the Commission was not fundamentally to concede anything of substance but to find something that would allow the hunger strikers to save face." Nothing could be conceded that would allow the prisoners to declare a victory. "What one wanted was to try and secure a formula which would at least have made the nationalists [the hunger strikers] feel that they had secured something, though not perhaps everything they had sought," but it had to be done in way that

would allow the government [to] retain its credibility with the anxious Unionist/ loyalist sections of the population in the face of what was a very special kind of pressure. . . . A clear-cut victory for the nationalists . . . would have been impossible for the government to concede without calling down on itself a lot of trouble from another quarter. . . . It's only in the aftermath of the conflict, of the resolution of the great contest of wills which was represented by the hunger strikes, that the actual issue could be dealt with rationally and calmly on its merits. But at the time I don't believe it was possible to have made concessions which would have ended the second hunger strike without their being represented [by the hunger strikers] as a form of victory in the battle of wills.

That is essentially what they were confronted with. "It was a test of strength and will. . . . [The government] could not put itself in a position in which it had been overturned and defeated manifestly by the use of this kind of pressure because the loyalist community would have thought, well, now this is the thin edge of the wedge and pressure is always going to produce concessions from the government. . . . [Our] eyes were on the feelings of the British public at large and the loyalist community in particular," he says, and "we couldn't see very much beyond that." It would have had "a disastrous effect" on the reputation of the government "if we had given in on our side and [it] could even have affected the outcome of the [next general] election." They were prepared to engage in "all sorts of attempts to find something that was face-saving [for the hunger strikers], something which had some real substance to it, but it couldn't be very big, it couldn't be very substantial, and it couldn't be on the scale implied by a willingness to die on the other side." The hunger strike weapon had to be tested to destruction. "Either it had to break the will of the government in a clear and manifest way or the government had to break the will of the nationalists in a clear and manifest way. . . . We had to retain the fundamental conviction within our consciousness that we were in control of the prison and that the prisons were run by the prison officers and not the prisoners." He never thought, given that parameter, "that the Irish Commission would be able to convey to the other side something which would be acceptable to them unless they were really looking for a way out"— and he was not convinced at the time that they were.

If Humphrey Atkins, Sir Ian Gilmour, and Michael Alison—two cabinet members and one minister of state—knew nothing of the talks between the IRA and the Foreign Office through the Mountain Climber intermediary, then who would? The obvious answer was the man at the top, the secretary of state for Foreign and Commonwealth Affairs himself, Lord Peter Carrington.

I wrote to Lord Carrington in early February 1989 setting out in broad terms what I was writing about without going into the matter of Mountain Climber and requesting an interview with him. In due course I received a short reply. "I would willingly see you but I really do not think I can be of much help to you," he wrote. "The Secretary of State for Northern Ireland obviously dealt much more with Irish affairs than I did during my period as Foreign Secretary. Although I saw the Irish Foreign Minister frequently, I did not really have much to do with the situation."

I followed up his letter with one of my own, thanking him for his willingness to see me and suggesting some dates in April, when I would be in London, on which we might be able to schedule a short interview. None of the suggested times suited him, however; his schedule was simply too full. When I was in London I hand-delivered another letter to his residence. This one asked specific questions: Whether he had authorized contacts between the Foreign Office and the IRA; whether contact could have taken place without his knowledge; whether he knew that the text of what Mrs. Thatcher would say in Ottawa should the hunger strikes end had been made available to the IRA.

A month passed. I telephoned his office twice inquiring as to when a reply might be forthcoming, and then in the last week of May I received a reply from his private secretary. "Lord Carrington," she wrote, "is very much abroad on business and has not had an opportunity to respond to your letter. He has, therefore, asked me to write and send his most sincere apologies but to say that he feels he simply has nothing further to add to his letter of 21 February." In short, Lord Carrington was not about to divulge anything.

From the beginning, therefore, the government saw the question solely in terms of the prisoners' statement of 5 February 1981: "We are demanding," they had said, "to be treated as political prisoners which everybody recognizes we are." And thus the government's further assumption: that the hunger strikes were not primarily directed at prison conditions, that this was obvious "from the disproportion," as the *Times* put it, "between the triviality of the improvements demanded in already good prison conditions and the gravity of a policy of serial suicide"; that any concessions offered would not be received on their merits but exploited by the IRA in pursuit of its objective, which was not penal reform but the furtherance of rebellion; that the IRA leadership was using the hunger strikes to showcase its power; that without power, "palpable and perceived," the IRA could not prevail against the authority and forces of the state; that it was, therefore, "vital" to the IRA that this display of power should in some way succeed and no less vital to the state that it should in no way succeed.

The government reduced the hunger strikes to a contest of wills. There would be no question of appearing to make concessions under duress, of seeming to back down in the face of the self-imposed death sentences of the hunger strikers, of appearing to be beaten. But once the hunger strikers bowed to the immovable might of the accommodating yet unyielding power of the state, forever vigilant in its war against catch-all terrorism, the compassion that benign governments dispense would be liberally exercised. Concessions would be granted once the concessions had ceased to be nonnegotiable demands.

Mrs. Thatcher knew her marketplace. Even in the wake of the massive media coverage of Sands's death and funeral, and the all but overwhelming international sympathy it generated for the hunger strikers, 92 percent of English and Welsh voters were opposed to the granting of political status, according to a MORI opinion poll, 89 percent had no sympathy whatsoever with the hunger strikes, and only a statistically insignificant 4 percent backed the prisoners' demands. When Father James Wixted, an Irish-born Catholic priest in Wantage, Oxfordshire, the parliamentary constituency of the murdered Airey Neave, announced that he would celebrate a mass for the repose of Sands's soul, there was a public outcry. His superior, the Right Reverend Anthony Emery, bishop of Portsmouth, forbade him from mentioning Sands's name during the mass. Mrs. Thatcher was angered at the priest's action. "It was," she told the Commons, "a matter on which a number of us feel very deeply indeed and why the feelings and thoughts of most of us are with the victims of the Provisional IRA." So it was with some satisfaction that the media reported that only five people showed up at Father Wixted's service. (Censure worked many ways: in Donegal, Church of Ireland minister Reverend Cecil Thornton, rector of Buncrana and Fahan, was rebuked by his superior, the Right Reverend James Mehaffey, bishop of Derry and Raphoe, for attending a prayer vigil for Sands in Buncrana, and when he visited Belfast in July, the *Times* reported that the head of the Church of England, Archbishop of Canterbury Right Reverend Robert Runcie, "was clearly upset by allegations that he had asked people to pray for the soul of Robert Sands.")

The *Times* once again succinctly expressed the British view. Sands, it editorialized, "committed suicide in the full knowledge of what he was doing and determined to reject all initiatives designed to save his life. He was not hounded to death. He was not in prison for his beliefs but for proven serious criminal offenses. He was not being oppressed or ill treated. There was only one killer of Bobby Sands and that was Bobby Sands himself." The *Daily Telegraph* damned with faint praise Sands's courage: "Courage he certainly had," was its verdict, "but it was courage of the ruthless and corrupted sort which holds human life in contempt."

Other papers delivered similar but less restrained judgments. "Sands' suicide," according to the *Daily Express,* was "contrary to the laws of his church and goes against the appeals of his Pope." Sands was "the fall-guy for an evil fanaticism . . . a fanatic who would have gone unnoticed in life, but who imagined—God help us—that he would serve Ireland in death." Young men like Sands, it went on, "committed suicide because they follow darkness, believing it to be a romantic dream. Hatred is their guide. Falsehood is their goal." The *Daily Mail* and the *Sun* echoed these sentiments. "Bobby Sands, willingly or not, killed himself to further an evil crusade," the *Daily Mail* said. "He was the tool of wicked conspirators who if they ever took control of Ulster would bring the province bloodshed, tyranny, and desolation." It called Sands's funeral "a macabre propaganda circus, the ritual of so-called full military honors at the graveside with masked gunmen solemnly firing volleys into the air, a gangsters' parody of the moving tributes which fighting men traditionally pay to comrades who fall in defense of honorable causes." Sands, said the *Sun,* left a legacy of evil. "He stood for tyranny—the dark tyranny of terror by the bomb cruelly placed to maim and kill unsuspecting innocents." He hoped "that from beyond the grave, his twisted sacrifice would impel other men into twisted acts of bloody revenge."

In the British view, nothing had changed. The poet and critic Seamus Deane writes, "the language of politics in Ireland and England, especially when the subject is Northern Ireland, is still dominated by the putative division between barbarism and civilization." The English, he writes, liken the conflict in Northern Ireland to "a battle between English civilization based on laws and Irish barbarism based on local kinship loyalties and sentiments." The barbarians come from "an area of dirt and desolation, not to be equalled in Western Europe, a blot on the fair face of the United Kingdom. Locked in a poverty trap, lost in a mist of sentiment and nostalgia, exploiting safeguards of the laws they [the Irish] despised, faithful to codes other than those of the English rite . . . they are not only barbarians, they are criminals." In contrast, their opponents "who wear uniforms, and live in barracks, and drive armoured cars, operate check points, etc., etc. kill with impunity, because they represent, they embody the Law. The terrorist embodies its denial."

Meeting the hunger strikers' demands for special status would undermine the basis of this equation, hence the undercurrents of anti-Irish opinion in the British media and government: there were still Irish who were "ineluctably criminal," who showed "remarkably consistent disrespect for English law, and, therefore, for the law as such."[1] Mrs. Thatcher's remark in the Commons following the race riots in Liverpool in early July—"Many of us did not think that these kinds of things could happen in our country"—was, in part because of its unintentional insensitivity, a perfect expression of mainland British attitudes. "Northern Ireland," the *Belfast Telegraph* somewhat acerbically observed in the wake of her comments, "which Mrs. Thatcher has insisted is a fully paid up member of the United Kingdom is obviously classed in a different light when it comes to her reaction to violence."

Moreover, both the official and the public attention span was short; other issues—race riots in English cities and the approaching royal wedding of Prince Charles and Lady Diana—pushed the hunger strikes aside when it became clear after Sands's death that the center would indeed hold, that the expectations of catastrophic violence which the media, often with the implicit encouragement of the government ("IRA READY TO BURN BELFAST" the *Daily Mail*'s front page announced following an Atkins statement), had cultivated with such assiduous anticipation would not materialize. During Mrs. Thatcher's twice-weekly fifteen-minute question time in the Commons on 9 July, less than a week after the death of the fifth hunger striker, Joe McDonnell, and the collapse of the talks between the Northern Ireland Office and the Irish Commission for Peace and Justice with each accusing the other of bad faith, none of the speakers who were called raised either matter.

One incident, perhaps, best illustrates the enormous perceptual gulf between the two traditions. On 1 July, Cardinal O'Fiaich met with Mrs. Thatcher. (There was a certain irony to the circumstances of the meeting. Cardinal O'Fiaich was in London for a service commemorating Oliver Plunkett, one of his predecessors as Archbishop of Armagh, who was hanged, drawn, and quartered at Tyburn in 1681 by one of Mrs. Thatcher's predecessors.) Mrs. Thatcher was herself: imperious, haughty, strident, in charge. At the beginning she spoke for perhaps twenty minutes without interruption, more intent, it seemed, on giving a sermon than in engaging in an exchange of views. She did not understand why the prisoners were on hunger strike. She had asked so many people. Was it, she asked somewhat rhetorically, to prove their virility? The Cardinal asked for changes in the prison regime that would allow the hunger strikes to end without loss of face. But she interrupted him: it would be wrong and dishonorable to make any concessions to murder and violence. She quoted the pope's plea at Drogheda to the men of violence to abandon their evil ways. She wondered why, despite two world wars, Britain and Germany managed to be friends but Ireland and Britain could not. At this point the cardinal could no longer restrain himself. It just might, he suggested, have to do with the fact that Britain did not occupy the Ruhr.

In accounts of the meeting, the cardinal's response often becomes the high point in the telling: the suggestion that he had somehow put Mrs. Thatcher in her place, that in the thrust and parry of repartee he had outmatched her, satisfied an atavistic urge to strike back. He had gotten one in for the home side. "She wasn't pleased by the response," Cardinal O'Fiaich recalls. "At that time we were just trying to score points. If we had got to a situation where we were really trying to help each other understand things, I wouldn't have made that response and she wouldn't have made some of her responses either. But it was quite obvious the meeting was going to produce nothing constructive, no meeting of the minds. At times it went very near to discourtesy on both sides." Later in the meeting when Mrs. Thatcher asserted that Mexico had as much right to interfere in the affairs of Texas as the Republic of Ireland had to interfere in the affairs of Northern Ireland, the Cardinal tried to give her some sense of how nationalists viewed the origins of the Northern Ireland state, how absurdly artificial the contours of the border were, how they divided dioceses and parishes—even his own parish was divided, with two churches in the North and one in the South—but she was not listening, a Cabinet meeting beckoned, and she went on her way, convinced that she was right, no better disposed to understanding the difficult and recalcitrant Irish, immune to the idea that perceptions of historical transgressions might have a place in a modern world view.

Mrs. Thatcher's response to the hunger strikes reflected Britain's sense of its position in relation to the larger conflict. It insisted on being seen only as peacemaker, honest broker between two warring communities in the turbulent province. "The Irish church and Irish state," a *Daily Telegraph* editorial reminded its readers, "find it convenient to imply that Mrs. Thatcher is rejecting available compromises, when they know quite well that the compromises could not be found, and that if Britain withdrew from the province, a Protestant state, with dire consequences for the Catholic population, would establish itself." Mrs. Thatcher, it asserted, "has made it clearer than ever that she understands the truth her opponents cannot bring themselves to admit."

Britain rejected out of hand nationalist Ireland's contention that the present conflict had its origins in the partition of Ireland in 1920. It refused to acknowledge that its inaction and inattention between 1920 and 1968, when parliamentary convention precluded matters relating to Northern Ireland being raised at Westminster, might have contributed to institutionalizing the discriminatory practices of the Unionist majority—or that its actions since 1969 might have been less than benevolently evenhanded. Britain saw itself as the one put upon, as the "good guy" keeping the unruly natives from tearing each other apart, as the bearer of standards of fair play and democracy not adhered to by its ruthless and cowardly opponents, as the mediator of good will in a dispute between two communities caught in a time warp of reformation theology and atavistic nationalism, as the disinterested, altruistic government pouring money, men, and arms into the province for the sole purpose of stopping two groups of incorrigible, belligerent Irish from executing their murderous designs on each other.

Britain refused to see itself as part of the problem or to acknowledge a historical liability, and its behavior—the sometimes resigned exasperation and the often unwitting condescension toward both communities in Northern Ireland—reflected its high opinion of its own good intentions. It would stay in Northern Ireland only as long as a majority of the people there wanted it to; it had no interests to protect, no territorial yearnings to satisfy, no national ambitions to fulfill. Meanwhile, it would discharge its responsibilities as the sovereign power. The government was not the inflexible party in the prison dispute; the hunger strikes were taking place solely at the behest of the Provisional IRA. The government's goal, Mrs. Thatcher told the Commons, was "to protect the law abiding and to defeat terrorism. To grant political status would be to give a license to kill." Accordingly, "the government [would] never grant political status no matter how much hunger striking there [might] be." Nor was she alone in her views. "The central question is this one of conceding political status," Michael Foot, leader of the Labour Party declared, endorsing Mrs. Thatcher's policies, "and that cannot be done without the government itself giving sure aid to the recruitment of terrorists."

Much was made of the facilities available to conforming prisoners: they could wear civilian-type clothing at all times including slacks, shirts, and pullovers of various colors provided by the prison. They could wear their own clothes for visits and during evening and week-end association. They were free to associate with each other for three hours every evening to watch television or play indoor games, and they could associate during the day on Saturdays and Sundays. They were allowed one hour's exercise a day, in the open if the weather permitted, and the use of the gymnasium and playing pitch for an additional three hours a week.

To underscore the government's commitment to maintaining and developing a humane and flexible prison regime, details of a typical working day at the Maze/Long Kesh were repeatedly highlighted during briefings for the increasing number of journalists, community leaders, churchmen, humanitarian bodies, and foreign visitors who trooped through the prison gates.

7:30 A.M.—unlock, ablutions, bed-making and cell-cleaning; 8:15 A.M.—breakfast in dining room; 8:40 A.M.—movement to industrial and vocational training workshops. Prisoners could take visits [they were allowed one statutory and three additional visits a month during this period or the afternoon work period and some attended education classes during the same time]; 12:15 P.M.—prisoners at the workshops returned to the H-blocks; 12:25 P.M.—lunch in dining room; 1:00 P.M.—exercise in open, weather permitting. Otherwise association in the dining room; 2:00 P.M.—prisoners return to cells for numbers check; 2:05 P.M.—prisoners return to workshops; 4:15 P.M.—prisoners return to H-blocks from workshops and are locked in their cells; 4:30 P.M.—tea in dining room; 5:00 P.M.—prisoners return to their cells; 5:30 P.M.—association in dining room or handicraft room or education room, or if a prisoner prefers in his own cell. In the summer, evening association could be spent in the exercises yard; 8:30 P.M.—prisoners lock up.

In short, from unlock at 7:30 A.M. to lock up at 8:30 P.M. the prisoners were actually locked in their cells for a mere 35 minutes. "We believe," Humphrey Atkins told Parliament, "that the conditions in the Maze Prison are superior to conditions in any other prison and I am convinced we are right."

Thus the British perspective: the strategic objective of the hunger strikes was for a category of prisoner that would vindicate the IRA's campaign of violence as a just war in which the forces of militant Republicanism were engaged with the security forces of the state and at the end of which prisoners of war would be released. In short, when the motive is pure, murder is no longer murder; violence committed in the name of war is not a crime.

And thus the form the propaganda war took: the British always couching the prisoners' demands in terms of political status, the prisoners never using the term, always referring only to the five demands or prison reform. Both sides chose terms that would have the most appeal to the broader public they were trying to manipulate, that would appear to make them more reasonable and their positions more tenable. ("Balanced statements" Sinn Fein spokesman Richard McAuley informed all and sundry, "which seek to temper criticism of one side with criticisms of the other help no one.")

To counter what appeared to be the international groundswell of admiration for Sands which his lonely death-stand had generated and the deepening perception that it was Mrs. Thatcher herself who was the inflexible party in the prison dispute, the Northern Ireland Office disseminated its own compilation, culled from new media accounts in nine countries and thirty-one separate publications in the United States, of editorial support for what the government clearly saw as its principled stand. Even Mauritius, the tiny island state of less than one million people hidden in the Indian Ocean, was not overlooked. "No sane person would starve to death to wear civilian clothes," the NIO reported *Le Cerneen,* the island's major newspaper, as telling its readers. "The immediate issue is about political status. The hunger strikers say they have the right to be treated as prisoners of war. There is little basis for this claim."

Sands, Humphrey Atkins said, had been ordered to die, had acted "under the instructions of those who felt it was useful to their cause that he should die." Atkins had no basis for making this assertion. His statement was part of the government's attempt to counter the enormous propaganda gains that had accrued to the hunger strikers after Sands's election to Westminster. It was, however, an indication of the level at which the propaganda war was conducted. Atkins said what he said not because it was true but because it was believable, because it fed the perception that the IRA, faceless and fanatical, with its disregard for public opinion and reputation for malevolence, was capable of going to any lengths to achieve its ends. Children, Mrs. Thatcher said, were being used "by evil men as shields and tools."

"In one area of Belfast," Atkins told the Commons, "the Provisional IRA are contemplating evacuating residents to other parts of the city, burning the emptied houses and by throwing the blame onto others further fuelling sectarian conflict. Already they have actually earmarked homes for those intended evacuees and the owners have been ordered to cooperate." Nothing remotely approaching the scenes of desolation Atkins had so vividly described occurred. And weeks later, he informed Parliament that the IRA "aim to destroy the government of the North, and following that . . . the government of the Republic.''

Thus the official line: invoke the pejorative term "terrorist" to describe the IRA at every opportunity, link the IRA to the larger, more menacing world of international terrorism, associate it with random acts of murderous and indiscriminate violence, predict its imminent demise, belittle the extent of its support in the Catholic community, insinuate that hard men of violence were coercing or otherwise persuading or ordering young men to fast to death, encourage mediation through establishment channels such as the ICJP, keep the psychological pressure on the hunger strikers, and hold out the olive branch of concessions—but only after the hunger strikes ended.

In the end, the British government's obsession with not appearing to be beaten consumed its more clever intentions. It won the contest of wills but little else. It lost the propaganda war, resuscitated an ailing IRA, and politicized militant Republicanism.

3 CONSEQUENCES

But who can talk of give and take,
What should be and what not
While those dead men are loitering there
To stir the boiling pot?

William Butler Yeats
"Sixteen Dead Men"

15   With the ending of the hunger strikes Northern Ireland quickly settled back into its unsettled ways. In September a new secretary of state, James Prior, was appointed. He held out the olive branch to the prisoners, once it was clear that the hunger strikers had given in, and by the end of 1981 the prisoners had been granted the substance of their demands. As a matter of right, prisoners could wear their own clothes at all times; they could associate freely within adjacent wings of the H-blocks during mealtimes, work, exercise, recreation, and weekends; they were given 50 percent of the remission they had looked for; and prison work was narrowly defined to include only a small number of activities that the prisoners could refuse to do without significant loss of privilege. There were the predictable noises: the Unionist parties condemned the government's gestures, accusing it of having won the war and lost the peace; Sinn Fein claimed victory; and the Dublin government, the Catholic Church, and the SDLP signaled their approval and relief.

In the broader political arena there was no question as to who had won and who had lost. Sinn Fein and the IRA were seen as indisputable winners, for although they had lost in the narrow sense that they had to call off the hunger strikes and accept what was on offer from the authorities, they won in the larger sense. They had two M.P.'s and two members of the Irish Parliament to show for their political intervention; they had shown that support for militant Republicanism was a lot higher than their opponents had insinuated; in the international community, their prisoners were accorded the political status Mrs. Thatcher denied them; and no one, outside of the Protestant community, and perhaps the British government, viewed the Republican prisoners as mere criminals or social deviants. Within their own community, whatever stigma of criminality or at least repugnance that moderate Catholics attached to the IRA's actions was assuaged; the IRA was legitimized, the human faces of the hunger strikers mitigating the hard edge of Republican violence. This generation had not been found wanting, and Sinn Fein would reap the harvest of their community's approval at the electoral polls. The old shibboleth, so smugly accepted, that only a few endorsed the actions of the men of violence, was exposed for the fiction it was. The community saw itself in danger only of the violence of the state.

But even if the hunger strikes were over, there was a lingering suggestion of unfinished business, an uneasy, unstated foreboding that something had changed—not for the better—and that the ledger books of revenge had yet to be properly balanced. The political parties in the South resumed their interminable squabbling, their increasingly shrill denunciations of one another an attempt to conceal the paucity of their own political agendas and the bankruptcy of their ideologies in the face of the rapid economic downturn. They were more conscious that in some parts of rural Ireland, at least, the fires of militant Republicanism still burned, not fiercely perhaps, but with a steady flame that would be difficult to douse without risk of a larger conflagration. The myths still had the power to move, even if they could not incite action.

The North was jaded, but like an addict whose overwhelming obsession with his next fix becomes a source of energy vanquishing every debilitation, it lurched toward new excess. The IRA, taking advantage of the moral stature the hunger strikers had bequeathed to it, shot dead the Reverend Robert Bradford, Official Unionist M.P. at Westminster for South Belfast, accusing him of being a rhetorical agent for sectarian violence during the hunger strikes, and raising fears that elected officials would join the paramilitaries' lists of "legitimate" targets—a step they had, to that point, shied away from. Ian Paisley, increasingly the dominant voice of an increasingly fearful Protestant community, once more ordered loyalists onto the streets for a "day of action" to protest the government's inadequate response to IRA murders; "third-force" commanders paraded their weaponry, threatening for the umpteenth time to take matters into their own hands and clear out IRA strongholds in the Catholic ghettos if the security forces would not; the political parties passed predictable resolutions at their annual conferences and received predictable responses.

The gulf between the two communities had widened, the psychological trauma of the hunger strikes reinforcing their perennial distrust of each other, undermining the impact of political initiatives before they could even get off the ground. Unawareness of others was compounded by obsession with self. Perceptions of self-interest were not confined to considerations of one's own situation but by one's perception of how others saw them. Too often, protagonists defined their realities not in terms of their own interests but in terms of the interests of others, reducing every possibility to a zero-sum toss-up. If your opponent was seen to gain, you were seen to lose. Thus Prior's attempt to resurrect a power-sharing Northern Ireland Assembly was stillborn. Protestants opposed his proposals because they saw power-sharing as a concession to Catholics; Catholics opposed them because they saw the absence of an explicit Irish Dimension as a concession to Protestants.

The hunger strikes mobilized the latent support for Sinn Fein and politicized a generation of young militant activists in the Republican ghettos, but they did not create that critical mass of support that would sweep across the Catholic community, generating its own momentum and leaving constitutional nationalism a casualty in its wake. The uprising might be imagined, but it would not be realized. If the death of ten men from hunger striking could not move the population, nothing could. The mythology was persuasive but no longer dominant.

But constitutional nationalism saw it differently. Sinn Fein's performance in the Northern Ireland Assembly elections in the fall of 1982, when they secured 30 percent of the Catholic vote, and in the British general elections in the summer of 1983, when they secured 43 percent of the Catholic vote, sent shivers of apprehension through the Irish political establishment. In the Republic, three general elections in the space of eighteen months had left the country exhausted, prone to wild speculation about how Sinn Fein might secure the balance of power in a hung parliament, vulnerable to loose talk about destabilization. The country had become unsure of itself, its finances were in a chaotic state, recession had taken hold, unemployment had begun to rise steeply, and the mood had turned from pessimism to a fatalistic resignation. Nothing would surprise anybody. Rumor was a distraction giving a sense of the melodramatic to what had become mundane.

In the North, the SDLP, with nothing to show for its years of advocacy of nonviolence, still truculently defensive about giving Sinn Fein a free rein in the two Fermanagh–South Tyrone by-elections, and increasingly perceived as middle aged and middle class, appeared to be incapable of holding off the Sinn Fein challenge. The proponents of "bad" violence, it appeared, were poised to become the authentic voice of the minority, unless something dramatic was done to halt them in their tracks.

Constitutional nationalism, North and South, remembered the past, remembered the fate that befell John Redmond's National Party after the 1916 Uprising when Catholics turned away from it in droves, not because they suddenly embraced the ideals of Pearse and Connolly or the cause of militant Republicanism, but because it was clear that no political initiative would emerge to fill the post-1916 political vacuum, and that Redmond's party could not, despite the concessions, accommodations, the unfailing willingness to be patient and trust the process, deliver Home Rule on terms that would be acceptable to a majority of Irish nationalists.

The New Ireland Forum was constitutional nationalism's immediate response to the crisis. Announced in March 1983, in time to allow the SDLP to say, during the British general election campaign, that it had been the SDLP's initiative, it brought together the major nationalist parties in Ireland—the Labour Party, Fine Gael, and Fianna Fail from the South, and the SDLP from the North—to spell out the way in which they hoped to achieve the unity of Ireland. It would show that these parties, which could claim to speak for 85 percent of Irish nationalists, spoke with one voice, offered a clearly articulated, unambiguous alternative to armed struggle, and had a common perception of the realities of the conflict and a common agenda for future action.

Every significant interest which had its say during the prison crisis—including the two governments and the wider communities they represented, the churches, and the political alignments within Northern Ireland itself—had reacted to the hunger strikes almost invariably on the basis of tribal imperative or with unconcealed prejudice that was all the more intense for being so specifically focused. It was hardly surprising, therefore, that their future actions would reflect these prejudices, albeit to a less pronounced extent. The hunger strikes had revealed the way in which the parties to the conflict adhered to their respective fictions; they had defined the principals to each other in ways that crystallized the often contemptuous attitudes they had toward each other. These sociopolitical touchstones would inform their future actions. Political initiatives would fail because the assumptions underlying them were informed by the prejudices, often unconscious, of the parties promulgating them.

"We are condemned to try and succeed because each of us if we fail or if we shirk this challenge, will be condemned by this and future generations as uncaring, unworthy and selfish politicians. Unworthy, not just of Ireland but of the human cause itself," John Hume, leader of the SDLP, told the opening session of the Forum on 30 May 1983. "There is no room, there is no time for opportunism or righteousness, or indeed, what is normally understood by 'politics.' Only then will those who doubt our good intentions—the Unionists in the North—and those who for centuries have found the pretext for their inexcusable neglect for this island in our divisions—the British—take us seriously and start to take their own responsibilities seriously."

Stirring, heart-felt words, words of hope that constitutional nationalism might rise to the occasion and fulfill the ambitious agenda it had set for itself. But it was not to be. In fairness, it did produce a plan: for the first time in sixty years the parties of constitutional nationalism came together to address the question of Northern Ireland without automatic recourse to the demand that partition must go. However, the Forum and the responses to it were to a large extent predetermined. What is normally understood as politics played, perhaps not surprisingly, a decisive role.

The hunger strikes had disturbed the uneasy relationship between constitutional and unconstitutional nationalism. The Forum could not complete the task it set itself without leading to discoveries and divisions that would make the task impossible, without rending in two not just the history of Ireland but Ireland itself. The Forum parties could not address the historical basis of Republican violence, could not examine the "bad" Republicanism of the present, without having to account for the facts that the "good" Republicanism of the past, using both the bullet and the Armalite of the day, had brought about the establishment of the Irish state; that the Irish government executed in cold blood or hanged seventy-two Irishmen between 1922 and 1923 for bearing arms on behalf of an independent Irish Republic—more than three times the number executed as cold-bloodedly by the British for bearing arms on behalf of the same cause between 1919 and 1921; and that both the IRA and Sinn Fein and the parties to the Forum shared a common view of Irish history, paying allegiance to a common pantheon of heroes whom they freely invoked to give legitimacy to their respective positions.

The Forum simply eschewed these questions, ignoring the fact that, historically, the proponents of the constitutional had proved themselves uncannily adept at using either the threat or the fact of the unconstitutional to gain their own particular ends, falling back on the traditional assertions that reflected the culture's dogmas about itself, and reducing the historical context to the partition of Ireland in 1920.

Partition, it said, imposed by Britain against the will of the majority of the people, was the cause rather than the consequence of division; the sole responsibility for that division was Britain's, and Britain's alone. And since partition became—by virtue of the need to avoid the question of the role of violence in the evolution of Catholic nationalism—the starting point of all explanations, the Forum could not place the Protestant tradition in its rightful historical perspective either, thus robbing it of its political and social texture, and making it appear as a dangling appendage to rather than an indispensable ingredient of the cultural mix. Far from being a catalyst that would lead nationalists to examine some of their most cherished assumptions and the validity of their aspirations, and to present a vision of a future that could be subscribed to by all traditions on the island of Ireland, the Forum became a political tool to undermine support for Sinn Fein.

The Forum Report, published in May 1984—in time for John Hume to trumpet its success before the 1984 European Parliament elections in which he had to contend with Sinn Fein opposition— reflects the key nationalist articles of faith: Britain wrongs Ireland; Britain can fix it; Protestants are Irishmen who mistakenly believe they are British or British subjects who can be persuaded to forego the British connection; there are combinations of constitutional and religious arrangements that will alleviate Protestant fears; Protestant consent to an all-Ireland state can be established as each of these fears is shown to be ill-founded; the British government always does an about-turn in the face of the threat of Unionist violence. When the safeguards offered to Unionists are sufficient to protect their interests, they will come around. The Unionist is disembodied; his concerns, even his psyche, can be disaggregated, compartmentalized into its separate elements, dealt with in discrete steps. Reconciliation is a matter of behavioral modification. Unity ultimately is inevitable because it is somehow historically ordained. Even if Unionists have the right to say no to a united Ireland, it is not an unqualified right. The wronged country is Ireland, the hurt community is nationalist, the responsible government is Britain.

But even if the Forum sidestepped the fundamental questions dogging Irish nationalism, there was a certain pageantry to its deliberations that captured the public imagination—the public relations version of what was going on became the accepted version. The imposing setting of Dublin Castle with its trappings of history, the spectacle of the country examining its conscience, making a public confession, albeit a very limited one, of its shortcomings of omission or commission, asking for forgiveness of a sort, and promising to make amends, to become more pluralistic, induced a vicarious participation. The country became Forum-conscious. Accounts of public sessions were carried in the media. The public session with the Irish Episcopal delegation was a first—the first time in the state's history that the church had submitted itself to being questioned on public issues by the state. As the months progressed and the deadline neared (failure to secure agreement by the time of the Euro-elections would reveal the bankruptcy of constitutional nationalism and vindicate Sinn Fein) the drama mounted: the parties were deadlocked. Mr. Haughey was holding out for more emphasis on the traditional precepts of nationalism; the SDLP's green and not-so-green wings were at loggerheads; the talks were about to collapse.

On the day of the report's publication, 2 May 1984, the proceedings were televised live. Even the fact of the Forum principals holding separate press conferences, disagreeing among themselves as to what it was they had agreed upon before the ink had even dried—Haughey insisted that the Forum called for a unitary state; Dr. FitzGerald disagreed; the report, he said, was not a blueprint but "an agenda for possible action"—was not sufficient to offset the general feeling of euphoria the exercise had generated. (The Forum's preferred solution was for "a unitary state achieved by agreement and consent, embracing the whole of Ireland and providing irrevocable guarantees for the protection and preservation of both the Unionist and the Nationalist identities." It also put forward two other options: a federal/confederal state and joint authority.) It was clear however, that the Forum had ducked the tough questions, merely restating the traditional aspirations of Irish nationalism, though dressing them up in a hue of less strident color; and that it was, for the most part, pedestrian in its analysis and unimaginative in its vision.

The people were forgiving. It was, after all, a political document, and, given the long-standing antipathy between Charles Haughey and Garret FitzGerald, the public was prepared to treat their joint signatures on a document as being more significant than their subsequent disagreements over what it was they had agreed to. After eleven months of deliberation, twenty-eight private sessions, thirteen public sessions, and fifty-six meetings of the four party leaders, the parties to the Forum could not be seen publicly to fail, since this would not only preclude further dialogue among themselves but almost certainly ensure further decline in the SDLP's political fortunes. What appeared to be an agreed-upon report allowed the parties to the Forum to go their separate ways. They could always argue that they were only disagreeing on the interpretation of the agreed-upon, not on the question of agreement itself. In short, the Forum report was a particularly Irish Catholic document, another example of an Irish solution to an Irish problem, reflecting contradiction, ambiguity, dual meanings, a propensity to sidestep unpleasant realities, and the passive-aggressiveness that is often the hallmark of the emancipated victim who continues to take refuge in a culture of learned helplessness. "In our Southern ethos we play with words," the Reverend Sydney Callaghan warned the Forum during his presentation to it. "We bandy them about; we throw them around and we know the ball game. We know many of them are not taken seriously. We live with that ball game; we understand it and we recognize it; it is a built-in recognition. So my Northern friends say, 'Say what you mean, mean what you say, but on the basis of your track record I frankly do not believe a word you politicians utter.' " The warning had fallen on deaf ears.

The Forum acknowledged that "the political arrangements for a new and sovereign Ireland would have to be freely-negotiated and agreed to by the people of the North and by the people of the South." But the Forum conspicuously failed to deal with the facts that Unionist consent does not exist, and will not exist in the foreseeable future; that Unionist opposition to being incorporated into an all-Ireland state is as strong now as in 1912; that opposition to any attempt to so incorporate them is the raison d'être of Unionism itself; that ultimately what is important to Unionists is not their Protestantism or their Britishness but their unrelenting opposition to any form of association with the rest of Ireland, an opposition that transcends in its intensity and durability any possibility of accommodation.

Irish nationalism, it was clear, ultimately rejected the Unionist position, insisting that there are some sets of safeguards—be they a bill of rights, quotas, weighted majorities, or a new Constitution, measures that nationalists would reject as being inadequate if applied to the protection of the Irish identity within Northern Ireland—that would somehow magically induce Unionists to sacrifice their position within Northern Ireland, where they enjoy a two-to-one advantage over nationalists, for one within an all-Ireland state in which they would be at a four-to-one disadvantage.

The Forum ignored the implications of its own requirements. Without the consent of Protestants, all its models were academic exercises. It simply put the onus on Britain to "re-assess its position and responsibility," accusing it of "crisis management," implicitly resuscitating the role of the Irish as victims, as being wronged, and restating the first commandment of holy nationalism: all that is wrong with Ireland is Britain's fault; the wrongdoer, that is, Britain, can fix things. The fact that Unionists immediately denounced the Forum's conclusions and belittled its analysis did not dismay the Forum parties. The report achieved its short-run goal, blunting Sinn Fein's performance in the Euro-elections. Moreover, it was not written for Unionist consumption but for British consideration.

The situation was familiar. Once again the Irish demanded action of some kind from the British, and once again the British ignored them. Once again the Irish pleaded with the British to take their deliberations seriously, and once again, the British dismissed their efforts. Once again the Irish, pleased with themselves, sought British approval, and once again they were angered and hurt when that approval was withheld. Once again Northern Ireland was a major item on Dublin's agenda, but a minor one on London's. Once again the powerlessness of the Irish, their resort to moral persuasion as the only diplomatic instrument at their command, had its counterpoint in the powerfulness of the British. Once again one was supplicant, the other master. And when the master chastised the supplicant, the supplicant, who had a long memory of being rebuked, was not disheartened. (In a terse statement issued to coincide with the Forum Report's publication, the British government noted that the Forum parties could not "expect the government to accept the Nationalist interpretation of past events which the Report expresses, or the dismissal of the strenuous efforts which successive UK governments have made in the past fifteen years to deal with the intractable problems of Northern Ireland." The Forum's account of the British position, it bluntly concluded, was "one-sided and unacceptable.")

The Forum parties continued to hold out for what they called the "considered" British response, something that would reflect in its depth of inquiry an effort commensurate with their own. Even when

Prior, with Mrs. Thatcher sitting at his side in the House of Commons, said that "there is one overriding and abiding reality and that is that consent is simply not forthcoming for any formulation that denies the Unionists their rights not only to belong to the United Kingdom but to be apart from the Republic," the Irish would not accept that this was the government's final response.

But they were not the only ones who were not listening. Aside from the M.P.'s from Northern Ireland, and a few diehard "Irish Question" M.P.'s, mostly either ultra-conservative supporters of the Unionist parties or Labour supporters of the SDLP, the chamber was virtually empty during the debate that followed. The intransigent preached to the irredentist, the convinced to the converted. An M.P. who evinced an interest in Northern Ireland without having to do so invited the banter of his colleagues. It was taken as a sign of eccentricity rather than of seriousness.

Mrs. Thatcher herself finally put to rest the question of a considered response during a press conference in November 1984 following her summit meeting with Dr. FitzGerald at Chequers. In response to a question relating to the Forum Report, she replied, "I have made it quite clear that a unified Ireland was one solution that was out. A second solution was a confederation of two states. That is out. A third solution was joint sovereignty. That is out. That is a derogation from sovereignty."

Mrs. Thatcher's remarks caused an uproar in Ireland, more for the manner in which she had delivered them than for the content itself. Anger at Mrs. Thatcher, stored up since the hunger strikes, exploded. Her response reminded people of her earlier responses, of her seeming contempt for all things Irish. The bluntness of her language, the quasi-aggressiveness of her demeanor, the barely concealed ill-temper at having the Forum Report brought up, as if it was a matter she had long since disposed of, once again underscored the Irish sense of being inferior, of being at the short end of Mrs. Thatcher's stick. Many argued, especially British commentators to the extent that they paid any attention to the matter at all, that Mrs. Thatcher was merely being herself. But the Irish saw her in a different light—in the context of their belief that she was anti-Irish, a myth perhaps, but not entirely a misperception.

Mrs. Thatcher's intervention, however, had at least one positive result for the Irish government. It gave greater urgency to the talks that had been under way between the two governments since March 1984, two months before the Forum had concluded its deliberations.

16   The Sinn Fein vote in the June 1983 British general election—43 percent of the nationalist vote, 15 percent of the overall vote compared to the SDLP's 18 percent, and the election of Gerry Adams to Westminster—had a traumatic impact in Dublin. The vote came close to legitimizing Sinn Fein as the majority voice of the Catholic community in the North, with the inescapable corollary that many Catholics there either supported the armed struggle or at least were not actively opposed to it. The vote demolished a few widely held beliefs: that the Catholic community in Northern Ireland did not support the IRA in large numbers, that militant Republicanism was an anachronism confined to small areas with long histories of irredentist nationalism, that almost all Catholics supported the constitutional route and peaceful means as the way forward. Dublin and the SDLP were faced with an electorate that increasingly was giving its approval to advocates of violence, to a war of attrition to end the British presence, to British withdrawal and a unified Ireland imposed against the wishes of the Protestant majority, if necessary. Militant Republicanism was on the verge of becoming the dominant nationalist tradition.

When FitzGerald met with Thatcher at Chequers in November 1983, he made the case for some dramatic political initiative to alleviate Catholic alienation in the North. If it was not forthcoming, he warned, Sinn Fein would become the majority voice of the minority community; if that were to happen it would signal the end of constitutional politics in the North, having consequences that would spill over into the South and possibly destabilize constitutional politics there, and that in turn would have serious repercussions for Britain.

Thatcher took heed. In March 1984 informal talks between the two governments got under way; a year later, formal talks began. The agreement that emerged after eighteen months of deliberations fell well short of the Forum options, but it did give the South a role in Northern Ireland. "The Anglo-Irish Agreement," FitzGerald told me, "is the result of the IRA's performance on the hunger strike. They may not like to accept that, just as they would claim at times there are things that we did that helped them, unintentionally, I'm sure. What they did helped Anglo-Irish relations enormously."

The agreement to which FitzGerald and Thatcher put their signatures on 15 November 1985 at Hillsborough, County Down, put British-Irish relations on a new footing. First, both governments affirmed that any change in the status of Northern Ireland (for example, incorporation by the Republic of Ireland) would come about only with the consent of a majority of the people of Northern Ireland. Both governments recognized that at the present the Protestant majority wished for no change in its status. And both governments promised to introduce and support in their respective Parliaments legislation to secure a united Ireland if in the future a majority of the people of Northern Ireland were clearly to wish for and formally to consent to the establishment of a united Ireland.

Second, the two governments agreed to set up an Intergovernmental Conference, serviced by a full-time secretariat with civil servants from both jurisdictions, that would be jointly chaired by the British secretary of state for Northern Ireland, currently Peter Brooke, and a "Permanent Irish Ministerial Representative"—at the present the minister for foreign affairs, Gerry Collins. The functions of the conference would pertain both to Northern Ireland and to relations between Northern Ireland and the Republic of Ireland, specifically with regard to political matters, security arrangements, the administration of justice, and the promotion of cross-border cooperation. A provision specifying that "determined efforts shall be made through the Conference to resolve any differences"—a binding legal obligation with precedent in international law—ensured that the Irish government's role was more than merely consultative, even though less than fully executive.

Third, both London and Dublin supported the idea of a "devolved" government, to deal with a range of matters within Northern Ireland, that would command "widespread acceptance throughout the community."[1] Should this occur, Dublin would nevertheless retain a say in certain areas affecting the interests of the Catholic minority (such as security arrangements and human rights). If devolution did not come to pass, then Dublin would continue to have a say in all matters that affect Catholics.

The agreement was designed to overcome Protestant opposition to power-sharing: the more willing Unionists were to share power with nationalists, the smaller would be the role of the conference, and hence the smaller the role of the South in the affairs of the North; the longer Unionists refused to share power, the larger and more permanent would be the role of the South.

It was an extraordinarily clever agreement, albeit a flawed one. It reflected an assumption about militant Republicanism—that there was some set of arrangements, some political formula, far short of conceding what the IRA wanted, that would lead to militant Republicanism either being rejected in its own community or being effectively sidelined to the role of bit player—that was as wishful in its intent as the Forum's assumption that there was some set of governance arrangements that would placate Unionist fears of a united Ireland. It was not, however, a time to question assumptions, which Mr. Haughey discovered to his dismay when his strident condemnation of the agreement as "copperfastening partition" fell on unreceptive ears, even within his own party.

The widespread enthusiasm with which the Irish, especially in the South (an *Irish Times*/MRBI poll taken a week after the agreement was signed showed a 59 percent approval rating for the pact and a 29 percent disapproval rating), embraced the agreement reflected their satisfaction with themselves and their belief that their obligations to Northern Catholics had been met, that something had finally been done for their coreligionists in the North that would alleviate their seemingly inexhaustive litany of grievances and get them, once and for all, off the South's already overburdened back. There was admiration for the manner in which Irish diplomats had romanced Tory backbenchers so that they responded favorably to the agreement, applause for the manner in which Mrs. Thatcher had been handled, for the skill with which the Irish side had moved the question up Mrs. Thatcher's agenda, given her notoriously short attention span when the issue of Northern Ireland surfaced. And they were pleased for other reasons. The camaraderie at the official level which the protracted negotiations engendered had evolved into a mutual respect; the new Intergovernmental Conference suggested that such respect would be exercised at the highest levels and would infuse Anglo-Irish relations generally; that a spirit of generosity if not quite mutual understanding was emerging that would allow Ireland to see itself as an equal in the partnership, not a junior member; that the agreement's promise that "determined efforts would be made to resolve differences" set a precedent for cooperative action.

There was also an element of smugness to their satisfaction—with their cleverness at having the British agree to have the summit at Hillsborough, the heart of British rule in Northern Ireland; with having persuaded the British to locate the conference secretariat in Belfast, thus ensuring the physical presence of the Irish government in the North; with the ambiguity of the agreement itself, which allowed the Irish to read it one way and the British another, and each to be able to say that the other's inconsistent interpretations were consistent with the terms of the agreement. The British could insist the agreement gave the Irish government only a consultative role in Northern Ireland and that its primary purpose was to ensure coordinated security policies to contain the IRA; the Irish could insist that their role was indeed more than consultative, implying an executive role consistent with the report of the New Ireland Forum.

The Irish government and John Hume went to extraordinary lengths to establish the relationship between the Forum report and the agreement, since it was necessary, as part of the overall design to undermine Republicanism, to show that one was the outgrowth of the other, that the agreement vindicated the wisdom of constitutional nationalism, that the path of nonviolence yielded more dividends than the path of violence, that constitutional nationalism, rather than being ideologically bankrupt, had proven itself superior in both tactics and strategy to militant Republicanism.

This obsession with securing the SDLP's base of support and isolating Sinn Fein overrode every other Irish consideration. At the heart of it was the explicit belief that the IRA posed a far greater threat to the Irish state than to the British government, and the implicit belief, given the necessity of seeing the IRA only in terms of "bad" violence, that support for militant Republicanism was the product of circumstance rather than conviction and ideology, that the IRA exploited the Catholic community rather than reflecting its essence. Thus the community could be detached from the IRA; the community could be "educated" to see its violence as wrong and perpetuating cycles of violence; the community could be wooed with a package of incentives that would be sufficient to convince it that continued support of the IRA was against its self-interest; the community could be turned against the men of violence who were exploiting it for their "evil" purposes.

Since the violence of the IRA was by definition "bad" violence, this fed the belief that the Catholic community which supported it did so mistakenly, or because it was somehow forced to do so, or because the perceived injustices of British rule make violence the most palatable alternative open to it. In short, support had nothing to do with conviction. The protest of the blanketmen and the hunger strikers could not be attributed to the absolute integrity of the Republicans' own beliefs but had to be ascribed to less worthy motives, at best to a strategic campaign to wrest political status from the British and gain the initiative in the propaganda war. The honesty of their motives could not be conceded; their actions had to be put down to their willingness to do whatever a bloody-minded IRA had in store for them. The motives of the Catholic community from which they came could not be conceded either. Thus the belief that there was some set of arrangements that would appear to grant the substance of the prisoners' demands, but which in reality would fall short of them, reflected the larger belief that there was some set of governance institutions that would appease the Catholic community and undermine support for the Republican movement, but which in reality would fall short of both British withdrawal and a united Ireland.

The agreement, the signatories believed, would detach Catholics from their current infatuation with Republicanism once they saw that the South vigorously pursued its role as the guarantor of Catholic interests, that their Irish identity had an equal standing with the Protestant identity, that their aspirations to a united Ireland were now legitimate; once the Flags and Emblems Act, which prohibited displays of the Tricolor of the Irish Republic, was repealed; once the police were more closely supervised and their practices made less repressive in the Catholic community; once the hated UDR was brought to heel and the Diplock courts were overhauled; once the Intergovernmental Conference, and especially the secretariat in Belfast, conveyed to Catholics that they were somehow "in union" with their coreligionists in the South. In short, you could enumerate Catholic grievances, develop a specific strategy to alleviate each of them, and at some point the overall level of grievance would diminish to the point where the community would turn its back on the IRA. You could undermine the ethos of militant Republicanism not by defeating it but by treating its symptoms.

But history says otherwise. Alleviating the grievances of oppressed groups rarely results in their being satisfied; concessions become irrelevant, once grievances are addressed, and serve only as a springboard for further demands. "Improved conditions," writes the political psychologist Jeanne Knutson, not only permit anger to arise; they equally create an emotional state of severe anxiety. As emotions are rekindled, the victim relives the terror of his victimization at full intensity, and realizes, for the first time, what might have happened. One never erases the identity of victim: those who live through the first injustice forever remain wary of the next attack by the identified source of aggression. Even if the aggressor loses his political, social or personal powers over the victim's life, fears are diminished, but never eradicated totally: a life preserving, primitive belief in personal safety has been breached. Once having been so terrorized, a victim thus simultaneously grieves over the past and fears the future.

Moreover, with the emergence of hope, "victims put aside ingrained feelings of traditional system support and the burdens of learned helplessness."[2]

Ironically, Catholic Ireland's attitude toward Northern Protestants was in many regards a mirror image of its attitude to Northern Catholics. It held that all things pertaining to Unionism—its Britishness, Protestantism, desire to maintain the higher standard of living that the U.K. economic link provided—could be compartmentalized and examined microscopically. Unionism had no organic essence; the whole was less than the sum of its parts. Opposition to a united Ireland was based on the Protestant desire to maintain a position of privilege rather than any deep-rooted ideological conviction. During the hunger strikes, Protestant opposition to a settlement that would appear to deny the prisoners the substance of their demands, but which in reality would go a long way toward meeting them, was simply dismissed as further proof of their intolerance. But this, too, embodied the larger belief that Protestant opposition to a set of governance arrangements that would appear to meet the Protestant demand not to become part of an all-Ireland state, but which in reality would go a long way toward doing just that, would simply typify their desire to maintain their privileged hegemony.

There is a broader process at work. Catholic public moral values are not the result of conviction arrived at through a process of consensus or the secular ethic of individual responsibility. They are a product, to a considerable extent, of the Catholic Church's imprint on the entire socialization process. They are immutable, fixed; they make no concessions to current orthodoxies. They are handed down from one generation to the next, their eternal truths promulgated by a hierarchy that is a compulsive guardian of Catholic values in the face of every threat, in constant fear of losing its power and position, unwilling to entertain any idea that might erode its authority. They are the teachings of the One, True, Holy, Catholic and Apostolic Church. They are written in stone, they are enduring, permanent, beyond question. Because the Irish Catholic moral value system is based on edict rather than arrived at through the consensual development of shared values, Catholics are not easily able to respond to value systems that evolve from a community's participation in the process that leads to the propagation of such shared values. Because their own value system often lacks the integrity of their convictions, they tend to dismiss the integrity of others' convictions.

Underlying Catholic Ireland's interpretation of the Forum Report and the Anglo-Irish agreement is its attitude toward Protestantism. Catholicism is "right," its values God-given; a united Ireland is historically mandated, a matter of inevitability. Protestants belong to the "wrong" religion; Unionists to the "wrong" state. Protestants should be converted to Catholicism, Unionists to a united Ireland. Acknowledgment of Protestant beliefs does not imply acceptance, approval, or concession of their legitimacy; acknowledgment of Unionism does not imply acceptance, approval, or concession of its legitimacy. The willingness to allow Protestants their Protestantism does not diminish the obligation you have to get them to see the errors of their ways; the willingness to allow Unionists their Britishness does not diminish the obligation you have to convince them that they are really Irish, or, at the very least, that their long-term interests would be more adequately safeguarded under some all-Ireland umbrella than in a British state.

Hence the logic of the agreement that prevailed in Catholic Ireland and, one should add, to a lesser but nonetheless significant extent in British government circles. A diminishing level of IRA violence was coupled with diminishing Protestant opposition to the agreement. Once it became clear to the Protestants that the constitutional status of Northern Ireland would be unaffected by the agreement, that their real interest in remaining part of the United Kingdom was adequately protected, that the Intergovernmental Conference was a reality both governments would not back away from, it was assumed by the two governments that Protestant opposition would decrease. Protestants would acquiesce in the agreement, even if they would not endorse it. Self-interest would move them to share power with Catholics, in order to minimize the purview of the conference. Power-sharing would further reduce support for the IRA since it would give Catholics an active voice in government itself. Protestant opposition would further diminish with increasing Catholic support of and membership in the ranks of the police. And, as their opposition eroded and their distrust dissipated, they would become increasingly responsive to new and more extended forms of cooperation between North and South.

The agreement is a superb exercise in the power of rationality: state the objectives, define the measures to implement them. It argues that specific grievances are more significant than the essence of grievance itself, and reflects the belief that tinkering with governance arrangements—a little overhauling here, a little fine-tuning there, get the sequence of reforms in proper order, get the pacing right; don't push too quickly or Protestant opposition will get out of control, don't go too slowly or Catholic disaffection will start to show itself again—can override the differences embedded in the mutually exclusive ideologies of both communities, or at least accommodate them sufficiently to undermine militant Republicanism, the aim of the Irish government, or to defeat terrorism, the aim of the British government.

However, since the agreement had to be simultaneously capable of accommodating Catholics without permanently alienating Protestants, it had to reflect this duality of intent. Thus its ambiguity and malleability; its emphasis on intent rather than fact; its adherence to process rather than specifics; its design as a framework rather than as a set of provisions. This accounted for much of its appeal to Catholics—it was written in a manner they could subscribe to—and for much of the opposition to it from Protestants—they could not understand it. Dublin said the agreement was more than consultative; Westminster said it was only consultative. Westminster said, or at least then secretary of state Tom King said, it ensured the perpetuity of the Union; Dublin said it did not. Dublin implied that the conference would have significant functions even in the event of power-sharing; London said it would not. London said Dublin had accepted that Northern Ireland was a legitimate part of the United Kingdom; Dublin said it had not, pointing with some pride to the wording of Article 1, which made no mention of the *constitutional* status of Northern Ireland, only to its *status*. Dublin said the agreement called for immediate and far-reaching changes in the administration of justice; London said it did not. London said that the agreement could be changed if Unionists engaged in talks; Dublin said it could not. London stressed security aspects; Dublin called attention to its contributions to decision making.

In the ambience of interpretation and counterinterpretation, Protestants took the only course they knew. They translated the agreement into the language they understood; they cut through the ambiguity, the nuances, the significant omissions, the balance and order of the arrangements it proposed, and got to the heart of the matter. The agreement mandated Dublin Rule.

Protestant reaction to the agreement was one of undiluted rage, rage that came from the wellsprings of their beings, an expression of anger and virulence at the British government so profoundly felt that it altered for all time the relationship between Protestant Ulster and Britain. The language of resentment used a vocabulary of hate. Mrs. Thatcher was "a Jezebel," "an unprincipled, shameless hussy" who had signed away Ulster Protestants' "inalienable right to citizenship in the U.K." ("We pray this night," Ian Paisley, leader of the Democratic Unionist Party and founding moderator of the Free Presbyterian Church, intoned to his congregation at Martyr's Memorial Church on the Sunday following the signature of the agreement, "that Thou wouldst deal with the Prime Minister of our country. We remember that the Apostle Paul handed over the enemies of truth to the Devil that they might learn not to blaspheme. In the name of Thy blessed self, Father, Son and Holy Ghost, we hand this woman, Margaret Thatcher, over to the Devil that she might learn not to blaspheme. . . . O God, in wrath take vengeance upon this wicked treacherous lying woman, take vengeance upon her, O Lord, and grant that we shall see a demonstration of Thy Power.")

The agreement fused the two most basic fears of Protestants—that they would somehow be outmaneuvered by the South and betrayed by the British—and convinced them that dark and perfidious deeds had been plotted behind their backs. They had been left out, the agreement presented to them as a *fait accompli*. To make matters worse, their adversaries, the SDLP, had been consulted at every level in the process by the Irish government, and had a veto over the final terms of the agreement itself.

Insecurity and the fears it breeds are, of course, permanent parts of the Protestant mentality. The Protestant colonizations of the seventeenth century were partial. At all times the new settlers lived in scattered enclaves and under precarious circumstances. Surrounded by a dispossessed and hostile native Catholic population, they were always vulnerable to attack. Initially the Protestants feared being overrun and massacred by the Catholic majority. Then came the fear of what would happen if the Act of Union of 1800 were ever repealed. Later it was the fear of Home Rule. And finally, ever since independence was achieved by the South, the Unionists have feared being abandoned by the British—or sold out by their own.

Protestant fears are ubiquitous. They encapsulate the entire Protestant experience in Ulster. Deeply rooted, pervasive, impervious to the passage of time, they seem almost genetically encoded, even necessary for the survival of the species. In moments of crisis, when the future threatens, Protestants resort to the strategies of the past. Ulster must "fight" to maintain its position in the Union, as it was prepared to do in 1912, and again in 1974. In each instance, the Protestants believe, only the threat of rebellion stayed Britain's hand. And thus in 1985, the Unionists raised once more the threat of rebellion—no matter that their constitutional position within the United Kingdom was guaranteed by formal international treaty.

From the Protestant perspective, the one element of the agreement that counted was the Intergovernmental Conference. The conference was viewed not as a small cooperative gesture but as a coalition government in embryo. In the Unionist view, the language in the agreement requiring "determined efforts to resolve differences" meant that Dublin would get its way fifty percent of the time. The conference was seen as a first step toward an all-Ireland state. Reconciliation was a code word for unification.

But Protestants reserved their most vituperative reactions for something that was not a part of the agreement—the secretariat's location in Belfast. This represented the greatest threat of all. The spectacle of Irish ministers coming to Belfast, the reality of Irish civil servants being permanently located there, struck the raw nerves of their most profound fears. The secretariat was the bridgehead, it penetrated the fortress, allowed the enemy to secure his foothold. "Dublin," the Democratic Unionist Party's Ivan Foster said, "not only [had] its foot in the door, the door was off the hinges."

They had been betrayed. Adding to their sense of betrayal was the fact that for once they had become slightly more secure in their own position. Mrs. Thatcher, after all, had stood firm during the hunger strikes; she had gone to war in the Falklands, at the far end of the Atlantic, eight thousand miles away, to maintain the right of eighteen hundred islanders to call themselves British and to protect British sovereignty in the face of Argentina's claim that the islands were part of its national territory; her "Out! Out! Out!" declaration had dealt a death blow to the New Ireland Forum.

Once again Ulster Protestants found themselves in near total isolation. The international community received the accord with acclaim, and the British political parties, in a rare display of unanimity, and being more than willing to have Britain's Ireland problem become Ireland's Ireland problem in some more obvious and visible way, gave it their unconditional imprimatur. The Unionists' cries that they had not been consulted reverberated in the dead air of the political wasteland they inhabited, their denunciations of the agreement, Mrs. Thatcher, the South—anything that came within range of their free-floating anger—obfuscating their cause for just complaint.

Forced to stand outside Hillsborough Castle to receive copies of the agreement, supplicants in the statelet they had once ruled with such hauteur, their sense of exclusion was complete. ("I stood outside Hillsborough," Harold McCusker told the House of Commons, "not waving a Union flag—I doubt if I will ever wave one again—not singing hymns, saying prayers or protesting but like a dog and asked the government to put in my hand the document that sold my birthright. They told me that they would give it to me as soon as possible. Having never consulted me, never sought my opinion or asked my advice, they told the rest of the world what was in store for me. . . . They could not even send out one of their servants to give it to me. At 2:45 P.M., fifteen minutes after the press conference had begun, I asked a policeman whether he would bring me the declaration that betrayed everything that I had stood for. A senior police officer went into Hillsborough Castle, asked for the document and brought it out to me.")

They saw themselves as the real victims of British misrule, deprived citizens in their own state. They were the ones whose birthright had been denied when their government was taken from them in 1972; they were the ones who had been brought to heel by Direct Rule; they were the ones who were being informed by dictatorial decree that the Act of Union of 1800—which, in their view, had conferred on Protestants an unalienable right to be British, ratifying a covenant made with the Crown, the symbol of continuity and perpetuity of order, rather than with the government of the day—had been abrogated. They were now conditional members of the United Kingdom, only part of the kingdom for as long as that was the wish of a majority—a far cry from Mrs. Thatcher's assurance in 1979 that

Northern Ireland was as British as Finchley (the constituency in North London that Mrs. Thatcher represents in Parliament). The goal of a united Ireland was now within grasp of the IRA. Violence pays.

The agreement impugned the one historical exigency of Protestantism—to uphold the settlement of 1689, to defend Protestant civil and religious liberty. It violated their mythic conception of self, their idealized experience of how they had emerged as a community, of how the Glorious Revolution had led to liberation from spiritual tyranny, the birth of the individual, the triumph of light over darkness, and, as James McEvoy writes, "the emergence of an ordered world of stable and finite realities—nation, crown, Parliament and property rights; in short, the final establishment of justice, under the active intervention of a favorable deity." Since "justice and the good-ordering of society, attunement to the wholeness of reality," brought with them peace and progress, industry and prosperity, "the truly ordering forces, which were possessed and released in virtue of the primordial act of ordering itself, could not operate for those who remained outside the framework of such attunement." Those people must remain in darkness, "in servitude to other forces, and suffer the consequence of ill-attunement to reality: poverty and backwardness." Thus basic to the Protestant interpretation of self was "the belief that the Protestant version of Christianity was inherently superior, both in itself and in the attitudes and actions to which it gave rise, to the Catholic Church,"[3] that they were to rule and not be ruled.

In their anger and terror, they invited substantiation of the truths of their own myths, desperately searching for the ritualistic acts that would recapture the primordial experience of order that had initiated their history. They were seeking the Protestant equivalent of the Republicans' hunger strikes, a form of protest so fused with the elements of the past, so evocative of their inner realities, that it would free them from the strictures of their predicament and provide them with a way out. Action had its parallels in the past: mass demonstrations in Belfast and the burning of Mrs. Thatcher in effigy to evoke the mass demonstrations of 1912 against Home Rule and the burning in effigy of Herbert Asquith; the Days of Action, bringing the province's industry and commerce to a standstill, to evoke the Ulster Workers' Council strike in 1974, which had brought down the power-sharing executive and the Sunningdale Agreement; the five hundred thousand signatures on a petition to the Queen calling for a suspension of the Agreement to evoke the Ulster Covenant in 1912.

"Ulster Says No" became the catchcry to rally the faithful. "Iron Lady be warned," their banners cried, "your iron will melt from the heat of Ulster." They would never accept the agreement. They would withdraw from Westminster, from local councils, from regional bodies. They would make Northern Ireland ungovernable. They would show that Northern Ireland could not be governed without the consent of the majority, and if their withdrawal from government meant that they ceded ground to the Protestant paramilitaries, the fault would not be theirs; responsibility for the sectarian violence that might result would lie with the two governments. The two main Unionist parties—the Official Unionist Party and the Democratic Unionist Party—closed ranks, the divisions between them put aside. Once again "the myth of Unionist siege [would have] its greatest social utility as an expression of a primary solidarity of purpose within a community principally defined by a determination to resist."[4] Their sheer determination not to accept the agreement under any circumstances or to engage in talks with nationalists unless the agreement was suspended would, they believed, ultimately prevail. They resigned their seats in the Westminster Parliament, calling the special elections held to fill them a referendum on the agreement. However, they lost one seat to the SDLP, and the total "no" vote fell under the five hundred thousand mandate they had sought. But they persisted. They had a simple objective, no grand design. In their fury they did not care whether their actions weakened their union with Great Britain. They were driven by their age-old fears: any association with the South would lead to the ineluctable absorption of the Protestant people of Ulster into an all-Ireland Catholic state. But the world had changed. The rituals that had once imparted an inner reality were now merely chimeric. They had lost their force.

4 LEGACY

We are closed in, and the key is turned
On our uncertainty. . . .

William Butler Yeats
"Meditations in Time of Civil War"

17   At first, Sinn Fein was non-plussed by the Anglo-Irish Agreement. The intensity of the loyalists' reaction to the agreement, the pure vitriol of their anger, and the uncompromising absoluteness of their rejection of it coupled with widespread nationalist support for it, caught Sinn Fein off guard, and its responses were uncharacteristically hesitant, reflecting the peculiar situation it found itself in. On the one hand, Sinn Fein said that the agreement was an "insult" which made "minimal concessions to the Irish government," offering only "cosmetic internal reform and a powerless consultative role" in return for "security collaboration." The agreement "was designed to defeat and isolate republicanism." Loyalist reaction was "deliberately provoked by Dublin and the SDLP in order to exaggerate the substance of the Treaty." The whole thing was a ploy that would allow the British government to "escape international criticism over its colonial occupation of the six counties" by being able to point to the Dublin government's involvement. On the other hand, Sinn Fein said that the agreement was "a compliment to Sinn Fein" since "never before had the Dublin and London governments been forced to spend so much time deliberating on how best to destroy Republicanism." Since the hunger strikes, it asserted, "Dublin and [its] Northern allies, the SDLP, had been struggling to claim back the high-ground of Irish nationalism." Whatever benefits the nationalist community derived from the agreement, partial and insufficient though they would be, were due directly to the sacrifices of Republicans, and were a vindication of the armed struggle. SDLP claims that Sinn Fein referred to the agreement as a "sell-out" were false. No Sinn Fein statement "had ever referred to the agreement as a sell-out"; the SDLP's attempts to sell this as the Republican position were designed to allow them "to have a monopoly or exclusive claims on whatever benefits [might] flow from the deal."

In the heady days following the hunger strikes there had been no hesitancy, no caveats. Nothing, it appeared, could go wrong. "Will anyone here object if, with a ballot box in one hand and an Armalite in the other, we take power in Ireland?" asked Danny Morrison to

thunderous applause at the Provisional Sinn Fein Ard Fheis in November 1981. Many in both parts of Ireland would indeed object,
but for a period many thought it at least possible.

The IRA settled in for the long haul; war-wariness in Britain itself,
it believed, would precipitate a collapse of the political will there to
pursue an indefinite and ultimately fruitless fight. It renewed its campaign, suspended since the mid-1970s, on the British mainland. In
July 1982, an explosion in Hyde Park killed eight soldiers; in December 1983, days before Christmas, a bomb went off in Harrod's, killing
five people; and in October 1984, the IRA made an attempt to kill
Mrs. Thatcher herself.

The decision to target Mrs. Thatcher had been made during the
hunger strikes. It was conceived as a revenge killing, since Republicans held her personally responsible for the deaths of the hunger
strikers. For three and a half years the IRA stalked her, tracking her
movements, observing her security arrangements, waiting for the
one opportunity to strike, finally settling on the Conservative Party
Conference in Brighton. The bomb, which IRA operatives had
placed, weeks before the Conference took place, behind the hardboard
back panel in a bathroom of a sixth-floor room of the hotel in which
Mrs. Thatcher was staying, failed to kill her, but it did kill five people,
including an M.P. and the wife of the government whip, and injured
thirty others, some permanently. "Today we were unlucky," the IRA
said in its statement claiming responsibility for the bombing, "but
remember, we have only to be lucky once. You [Mrs. Thatcher] will
have to be lucky always." Armed struggle would become armed
propaganda; violence itself, when possible, a backdrop to the manner
in which it was represented. "The tactic of armed struggle is of
primary importance," wrote an increasingly visible Gerry Adams,
"because it provides a vital cutting edge. Without it the issue of Ireland
would not even be an issue."[1]

The hunger strike provided the catalyst for change; the decision
to contest Northern Ireland elections was hastened by the success of
Bobby Sands and Owen Carron in the Westminster by-election in
1981. The Northern figures in the movement, led by Gerry Adams,
who had come to prominence during the hunger strikes, took control.
In 1982, Sinn Fein abandoned the federalist Eire Nua (New Ireland)
policy in favor of a policy calling for a unitary all-Ireland state; in
1983 it elected Gerry Adams president; in 1985 Sinn Fein candidates

elected to local councils took their seats; and in 1986 Sinn Fein dropped its abstentionist stand in the Dublin parliament.[2]

(The case for abandoning abstentionism was made by the H-block prisoners in the middle of the hunger strikes. In the depth of their anguish, the prospects for a settlement long gone, and facing nothing but a future of death and more death, the prisoners still held to the revolutionary dream that there, within the eight-by-ten-foot spaces of their cells, they were creating the future. Abstraction made the present bearable. There was a plan, a grand strategy. They, the prisoners, had it all figured out. Their deaths were just a passing thing, the fate of front-line soldiers, part of the larger design. They would not be distracted by casualties. There were larger issues to be thrashed out, plans to be implemented, philosophies to be redefined.

"We are talking of exploiting our situation to the fullest for maximum gain on the ground, especially in the Free State," McFarlane had written Adams in July 1981. "The climate is ripe to make significant progress and establish a firm base down there which is a necessity for future development and success in the final analysis. To allow opportunities to slip by would be a grave mistake. We are examining the possibility of contesting elections and actually making full use of seats gained—i.e. participating in the Dail. Such an idea presents problems within the Movement. How great would the opposition be and what would be the consequences of pursuing a course which did not enjoy a sizable degree of support? There are obvious dangers in promoting ideas that could and possibly would be viewed as departures from policy. . . . Anyway, we are thinking along these lines at present.")

Adams talked of developing the movement's "potential," of having "to move into the mainstream of political relevancy," of "break[ing] down self-isolation," and of cracking "the compartmentalized attitude" many Republicans had "whereby they pursued Republican 'politics' in isolation from their involvement in other activities." Sinn Fein dressed itself up in a new consciousness, becoming a platform for all kinds of militancies. One could hardly be against British oppression and not against oppression between the sexes; one could hardly demand the right to self-determination and ignore the demands of the Palestinians or South Africa's blacks. As Sinn Fein moved out of the ghetto, it found itself increasingly becoming a forum for elite special-interest groups who wanted to include their causes on the revolutionary agenda. No perceived injustice would be overlooked. With no immediate prospect that a united Ireland would come into being, political liberation movements around the world became surrogate revolutions.

The Palestinians were "comrades in struggle." The withdrawal of the PLO forces from Beirut was "reminiscent of the flight of the Wild Geese after the Siege of Limerick." Republicans were "the real Palestinians of Western Europe." Sinn Fein supported the Polish people in their struggle. Sinn Fein expressed solidarity with its "black brothers and sisters in Africa"; it stood "shoulder to shoulder with [the ANC] in their right to develop their struggle by whatever methods are forced on them"; it supported the Basques, the Salvadorans, the Nicaraguans, the Chileans, and "all men and women denied freedom." Their successes were Sinn Fein's successes; their victories were a victory for Republicanism.

The Republican struggle became for Republicans part of a wider struggle, part of the larger cultural dispossession where oppressed people struggled to regain what was theirs and to assert their individual and collective freedoms. Republicans identified with freedom fighters, but not terrorists. They supported "legitimate struggles for national liberation and self-determination throughout the world," but condemned unequivocally "such groups as the Red Army Faction, Direct Action and the Red Brigades." The left wing of the Labour Party in Britain made friendly overtures. Sometimes the graves in Bellaghy and Tamlaghtduff appeared to be remote, and Francis Hughes, the soldier, would have had trouble knowing what all the resolutions passed at Sinn Fein's Ard Fheiseanna had to do with freeing Ireland.

The push in new directions came up against new, unexplored constraints, exposed contradictions, ultimately entrapping the movement in a dilemma of its own making, for once having made the leap into the constitutional process of elections, it cannot leap back out. Once having submitted itself to the test of the ballot box, it cannot unsubmit itself when elections do not go its way, without losing its credibility and its claim to legitimacy. Once having held up its electoral success as a measure of the support it enjoyed in the Catholic community, it must hold up its lack of support to the same yardstick. Once having sought to broaden its base, it cannot indefinitely attribute its failure to do so to having nothing to do with the armed struggle. The ongoing commitment to participation in the electoral process in the

South is a far cry from intervention in elections in extraordinary circumstances where one or two Sinn Fein seats might make a difference in a hung parliament—the rationale for the intervention during the hunger strikes.

Sinn Fein has not quite figured out where it is going, even if its electoral tactics are successful; it has no idea where it is going if its tactics are unsuccessful. Success at the ballot box justifies Sinn Fein strategy; failure ultimately will bring into question the legitimacy not merely of the movement itself but of the armed struggle it advocates. The hunger strikes, once undertaken, could not be abandoned—the options open to the hunger strikers made the cost of stopping prohibitive. Likewise, participation in constitutional politics, once undertaken, cannot be abandoned either, for again, the cost of doing so would appear to be too great. Failure at the ballot box, however, especially in the South, may involve a cost that is just as great.

Sinn Fein struggled to find a new voice in the late 1980s, a proper balance between its new-found pragmatism and its old-time righteousness that would reconcile its contradictory impulses—to adopt the language of the democratic process and the sanction of the ballot box and to assert simultaneously that no argument, no countervailing constitutionalism, could derogate the IRA's absolute right to conduct the armed struggle—that were the hallmarks of the new strategy. The people were right—but only up to a point; their wishes were paramount, but only when they had the right wishes. They did not have the right to be wrong on the national question. Sinn Fein wanted "a sovereign, independent, united Ireland." However, Gerry Adams declaimed, "partitionists, North and South," had manipulated the people to the point where they could count on "the passive acquiescence of a majority" to maintain their position. In short, the people were not to be trusted. They were either dupes, complacent, unthinking, or unconcerned. There was "no such thing as constitutional nationalism" if it countenanced the maintenance "of a six-county colony." The Dublin government was "a partitionist institution," not "the head of a sovereign nation as envisaged in the 1916 Proclamation." The Dublin government had no right or authority to negotiate "any treaty about any issue with the British government while that government claims jurisdiction over any part of Irish national territory"; it had no right to speak on behalf of Republicans. People in the South did not understand abstentionism—"ninety-five percent of them accepted Leinster House as being their government." They were wrong, of course, but Sinn Fein "had a duty to win them over to [its] view" at "their level of understanding." The struggle could not be built "merely on the Republican perception of things." Sinn Fein could "only proceed from the objective reality of the peoples' consciousness."

However, no consideration of the objective reality of the "peoples' consciousness" entered the picture where the armed struggle was concerned. Here, the IRA had "the right to do what is forced on them"; its legitimacy predated and superseded the paraphernalia of constitutionalism; it stemmed from "organized, popular resistance to British rule in Ireland," which "has been a fact of history since Britain first encroached on Irish sovereignty 800 years ago." All deaths and all the bloodshed are the fault of the British. The IRA is right. The Republican position "is clear and would never change. The war against Britain" will "continue until freedom is achieved."

At the core of the new strategy ("armed struggle in the six counties in pursuance of British withdrawal and political struggle throughout the whole 32 counties in pursuance of the Republic, breaking out of isolation and becoming politically relevant, [blending] the national struggle with contemporary reality as perceived by the majority of people in the 26 counties" is how *An Phoblacht* articulates it) is a contradiction. The greater the commitment to armed struggle in the North, the less the appeal of Sinn Fein to voters in the South who are being asked to sanction "bad" violence. The poorer the performance of Sinn Fein in the South, the more it exposes the IRA's lack of legitimacy. The drive for success at the ballot box will create pressures to subordinate the armed struggle to political pragmatism; lack of success will simply reflect the real lack of support for the IRA's campaign of violence. "Without politics you may be able to bomb and shoot a British connection out of existence but you will not bring anything into existence," writes Gerry Adams.[3] But what if the violence makes the politics impossible? Between November 1987 and the end of 1988, twenty-two of the people killed by the IRA—one-quarter of the number it killed during this period—were "mistaken" victims, often members of the Catholic community. Indeed, the recurring public revulsion at these killings led the IRA to disband its West Fermanagh unit in January 1989. At the Sinn Fein Ard Fheis later that month, Gerry Adams gently rebuked the IRA: "At times the fate of this struggle is in your [the IRA's] hands. You have to be careful and careful again. These are the feelings of the broad mass of the Republican people, feelings which are shared by Republican activists and which now call for more circumspection than ever before. The morale of your comrades in jail, your own morale and [that] of your comrades in the field can be raised or dashed by your actions. You can advance or retard this struggle."

In the end, Sinn Fein's identity is inseparable from its relationship with the IRA. Without that relationship it is little more than a left-leaning, essentially working-class party with a limited constituency and of limited consequence. With that relationship it exerts an influence on events out of all proportion to popular support for its policies. The movement's power comes out of the barrel of a gun.

For some, of course, any deviation from Republican orthodoxy was heresy. A number of senior Republicans, including Ivor Bell, the OC of the Northern Command, who took issue with the direction in which Adams was taking the movement, were "retired," and on the question of abstentionism the movement split—as it had on the issue in 1969. Led by former President Ruairi O'Bradaigh, a number of the hardline traditionalists walked out of the 1986 Ard Chomhairle and joined Republican Sinn Fein, which waits for the policies of the present to collapse, for disaffection within the IRA to emerge with what Republican Sinn Fein sees as the inevitable subordination of physical force to politics. The pure will not be found wanting.

18   Galbally, County Tyrone, is tiny. On one side of the road there is a Catholic Church with a graveyard beside it, a credit union office, and a few houses. Across the road there is a grocery shop and a large bar, and a short distance outside the village a small housing estate and a primary school. Here, on a small farm where the land is good only for grazing cattle and raising a few pigs, the hunger striker Martin Hurson grew up, and here, in the small graveyard adjoining the Parish Church, he was laid to rest.

"Martin Hurson," said Sean Lynch, a former chairman of the Longford County Council, in his eulogy to the dead hunger striker, "calls like a voice from heaven, filling young hearts with courage and determination, lighting young minds with the deathless glow of unselfish patriotism and keeping the flag of the Republic of Ireland free from stain of dishonor, cowardice, brutality or shame, so that one day all true patriots will rally to it again and bear it proudly to victory, unity and peace."

Listening that day, thirteen-year-old Sean Donnelly and fifteen-year-old Declan Arthurs, neighbors of the Hurson family, heard the call. Six years later, just two months short of the sixth anniversary of Hurson's death, they too were laid to rest in the same small graveyard, and they too became, no doubt, voices from heaven for other young men.

They died in Loughgall, a village no bigger than Galbally, in County Armagh, on 8 May 1987 when they and six other IRA volunteers—twenty-four-year-old Tom Gormley, twenty-five-year-old Eugene Kelly, thirty-year-old Paddy Kelly, twenty-six-year-old Padraig McKearney, twenty-nine-year-old Gerard O'Callaghan, and thirty-one-year-old Jim Lynagh—were gunned down by the RUC and British army undercover security personnel, who were lying in wait for them, as they launched what was supposed to be a surprise attack on the local RUC police station.

It was a devastating setback for the IRA, practically decimating the East Tyrone brigade to which the eight had belonged, the largest number of casualties it had suffered since the Anglo-Irish war of 1920, and, given the movement's new "lean" look and its reliance on a small number of active service units, an incapacitating dilution of its manpower and seasoned leadership. The British government pronounced itself well satisfied; the operation proved that the war against terrorism was being won. There was also an element of benign triumphalism in official circles, not too subtle hints that, for once, the IRA had received some of its own medicine, that the security forces were, in a sense, only evening the score. (The *Times* set the tone: "Occasions on which the security forces strike back and seem to do so," its editorial declared, "help boost the confidence which must have been eroded in many law abiding minds in Northern Ireland.")

Nationalists were wary. At first the Dublin government put the blame for the deaths on the IRA leadership, whom they accused of putting "young lives at risk" (the IRA rather ruefully pointed out that a number of its more seasoned veterans had died in the incident), but some days later, as more details of the killings emerged and it became clear that the security forces had ample foreknowledge of the IRA's operation, old ambivalences began to assert themselves, and Dublin drew back, voicing its reservations.

Father Faul was the first to articulate what many Catholics, North and South, were feeling. "If the RUC," he said, "had prior information they should have prevented the gun battle. They should have arrested the people. It smacks of revenge and retaliation." Moreover— and he stated what was for many a truth they could not acknowledge—"as much as you condemn the Provisional IRA, the sight of an English soldier shooting an Irishman in Ireland produces a gut reaction."

The gut reaction began to make itself felt, though it expressed itself in the usual ambiguous way. For though it was clear that the IRA had planned to blow up the police station and to kill whomever was in it, that they had, in fact, come to Loughgall with murder on their minds, it was also clear that the decision to kill them had been made prior to the stake-out itself.

As always, constitutional nationalists put the matter in the context of their own interests: their fears that Loughgall would redound to the advantage of the IRA, that it would somehow undermine the Anglo-Irish Agreement, show that the agreement was a lot less than it had been hyped up to be, that it had not made a difference. (In the first four months of 1987, forty-seven persons had died violently, fifteen of them at the hands of the IRA in the five weeks prior to Loughgall.) Leading members of the SDLP, disquieted that the shootings had taken place on the eve of a British general election in which its main opposition would once again be Sinn Fein and the results taken as a barometer of the success of the agreement, called for a public inquiry into the killings.

Nationalist condemnation of the IRA's intentions quickly became tempered with a largely unarticulated anger at the British government for what appeared to be a cold-blooded decision simply to get the IRA operatives, and with the IRA for once again forcing constitutional nationalism to face the demons of its own contradictions. And in the subconscious there were the old beliefs: that the British had no regard for Irish lives, that their abhorrence of the IRA masked a larger disdain for the Irish at large, that the continuous vilification of the IRA as terrorists and murderers and evil men and somehow subhuman sanctioned a shoot-to-kill policy; in short, that Irish lives were cheap and good riddance. For many it seemed that the British were treating the IRA as an armed enemy to be ambushed and shot on sight rather than as a criminal organization whose members would be arrested, charged, tried, and convicted. Were the police and army abrogating to themselves the right to act as judge, jury, and executioner? Was the British government acceding to the IRA's view that what was happening in the North was war? These questions went unanswered, as they could not be addressed in the sanitized communiqués that invariably followed meetings of the Intergovernmental Conference.

It was, of course, the issue of war that raised the most discomfort. For if the British government by its actions began to treat the IRA as an army, and to behave as though it were in a war situation, it would vindicate the IRA's unswerving contention—a contention for which the ten hunger strikers had given their lives—that Northern Ireland was a war situation in which the legitimate army of the Irish Republic was engaged in an armed conflict with the army of the United Kingdom. In fact, the government's actions would validate the Republican movement's interpretation of the conflict and once again confer on the IRA the legitimacy it had fought so tenaciously to achieve. "We cannot treat persons convicted of criminal offenses as prisoners of war," Margaret Thatcher coldly informed Cardinal O'Fiaich in May 1981, when O'Fiaich pleaded with her following Sands's death to do something to end the prison crisis; the question now was whether the British government was shooting those not convicted of criminal offenses as soldiers of war.

For constitutional nationalists, North and South, anything that suggested that the conflict was, in fact, a war undermined yet again their ever-so-careful distinction between "good" violence and "bad" violence. Actions of the British government which implied that it acceded to the IRA's view of the conflict made it increasingly difficult to maintain that the IRA violence was bad. In the circumstances of what could be construed as a shoot-to-kill policy, the violence of the British government became the "bad" violence; the insinuations, widely believed, that the security forces had not just killed the IRA men in a shoot-out but had mercilessly massacred them with firepower ferociously excessive for the occasion invoked folk memories of the Black and Tan war, stirred in the dim recesses of many minds stories of reprisal killings in the old days, once again collapsing time, compressing the historical moment, impelling comparisons with the past. The more British violence could be seen as "bad," the more difficult it became to see the IRA's violence as bad; the gut reaction was in danger of becoming the prevailing reaction.

The Republican mythology apparatus enfolded events, providing the context of a larger struggle in which to place the killings, seizing and holding the moral high ground, finding no contradiction whatsoever in calling the ambush murder even though the foiled operation was itself precisely ambush with murder in mind.

There was, of course, the inevitable historical analogue that would give Loughgall its rightful place in the hierarchy of atrocities committed against Republicans: Clonmult in County Cork, 20 February 1920. On that occasion, Black and Tan auxiliaries, acting in line with what the Republican writing of history had deemed to be an officially sanctioned shoot-to-kill policy, opened fire on a party of fifteen IRA volunteers after they had surrendered following an armed encounter. "The Auxiliaries," Republicans were reminded in *An Phoblacht/Republican News*, "fell on them 'like wild beasts,' killing twelve and tearing from the dead and wounded watches, pens, religious medals, shouting and cursing the whole time." The Clonmult ambush was a setback for the IRA in Cork, but the following month it rebounded: "far from being defeated [it] demonstrated that [the IRA] could carry out devastating attacks on the British occupation forces."

There was an absolute order to history and absolute order demanded absolute acts. The volunteers, *An Phoblacht/Republican News* said, had gone to Loughgall "with courage and skill and above all with comradeship and a firm belief in the correctness of their action. They went as Republican soldiers who had carefully planned and hoped to successfully inflict a major blow against the British war machine." They "were greatly outnumbered and outarmed by an occupying army with a vast array of military equipment and surveillance technology at its disposal." They could have been arrested "but the SAS planned to take no prisoners and they took none." They had been murdered—"murder planned at the very highest level of the British government's administration." Loughgall happened "because the British needed revenge," because the British "had been defeated and demoralized by the IRA." "The young men who were there [at Loughgall] with guns in their hands had every right and every justification to be there. They were there for the Irish people. The people who laid in wait, the people who murdered them, they were the terrorists. . . . Margaret Thatcher and Tom King and all the other rich and powerful people would be sorry in their time."

Once more the eulogists composed their eulogies. What happened at Loughgall "would forever be remembered by those thousands and thousands of Irish people shocked and angered at the wanton murders of nine [sic] young Irishmen by the soldiers of a foreign army holding no legal or moral right to bear arms on Irish soil." The Loughgall martyrs would "never die"; they would "forever be remembered." They were "legends." The legends "would never die." They were "heroes, freedom fighters, peace soldiers." They had "sacrificed their lives," and out of the sacrifice would come "a greater number of IRA recruits." They were historical people.

In the small villages of Armagh and Tyrone they understood. The talk from Dublin that the IRA leadership was "trapping people into violence" could have been the propaganda of a foreign government, the talk from London of taking the fight to the terrorists nothing more than the triumphalist importunings of the old enemy. In Dungannon, black flags fluttered in every window, thousands lined the funeral routes: country people, respectable people who believed that the volunteers—the sons of their neighbors, hard-working decent members of their communities, husbands and fathers—had been needlessly shot in a show of premeditated vengeance. The priest presiding over the requiem mass for the funeral of Paddy Kelly, the commander of the East Tyrone Brigade (the brigade was reputedly responsible for killing sixty UDR members, fifty RUC personnel, and at least five civilians since it began operations in 1971), told the mourners packed into St. Patrick's Cathedral in Dungannon that Kelly was "an upright and truthful man who loved his family, his Irish culture and his country." ("That sermon," Ken Maginnis, Official Unionist M.P. for Fermanagh–South Tyrone, told me, "did more harm than the eleven people who were killed at Enniskillen[1] to the Unionist understanding of what Irish Nationalism and the Catholic community was really about." The Catholic Church seemed to be holding up to emulate "a man who was out to commit cruel cold murder.") To Kelly's wife, Kathleen, who was expecting their fourth child when he died, he was a dedicated soldier. "He was a brilliant fighter and he was cool," was Padraig McKearney's nine-year-old niece's appraisal of her uncle. McKearney was buried thirteen years to the day that his brother Sean was killed on active service in 1974; another brother, Tommy, had been in the H-blocks for eleven years. Tom Gormley, Eugene Kelly, Sean Donnelly, and Declan Arthurs had come to age when Martin Hurson died. Hurson was the hero to whom they looked, the one who had set the example, provided the

inspiration. Theirs was a closed world with an unchangeable, un-
ambivalent internal code of its own, of people shaped since childhood
by the same common experiences and struggle, who maintained a
system of mutual support and an assiduous sense of ideological and
personal commitment to each other. It was a world in which the
Anglo-Irish Agreement played no part, in which the promise of two
governments to consult and the right of the Irish government to put
forward views and proposals were abstractions, irrelevancies, in
which the Irish government was still the Free State government, a
partition government that collaborated with the British to destroy
Republicanism. In Galbally, Aughnaskea, Cappagh, and Moy they
knew their responsibilities to the dead.

The Anglo-Irish Agreement achieved its immediate goal:
stemming the flow of nationalist support for Sinn Fein. The Westminster special by-elections in January 1986, called when the Unionists resigned their seats and thus forcing by-elections that they hoped
would reveal the depth of Protestant opposition to the agreement,
showed a 35 percent swing away from Sinn Fein in the constituencies
in which it went head-to-head against the SDLP. In three elections
in the North since then—local elections in 1985, a general election in
1987, and local elections again in 1989—Sinn Fein's share of the vote
has fluctuated between 11.3 percent and 11.8 percent. In a fourth
election—the Euro elections of 1989—Sinn Fein's share fell from its
1984 level of 13.3 percent to 9.2 percent of the vote, a drop of almost
one-third. In the short run, at least, it is clear that Sinn Fein will
remain the voice of the minority. In the South the omens are not
promising. Sinn Fein's forays into the Republic's general elections in
1987 and again in 1989 were disastrous. It received 1.9 percent of the
vote in 1987, and its share fell to 1.2 percent in 1989, a drop of 47
percent in two years. Its 1989 Euro vote in the South, 5.2 percent of
the vote, offered some solace but not much. Militant Republicanism,
Brits out, the Armalite and the ballot box, had no electoral constituency in the Republic, where they could not be put in the immediate
context of martyrdom or persecution. (The Irish public makes a distinction between the actions taken by the authorities in the South
against the IRA and actions taken by the British government against
the IRA in the North. Public opinion surveys in the South consistently
show that more people are in favor of the Irish government taking a

tougher stand toward the IRA than are in favor of the British government doing so.)

In time, when it became clear that the Protestant backlash against the agreement had slowed the agenda of reform, especially in the administration of justice and the judiciary, Sinn Fein became more emboldened in its criticisms of the agreement; by November 1987, Adams was disparaging it as "a mediocre agreement" that was "not worth the loyalist backlash it had provoked," condemning it out of hand as "part of the nationalist nightmare."

However, the problem wasn't so much the lack of progress on issues that nationalists regarded as germane to the agreement's success that contributed to the erosion of their confidence in its efficacy, as its irrelevance to their everyday lives, defined as they were by their profound sense of grievance and their propensity to perceive every reality in terms of the metaphysics of conflict. The sense of larger grievance, the embedded psychic sense of being wronged, could not be alleviated when it was reinforced on a continuing basis by the sense of everyday grievance generated by the actions of the state.

There is always an issue, one issue that becomes at one point in time the symbolic lightning rod for all grievances, that rekindles the anguish that compels the Catholic community to see itself as the perpetual victim of injustice. The Republican movement taps this psychic nerve, translates every government response to militant Republicanism into the language of victimhood that the larger Catholic community speaks so fluently. Internment in the early 1970s, interrogation techniques in the mid-1970s, prison conditions in the late 1970s, the hard-line stand during the hunger strikes in the early 1980s, the use of supergrasses (paid informants) in the mid-1980s, the policing of Republican funerals, allegations of shoot-to-kill policies, the suppression of the Stalker/Sampson Report into these allegations, the verdict of the Court of Appeals in the case of the Birmingham Six, the steps to make the Prevention of Terrorism Act permanent, the fatal shooting of three unarmed IRA members in Gibraltar in the later 1980s[2]—each in its time was seen as an action aimed specifically at Catholics rather than at "known Republicans"; each became a magnet for protest drawing to it thousands who found a parallel experience of perceived oppression in their own lives. Each stoked the dying embers of grievance, each raised anew old questions of good and bad violence, each reinforced the deepest beliefs of Catholics that they would always be wronged, that nothing would ever change, making them the unwilling accomplices in the propaganda of the IRA.

19   If the hunger strikes established the upper bound of support for the Republican movement, Enniskillen established the lower bound; if the hunger strikes ensured that the IRA would not prevail, Enniskillen ensured that it would not be defeated; if the bombing of the Remembrance Day Parade at Enniskillen would not undermine the IRA and dry up support for it in the Catholic community, nothing would.

Enniskillen is the largest town in Fermanagh. A town of ten thousand people, almost equally divided between Catholics and Protestants, nestled between lower and upper Lough Erne in a spectacular natural setting, it had become something of a haven for Protestant families in the area with security force connections, and many had moved there from outlying farm areas prone to IRA attack.

There, on 8 November 1987, Remembrance Day, the day on which people all over the United Kingdom gather at the cenotaphs in their towns and villages to remember those who died in two world wars, a bomb packed with about thirty pounds of explosives left inside the community center adjacent to the war memorial blew a gable wall out on top of the crowd that had come to watch the services, killing eleven people—all of them civilians and Protestant—and injuring sixty-three others, many of them seriously.

After a thirty-hour silence the IRA accepted responsibility for the bombing and expressed regret for it. "The bomb," it said, had been "aimed at catching Crown Forces security force personnel on patrol in connection with the Remembrance Day service but not during it." The bomb "blew up without being triggered by [the IRA's] radio signal."

The reaction was immediate, the condemnation without qualification. A groundswell of outrage gathered across the land, gathering force with each new voice of denunciation, sweeping all before it in its censorious folds, becoming an avalanche of damnation. Political and religious leaders vied with each other for adjectives that would best describe their abhorrence of the deed. It was "a blot on mankind" (Margaret Thatcher), "an atrocity against ordinary people" (Labour

Party leader Neil Kinnock), "an unspeakable act" (Irish Prime Minister Charles Haughey), "a brutal massacre so inhuman it could only be described as satanic" (Presbyterian Moderator Reverend William Fleming), "a heinous crime" (Cardinal Tomas O'Fiaich), "nothing short of barbarous murder" (Fine Gael leader Alan Dukes), "an act of savagery" (SDLP leader John Hume), "a blasphemy" (Archbishop Runice of Westminster). Even *Tass,* heretofore sympathetic to the IRA, weighed in, calling it "a barbaric act."

There were worse atrocities during the eighteen years of the conflict, but none, perhaps, that drew the level of condemnation that Enniskillen did. The killing of members of the security forces or tit-for-tat sectarian assassinations, abominable as they are, at least fit into the established ground rules of the conflict. The fact that the bombing was incomprehensible, so obviously sectarian, so willfully an act of random murder aimed at the defenseless and vulnerable, so blatantly a case of Protestants being killed simply because they were Protestants, threatened to disrupt the delicate social mechanisms the two communities employ to regulate and control their relationships. Enniskillen broke the ground rules; acceptable violence had degenerated into unacceptable violence. The bad violence was unmistakably bad; ambivalence, for once, it appeared, could unequivocally resolve itself with moral certainty.

Remembrance Day commemorated the most sacred of Protestant Ulster's memories: the thousands who had laid down their lives at the Somme during World War I. To attack people gathered to honor the memory of their dead was seen as obscene, something that violated the most fundamental human rites: remembering the dead, grieving for the lives given on behalf of the community. "They [the IRA] picked the most solemn day in the calendar," said the *Belfast Telegraph;* their victims were "ordinary decent civilians paying tribute to those who died in the cause of freedom. A greater contrast between those who went to their deaths on the battlefields of France and those who crept into a community center to plant a bomb cannot be imagined." It was an act that appeared to be aimed at not just Protestants in Enniskillen but at Protestants collectively. The intent, if one could be discerned, was to kill not just Protestants but the concept of a Protestant identity.

Constitutional nationalism turned on the IRA, excoriating its adherents, sensing that here at last was an opportunity to isolate it from the community supporting it, to brand it as irrevocably bad. The

Irish News—the largest selling province-wide middle-of-the-road Catholic newspaper—denounced the IRA in a series of scathing editorials. The bombing "was a criminal act of carnage," "the biggest mistake ever by the IRA." They had "surely, finally put themselves beyond the pale." They were "not fit to have any role in deciding [the minority's] future. Tawdry and misguided romantic images of freedom fighters espousing a justifiable cause deserve contempt and ridicule. There [was] nothing romantic about the placement of no-warning bombs, the firing of bullets which strike victims from close range or the destruction of decency and fairmindedness through the use of malice-laden rhetoric. There [was] no distinction between the killing of a young British soldier or member of the RUC and the blowing up of pensioners in their seventies." The Catholic community had to "decide in all conscience whether they can support in even the most tenuous manner the activities of the IRA in its so called armed struggle" and the morality "of giving public support to the political parties that support the IRA."

Catholic bishops weighed in with their strongest condemnation of violence. "After nearly twenty years of violence in the North the language of condemnation has become worn and emotions have even dulled by too long exposure to atrocity and tragedy," they said in a statement read at every mass throughout Ireland. "Yet recent events have evoked among our people a new sense of revulsion and shame at the depth to which our country is being dragged." "There is," it went on, "no room for ambivalence. In the face of the present campaigns of Republican violence the choice of all Catholics is clear. It is a choice between good and evil. It is," they warned, "sinful to join organizations committed to violence or to remain in them. It [is] sinful to support such organizations or to call on others to support them." People who provide safe houses or who store weapons "share in the awful crime of murder. People must choose. There is no longer any room for romantic illusion. There is no excuse for thinking that the present violence in Ireland can be morally justified."

In the South whole communities outdid each other in their eagerness to distance themselves from the horror, to disown the perpetrators, to separate themselves from those who committed the act and presumed to speak in their name. In Dublin, 4,000 people attended a memorial service for the victims in St. Patrick's Cathedral—the largest crowd ever to attend a service there—and the country came to a complete stop on 15 November. Everything—traffic, radio, television, work, play—came to a halt for one minute; 45,000 people trekked into the Mansion House in Dublin to sign a book of condolences; and Mrs. Carmencita Hederman, Lord Mayor of Dublin, went to Enniskillen and broke down and wept on behalf of her city for Enniskillen's dead.

And out of the shame and the guilt and the horror sprang hope. Enniskillen would be a watershed; out of the atrocity would emerge a togetherness, a recognition in both communities in the North of the need to find a political solution to their problems, to reach some kind of rapprochement between North and South. "There are distinct signs that Enniskillen has changed the political climate in a way that nothing else could have done," observed the *Belfast Telegraph*. Prominent church leaders spoke to ecumenical congregations North and South: Enniskillen "could be a turning point in the history of Northern Ireland"; "a watershed for the people of the North, highlighting more than any other incident the obscenity of what was happening."

"The whole of Enniskillen has turned into a war monument," playwright Frank McGuinness, author of the celebrated play *Observe the Sons of Ulster Marching towards the Somme,* wrote in the *Irish Times*. "For the sins of the fathers revenge has been taken against the children of Enniskillen. From the day of this bombing they will date their lives. That is the legacy bestowed upon them. They in turn will bestow theirs on us, making us all children of Enniskillen stumbling together through this island, crawling forward through the mess of our history, living forever in a house that is now forever divided. All is changed after Enniskillen."

But all was not changed. The intensity and sheer volume of the condemnations created the momentary illusion that something was actually happening, that Enniskillen had provided constitutional nationalism with the moral ammunition to confront the guns of unconstitutional nationalism. The good and right-sounding expressions of sympathy were, however, mostly platitudes, the products of a debilitating passiveness rather than the manifestation of an empowering resolution. The ideology of denunciation had become empty of meaning. The righteous took pride in their righteousness, pleasure in their disavowals of violence; the proper displays of shared grief absolved constitutional nationalism of compliance in the acts of unconstitutional nationalism, and, genuine though these displays were, they were an escape. There was no need for constitutional nationalism to question itself when the acts of unconstitutional nationalism provided such a convenient target of disapproval. Its motives became obviously pure when the actions of unconstitutional nationalism were so obviously bad.

Beneath the surface the old antagonisms lurked, biding their time, waiting for the fever of commiseration to burst in the heat of its own excesses; behind the fine words and apt phrases, the old ambivalences remained, less blatant but no less pervasive. Only 47 percent of respondents in a public opinion survey conducted on behalf of the *Irish Times* immediately following the bombing approved of the implementation of an act that would make it easier to extradite IRA members wanted in connection with terrorist acts committed in the North. Neither the SDLP nor the Irish government sent official representatives to the Remembrance Day memorial service held in Enniskillen two weeks after the bombing. No Fianna Fail or Labour T.D. attended, no senior SDLP person, no Catholic bishop. There were, of course, disclaimers: it was a religious ceremony, they did not want to intrude; they would have been unwelcome; their presence might incite protest. "Can it be," asked the *Irish Times,* "that after all the grand phrases of condemnation and of reconciliation, nationalist politicians, North and South, still find it impossible to attend a ceremony which is associated with Poppy Day? Even when it also commemorates the callous killing of eleven fellow countrymen?" The answer was yes.

The red poppy, the symbol of remembrance, was itself a symbol of division.[1] "How much we limit ourselves," wrote Mary Holland in the *Irish Times,* "and the part we played in Europe's history by denying the Irish men and women who fought in both world wars. How pitiable that we think it will diminish the sacrifices made by those who died on Irish soil for independence if we recognize that other Irish people shed their blood in other fields." "It was," she went on, "Irish nationalists, first in the Forum Report and then in the Anglo-Irish Agreement, who wanted the rhetoric about respecting both traditions in this land." Yet in the South, "where it poses no threat, we have yet to come to terms with the Remembrance Day Poppy and what it commemorates."

In the Protestant community, angry voices strove to make themselves heard over the vertiginous clamor of reconciliation emanating from ecumenical memorial services. In Fermanagh they remembered that their neighbors had freely elected Bobby Sands, Owen Carron, and eight Sinn Fein councilors, that almost 200 members of the local security forces, UDR and RUC men—members of their community, upholders of their traditions—had been assassinated in the previous fifteen years in circumstances where they had little chance of defending themselves, that the information their murderers acted on undoubtedly had been provided by their Catholic neighbors, that no member of the IRA had ever been arrested in connection with these deaths, that murder brought silence, and silence complicity. No one knew anything, and so it proved with Enniskillen—no information came out of the Catholic community, no leads to follow up on, no knowledge of anything untoward. Its whispers were for itself; the dark and terrible secrets it harbored imprisoned it in consenting silence, and no arrests were made. Their neighbors voted for men and women who were committed to violence, to murdering Protestants, to killing members of their community, and yet somehow they were held to be the sectarian bigots. Why, they asked, does no one step forward? Why does the Catholic Church not excommunicate members of the IRA? (Bishop Cahal Daly answers: "Excommunication could not make any more explicit or more formal the condemnation by the Church of the IRA which is well known to the IRA themselves. . . . It would be a very clumsy and crude kind of weapon and would be pastorally counterproductive. . . . Excommunication in Irish history has been ineffectual. . . . Broadly speaking the Catholic community would not feel it was the way to handle the situation. . . . In some sense the IRA is still within hearing range of what the Church is saying. It still feels uneasy in conscience that the Church is not supporting it, that the Church instead is condemning it.")

Many Protestants asked the question a *Belfast Telegraph* letter writer posed: "We have had the usual platitudes from the hypocritical trinity, O'Fiaich, Haughey and Hume," the letter said. But "if the scum responsible for this outrage were caught, found guilty and imprisoned and then went on a hunger strike 'for political status' would the above trio support their action?" Many believed they knew the answer.

There was a feeling in the Protestant community that Catholics somehow had appropriated the tragedy to their advantage. "Unbelievably," wrote the *Newsletter,* "Unionists have been treated to the spectacle of one of the most astonishing heists in recent times. Skilled propagandists and their unwitting aides have succeeded to a remarkable extent in presenting the Enniskillen massacre as a plus point for the Hillsborough Agreement and the SDLP to the disadvantage of the Unionist people."

Moreover, if the two communities were talking about watersheds, they were different kinds of watersheds. Nationalists continued to emphasize the need for Unionists to accept the reality of the Anglo-Irish Agreement. Unionists held the agreement to blame for all their travails. The agreement, they insisted, had failed. Enniskillen was only the final and most obvious manifestation of its failure. It had not brought peace, or stability, or better security, or a diminution of violence. But how, asked nationalists, can it be expected to work when Unionists refused to budge an inch from their age-old slogans? There was the implied suggestion that Unionists themselves were to blame for the violence being inflicted on them. Only political dialogue, it was said, could bring about a reduction in violence. The implication: as long as Unionists put themselves beyond the pale of dialogue, the violence would continue. "The impression is given by such calls for Unionists and Nationalists to talk," wrote Mervyn Pauley, the *Newsletter*'s political commentator, "that atrocities like Enniskillen could be avoided if only local politicians would sink their differences and smoke the pipe of peace in a veritable outpouring of togetherness." But since the Anglo-Irish Agreement "was the great impediment" to talks, the calls for talks were "dishonest, a subtle attempt to shift some of the blame onto the usual scapegoats, the bad old foxholed Unionists."

The Republican movement was in a foxhole of another kind. Nothing better illustrates its sense of high-mindedness, purity of purpose, and fanatical self-righteousness than its response to Enniskillen. The bombing offended its puritanical understanding of its own moral rectitude, but did not impugn it. The IRA could make mistakes but it could do no wrong.

At first, before the IRA took responsibility, Sinn Fein councilors in Enniskillen suggested that the bombing was the work of the government using undercover operatives, probably the SAS (an elite commando group used for undercover operations), to create a climate in which the IRA would be blamed and the Dublin government pressed into implementing the Extradition Treaty. When the IRA owned up to the bombing, they accepted the responsibility but not the blame. The bombing was "an appalling tragedy and should never have happened . . . [the] IRA had no intention of injuring civilians

. . . did not themselves detonate the remote control bomb . . . did not anticipate the tragic results of the premature explosion of the bomb." It was "a monumental error" for which the Republicans "[had] paid and [would] continue to pay dearly."

The Republican movement did not "try to excuse or defend the action. The most telling criticism of this disastrous IRA action had come from Republicans themselves." However, "accidents do happen and people get killed who are not intended to get killed." What had happened in Enniskillen "was part of an ongoing struggle and however appalling and tragic it might have been it [had] to be looked at in the overall context of that struggle." It was "a terrible tragedy," but there was a more terrible tragedy—"the fact that the Irish people [had been] denied the right to self-determination." That was the "root cause of unrest. All deaths, injuries and injustices stem[med] from that undeniable fact." Ultimately, the British occupation of Ireland was to blame. The Irish people had "the right to seek freedom from England." There had been "a massive effort to convert the natural revulsion of ordinary people about what happened at Enniskillen into anti-Republican sentiment, to try and invalidate the entire struggle on the basis of the Enniskillen tragedy." It would not succeed. The war would go on. "Armed resistance to British rule [would] bring freedom." Meanwhile, "the sympathy of Republicans went out to the families and friends of the dead and the injured." Bereavement and suffering "were things Republicans deeply understood" because they had experienced them at first-hand so many times. Republicans would "never forget" Enniskillen and "in the struggle to end injustice and bring about a free, peaceful Ireland they would carry it in their hearts and minds forever." In short, the Republicans simply appropriated the tragedy and made it their own. The ideology of justification was as bankrupt as the ideology of denunciation. Not that their ghettos did not understand. They did. "The Brits, through ignorance or whatever, turned the event to the IRA's advantage by harping on and on about it," says Father Matt Wallace, a curate in the parish that includes the Lower Falls, part of the heartland of Republicanism. "It was played out. It was like a long-playing record. The event was horrific, but what became more horrific to the people was that the British would use it as propaganda."

"One is left with the suspicion," said a letter to the *Belfast Telegraph,* "that it's all been heard before and that Enniskillen is destined to take its place amongst previous Northern Ireland nine-day wonders." And so it was to prove. The shock, horror, shame, and vulnerability it evoked soon subsided. Each player played his part, performed the ritual role, engaged in the symbolic act. The middle classes filled their churches. Small ecumenical gestures became more significant because they were so occasional.

But the attempt to share grief was compromised by other realities. The Protestant community was resentful of the intrusion of Catholics who came to sympathize but not to yield on their demands—demands that were, in Protestant eyes, responsible for the deaths. Even questions of theology intruded. Dr. William Fleming, the then Presbyterian moderator, admonished Cardinal O'Fiaich for announcing "that Mass would be celebrated and prayers said for the souls of the departed who had died in the bombing," since "to pray for the repose of the soul undermines the whole message of the assurances of the blessedness of the Christian in the after life."

The conflict is about permanent identity-in-opposition, requiring every occasion to splice itself, like some feat of genetic engineering, into its tribal components, precluding a shared sense of grieving, the rhetoric of exclusion accommodating only a mutual sense of betrayal. It is the conflict itself which provides the meaning, the structures of understanding and purpose that prevent social disintegration. The "ideology of . . . conflict," the sociologist Peter Marris observes, "does not press claims or demand rights only for their own sake, but to sustain the conflict itself. Its intransigence wards off the unbearable strain of incorporating the contradictions, and cannot help being identified with both sides."[2] They were not all the children of Enniskillen now. They had become inured to the brutality, capable of being shocked but not capable of being changed. When the condemnations subsided, the people who mattered to the Republican movement would accept their explanation, that it was a mistake, an attempt to kill members of the security forces taking part in the Remembrance Day activities that had gone wrong; that it was carried out by a local unit with the approval of the local brigade staff; that because of its limited intent it had not been cleared with either the Army council or GHQ; that the unit carrying the bombing out had mistakenly believed that members of the UDR usually took up a position close to the gable wall; that there had been no intention to kill civilians; that something had gone horribly wrong, that it wouldn't happen again, that all wars have innocent casualties, that ultimately Britain was to blame for the situation that makes violence necessary. "When people live in the shade of violence," writes Frank Wright, "they also live in fear of the worst things said and done in their name, because they know they are in danger of being held responsible for them by the other side. It becomes difficult to repudiate 'our' confrontationalists when the same people may be 'our' defender against whatever they provoke."[3] Once, when Eileen Doherty, wife of Paddy Doherty, a longtime Derry Republican who has one son serving a twelve-year term in the Maze/Long Kesh for IRA activities and a son-in-law who had been executed by the IRA for being an informant, despite the family's intercessions on his behalf and belief in his innocence, was asked whether she still supported the IRA, she replied, "There'll never be peace in Ireland until the British go. It's as simple as that. I want to see a united Ireland even if we have to pay a high price for it."[4] In Park and Moy and Galbally and Bellaghy and Tamlaghtduff they have paid a high price: no number of Enniskillens will change their minds.

20   **They** still march in Belfast on 5 May, the anniversary of Bobby Sands's death. The crowds grow a little thinner each year, memories a little more dim, the rhetoric a little more worn. In a paradoxical way there is too little memory in a country which prides itself on too much. "We will always remember you, Jimmy Sands"— the graffiti on the gable wall is a poignant reminder that militant Republicanism provides the martyrs for a culture that devours and forgets. Yet the appetite remains insatiable, the role of martyr too fatally attractive. In the Catholic ghettos they remember the hunger strikes. But the names no longer trip off the lips—memory is collective, not personal. Too much death has robbed people of their memories.

It was with some trepidation that I approached the families of the hunger strikers. I felt that I would be intruding on their grief, invading their private worlds, a voyeur looking for that extra detail that would make the macabre more memorable, implicitly faulting them perhaps for events that were beyond their control, making judgments from a perspective that was irrelevant in the circumscribed world they inhabited.

Sinn Fein was of no help in arranging introductions. It had decided, I was informed, that it would not facilitate the introduction of any more writers to the families. Too many had already talked to them; too much had already been written, some of it not to their liking. They were tired of being imposed upon, upset by some of the things written about them.

I waited, took my time to establish and maintain contacts with friends of the families, trying to assure them of my own credentials, anxious for them to understand that I was not there to exploit the families but to learn from them, that the families, too, whether they liked it or not, were part of history and had their responsibilities toward it. It took time—close to three years in some cases—before the proper introductions were made and members of the hunger strikers' families consented to talk.

But still I was troubled. For it seemed to me that there was no way to write about the hunger strikers without hurting their families, without somehow invading their memories of sons, brothers, and husbands, without insinuating a sense of betrayal. They were in search of validation, I was in search of understanding, and the two didn't converge at convenient points of commiseration. I wanted to dissect conventional wisdoms, they wanted to embrace them. They were grounded in a sense of place that formed an integral part of their identities; for me place was a matter of geography. The language of our differences, I felt, would overwhelm our understanding of the events; their sense of the wrong done to them would not accommodate questioning. For how was I to convey to them that I wanted desperately to understand but could not approve, that when all the slogans and posturing and politics were put aside we were left with the insanity of it, a self-perpetuating cycle of death that no one seemed able or willing to stop, that the disproportion between cause and probable effect was beyond the bounds of the morally acceptable?

I spoke with members of seven families: the McDonnells, Lynches, McCreeshes, Hursons, McElwees, O'Haras, and Devines. Bobby Sands's family has kept its silence since Bobby's death; the Dohertys did not want to talk; and Mrs. Hughes, Francis Hughes' mother, preferred not to be disturbed.

I met with the families in their homes, usually in the front-room parlors, surrounded by the memorabilia of the dead hunger strikers— striking portraits that dominated living rooms, commanding attention, reminding you of how young they really were; Celtic crosses and harps carved in wood by comrade-prisoners in the Maze/Long Kesh; plaques eulogizing their deeds; testimonials from abroad paying due tribute. The paraphernalia of commemoration suggested an order and coherence that the hunger strikes never had; it put their deaths in the context of their own history, providing the comfort that, since so many had cared, their cause must have been just, ensuring that in their own homes at least they would never be forgotten.

For the hunger strikers' families the hunger strikes are fixed in time, every detail either recounted with total recall as though the events took place only yesterday or entirely blocked out. Some memories are too painful to recall. They have attached themselves to their dead sons and brothers, arresting the mourning process, leaving in its place unresolved grief, implacable pain, and a certain kind of fatalism—their lives were interrupted during the hunger strikes and they have never fully resumed them. Everything is incomplete.

The families I spoke with were extraordinarily open, as if recounting their story to a stranger helped them to better understand it themselves. They were looking for implicit affirmations of the decisions they made, eager to put me in their place, to have me make the terrible decisions they were called on to make, challenging me to say that something other than what they did could have been done, given the circumstances. They were voices asking for empathy, sometimes demanding it, but never pleading for it. Yet theirs were also the voices of acceptance, the easy admission of their own powerlessness an excuse of sorts—powerlessness itself was a refuge, providing comfort in the face of the overwhelming.

Often I could sense the under-the-surface pain of the disagreements family members had had among themselves, families split down the middle, some members advocating intervention, others opposing it, the final decision invariably resting with the mother—mothers who were called on to attest to their love for their sons by acceding to their sons' requests that they be allowed to die.

There were common themes: the prevailing view that if Mrs. Thatcher had been a man the hunger strikes would have been settled, that she was trying to prove that she was stronger than any man; mild criticism of the Catholic Church hierarchy for not coming straight out on behalf of the five demands; harsh criticism of the South's government for its unwillingness to confront the British on the issue; confirmation that the British were duplicitous; a belief that the Irish Commission's proposals would have resolved the hunger strikes if only the British had kept their word and sent an official into the Maze/Long Kesh to guarantee the settlement; a conviction that their own son or brother would not die—a hope they maintained to the very end, even when there were absolutely no grounds for it; an insistence that the hunger strikers had won, either by having their demands subsequently met or by showing the British what Irish courage was; the reawakened pain whenever they would see other men who had done time with a dead hunger striker on the street or in a shop—the knowledge that their sons and brothers would be out too, young men in the prime of their lives; an unwavering conviction that the dead hunger strikers were still with them, living presences with whom they communicated.

Our conversations were intense and emotional as questions triggered stream-of-consciousness replies, replies that often reflected a tentativeness about what had happened, a hesitancy to trust a reality that was behind them or even to let memories of it surface. Often they would cry—and I would cry too—responses punctuated by long periods of silence. I was privy to their grief and it humbled me. For it was clear that the hunger strikers came from loving, caring, close-knit families who believed that their sons died to free Ireland: they had to believe this if only to provide themselves with a context that made sense of the madness. At some point during our talks some small detail would unleash the sorrow that was always there or the act of recollection itself exposed the incomprehensibility of it all. There was, they invariably claimed, nothing they could have done. They too were prisoners—prisoners of the circumstances in which they had found themselves.

"Everything died with Joseph," Joe McDonnell's sister Maura tells me, "and we were left to carry the burden of guilt. I really felt that it was me that actually let him die. I have to carry that with me the rest of my life. It's the sort of guilt that you don't want to be here anymore, you want to be with him. . . . He never leaves my mind, even after he died I dreamt about his waiting for me coming to help him."

The family can't talk about Joe's death among themselves, can't share the grief, afraid of what the accusing finger might bring into the open. "It is all hushed up," Eileen McDonnell, Joe's mother, explains. "We don't explore anything here, we keep it all to ourselves—it would become a crying matter—what we should have done.

If people had asked me, 'Do you want a free Ireland or do you want your son?' I would have said, 'I want my son.' I can prove I want a free Ireland as much as anybody else but when it came to giving up your son for it, no, I wouldn't have given up my son for it, definitely not."

But you sense that her certainty about what she would have done has a lot to do with the fact that she didn't have to do it. The McDonnell family were cut out of the decision-making process. It was Joe's wife, Goretti, who made the decision not to intervene, and Goretti never discussed it with any member of the McDonnell family. "I never got a chance to ask my own son if he wanted to die; his wife never consulted me," Eileen McDonnell says, and the family's sense of exclusion paralyzed their ability to act. Their anger at Goretti, who has since remarried, although not openly expressed, is easy to detect. It lingers like a bad taste.

None of them believed that Joe would die. Not at any time, not even at the end. The Irish Commission for Peace and Justice convinced them that the hunger strike would be over once an NIO official visited the prison to put his imprimatur on the agreement the Commission believed it had worked out with Alison, and that Joe would be saved. The ICJP said it would be settled, the prison chaplain said it, an NIO official said it, even the prison warders said it.

Campaigning up and down the South on Joe's behalf (Joe was a candidate in the South's general election in the Sligo-Leitrim constituency) they hadn't even the time to consider that Joe might be dying. "I didn't realize he was so bad," says Eileen McDonnell. "They [other family members] were coming down [from visits] and I was saying 'How is he?' and [they would say] 'great' and they should have been saying to me, 'Mammy, you may as well get it into your head Joseph is going to die.' "

And when Joseph died?

"That's when you realized all the things you should have done— I should have done. I couldn't sleep. I lay in bed and kept saying, 'I should have done this and I should have done that.' But at the time you didn't think. You just thought he was going to live. I never for a minute thought he was going to die."

And how have they dealt with their grief?

"I've never talked to anyone about my grief," his sister Eilis says. "The way I felt after Joseph died, it was just the way the prophet said to Our Lady, 'The sword of sorrow shall pierce your heart.'

Every morning I got up it was as if there were dozens [of swords] piercing me. You could actually feel it and that's the way it went on all day for about two years. Although I didn't really speak much about it, I used to remember getting my kids to bed at night and getting the house to myself and running into the dinette and getting down on my knees and screaming, but nothing came out."

"Some people would say [the hunger strike] has done a lot of good, other people would sort of feel it was in vain," says Maura. "I just think that it has ruined the family. When the hunger strike ended, then you felt that maybe you should have done something, and therefore it left you with a terrible scar that you were actually guilty of letting him go ahead and go through with it. . . . We'll never get over our grief because it wasn't natural. When you look around and see young men who are now out you realize that he would be out too. You keep waiting for him to come home and he never will."

Have they ever gotten together with the families of the other hunger strikers to talk among themselves about their experiences of having to deal with the hunger strikes' aftermath?

"You can't," Maura says. "You can't because it's too emotional. I see Mrs. Doherty [Kieran's mother] now and again and as soon as we see each other, we just can't talk to each other because she just looks at me and I just look at her and the two of us break down. We can't actually sit down and talk about it. . . . You sort of feel there was something wrong with you when it was all happening. . . . But it's too emotional a thing to sit down and say, What way do you feel? You can't change it, you can't bring anyone back and we can't even sit down and talk about it."

When the funeral was over, the orations given, the military rites performed, and the crowds dispersed, they were on their own, face to face with a grief they could not come to terms with and at the same time cannot let go of. "You turn around and say Christmas seems like years ago but you do not say Joe's death was years ago. Joseph's death was only yesterday," says Maura.

Mrs. McDonnell shows me a collection of press cuttings about Joe's hunger strike and funeral and a copy of a poem called "The Patriot Mother" that someone had written for her:

> A mother kneels in silent prayer, a flower clasped to her breast,
> She lays it on a lonely grave where her fallen son now rests
> No tears blur her deep blue eyes, they shine with loving pride,
> She knows he fought for freedom, for liberty he died.

I recite the words, and she sits there holding her memories and quietly cries.

For Bridie Lynch, Kevin Lynch's mother, Kevin, too, lives in the present. We sat in the front room of her home in Dungiven, looking at the cemetery across the street where Kevin is buried. In winter when the trees are bare you can see the outline of the Celtic cross headstone that marks the grave.

How does she remember Kevin now, I ask her.

"Would you believe this," she says. "I remember him when I go to make the beds. I remember Kevin as a wee thing four years of age and when I'd be putting the clothes on the line to dry after washing them, he'd say, 'Mammy's on the line, Daddy's on the line,' naming everyone in the family, and every day that comes through my head and I remember Kevin, no matter what I'd be doing. I talk to him, I talk to Kevin. And he'll never leave."

For the first six months that Kevin was in the Maze/Long Kesh he wouldn't wear the prison uniform, even for the monthly statutory visit. "I went to Lourdes," says Mrs. Lynch, "with the intention that I would get a visit, that he'd break his silence, and when I came home from Lourdes the visiting card was in the house."

The grief is something she will never get over. "I'm reconciled to God now that it happened the way it happened," she says. When Kevin went to work in England in the early 1970s she prayed that he would stay there—too many young people in the area were being lifted (arrested). And Kevin's death, she confides, has relieved her of having to worry that Kevin, once out of prison, would have become involved again and killed someone—something that would have caused her even greater pain and grief than Kevin's own death. "Kevin killed nobody, thank God. He didn't bomb anybody, he didn't shoot anybody and that's a relief to me. No mother would have been as glad to see their son coming home to us, but at the same time if he'd been out and running about now, after all they had to suffer in Long Kesh and on the blanket protest, I'd be worried. It would bother me that he would be out running about for fear of him getting into serious trouble. There are times when you think they're better off in heaven than here." Mrs. Lynch is at peace with her decision not to intervene. She would do nothing differently. "All you have is your word," she says, "when you break your word you have nothing. There's nothing we could have done other than what we did do. I'm content that I gave Kevin his wish."

Was there a lot of pressure on her to take Kevin off the hunger strike?

"No. I'm not one of those people who like to tell lies. It was said that this one and that one were pressing to get Kevin off. But it wasn't true. Not one priest told me to [except for] the parish priest across the road. He was very anxious for Kevin to come off and I told him the story [of the promise she had given to Kevin]. I told him that I had promised him faithfully that I would stand by him and I says, 'All you have is your word.' And he says, 'If you can't do it, can't his father do it if he didn't promise him.' But Paddy [her husband] said he wouldn't."

She was in the prison hospital the evening Paddy Quinn took a turn for the worse. She and Mrs. Doherty were put in a waiting room. "We were told to stay in there and not to open the door. We didn't. We prayed all the time. When the door opened it was Father Toner [the prison chaplain] and my own daughter Mary coming in from visiting Kevin and I said, 'Is Paddy Quinn dead?' 'No,' my daughter Mary says, 'he's not dead, he's going to an outside hospital.' I thanked God. I thanked God for his mother because she was a widow woman, and a terribly kindly woman, a very good woman. But I couldn't have acted myself because I had given Kevin a promise."

When the government referred to Kevin as a terrorist, a criminal, how did that make her feel?

"I call Maggie Thatcher a bigger criminal than what my son was and do to this day. If you judge you have to be judged yourself. I wouldn't like to be in Maggie Thatcher's shoes to meet God."

Kevin's father, Paddy Lynch, who was vehemently opposed to keeping Kevin on the hunger strike, continues to nurture his grief. "I would say the father took it worse than me and I loved him," says Mrs. Lynch. "Even if he comes into this room twenty times a day, he looks at Kevin's photo." Each evening at five o'clock Paddy Lynch crosses the street from his home to the cemetery where Kevin is buried and stays there until seven—the vigil at Kevin's grave has become part of his own ritual of sorrow, as if he believes that the pure persistence of his nightly pilgrimage can will Kevin back to life.

Before I go Mrs. Lynch insists on the ubiquitous cup of tea. After-wards the two of us cross the street and visit Kevin's grave. "Many's a time on Sunday when I go to the graveyard," she says. "I see young ones of ten, eleven, and twelve years of age, and I haven't a clue who they are but they know where Kevin is lying."

"If you close your eyes for a moment," I ask Father Brian McCreesh, Raymond McCreesh's brother, "and look back to Raymond's hunger strike, what images come immediately to mind?"

None, he says, no particular images at all.

Well, how about the impact of the hunger strike itself. Has it had a lasting effect?

"The abiding impact the hunger strike had," he replies, "was the very strong sense that the people to whom I belong and the people to whom the hunger strikers belonged are on their own. The oppressed people of the North, people with a very strong sense of Irish identity, are on their own."

The Catholic Church, he continues, "had been silenced by the British." That was one of the great successes of British rule in Ireland in modern times. The Dublin government had turned its back on the North. They had been abandoned.

When the bishops made statements that the IRA is an evil organization and that anyone who supports it or is a member of it is committing a mortal sin, what was the reaction of the Church on the ground, of members of what he would call the oppressed community?

"What you call the church on the ground and ordinary people are more aware of the complexities of the situation," he says. "Very often bishops' statements seem to lack that sort of sense of complexity which there is. For example, we had a statement from the bishops last November, the day after the Enniskillen bomb, which was to be read out at all masses the next Sunday, a rushed, hasty statement, in which it was stated that there can be no ambivalence about violence, which totally flies in the face of reality because the thing is full of ambivalence and ambiguity. It's just there, it's a reality. . . . Statements like that do more harm than good because they're not credible."

The hunger strike was symbolic.

I think a lot of us who live in the Six Counties, occupied Ireland, have a very deep sense of identity with prisoners because we all feel like prisoners and this little statelet to which we belong is for us a prison. It's an open prison, but it's a prison in which our identity as Irish people is either totally denied or degraded. We don't feel free, we feel persecuted, spied upon, and it's very easy to identify with people who are in prisons surrounded by barbed wire, concrete walls, watched over by prison guards because one of the realities here in the Six Counties is that people with a very strong sense of Irish identity are prisoners in their own land . . . as the agents of the British government, the whole Unionist population are our prison warders, our prison guards.

With his knowledge of Raymond, what did he think were the special qualities in him that led Raymond to the momentous decision to go on the hunger strike?

No particular quality. Just a sense of humanity and a sense of dignity and a very strong sense of Irishness. A sense of justice. A sense of history. What those men died for was their identity. The whole thing was much deeper than the five demands. It was just an awareness of who they were, that's basically why they died. Because their identity was being denied and degraded. They just died because they were Irish and they weren't free. The hunger strikers demonstrated a spirit of determination and resolve in our people which will have a lasting effect. That people are willing to die rather than to suffer oppression and injustice.

How did Raymond make his decision to go on hunger strike? Did he say, "I'm going on hunger strike and I don't want to be taken off, I want to remain on, I want to resist all pressures?"

Father McCreesh couldn't remember all the details at this point. "I don't even know if it was made as explicit as that," he says, "but it certainly would have been understood. He had made his decision and the family respected that and stood by him in it."

Looking back, was there anything in retrospect that he should have done differently?

No. Our fundamental decision as a family was to stand by Raymond. He had made this decision and I think we were happy that he made it in clarity of mind.

Our parents didn't see Raymond from the day he was convicted and sentenced until the day he asked to see them to tell them he was going on hunger strike. [McCreesh had refused to put on the prison uniform for the monthly statutory visit. As a result his family hadn't seen him for four years.] We had a lot of our grieving done in those years. We went through it that time even more so than during the hunger strike. We had a lot of grieving over us during the time Raymond was in prison. And even though he came out of Long Kesh dead, in a coffin, at least he came out of it and there was a real sense of relief that he was out.

Long Kesh, he says, is very anti-Irish and anti-Catholic. "There's always a strangeness about saying mass in Long Kesh. While saying mass you would have felt very much a sense of the terrible injustice of it all. I'd have no difficulty really identifying with the prisoners, they shouldn't have been there at all."

One of the consoling things for him was the fact that "Raymond's death on the hunger strike was a victory at a very personal level. It was a personal victory for him as it was for all the hunger strikers. They were defeated in every other way. Yet nobody could stop them from dying—it was a victory."

What stands out for him as being the most difficult thing he and his family had to face during Raymond's hunger strike?

"The lies of the British establishment. In this community the oppressor has access to all the means of communication and is ruthless in falsifying situations. Britain is a liar. We're a lied-against people with very little power to counter that. Our own family was subjected to a whole campaign of lies during the hunger strike. They concocted this whole story about Raymond wanting to come off the hunger strike and the family and mainly myself forcing him to stay on it. Total lies, and yet they broadcast that throughout the world and kept it up even after his death. You had lies coming at you all the time." (On Saturday, 16 May 1981, the fifty-seventh day of McCreesh's hunger strike, the NIO reported that McCreesh had considered ending his hunger strike but had been deterred from doing so following a visit from his family. The report said that McCreesh had asked for nourishment late on the Saturday night in question, that his family was sent for, and that following the visit McCreesh changed his mind. The report was angrily denied by the McCreesh family in a statement issued through the Republican Press Center in Belfast. "We are respecting his wishes not to be revived should he again lapse into a coma. None of us has witnessed him asking for food," their statement read, "and he is clearly determined to continue with his hunger strike.")

He walks me to the door of the Parochial House at the Church of Our Lady in Coalisland. It is a cold and blustery November afternoon. "It is a strange thing," he says, "but people often call me Raymond since the hunger strike." He has had letters addressed to Father Raymond McCreesh; people introduce him to other people as Father Raymond McCreesh. "Strange," he says. We make our goodbyes and I leave him still hearing his voice: "As long as there is one person in prison, we're all in prison. As long as one is oppressed, we're all oppressed. As long as one is in mourning, we're all in mourning."

Martin Hurson's sister-in-law, Sheila, the wife of his brother, Brendan, believes "the hunger strike proved how determined the Irish people really are. They didn't give in. Maggie Thatcher would never budge an inch. Well, they didn't budge an inch either. They stuck their ground, they couldn't do any more. They were the only ones who stood up to Maggie Thatcher. They gave everything they had. So they must have proved something. Who else proved as much?"

Both Sheila and Brendan castigate the Dublin government for doing nothing, both feel abandoned by their coreligionists in the South, and both belittle the Anglo-Irish Agreement for achieving nothing, for being little more than a security collaboration between Dublin and London. "We're actually worse off with harassment," says Brendan. "It has given the security forces the upper hand. They can do what they like and the way I look at it that's coming from Dublin and London, from the conservative government in London and the government-of-the-day in Dublin." Nevertheless, "the Nationalist people of the Six Counties will fight and they'll keep it going," no matter what Dublin does. "They've that much determination, we've suffered that much. We've lost that much with no help from anyone."

Is the Catholic Church wrong to condemn the IRA?, I ask. "Yes it is," he answers. "They know actually what is happening. They know the root evil of it. Why do they not condemn it?" He would talk to different priests and get them to the point of admitting that there was something wrong but still they wouldn't come out in public and say it. "It was the same during the hunger strike," he says. "There were more clergy, more priests came here to the house and they thought it was terrible. You get priests coming from different parts and they came offering sympathy and said mass in the house, and then you get a certain number of priests condemning it."

The security forces were still doing house-to-house searches in the area around Galbally. The extent of the harassment preoccupies them both. I want to talk about Martin, they want to talk about harassment. "There's homes in this district and once a month their whole house is tipped upside down—every letter, every cupboard, every book examined," Brendan explains. If you go out at night you are sure to be stopped and harassed by a UDR patrol. "I wouldn't go out the lane on my own at night because you never know whether you're going to be stopped," says Sheila. "Any young lads that's on the road at night on their own will get stopped, they get a hassling and ten chances to one they get a beating." If Brendan is out on his own at night Sheila worries. "He went over one night to a neighbor's house, maybe an eighth of a mile up the road, and he had to get his hair searched. His hair was searched by the UDR. They stopped him and took him out and used bad language and searched him."

"I could show you things they have actually done, uncalled-for things," says Brendan. "People trying to make a living have to struggle to put up with it on a day-to-day basis. You don't hear it mentioned in the papers. The people know about it but it's not being published. It's getting no headlines at all and it's still going on."

What, I want to know, did their children (they have three boys and five girls) know about Martin?

"The children ask about Martin all the time. 'Was our Martin,' they would ask, 'an IRA man?' And they would be told yes, and when some of the younger ones might say 'Aren't the IRA bad men?' you had to explain to them that that's not the way it is, that the IRA is fighting for a cause. You explain that Ireland's split, that the soldiers and the UDR and the RUC shouldn't be here, that it's a war situation." They worry that their own boys might get involved with the IRA when they grow up, in the belief that if Martin was in it, it must be all right—even the wee ones had all the Republican songs at the tip of their tongues. And they worry, too, that the Donnellys down the lane—their next-door neighbors, in fact—whose son, Sean, was shot dead at Loughgall, might somehow be blaming Martin for getting their son involved.

"There was an awful gentleness in Martin. He was really like a big child," says Sheila. Once he ran over a kitten belonging to one of their children and killed it. "Well, to him," she says, "that was a wild crime. He was in an awful state, he was worse than a child about the cat. He wasn't in prison a month until that wood carving [of a cat] came out to give to the children in place of the cat. The children had forgotten about the cat but Martin wanted the carving given to the child that owned the cat he had killed. He wasn't a bad man. He had a heart. It touched me, that; I thought there was an awful lot of goodness in him." And they remember the outpouring of support at the time of Martin's death. "There's boxes and boxes of letters in this house that came from all parts of the world. They came from France, Germany, Holland, America, Canada, Australia, New Zealand—you name any part of the world." And people still come to visit. Two or three people a year at least. Maybe to write about the hunger strike like myself or to see where Martin lived or to visit his grave.

Brendan was with Martin when Martin died. He is still angry at the way he was treated. He wasn't allowed to make a phone call to inform the rest of the family of Martin's death for two hours—in fact, the family had heard the news on the radio before he was able to get in touch with them. "They put me into a room and locked the door," he says. "And when I came out again the body was gone." (It has been taken to Omagh for an autopsy but the family had to ferret out this information themselves. For hours nobody knew where the remains had been taken.) And it is this memory that shapes his personal history of the hunger strikes—the way the family was treated in the prison when they went in on visits, the constant hassle, the barely concealed contempt for them, how routine processing procedures were made interminably difficult, the way he himself was treated the night Martin died. On Sheila Hurson's mind one memory is indelibly imprinted: seeing Martin's dinner sitting at the bottom of his bed. A fresh dinner sent in every day and dessert sitting beside it. "How could he stand the smell of that," she wonders, "and not give in?"

Before I go I have a few words with some of their children. ("Does that man talk to all the hunger strikers' mammies and daddies?" the six-year-old wanted to know.) What, I ask them, do they know about their Uncle Martin? And they answer in unison: He died to free Ireland.

Peggy O'Hara, Patsy O'Hara's mother, remembers the dinners, too. They were brought in right up to the day Patsy died. The smell of the food sitting on the tray at the end of his bed made Patsy vomit. For her, too, Patsy is a constant presence. "I have Patsy in my mind from the moment I arise in the morning until I go to bed at night," she says. "I seem to have got the idea that Patsy's with me, with every decision I make. I've a big picture down in our house and when I rise in the morning before I go to my work I smile at him—it seems to console me. If I'm going to do anything important I will talk to Patsy. He seems to be guiding me. He's always in the conversation. I don't think Patsy's up there [in the graveyard]. I think Patsy's more with me everywhere I go."

Had Patsy said anything to her beforehand, such as "When I get very ill or become unconscious promise not to take me off"?

"No, Patsy wouldn't have said that to me," she says,

because Patsy knew the nature of me. He might have said it to Elizabeth [his sister] but he wouldn't have said it to me because I would still have taken him off. I told my family that there was no way I was going to let Patsy die and that I didn't care about Ireland or the whole world. That night when he said those words to me ["I'm sorry, Mammy, we didn't win. Please, Mammy, let the fight go on"], I still would have took him off but Patsy died the next day. That's the way that I was, I didn't know he was so near death. . . . Even when Raymond [McCreesh] died I still didn't think Patsy would die. Patsy was a big strong young fellow. I just didn't think that Patsy would die.

In retrospect is there anything she would have done differently?

"If it was today, and knowing what I know now, I'd have talked to Patsy. I'd have talked to Patsy with all the experience I have now and Patsy would have listened to me. I would have talked to Patsy and to the rest of those young fellows and then told them they still would be coming out of Long Kesh, if it hadn't been stopped. Maggie Thatcher wouldn't have given in to them—even though she's supposed to be a mother—so what was the point?"

And what did she think came out of the hunger strikes?

Not very much, she says. Some people say lots of things came out of it, but she doesn't think so.

Is she bitter, I ask.

"No," she says, "because life is too short to be bitter. The way I look at it, at the beginning we thought it was Maggie Thatcher and Charlie Haughey but when I became aware of the fact that it was the whole cabinet, people that you don't even know, how could you be bitter about people you don't even know? The only thing I can say is them people have to make answer to their own consciences for what they let happen to them young fellows." If the Catholic Church and the Irish government had stood up to the British, perhaps something might have happened.

Her most vivid memory of Patsy?

"I got Patsy a Rover and before Patsy would go anywhere he would ask me and my husband where we wanted to go and I saw Ireland, which I never would have only for Patsy. Patsy was a great young fellow. We used to take sandwiches and we'd go here one day and there the next. Everybody would look at the young fellow in the Rover because a Rover in them days was special—I paid six hundred fifty pounds for it—now you'd pay near eleven thousand for it. It was a great car and he loved that car and he used to take us here, there and everywhere in it."

She tells the story of how she herself got "involved." One day a customer came into the bar the family owned and said, "Your son Sean Seamus is down at the Guildhall [Derry City Hall] with a placard around his neck." She took the bus down to the Guildhall, "and there was Sean Seamus and so many other young fellows going around in a circle with placards and I went over to my son and I said to him, 'Who told you to put that placard on?' and he pointed over to a young fellow, Finbar, and I took the placard off Sean and I went over and put the placard around Finbar's neck and I told him to march up and down with the placard and I hit him with my umbrella. That's how much I was involved with politics." Later on that day there was a march and she went down to Duke Street to make sure Sean Seamus wasn't getting into more trouble. It was the first time she saw water cannons. "Everyone was getting battered to the ground and when I saw that, that changed my attitude. I never was involved before but that kind of changed my attitude that they couldn't have a wee march. That's all they were doing. They were marching for civil rights and they weren't allowed to march."

Elizabeth, her daughter, she says, had to leave Derry. "Every time it was coming up to Patsy's anniversary it was more the women cops than the men, although they helped too. They would call out names about Patsy, about what was it when he died on the hunger strike, how many stone he weighed, and finally she just left to make herself a new life [in the United States] because you'll never get any satisfaction here."

And how do the family grieve—do they talk about Patsy's hunger strike or do they grieve on their own?

They do it together. "Patsy's ours to share. We talk about Patsy as if he's there.

"I made a terrible lot of good friends," she says, "genuine friends who I never would have had that I can go to, important people that I wouldn't ever have known. So, the young fellows have achieved something. Important people wouldn't have known me and I suppose the rest of the mothers are the same. When we die we'll just be a memory but those young fellows will live forever. All the generations will remember them."

She has survived, emptied of anger—she and her Patsy will always be together.

"You're welcome down at my house anytime," she says when I go to leave. "When you come down you'll see Patsy's picture. It's a portrait an artist did in America. Whatever way she's captured the picture, he's smiling no matter what way you go his eyes are looking at you. You could sit and look at him all day."

The visiting. That was the hardest part for Alice McElwee, Thomas McElwee's mother. "Going to visit them during the hunger strike. Going to visit Thomas and then not seeing Benedict. [Thomas's brother, Benedict, was also doing time in the Maze/Long Kesh for offenses connected with the same bombing incident for which Thomas was convicted.] Being in the same place and not being able to see Benedict was awful hard. Benedict was kept away from Thomas all the time. He never saw him during the whole time of the hunger strike. On the morning Thomas died, Benedict was on his way over to see him, and he didn't even know he was dead until he was near at hand and they told him to come and identify the body."

"On the morning Thomas died," she continues, "we were all in a very sad state. We didn't know at the time Thomas was dead, but we knew he wasn't very well and we all went to mass that morning. I have infants buried in the graveyard and on the way home I went down to visit their graves and I just knew there was something really wrong. We had a weight of bother hanging down over us that day. I just couldn't get it lifted. I knew something was going to happen." They were back in the house for perhaps half an hour when the phone rang; it was Father Toner calling to tell them that Thomas had died suddenly that morning.

Did they ever wonder what they might have done if Thomas had slipped into unconsciousness?

"We did. We wondered," she says.

We just felt helpless. He always said, "Stick by me," and we promised that we would stick by him, but we never thought it was going to go so far. Every day we were just living through hope that the government would see their point and give them the five demands they wanted. It wasn't that much that they wanted and we always lived in hope. That's what kept me going and able to handle things. The hope that it would come today or tomorrow and that if it didn't come today it would come tomorrow. We always thought that [the five demands] were so simple that the government would give in to them because it was really nothing. That's the point: it was just their clothes and their work and freedom of association.

It has taken the McElwees a long time to recover from Thomas's death. "There was just an emptiness there, not knowing where to turn to, a lost feeling." One sister who had been very close to Thomas almost had a nervous breakdown. "It was hard on all his sisters and the brothers were just speechless. They just closed up, kept it bottled up inside them."

Has she one memory of Thomas that stands out for her?

"I remember him buying me a Christmas box one Christmas," she says. "It was a big picture of wild ducks over a lake—a beautiful painting. And Thomas said, 'I hope you like it, Mammy, I remember you and the ducks'—we used to keep ducks. And then I looked at the picture and I pointed this wee defect to Thomas, and he says, 'No problem, I'll get it fixed for you.' And away he went the same night and got it fixed. He was quick like that to please, having everything perfect."

But Thomas's sister, Enda, has not yet worked out her grief. "It's still very much there," she says. "To me Thomas is still here." The family is "incomplete." It doesn't surprise her that Thomas gave up his life for the rest of the prisoners—that was just him. "It was just like a family inside, they all got so close. They lived for each other."

Her most vivid recollection of Thomas?

"The last time we saw him. He admired how nice I was and what a good-looking girl I was and how well I was dressed." Alice McElwee remembers that last visit too—the night before Thomas died. "We talked about the clothes we wore," she recalls, "how well we looked in our clothes. He had a great interest in clothing," which they found a little ironic since one of the prisoners' demands was to wear their own clothing. Thomas had always been a smart dresser. In fact, to this day, whenever Mrs. McElwee sees smart-looking clothing in a shop window, Thomas immediately comes to her mind and she will find herself saying, "He'd have looked well in that now."

How had Thomas's death changed their lives?

"You feel bitter against the British," says Enda, "at the same time you try not to, you try to live as normally as you would have." But some things have changed: the UDR and RUC put them in a special category. "If my brothers," says Enda, "are out in the car and they are stopped and then the name McElwee comes up, they'll pull you in and it's the same with cousins—anyone with any connection at all to the family is treated differently. They [the UDR and RUC] haven't lost their memories." "Even in jobs we're treated differently," Mrs. McElwee adds. "My youngest daughter didn't get a job because of her name in any work for a long time."

Did they find it easier or harder, as time went by, to talk about the past?

Both Alice and Enda say it has become harder. "To be perfectly honest with you, I couldn't actually talk about the time he was on hunger strike and the way he looked," says Enda. "When he was deteriorating, you try and not think about it." Her grief today is as strong as it was when Thomas died. She can still see him, and she dreams about him. In her dreams Thomas is always at home, dressed in the boiler suit that he wore to work, stretched out on the living room couch—just as he used to do every evening when he came home from work.

Thomas is a soldier who died for his country. One of Mrs. McElwee's grandchildren, a five-year-old, is named after him. "He goes over to the neighbor's house and he tells them why he was called Thomas," says Mrs. McElwee. "He says, 'I got my name from my Uncle Thomas and he was a soldier.' He's proud of his Uncle Thomas." When Enda has children of her own, she too, will tell them the story of their Uncle Thomas, an Irish soldier who fought for his country and died, who was put in jail and when the prisoners were denied the right to wear their own clothes and get their other demands, he put his name forward to go on a hunger strike to get the demands granted, that he went on a hunger strike for the love of his fellow prisoners. "We'll never forget," says Enda, "when he died the family was never complete anymore."

What do they think Thomas died for?

"It's obvious that he was doing it for love of his comrades and love of his country," says Enda. "They could never have gone on with the blanket protest. They had to take a stand and Thomas put his name forward. I wasn't surprised because that's the kind of person he was like. He says, 'I hope you will understand.' That was him. So we just went along with him. Some of us may not have liked it but we stood by his wishes."

Did they ever consider that Thomas might be committing suicide?

"I dealt with that fair enough," says Mrs. McElwee. "I knew rightly it wasn't suicide. The fellows didn't want to die, not one of them. If they had known they were going to die, they wouldn't have went that far."

Did she ever think that perhaps Thomas had died in vain?

No, she didn't. "The young men left behind got their dignity, got their clothes, and they got their other demands."

And the Catholic Church, how supportive was it?

"Sometimes we were disappointed. We thought they could have done more [to get the five demands]. In a way we were disappointed with them." Thomas had hoped that the Irish Commission proposals would work; the families thought they were fair and acceptable, but even when the effort fell apart, "Thomas kept his hope up to the very end." The prison chaplains, however, were good men. "Father Toner came with Communion every day. On the day Kieran Doherty died, Father Toner wasn't able to come into Thomas and he made the remark to Father Toner how he missed the Lord that day. That's what he said to Father Toner: he missed the Lord that day. He looked forward to Holy Communion."

It was dark when I left their home, a few miles outside Bellaghy. Enda told me to be careful—the UDR and RUC were likely to be out there patrolling the country roads. The harassment was as constant as ever. Just after Benedict had gotten out of Long Kesh, her own fiancé had been badly beaten by the UDR one night and not long ago on her way home she passed a carload of young people standing spread-eagled against a wall with their hands up and their legs out. There is one last thing I want to know. Who made the beautiful hand-carved crucifix mounted on a mahogany base on which the stations of the cross had been delicately inscribed in great detail and with great craftsmanship? It had been made in Port Laoise by Dominick McGlinchey, the head of the INLA, Mrs. McElwee says, and sent to her after Thomas died. I have difficulty reconciling the beautiful carving with the notorious "Mad Dog" McGlinchey, at one time the most wanted man in both the North and South, the man with the reputation as a psychotic killer.

Margaret Devine is getting better. For almost eight years she could not accept that Micky was dead, she obsessed about him, limiting her world to her memories of him, distorting the past, ruining the present. Now she is in therapy, getting regular counseling. "It's seven years now and I just got over it—I'm not really over it properly but I would say I'm just starting to learn to get over it. I learnt a lot. I learned that he died for his country, that he had to die for his beliefs."

How do her children, Michael and Louise, remember their father?

"My oldest son Michael remembers him well," she says. "He was three years old when Micky was lifted, but he remembers him pretty well. He remembers going out to play football with him and he remembers sitting on the bed asking his father to give up the hunger strike and he was saying, 'Please, Daddy, don't die.' And Louise remembers it too. She was only five. They say children have no memories but they do. Children have hearts and memories."

Do they remember Micky as a soldier who died for his country?

I tried to pump it into their heads but as they got older Michael thinks that his father was no big hero. He has really turned against him in a sense of, he should have been there to look after him. I try still to pump it into his head that "Your Daddy died for Ireland, he was that dedicated to the cause. You should be very proud of your father." I think he's grieving quietly himself. Michael is trying to block his father out. He feels that he rejected him or something. Once you mention his name it's like a big bad name to him. He says, "My father was never there." You can feel that in him, "Well, my father didn't care about me," that's the feeling you get from him when you are talking to him. . . . Michael has curly hair just like Micky and he had it restyled and I says, "Why are you getting your hair shaved up like that? You've lovely red hair like your father." And he said, "That's the reason why."

And Louise?

"Louise would see her father as a hero because she talks about him a lot. She sees him as a hero all right."

"In the primary school," she continues, "they [Michael and Louise] went through hell when Micky died. The children would taunt them with, 'Your father committed suicide and he starved himself to death. At least my father didn't starve himself.' The children would come home crying and they wouldn't go to school for about a week and I would have to go to the school and explain what happened. Sometimes I think they still feel sore when people talk about their father."

After Micky's death, I ask her, whom did she rely on for comfort and support?

"There was nobody," she says.

The first help I got was this year [1988] with the Northlands Centre [a hospital for mental health care in Derry], and they taught me a lot, how to cope with life. I just couldn't live. My life was just unbelievable. I really thought I was crazy, but all the time it was over Micky and I didn't realize that. I thought, God, what's happening to me, and all the time it was that I was thinking too much of the olden times me and Micky had. I was playing sentimental music and looking at pictures and crying about Micky. I couldn't believe that I didn't grieve properly. . . . When somebody would say to me, "What's wrong," I would say, "I miss Micky," and they would say, "How can you miss Micky? Sure you're living with another man," and I would say, "That's not the same thing." I would say, "I don't love that person. I love my own husband," and they couldn't understand what I was talking about. That I never let Micky's love go.

How about the Catholic Church? Was she able to turn to it for solace?

"Many's the time I went to the priest, saying to the priest, 'Father, I can't get over Micky's death,' and everybody keeps telling me I'll get over his death, and the priest would say to me, 'That's right. You'll never get over his death. Don't let anybody fool you by saying everything will be all right. You'll never get over his death.' "

What did she think Micky meant when he sent a last message out of the prison to her saying that he had forgiven her?

"I thought Micky was blaming me for his death. I thought, what is he forgiving me for? What did I do? Is he forgiving me for not signing the papers? Is this what it is? I couldn't get it out of my head. I started thinking it was my fault that he died. I took the whole blame. I just crucified myself and that's when I started drinking heavier and heavier and saying, 'I killed him,' and telling everybody that I had killed my husband."

However, because of the treatment she is receiving at the Northlands Centre—she gets weekly counseling—she has come to accept that Micky allowed himself to die for what he believed in, that it wasn't her fault.

The doctor said to me, "Micky had nothing to forgive you for because you tried your best," and the doctor said it was me who should forgive him for dying and leaving me with two young children to cope with and look after. So eventually I got that out of my system and I see things more clearly. I saw that he was dedicated to the movement, dedicated to fighting for Ireland—what he always talked about—a free Ireland. He always said, "We'll have a free Ireland," and even in his letters he would write about that, we'll all have a free Ireland sometime soon, and soon never came because I was always waiting for this free Ireland. "It's coming now," he'd write. "We'll soon have a free Ireland. I'll soon be let loose," and I would wait and wait and still no free Ireland. . . . [The doctor] told me at one stage to take Micky's photographs and pictures off the walls, that if they were off the walls I would come to grips with his death quicker. They said while you have his pictures plastered on the wall, you're going to be there with this grief, you're always going to live with it. They said put them in a box where they can be for the children when they grow up.

And now?

Now I get counseling every week about how to cope with life without grieving for Micky and I feel it helps me a terrible lot because if I hadn't gone to those people [the Northlands Centre] I would still be sitting here and I wouldn't have spoken to anybody and I wouldn't have told them how I felt inside. I was shattered inside about losing him. Everybody thought, well, she's living with another man, she's okay, but that wasn't the problem. The problem inside me was that I still loved Micky and he's away now and I couldn't believe it. People thought, sure she's having children. I said that's no problem, it still doesn't make you lose the memory of what you had years ago.

"Micky was my first boyfriend. I loved him too much. I depended on him, too, and when he left me I didn't know where to turn or what to do because he had all the brains inside him and I felt I was so stupid. I had to learn that I wasn't stupid, that I could use my own brains. I've learnt now that I can cope on my own.

I came away from my meetings with the families distraught and deeply unsettled. The almost pervasive fixation they had with the idea that the hunger strikers were still with them—an existential denial that the hunger strikers were dead—ensured that the claims of the past would continue to outweigh the possibilities of the future. Their recollections had a dreamlike quality; they remembered some events vividly, called up graphic images, embellished the details, but at the same time they appeared to be detached from what had gone on, so that sometimes I felt as if they were observers of the events we were talking about rather than participants in them.

Many still weren't sure what had actually happened or even how it happened. They found it hard to believe that the IRA couldn't have ordered an end to the hunger strikes, and in some cases they were not beyond believing that the IRA had ordered the men to continue. The IRA, after all, was known for the power it wielded within their communities and for the ruthlessness it employed and the harsh discipline it imposed. They were given explanations but not satisfactory ones. It was up to the men themselves, they were told, the Republican movement could do nothing about it, but that explanation seemed insufficient to them, at odds with their own understanding of how things worked. They had traveled much during the hunger strikes— the length and breadth of Ireland—pleading their sons' and brothers' and husbands' cases, doing what they were told unquestioningly, so that they rarely had time to think about what was actually going on, always believing that no matter what else happened their own would somehow be saved. They surrendered to their powerlessness—they couldn't be seen to let their own side down or to be the ones who put their sons and brothers and husbands in the position of having to do so. They had no need to make a decision regarding intervention because they believed they wouldn't have to—the hunger strikers' demands would be met before their own sons and brothers and husbands reached the critical phase of their fasts.

The families are, of course, the real victims of the hunger strikes, chattels the Republican movement and the ICJP fought over, objects of an even more bitter battle between Father Denis Faul and Sinn Fein. In their victimhood they looked for meaning, for some way to make sense of it all, to rationalize their own actions or lack of action, to assuage their guilt for not having done something more. And they found it in the mythic past. Their sons were "soldiers," they were dying "to free Ireland," "for the love of their country," "as an expression of their Irishness." They were folded into the embrace of the eight-hundred-year struggle against the English.

I had started my inquiries into the hunger strikes at the Stella Maris School in Rathcoole, which Bobby Sands had attended, and I went back there to finish them. I wanted to find out how students there felt about the school's most celebrated graduate, to talk with a cross-section of students who either would have been old enough to remember something of the hunger strikes or would have been told stories about them. I wanted to see how the hunger strikes had entered the mythology, how one generation created the myth and passed it on to the next, who in time would mold it to its own particular aspirations. But Father Hugh Croffan, a member of the Management Committee for Stella Maris, wouldn't hear of it. There would be no interviewing students regarding Bobby Sands, the hunger strike, or for that matter on anything having to do with the conflict. Bringing up the past was taboo. He didn't want to know what the students thought about these things. Other than that I was free to ask whatever questions I wanted to, as long as I submitted them in advance and agreed to have a teacher in the classroom to ensure that I didn't exceed my guidelines—conditions that would have made the exercise meaningless.

Late one November afternoon I sat in Vice-Principal Tom Cunningham's office and we talked about the school. The student population, which had been close to 1,100 in 1969, was now down to 200, the result of the demographic shifts in population in the early 1970s when each community retreated to its own enclaves. There were still instances where students were intimidated on their way to and from school—one reason, he suggested, why Father Croffan didn't want me to start digging into the past. How many Stella Maris students had been killed since the conflict erupted, I ask him. He smiles slightly, opens the drawer of his desk and takes out a bundle of passport-size photographs—photographs of the faces of young boys, twelve or thirteen years old, reflecting the self-consciousness and awkwardness of adolescence. He flips through them, arranges them in order, and starts to put one after another on his desk, naming the boy in each photograph. "John Erlean, Samuel Hughes, and Charley McCrystal killed by a car bomb of their own making. Thomas Donaghy, Bernard Reynolds, Gerald Gilmore—all assassinated. John Rolston assassinated, Liam McDowell assassinated . . ." and on he goes, tears streaming down his cheeks, as he matches each picture with a name. "Myles Grogan shot as an informer by the Republican movement; Gerard McKeown killed in a bar by a bomb planted by Loyalist paramilitaries; Denis Maguire who joined the RUC and was killed by the IRA, Denis Price who was killed in the mortar attack on the RUC station in Newry"—twenty students in all, victims of either random assassination or bombing or deliberate intention. And we sit there in silence, the two of us, in the fading light of the winter afternoon, the waste of it all overwhelming. There is nothing left to say.

This book has been a voyage of self-discovery, the narrative in part reflecting my own struggle to come to terms with the myths of my Irish past, to better understand the psychological causes that separate the people who share the island of Ireland.

Some concluding observations: The hunger strikes brought into sharp focus the religious dimension of the conflict—differences in the definition and meaning of moral concepts underwriting our notions of right and wrong that make reconciliation difficult, differences that transcend the politics of the conflict. We ignore it, of course, because it makes us uncomfortable to think of ourselves, part of the civilized Western world, as being parties to something as preposterously pre-modern as a religious conflict.

There is no understanding of the Protestant mind in Catholic Ireland and the common belief that Northern Protestants can be accommodated in a thirty-two-county all-Ireland state is delusionary—their obdurate resistance to being incorporated into one is a primary component of their identity. Catholic Ireland does not understand them and makes little attempt to do so. It does not take them seriously; it treats them, at best, with benign condescension, at worst with benign bigotry.

Even after twenty years of conflict, ambivalence about violence—in ways that are difficult to discern but are there nonetheless—continues to plague constitutional nationalism. In the South, the myths are fading but they still hold the state hostage to their power; hence the South's propensity to react to every British action in Northern Ireland almost entirely in the context of whether it will increase support for the IRA. Condemnations of violence have become so routine, the phrases of condemnation so repetitious, that they vitiate the language itself. They are a manifestation of the bankruptcy of ideas, an excuse for the passive behavior of constitutional politicians on both sides of the border.

The propensity by constitutional nationalism to simply denounce the IRA as an evil, to insist that young men are being manipulated by the "godfathers" of violence, aggravates the situation because it distorts our understanding of it. The IRA will not go away, as long as British troops remain in Northern Ireland. They can't defeat the British security forces and the security forces can't defeat them—a mutual standoff that perpetuates an acceptable level of instability. Members of the Republican movement I have spoken with in the course of this inquiry were highly intelligent, extraordinarily motivated, relentlessly committed to their course of action, imbued with a puritanical obsession—you might even say a tyrannical obsession—with wanting to do right and to be seen to do right, which makes their actions all the more frightening. It is the certitude they bring to their beliefs rather than the beliefs themselves that turns abstractions into instruments of death, the narcissistic self-righteousness that condones the lunacies, the schizophrenic contradictions that pass for the precepts of a hallowed nationalism. We must understand them, understand that they have a set of moral values that legitimizes the use of violence and vindicates the armed struggle. Their bishops may argue to the contrary but many of their priests do not. They are us, the Catholic Irish, by-products of our culture and values, and yes, there but for the grace of God go I. They cannot be weaned from their convictions by political arrangements that attempt to undermine support for them in their communities, because they and their communities are inextricably intertwined.

In the end the hunger strikes were about the actions of men who had reached the breaking point, who chose the ultimate form of protest in order to resolve the prison issue one way or the other. They had two choices: either unending years on the dirty protest or surrender; one was impossible, the other unthinkable. "What the hunger strike became," Gerry Adams told me, "was a struggle of wills as personified by Thatcher's public utterances—'the IRA are playing their last card, we're not going to give an inch'—and as personified by what Bobby [Sands] was writing about—'we are an Irish nation, we have the right to be free, I'm a political soldier, I'm a political prisoner, I'm not a criminal.' " This, of course, is precisely what the British were saying all along—that the issue was not about improving prison conditions or making a concession or two, but about political status. Indeed, the British and the IRA understand each other perfectly. Twenty years of conflict have fashioned an unholy psychological alliance between the two.

And the British? For the most part they do not care or if they do it is a forced caring. When I raised the issue of the hunger strikes with British officials, they would often pause, apologize for not being able to recall very much about them, and invariably get names and dates wrong. Perhaps it is understandable. For the British, Ireland is just one of many problems; for Ireland it is *the* problem. What is lacking, however, is a generosity of spirit—an acknowledgment that they too share responsibility for the conflict. Because they refuse to call it a war, preferring instead to fall back on another myth—that it is all about law and order—they are slowly eroding the values indigenous to their own democracy. But that aside, this conflict is essentially an Irish conflict, a conflict between the peoples who share the island of Ireland, between two traditions that define themselves in mutually exclusive terms. They have yet to confront each other directly, primarily because the war is being fought by their surrogates—the IRA and the British security forces.

"The long duration of the conflict between Catholics and Protestants over three centuries," writes sociologist John Darby, "has led to the evolution of social mechanisms to regulate and control their relationships; unable either to remove each other and unwilling to assimilate, they gradually evolved forms of relationships which regulated rather than resolved their antagonisms."[1] The hunger strikes tested the limits of these social mechanisms, but they held, and that perhaps is reason for hope.

I will give the next-to-last word to Alasdair MacIntyre: "The coming together of two previously separate communities, each with its own well-established institutions, practices, and beliefs, either by mi-gration or by conquest, may open up new alternative possibilities and require more than the existing means of evaluation are able to pro-vide," he writes in *Whose Justice? Which Rationality?* "What responses the inhabitants of a particular community make in the face of such stimuli toward the reformulation of their beliefs or the remaking of their practices or both will depend not only upon what stock of reasons and of questioning and reasoning abilities they already possess but also upon inventiveness."[2]

In Ireland, where the parties to the conflict, both immediate and peripheral, are entrapped in an action-response pattern that endlessly repeats itself, there is little of this reasoning and questioning, and certainly no inventiveness.

There are no grand conclusions to be drawn, no prescriptions or solutions to offer. I believe the conflict will last at least another twenty or thirty years, that the competing claims to legitimacy will never entirely resolve themselves. The IRA must be understood in terms of its tradition—a tradition which has its own standards of reasoning, its own background of beliefs. Attempts to show that these beliefs are wrong or somehow invalid will get us no place. They merely state that the beliefs and claims of another tradition are superior. But it is an Irish problem—not a British one—and at some point the British will have to leave us on our own, if only to compel us out of necessity to inventiveness.

And perhaps we will not be able to. Perhaps the solution is already with us, perhaps it lies in the unending, wearisome, self-perpetuating little war from which most people in Northern Ireland can safely insulate themselves; a class war, containable, and in the larger context of war and peace a small thing; a self-sustaining war, because the conflict is about the conflict, and to take it away from people would be to take away their feeling of somehow being special, and, therefore, worthy of special attention.

NOTES

Chapter One

1. Alasdair MacIntyre, *Whose Justice? Which Rationality?* (Notre Dame, Ind.: University of Notre Dame Press, 1988), ix.

2. Robert Elias, *The Politics of Victimization* (New York: Oxford University Press, 1986), 233.

Chapter Two

1. George Dangerfield, *The Damnable Question* (Boston: Little, Brown & Co., 1976), 218.

2. Patrick Bishop and Eamonn Mallie, *The Provisional IRA* (London: Heinemann, 1987), 67.

3. See note 2, p. 290.

4. The cells were cleaned on average about every ten days by volunteer prison officers dressed from head to foot in heavy rubber protective clothing and using an industrial steam-cleaning machine specially purchased for the task.

5. Seamus, Deane, "Civilians and Barbarians," *A Field Day Pamphlet*, no. 3, 1983, 41–42.

6. Father Raymond Murray, "Ill-Treatment of Prisoners and Human Rights," in Denis Faul and Raymond Murray, *H-Blocks: British Jail for Irish Political Prisoners* (Dungannon, 1977), 3.

Chapter Three

1. Sean MacStiofan, *Revolutionary in Ireland* (Edinburgh: Gordon Cremonsi, 1975), 361.

Chapter Four

1. Marc Fried, "Grieving for a Lost Home," in *The Urban Condition* (New York: Basic Books, 1963), 153.

2. John Mack, "Nationalism and the Self," *The Psychohistory Review* 2, no. 3 (Spring 1983): 47–69.

3. Vamik D. Volkan, "Psychological Concepts Useful in the Building of Political Foundations Between Nations: Track II Diplomacy," *Journal of American Psychoanalytic Association* 35, no. 4 (1987): 906.

4. Frantz Fanon, *The Wretched of the Earth* (New York: Grove Press, Inc., 1968), 147.

5. Ibid., 94.

6. Ibid., 50.

7. Patrick Pearse, "The Coming Revolution," in *Political Writings and Speeches* (Dublin: Talbot Press, 1962), 98.

8. George Jackson, *Blood in My Eye* (New York: Random House, 1972), 14.

9. Huey P. Newton, *Revolutionary Suicide* (New York: Harcourt Brace Jovanovich, 1973), 4.

10. Peter Marris, *Loss and Change* (London: Routledge & Kegan Paul, 1986), 97.

11. Leon Uris, *Trinity* (New York: Doubleday, 1976), 731.

12. Ibid., 466.

13. William Irwin Thompson, *The Imagination of an Insurrection* (Oxford: Oxford University Press, 1967), 87.

14. Ibid., 77.

15. Richard Kearney, "Myth and Terror," in *The Crane Bag Book of Irish Studies (1977–1981)* (Dublin: Blackwater Press, 1982), 277.

16. Ibid., 276.

17. Peter Gilliman, "In the Shadow of the Sun—A Deep Concern for the Loos and Drains," *The Sunday Times* (London), 8 May 1983.

18. Thompson, "The Mythic Past and the Present Moment," in Robert O'Driscoll, ed., *The Celtic Consciousness* (New York: George Braziller, 1981), 597.

19. Ruth Dudley Edwards, *Patrick Pearse: The Triumph of Failure* (London: Faber & Faber, 1979), 308.

Chapter Five

1. Camilo Torres, 15 June 1965, at a conference in Grandcolonbiano, Columbia, quoted in John Gerassi, *Revolutionary Priest: The Complete Writings and Messages of Camilo Torres* (New York: Vintage Books, 1971), 27.

2. On 7 July 1972, a party of Provisional IRA leaders, including Gerry Adams, was secretly flown to London for talks with William Whitelaw, the secretary of state for Northern Ireland. The talks were unproductive. Two days later the truce which the Provisionals had announced on 22 June collapsed. It had lasted just thirteen days. After secret talks between IRA leaders and Protestant clergymen at Feakle, County Clare, on 10 December 1974, meetings took place between British government officials and members of Provisional Sinn Fein. The cease-fire which the IRA had announced on 22 December 1974 was extended first to 16 January 1975 and then to 10 February, when an open-ended cease-fire was announced which lasted a year.

3. Robert Jay Lifton, quoted in Terence Des Pres, *The Survivor: The Anatomy of Life in the Death Camps* (New York: Oxford University Press, 1976), 39.

4. Liam McCloskey quoted by Liam Clarke, *Broadening the Battlefield* (Dublin: Gill & Macmillan, 1987), 197.

5. Comms that McFarlane sent to Gerry Adams.

6. Joel Brockner and Jeffrey Z. Rubin, *Entrapment in Escalating Conflicts: A Social Psychological Analysis* (New York: Springer Verlag, 1985), 5.

Chapter Seven

1. Jeanne N. Knutson, *Victimization and Political Violence: The Sceptre of Our Times,* uncompleted book MS, 1981, 73.

2. Erik H. Erikson, *In Search of Common Ground: Conversations with Erik Erikson and Huey Newton* (New York: Dell, 1973), 46.

3. Knutson, *Victimization and Political Violence,* 75.

4. Terence Des Pres, *The Survivor: The Anatomy of Life in the Death Camps* (New York: Oxford University Press, 1976), 5.

5. Father Denis Faul and Father Raymond Murray, "The Caves of Long Kesh," *H-Blocks: British Jail for Irish Political Prisoners* (Dungannon, 1977), 91.

6. Patrick Graham, quoted by Padraig O'Malley in "Art and Politics: Four Irish Expressionist Painters," Symposium at the Museum of Fine Arts, Boston; *Working Papers in Irish Studies* 86, nos. 4/5 (1986), 27.

7. Editorial in *New York Times* quoted in Jeanne Knutson, *Victimization and Political Violence,* 75.

8. Patrick Pearse, quoted in F. S. L. Lyons, *Culture and Anarchy in Ireland* (Oxford: Claredon Press, 1979), 88.

9. Patrick Pearse, quoted in Lyons, *Culture and Anarchy in Ireland,* 91.

10. Richard Kearney, *Transitions: Narrations in Modern Irish Culture* (Manchester: Manchester University Press, 1988), 223.

11. William Irwin Thompson, *The Imagination of an Insurrection* (Oxford: Oxford University Press, 1967), 139.

12. Quoted in Kearney, *Transitions,* 236.

13. Shiva Naipaul, *Journey to Nowhere* (New York: Simon and Schuster, 1980), 157–58.

Chapter Eight

1. Patrick Pearse, quoted in Ruth Dudley Edwards, *Patrick Pearse: The Triumph of Failure* (London: Faber and Faber, 1979), 314.

2. Ernest Jones, *Psycho-Myth, Psycho-History: Essays in Applied Psychoanalysis,* vol. 1 (New York: Stonehill Publishing, 1974), 107.

3. A. Norman Jeffares, ed., *W. B. Yeats: Selected Plays* (London: Pan Books, 1974), 256.

4. Margaret MacCurtin, "The Religious Image of Women," in *The Crane Bag Book of Irish Studies (1977–1981),* ed. M. P. Hederman and R. Kearney (Dublin: Blackwater Press, 1982), 542.

5. Jeanne N. Knutson, *Victimization and Political Violence,* 69.

Chapter Ten

1. Patrick Pearse, quoted in F. S. L. Lyons, *Culture and Anarchy in Ireland 1890–1939* (Oxford: Oxford University Press, 1979), 85.

2. Margaret O'Callaghan, "The Church and Irish Independence," *The Crane Bag, Forum Issue* 7, no. 2 (1983): 65–76.

3. Robert Kee, *The Green Flag: Ourselves Alone,* vol. 1 (London: Quartet Books, 1976), 51–78.

4. Denis Donoghue, " 'Letter from Dublin.' Inside the Maze—Legitimising Heirs to the Men of 1916," *The Listener* (3 September 1981), 1–3.

5. Quoted in U.K. Foreign and Commonwealth Office, *Northern Ireland Briefing Pack* (London: Her Majesty's Stationery Office, 1981), 12–2.

6. Ibid.

7. Kee, *The Green Flag,* 3:127.

8. Excerpt from the *Irish Catholic Directory, 1923,* 2 April 1922, 608, quoted in Margaret O'Callaghan "The Church and Irish Independence," 66.

9. O'Callaghan, "The Church and Irish Independence," 67–68.

10. Kee, *The Green Flag,* 3:61.

11. Warren E. Susman, *Culture as History: The Transformation of American Society in the Twentieth Century* (New York: Pantheon Books, 1984), 271–85.

12. Author interview with Garret FitzGerald

Chapter Eleven

1. Frank Wright, "Reconciling the Histories of Protestant and Catholic in Northern Ireland," in *Reconciling Memories,* ed. Alan D. Falconer (Dublin: Columba Press, 1988), 75.

2. A.T.Q. Stewart, *The Narrow Ground* (London: Faber and Faber, 1977), 22. On 4 September 1607, the O'Neills and O'Donnells and a large number of their kinsmen sailed to the Continent. "In song and romance the 'Flight of the Earls' had become a poignant exodus of what remained heroic and quintessentially Gaelic in Ireland," writes Karl S. Bottigheimer in *Ireland and the Irish* (New York: Columbia University Press, 1982), 118.

Chapter Twelve

1. Terence Brown, "The Whole Protestant Community: The Making of a Historical Myth," *A Field Day Pamphlet* 7 (1985), 8.

2. Ken Heskin, *Northern Ireland: A Psychological Analysis* (New York: Columbia University Press, 1980), 29.

3. Ibid., 30.

4. Terence Des Pres, *The Survivor: An Anatomy of Life in the Death Camps* (New York: Oxford University Press, 1976).

5. A.T.Q. Stewart, *The Narrow Ground* (London: Faber & Faber, 1977), 16.

6. Vincent Crapanzano, *Waiting: The Whites of South Africa* (New York: Random House, 1985), xxii.

7. Ibid.

Chapter Thirteen

1. Tomas O'Fiaich, "The Clergy and Fenianism, 1860–70," *Irish Ecclesiastical Record,* 109 (February 1968), 93.

2. These excerpts from the Catholic Church's 1983 *Directory of Mixed Marriages,* quoted in "Arguments and Disagreements of Irish Presbyterians and Roman Catholics," published by the Presbyterian Church in Ireland, June 1988.

3. Alasdair MacIntyre, *Whose Justice? Which Rationality?* (Notre Dame, Ind.: University of Notre Dame Press, 1988), 378.

4. Donald Davidson, quoted in ibid., 370.

5. Ibid., 381.

6. Denis O'Callaghan, "Hunger Strikes: The Rights and Wrongs," *Irish Press,* 14 November 1980.

7. Denis O'Callaghan, "A Moral Dilemma," *Irish Times,* 15 June 1981.

Chapter Fourteen

1. Seamus Deane, "Civilians and Barbarians," *A Field Day Pamphlet,* no. 3, 1983, 7–12.

Chapter Sixteen

1. Since 1972, when Britain abolished the Northern Ireland government, the North has been ruled directly from London; "devolution" refers to the reestablishment of a provincial government authority.

2. Jeanne N. Knutson, *Victimization and Political Violence* (1981), 73–76.

3. James McEvoy, "Catholic Hopes and Protestant Fears," *The Crane Bag* 7, no. 2 (1983): 101–2.

4. Terence Brown, "The Whole Protestant Community: The Making of a Historical Myth," *A Field Day Pamphlet,* no. 7, 1985, 10.

Chapter Seventeen

1. Gerry Adams, *The Politics of Irish Freedom* (Dingle, Co. Kerry: Brandon, 1986), 64.

2. Abstentionism from the parliaments of Dublin and Belfast was raised to the level of principle between 1921 and 1985 on the grounds that both Irish states were illegal assemblies, in violation of the Republic declared by the first Dail in 1919. The Westminster parliament was boycotted because the British presence in Ireland was regarded as illegal. Sinn Fein's and the IRA's recognition of the Dublin parliament was an acknowledgment of a reality—the overwhelming number of people of the South recognized it as a legitimate government.

3. Adams, *The Politics of Irish Freedom,* 64.

Chapter Eighteen

1. On 8 November 1987 the IRA detonated a bomb during Remembrance Day ceremonies in Enniskillen, killing eleven people. See chapter 19.

2. In late 1982, six unarmed nationalists were shot dead by members of the RUC. Accusations of an RUC "shoot-to-kill" policy resulted in an independent investigation into the deaths led by John Stalker, deputy chief constable of the Greater Manchester Police. The investigation showed the RUCs' account to be

untrue. Stalker was removed from both his position and the case before completing the investigation, and was accused but subsequently acquitted of consorting with criminals. The Stalker Report, completed under the direction of Chief Constable Colin Sampson, was submitted to Sir Patrick Mayhew, the British attorney general, in January 1988. For national security reasons, the report's findings were not made public and no disciplinary action was taken.

On 21 November 1974, two pub bombings in Birmingham killing nineteen people led to the conviction of six Irish nationalists. When subsequent evidence of their innocence emerged, an appeal was granted. In February 1988, the Court of Appeals ruled against the defendants.

Questions about a shoot-to-kill policy were raised again by the deaths of three unarmed members of the IRA at the hands of British security forces in Gibraltar in March 1988. These questions remain, despite the subsequent inquest and acquittal of implicated security personnel.

Intended as a temporary measure following the 1974 Birmingham pub bombings, the Prevention of Terrorism Act allows the government to detain people suspected of terrorism for up to seven days without bringing charges and to deport them. Aimed mostly at Irish people living in or traveling to Britain, the act must be renewed every year.

Chapter Nineteen

1. On Remembrance Day Britain honors her war dead. The red poppy is the symbol of remembrance. The Republic of Ireland does not recognize Remembrance Day, since the occasion is equated with honoring the British army, despite the fact that tens of thousands of Irishmen died fighting on behalf of Britain in World War I (far more than ever died on behalf of Ireland for Ireland's freedom), when Ireland was still part of the United Kingdom, and many more died in the service of the British army during World War II, when Ireland was neutral. On Remembrance Day services are conducted at St. Patrick's Cathedral, Dublin, but there is no official government representation. Ireland has its own National Day of Commemoration when it honors its war dead, including those who died in both world wars, although all reference to their having served in the British army is omitted.

2. Peter Marris, *Loss and Change* (London: Routledge & Kegan Paul, 1986), 96.

3. Frank Wright, "Reconciling the Histories of Catholics and Protestants in Northern Ireland," in *Reconciling Memories,* ed. Alan D. Falconer (Dublin: Columbia Press, 1988), 79.

4. Elizabeth Shannon, *I Am Ireland: Women of the North Speak Out* (Boston: Little Brown, 1989), 48.

Chapter Twenty

1. John Darby, *Intimidation and the Control of Conflict in Northern Ireland* (Dublin: Gill & Macmillan, 1986), 168–69.

2. Alasdair MacIntyre, *Whose Justice? Which Rationality?* (Notre Dame, Ind.: University of Notre Dame Press, 1988), 355.

GLOSSARY

Black and Tan War The War of Independence of 1919–21 is sometimes called the "Black and Tan War" or the "Tan War." Members of the Royal Irish Constabulary (RIC), the Irish police force, for the most part Catholics, began to resign because of the campaign of assassinations the IRA was conducting against them. Their places were taken by recruits from Britain, men who had been demobilized by the British army. What the authorities never really clarified was whether they were to behave like soldiers or like police. Their mixture of army and police uniforms symbolized their ambivalent role and gave them the nickname the "Black and Tans." In all, seven thousand members of the RIC were recruited in this way. On average they served in Ireland for about eight months. A new specially trained Auxiliary Division of the RIC came into being in July 1920. It was this Auxiliary Division, about fifteen hundred men, who were to hunt the IRA in motorized packs across the Irish countryside, which became indelibly associated in the public mind with the Black and Tans. Often, they took the law into their own hands and committed many acts of reprisal against innocent people whom they suspected of supporting the IRA.

Democratic Unionist Party (DUP) Founded in 1971, the DUP regards itself as being "right wing in terms of being strong on the Constitution but to the left on social policies." It represents hard-line Unionism and political Protestantism. It opposes power sharing and an Irish Dimension, and strongly opposes the Anglo–Irish Agreement of 1985. Its leader is the Reverend Ian Paisley, founder of the Free Presbyterian Church.

Diplock Courts Following the report of the Diplock Commission, headed by Lord Diplock, in 1972, the government adopted its proposals calling for nonjury trials for a wide range of political/terrorist offenses. The Commission argued that these cases should be heard by a single judge sitting alone because of the risk of jury intimidation. The courts became known as "Diplock Courts," with a High Court judge sitting for the more serious cases.

Direct Rule In March 1972, the British government suspended indefinitely the Northern Ireland Parliament after Brian Faulkner, the province's prime minister, balked at handing over all security power to Westminster. The British government took full control of Northern Ireland, appointing a secretary of state for Northern Ireland to implement Direct Rule and a Northern Ireland Office to administer it.

Fenian The Fenian Brotherhood, a Republican physical-force movement founded in 1858, was active in the nineteenth century in Britain and the United States. The term is often applied to Catholics by loyalists.

Fianna Fail Fianna Fail is the largest political party in the Republic of Ireland. It originated in the Republican wing of Sinn Fein, which opposed the Anglo-Irish Treaty of 1921. It came to power in 1932 and has ruled the country for most of the period since, except for 1948–51, 1954–57, 1973–77, mid-1981 to March 1982, and December 1982 to March 1987. Fianna Fail is a staunchly nationalist party. Its leader is Charles Haughey.

Fine Gael Fine Gael is the Republic of Ireland's second largest political party. It originated in the pro-treaty wing of Sinn Fein. It has never been able to form a government from its own ranks. It is regarded as being less "nationalist" than Fianna Fail. Dr. Garret FitzGerald is a former leader; Alan Dukes is the current one.

Irish Dimension A term which came into popular usage in 1973, it is an acknowledgment of the desire of the majority of the Catholic community in Northern Ireland for an eventual united Ireland. It is a counterbalance to the British Dimension, the term used to express the Unionist attachment to Britain. It was given institutional expression in the plan for a Council of Ireland in the Sunningdale Agreement. Today it has institutional expression under the Anglo-Irish Agreement of 1985 in the form of the Intergovernmental Conference.

Irish National Liberation Army (INLA) *(see also* **Provisional IRA)** In 1976, the Official Sinn Fein movement split, the more radical and militant wing becoming the Irish National Liberation Army, and its political counterpart, the Irish Republican Socialist Party (IRSP). INLA, which is not a very large paramilitary organization, has, however, been associated with many ruthless acts of violence, including the car-bomb killing of Airey Neave, the Conservative Party's spokesperson on Northern Ireland and a close confidant to British prime minister Margaret Thatcher, in March 1979. In the hunger strikes three INLA prisoners died—Patsy O'Hara, Kevin Lynch, and Micky Devine.

Loyalist, Loyalism A more extreme form of Unionism. Loyalists, ironically, are likely to place more emphasis on not becoming part of an all-Ireland state than with the maintenance of the United Kingdom link. The union with Britain is seen as a safeguard against absorption into the Irish Republic. Loyalists are more likely than Unionists to be working-class.

Nationalist Nationalists give their allegiance to the precepts of Irish nationalism—the abolition of the border between the North and the South of Ireland and the unification of Ireland. Invariably, though not necessarily, nationalists are Catholic. Nationalists support constitutional politics and a united Ireland obtained with the consent of a majority of the people of Northern Ireland.

Official IRA (OIRA) (see also Provisional IRA) The military wing of Official Sinn Fein. It has been disbanded. Official Sinn Fein is now the Workers' Party. Official Sinn Fein entered constitutional politics and at present holds two seats in the Irish parliament.

Official Unionist Party (OUP) Also known as the Ulster Unionist Party. The OUP traces its origins to the Ulster Unionist Party, which was founded in 1892 and remained the sole voice of the Protestant population of Northern Ireland until the late 1960s, and the governing party from 1920 to 1972. The monolith, however, collapsed during divisions that ensued over civil rights, the fall of Stormont, and power sharing with Catholics. The OUP remains the largest political party in the province. The OUP is split between integrationists—those who want full integration with Great Britain—and devolutionists—those who want a return to devolved government in Northern Ireland. They also oppose the Anglo-Irish Agreement of 1985.

Orange Order The Orange Order was founded in 1795 after a clash between Catholics and Protestants at the "Battle of the Diamond." It is the largest Protestant organization in Northern Ireland, where it has between 80,000 and 100,000 members. About one adult Protestant in three is a member. Its annual Twelfth of July demonstrations at more than twenty centers in Northern Ireland celebrate King William's victory over King James II at the Battle of the Boyne in 1690. In religious terms the Order stands for "good, clean Protestant living, fundamental sabbatarianism, and vehement opposition to the Catholic Church." In political terms the Order is pledged to "support and maintain the laws and constitution of the United Kingdom and Protestant succession to the throne."

Provisional Irish Republican Army (PIRA) The Provisional IRA, also called "The Provies," "The Provos," or simply the IRA, and its political wing, Provisional Sinn Fein or just Sinn Fein, came into being in January 1970 after the IRA Army Council voted to give token recognition to the parliaments in Dublin, London, and Belfast, which effectively meant the end of abstentionism. (Sinn Fein candidates would sometimes run for seats in one of these parliaments. However, if elected, they would not serve since they regarded these institutions as being either illegal or foreign.) Those who disagreed with the Army Council's ruling walked out, splitting the Republican movement into the Provisional IRA and Provisional Sinn Fein, founded by those who had walked out, and the Official IRA and Official Sinn Fein. The Official IRA abandoned its military activities in 1972 and disbanded sometime afterward. PIRA, however, has sustained a twenty-year military campaign to end what it terms the "British occupation" of Ireland. Sinn Fein publishes *An Phoblacht/Republican News*.

Republican, Republicanism A more extreme form of nationalism. Republicans support a thirty-two county Republic. The term has become synonymous with support for Sinn Fein with its socialist orientation and the IRA's military campaign, although not all Republicans would necessarily support either. Republicans call for British withdrawal or a declaration of intent to withdraw as the first step toward bringing about a united Ireland.

Royal Ulster Constabulary (RUC) The Royal Ulster Constabulary is the Northern Ireland police force. It is about 90 percent Protestant.

Sinn Fein: *See* Provisional Irish Republican Army.

Social Democratic and Labour Party (SDLP) The SDLP speaks for a majority of Catholics in Northern Ireland. Founded in 1970 by a group of ex-civil rights activists, it is an umbrella party. It brought together the remnants of the old Nationalist Party, which stood for unity with the rest of Ireland and little else, the National Democratic Party, and the Republican Labour Party. Its long-term goals are a socialist state in the European social democratic tradition, and Irish unity based on the consent of a majority of the people of Northern Ireland. It is generally split between those who hew to a strictly nationalist line—the "Greens"—and those who do not. The party leader is John Hume.

Stormont The Northern Ireland Parliament at Stormont, on the outskirts of Belfast. Hence the phrase "Stormont rule."

Sunningdale Agreement The Sunningdale Conference was held at Sunningdale (Berkshire) Civil Service College from 6 to 9 December 1973. Participating were the British and Irish governments and the three parties—the Unionist party, the SDLP, and the Alliance party—that had formed a power-sharing executive in Northern Ireland in 1974. The Sunningdale Agreement provided for a Council of Ireland; thus the "Irish Dimension." The first tier of the Council would have consisted of seven ministers from both the Dail (Irish parliament) and the Northern Ireland Assembly. Decisions would have required an unanimous vote. A second tier would have had a consultative role. The Sunningdale Agreement and the power-sharing executive collapsed following the Ulster Workers' Council Strike in May 1974.

Ulster Defence Association (UDA) Started in September 1971 as a coordinating body for a great variety of loyalist vigilante groups, the UDA is Northern Ireland's largest Protestant paramilitary organization. It is legal although its military wing, the Ulster Freedom Fighters, is proscribed. The UDA advocates independence for Northern Ireland. It publishes *Ulster*.

Ulster Defence Regiment (UDR) The Ulster Defence Regiment, which became operational in April 1970, is a locally based regiment of the British Army. Its members are drawn exclusively from Northern Ireland. It provides back-up services for Northern Ireland's police force. The UDR is about 98 percent Protestant. One-third of its members are full-time soldiers and two-thirds serve in a part-time capacity. The UDR accounts for over 40 percent of the military forces in Northern Ireland.

Ulster Protestant Action Group A splinter Protestant paramilitary organization.

Ulster Volunteer Force (UVF) An illegal Protestant paramilitary force, it is sometimes described as the "secret Protestant army." In 1966 it revived the title of the Unionist force established in 1912 to fight Irish Home Rule.

Unionist Unionists give their allegiance to the precepts of Unionism—the maintenance of the union between Northern Ireland and the United Kingdom. Invariably, though not necessarily, Unionists are Protestant.

SOURCES

Interviews

Gerry Adams President of Sinn Fein. Abstaining member of British Parliament for West Belfast. Was vice-president of Sinn Fein during hunger strikes. Headed the Sinn Fein Committee that advised the hunger strikers. (25 March '85; 23 May '85; 17 August '85; 4 September '86; 30 August '88; 4 April '89)

David Aiken Democratic Unionist Party; member of Omagh District Council. (1 September '86)

Michael Alison Member of British Parliament (M.P.); minister of state for Northern Ireland during the hunger strikes. (24 September '86; 23 November '88)

Chris Anderson Former member of the Star of the Sea Youth Club. (29 December '88)

Humphrey Atkins Now Lord Colnbrook; secretary of state for Northern Ireland during the hunger strikes. (27 November '88)

Sean Banner Former member of the Republican movement. (29 August '86)

Robert Bell Curator of the Northern Ireland Political Archive in Linenhall Library, Belfast. Former resident of Suffolk, a Protestant enclave in West Belfast. (23 June '86)

Ellen Bell Resident of Suffolk. Robert Bell's mother. (23 June '86)

Neil Blaney Member of the European Parliament; Member of Dail Eireann (Irish parliament). (2 February '89)

Sir John Blelloch Permanent under secretary of the Northern Ireland Office; deputy secretary at the NIO during the hunger strikes. (23 September '86; 23 November '88)

John Boy Resident of Suffolk. (30 August '86)

Ann Boyle Resident of Suffolk. (30 August '86)

The Very Reverend Dr. Godfrey Brown Former moderator of the Presbyterian Church in Ireland. (5 January '89)

Jean Brown Resident of Suffolk. (31 July '86)

John and Maeve Cadoo Aughnacloy, Co. Tyrone. Their son Franklin, a part-time member of the UDR, was shot dead by the IRA on 10 May 1979. (25 August '86)

The Reverend Sydney Callaghan Former president of the Methodist Church in Ireland. (30 December '87)

Gregory Campbell Democratic Unionist Party; member of Derry City Council. (23 August '86)

Jerome Connolly Secretary of the Irish Commission for Justice and Peace. (19 November '85; 1 February '86; 30 January '89)

Jim Craig Member of the Ulster Defence Association; shot dead by the UDA on 15 October 1988 for racketeering and complicity in the death of John McMichael (see below). (25 August '86)

Colin Crawford Worker at Maze/Long Kesh Prison for the Northern Ireland Probation Service, 1974–80. (24 November '88)

Father Oliver Crilly Member of the Executive Committee of the Irish Commission for Justice and Peace. (25 November '88)

Tom Cunningham Vice-principal of the Stella Maris Secondary School. (2 September '88)

Austin Currie Social Democratic and Labour Party (SDLP). The local Fermanagh–South Tyrone Constituency Committee nominated him to run for the seat left vacant in the wake of Frank McManus's death. Its decision was overruled by the Party Executive. (3 January '89)

John Cushnahan Former leader of the Alliance Party. (24 July 86; 29 August '86)

The Most Reverend Dr. Cahal B. Daly Bishop of Down and Connor. (8 November '88)

The Most Reverend Dr. Edward Daly Bishop of Derry. (1 January '86)

Margaret Devine Wife of hunger striker Micky Devine. (1 February '89)

Paddy Devlin Interned under Special Powers Act, 1942–45; founding member of the Northern Ireland Civil Rights Association; cofounder of the SDLP; resigned from the party in 1977; obtained the largest single vote in the 1977 District Council elections; full-time district secretary to the Irish Transport and General Workers' Union. (21 November '88)

Paddy Doherty Republican; founder of the North West Learning Centre, Derry. (28 August '86)

Jimmy Drumm Senior Sinn Fein official; in charge of families and funeral arrangements during hunger strikes. His wife, Maura, a vice-president of Sinn Fein, was assassinated in March 1976. (29 December '88; 5 January '89)

The Most Reverend Dr. Robin Eames Anglican primate of All Ireland; archbishop of Armagh; bishop of Down during the hunger strikes. (31 December '87; 7 November '88; 5 January '89)

Edith Elliott Charlemont, Co. Armagh. Her husband, George, a part-time member of the UDR, was shot dead by the IRA in 1980; her brother, Jack Donnolly, also a part-time UDR member, was shot dead by the IRA on 16 April 1981. (3 January '89)

Father Denis Faul Dungannon, Co. Tyrone. Activist through the seventies for prison reform; frequent visitor to Maze/Long Kesh Prison; brought families together to end the hunger strike. (23 November '85; 26 August '88)

Brian Feeney SDLP; member of Belfast City Council. (30 July '86)

Seamus Finucane Sinn Fein; former internee; former blanketman in Maze/Long Kesh who participated in the Dirty Protest. (4 September '86)

Garret FitzGerald Former leader of Fine Gael; Taoiseach (prime minister) of the Republic of Ireland, 1981–82, 1982–87. (2 January '89)

The Very Reverend Dr. William Fleming Former moderator of the Presbyterian Church in Ireland. (31 December '87)

The Reverend Ivan Foster Democratic Unionist Party; minister in the Free Presbyterian Church (founded by Ian Paisley). (25 August '86)

Brian Gallagher Chairman of the Irish Commission for Justice and Peace. (30 January '89)

The Reverend Eric Gallagher Former president of the Methodist Church in Ireland. (29 December '87)

Oliver Gibson Democratic Unionist Party; member of Omagh District Council. (1 September '86)

Sir Ian Gilmour Lord Privy Seal and senior cabinet member who served as deputy to the secretary of state for foreign and commonwealth affairs at the time of the hunger strikes. (6 April '89)

Tommy Gorman Sinn Fein; former blanket man in Maze/Long Kesh who participated in the Dirty Protest. (19 August '86; 26 August '86)

The Right Reverend Victor Griffin Church of Ireland; dean of St. Patrick's Cathedral, Dublin. (28 December '88)

Jack Hanvey Resident of Suffolk. (22 July '86)

Rubie Harris Mother of Hugh Harris, who was killed during the Bayardo bombing in 1975. (27 November '88)

William Haye Democratic Unionist Party; member of Derry City Council. (28 August '86)

Father James Healy, S.J. Teacher of moral theology, the Institute of Theology and Philosophy, Milltown Park, Dublin. (2 January '89)

Gerard Hodgins Sinn Fein; former blanketman at Maze/Long Kesh who went on the Dirty Protest; joined the hunger strike on 13 September 1981; ended hunger strike on 3 October 1981. (5 September '86)

John Hume Leader of the SDLP; member of British Parliament for Foyle. Member of European Parliament. One of the architects of the New Ireland Forum. (28 August '86; 10 March '89)

Brendan and Sheila Hurson Brother and sister-in-law of hunger striker Martin Hurson. (22 November '88)

Jake Jackson Sinn Fein; former blanketman in Maze/Long Kesh who went on the Dirty Protest; member of Brendan McFarlane's leadership circle. (6 January '89; 29 January '89)

Alan Kane Democratic Unionist Party; member of Cookstown District Council. (27 August '86)

Father Myles Kavanagh Holy Cross Cathedral, Ardoyne. (29 August '88)

Hugh Logue SDLP; member of Irish Commission for Justice and Peace. (27 December '88)

Bridie Lynch Mother of hunger striker Kevin Lynch. (22 November '88)

H. A. Lyons Psychiatrist, Purdysburn Hospital, Belfast. (1 September '88)

Ken Maginnis Official Unionist Party; member of the British Parliament for Fermanagh–South Tyrone. He was defeated by Owen Carron in August 1981. However, in the 1983 general election, both Sinn Fein and the SDLP fielded candidates, split the Catholic vote, and ensured the election of Maginnis. (31 December '85; 13 July '86; 25 August '86; 3 January '89)

Eamonn Mallie Co-author of *The Provisional IRA;* reporter for Downtown Radio Belfast. (3 January '89)

Seamus Mallon Deputy leader SDLP; member of British Parliament. (17 March '87)

Bernadette Devlin McAliskey One of the leaders of the National H-Block/Armagh Committee. (25 November '88)

Paddy McCabe Sacristan, Holy Cross Cathedral, Ardoyne. (27 November '88)

James McClure Democratic Unionist Party; member of Coleraine District Council. (27 August '86)

Jeanette and Walter McCreery Residents of Suffolk. (29 August '86)

John McCrillen Sinn Fein; former Republican prisoner; was on remand at Crumlin Road Jail during first hunger strike; joined a three-day fast to signify solidarity with the hunger strikers; was on same wing in the H-blocks as the hunger striker Joe McDonnell. (26 August '86)

Father Brian McCreesh Brother of hunger striker Raymond McCreesh. (25 November '88)

Harold McCusker Deputy leader of Official Unionist Party; member of the British Parliament for Upper Bann. (29 July '86)

Maura, Eilish, and Robert McDonnell Sisters and brother of hunger striker Joe McDonnell. (20 November '88)

Eileen McDonnell Mother of hunger striker Joe McDonnell. (1 February '89)

Alice McElwee and Enda McElwee Mother and sister of hunger striker Thomas McElwee. (5 January '89)

Pat McGeown Sinn Fein; former blanketman in Maze/Long Kesh who went on Dirty Protest; went on the hunger strike on 10 July 1981; wife intervened on 20 August. (4 August '86; 19 August '86; 5 September '86; 28 January '89)

Eric McKee Member of Ulster Defence Association. (29 August '86)

John McMichael Senior UDA official and author of the UDA document *Common Sense,* which urged the Unionist Parties to participate in a power-sharing government with Nationalists. Assassinated by the IRA in December 1987. (20 November '85; 5 August '86)

Jim McMullan Sinn Fein; former blanketman in Maze/Long Kesh who went on Dirty Protest. (5 September '86)

Billy McQuistan Ulster Defence Association; went on the UDA blanket protest and the short-lived UDA hunger strike in December 1981. His father (who has special-category status) is serving a life sentence in the H-block compounds. (21 August '86; 29 August '86)

Danny Morrison National director of publicity for Sinn Fein; was editor of *An Phoblacht/Republican News* during hunger strikes. (20 November '85; 24 July '86; 4 April '89)

Kevin Mulgrew Sinn Fein; former H-block remand prisoner before hunger strikes; served time in the H-blocks after the hunger strike. (5 August '86; 19 August '86; 26 August '86)

Joe Mullan Twinbrook resident during hunger strike; played football with Bobby Sands as a youth. (23 November '88)

Father Liam Mullan Parish priest in Twinbrook during hunger strike; presided over funeral services for Bobby Sands. (21 November '88)

Ray Mullan Teacher of social studies at St. Louise Comprehensive College for Girls. (25 November '88)

Pat Murphy Ardoyne; friend of Brendan McFarlane. (26 November '88; 30 December '88)

Denis Nellis Former H-block blanketman who went on the Dirty Protest. At one point in May 1981 he was on McFarlane's short-list for the hunger strikes. (28 August '86)

Father Piaras O'Duill Chairman of the National H-Block/Armagh Committee, Dublin. (1 February '89)

Tomas Cardinal O'Fiaich Archbishop of Armagh; primate of All Ireland (3 January '86; 4 January '89)

Peggy O'Hara Mother of hunger striker Patsy O'Hara. (26 November '88)

The Right Reverend Dermot O'Mahony Auxiliary bishop of Dublin; chairperson of the Irish Commission for Justice and Peace. (31 January '89)

Brigid McKenna O'Neill Mother of Sean McKenna, whose imminent death ended the first hunger strike. (1 January '86)

Brian Palmer A Northern Ireland Office official responsible for prison issues. (3 July '86)

Desmond Rea Professor at the University of Ulster; general lay secretary of the Methodist Church Council on Social Welfare. (29 December '87)

Jackie Redpath Editor of *Shankill Bulletin*. (25 July '86)

Joe Reid Ballymurphy community activist. (1 September '88)

Peter Robinson Deputy leader of the Democratic Unionist Party; member of British Parliament for East Belfast. (26 November '85; 30 December '85; 30 July '86; 3 September '86; 6 July '87; 29 August '88)

Father Sean Rogan Curate in Twinbrook during hunger strikes; assisted Father Mullan during funeral services for Bobby Sands. (4 January '89)

Chris Ryder Former reporter for the *Times* in Northern Ireland. (4 January '89)

Kevin Sheehan Former blanketman at Maze/Long Kesh who went on the Dirty Protest. His brother Patrick joined the hunger strike on 17 August and came off on 3 October. (5 August '86; 26 August '86; 4 September '86)

Dr. Daniel Sloan Deputy chief medical officer of the Department of Health and Social Services, who oversaw treatment of hunger strikers. (27 August '86; 25 September '86)

Ruby Speer Desertmartin, County Derry. Her husband, James, a part-time member of the UDR, was assassinated by the IRA in November 1976. (31 December '85)

Gusty Spence The UVF commander in the Shankill Road, who served eighteen years in the Compounds with special-category status in connection with the murder of a Catholic in 1966. Currently leader of the Progressive Unionist Party. (9 July '86; 25 September '86)

Charles Steele Democratic Unionist Party; member of Ballymoney District Council. (26 August '86)

Paddy Straney Uncle of hunger striker Joe McDonnell. (19 November '88)

Denis Sweeney Former member of the Star of the Sea Youth Club who played with Bobby Sands on the Club's soccer team. (1 September '88)

The Right Reverend Norman Taggart General ministerial secretary of the Methodist Church in Ireland. (29 December '87)

Brian Turkington Resident of Suffolk. (22 July '86)

Andy Tyrie Supreme commander of the UDA who was forced to resign from his position in 1988 in the aftermath of John McMichael's assassination. (27 November '85; 6 July '87)

Father Matt Wallace A curate in Lenadoon when Joe McDonnell was on hunger strike (18 November '88)

Alfie Watson Former prison warder in the H-blocks. His son Jim is currently serving time in Maze/Long Kesh for the attempted murder of Bernadette Devlin McAliskey. (2 September '86; 5 September '86)

John Watson Principal of St. Colm's Secondary School, Twinbrook. (2 September '86; 5 September '86)

Sammy Wilson Democratic Unionist Party; former lord mayor of Belfast. (29 August '86)

In addition, fifteen other people gave interviews on the condition that their names would be held in confidence.

Newspapers

Andersonstown News (Belfast)
An Phoblacht/Republican News (Dublin)
Belfast Telegraph (Belfast)
Daily Express (London)
Daily Mail (London)
Daily Telegraph (London)
Guardian (London)
Hot Press (Dublin)
Independent (Dublin)

Independent (London)
Irish News (Belfast)
Irish Post (London)
Irish Press (Dublin)
Irish Times (Dublin)
Newsletter (Belfast)
New York Irish People
Sun (London)
Times (London)

Periodicals and Occasional Publications

Alliance (Belfast)
Church of Ireland Gazette (Lisburn)
Fortnight (Belfast)
H-Block/Armagh Bulletins (Belfast)
Irelande Libre (Paris)
Irish Democrat (Dublin)
Iris (Dublin)
Irish Prisoner (London)
Irish Socialist Review (Dublin)

Magill (Dublin)
Northern People (Belfast)
Orange Torch (Glasgow)
Orange Standard (Belfast)
Peace by Peace (Belfast)
Prison Struggle (Belfast)
Protestant Telegraph (Belfast)
Ulster (Belfast)
Ulster Defiant (Belfast)

Statements and Press Releases

Don't Let the Irish Prisoners Die Committee (London)
National H-Block Committee (Dublin)
Northern Ireland Information Services (London/Belfast)
Republican Protesting Prisoners in H-Block/Long Kesh
Sinn Fein (Belfast)

Other

British Broadcasting Corporation. "Sister Genevieve." 8 October 1981.
————. "Old Scores." 6 August 1983.
Beresford, David. *Ten Men Dead* for excerpts from comms between
   Brendan McFarlane and Gerry Adams.

BIBLIOGRAPHY

Abramson, Lyn Y., Martin E. P. Seligman, and John D. Teasdale. "Learned Helplessness in Humans: Critique and Reformulation." *Journal of Abnormal Psychology* 87, no. 1 (1978): 49–74.

Adams, Gerry. *Falls Memories*. Dingle, County Kerry: Brandon, 1982.

———. *The Politics of Irish Freedom*. Dingle, County Kerry: Brandon, 1986.

———. *A Pathway to Peace*. Dublin: Mercier Press, 1988.

———. "The Way Forward." Address in Belfast, 10 May 1989.

———. *Signposts to Independence and Socialism*. Dublin: Sinn Fein Publicity Department, October 1988.

———. *Selected Writings*. Dublin: Sinn Fein Publicity Department, 1989.

———. "Presidential Address by Gerry Adams to the 80th Sinn Fein Ard-Fheis." *An Phoblacht/Republican News*, 8 November 1984.

———. "Presidential Address by Gerry Adams to the 81st Sinn Fein Ard-Fheis, 1984." *An Phoblacht/Republican News*, 7 November 1985.

———. "Presidential Address by Gerry Adams to the 82nd Annual Sinn Fein Ard-Fheis." Mansion House, Dublin, November 1986. Sinn Fein Publicity Department.

———. "Presidential Address of Gerry Adams to the 83rd Sinn Fein Ard-Fheis." *An Phoblacht/Republican News*, 5 November 1987.

———. "Presidential Address by Gerry Adams M.P. to the 84th Sinn Fein Ard-Fheis." Mansion House, Dublin, 28 January 1989.

Amnesty International. *Annual Report 1979*. London: Amnesty International, 1980.

———. *Annual Report 1980*. London: Amnesty International, 1981.

———. *Annual Report 1981*. London: Amnesty International, 1982.

Arendt, Hannah. *On Violence*. New York: Harcourt, Brace & World, Inc., 1969.

Bazerman, Max H., Tony Giuliano, and Alan Appelman. "Escalation of Commitment in Individual and Group Decision Making." *Organizational Behavior and Human Performance* 33 (1984): 141–52.

Bell Geoffrey. *The Protestants of Ulster*. London: Pluto Press, 1976.

Bell, Robert. *The Book of Ulster Surnames*. Belfast: Black Staff Books, 1989.

Beresford, David. *Ten Men Dead*. London: Grafton Books, 1987.

Berry, Steve. " 'To the Bitter Climax of Death If Necessary': The H-Block Hunger Strike and the Struggle for Political Status." London: Socialist Workers Party, n.d.

Bishop, Patrick, and Eamonn Mallie. *The Provisional IRA.* London: Heinemann, 1987.

Bolger, Dermont, ed. *Letters from the New Island: Sixteen on Sixteen, Irish Writers on the Easter Rising.* Dublin: Raven Arts Press, 1988.

Bottigheimer, Karl S. *Ireland and the Irish.* New York: Columbia University Press, 1982.

Boyle, Kevin, and Tom Hadden. *Ireland: A Positive Proposal.* Middlesex: Penguin Books, 1985.

Brockner, Joel, Myril C. Shaw, and Jeffrey Z. Rubin. "Factors Affecting Withdrawal from an Escalating Conflict: Quitting Before It's Too Late." *Journal of Experimental Social Psychology* 15 (1979): 492–503.

Brockner, Joel, Jeffrey Z. Rubin, and Elaine Lang. "Face-Saving and Entrapment." *Journal of Experimental Social Psychology* 17 (1981): 68–79.

Brockner, Joel, Jeffrey Z. Rubin, Judy Fine, Thomas P. Hamilton, Barbara Thomas, and Beth Turetsky. "Factors Affecting Entrapment in Escalating Conflicts: The Importance of Timing." *Journal of Research in Personality* 16 (1982): 247–66.

Brockner, Joel, and Melissa Elkind. "Self-Esteem and Reactance: Further Evidence of Attitudinal and Motivational Consequences." *Journal of Experimental Social Psychology* 21 (1985): 346–61.

Brooke, Peter. *Ulster Presbyterianism.* Dublin: Gill & Macmillan, 1987.

Brown, Terence. *Ireland: A Social and Cultural History 1922–1985.* 1981. Revised. London: Fontana Press, 1985.

———. "The Whole Protestant Community: The Making of a Historical Myth." *A Field Day Pamphlet,* no. 7, 1985.

Browne, Vincent. "H-Block Crisis: Courage, Lies and Confusion." *Magill* (August 1981): 6–14, 56–60.

Bruce, Steve. *God Save Ulster.* Oxford: Oxford University Press, 1986.

Buckley, Vincent. *Memory Ireland.* Australia: Penguin Books, 1985.

Burton, Frank. *The Politics of Legitimacy.* London: Routledge & Kegan Paul, 1978.

Campbell, Joseph. *The Hero with a Thousand Faces.* 2d ed. Princeton, N.J.: Princeton University Press, 1968.

Campbell, Joseph, with Bill Moyers. *The Power of Myth.* Edited by Betty Sue Flowers. New York: Doubleday, 1988.

Chopp, Rebecca S. *The Praxis of Suffering.* Maryknoll, N.Y.: Orbis Books, 1986.

Clarke, Desmond M. *Church and State: Essays in Political Philosophy.* Cork: Cork University Press, 1985.

Clarke, Liam. *Broadening the Battlefield.* Dublin: Gill & Macmillan, 1987.

Collins, Tom. *The Irish Hunger Strike.* Dublin: White Island Book Co., 1986.

Comerford, R. V. *The Fenians in Context.* Dublin: Wolfhound Press, 1985.

Common, R. "A Community Under Siege 1970–1977." Belfast: Renewal Design and Print, n.d.

Coogan, Tim Pat. *The IRA.* London: Fontana, 1987.

———. *On the Blanket: The H Block Story.* Dublin: Ward River Press, 1980.

———. *Disillusioned Decades: Ireland 1966–1987.* Gill & Macmillan, 1987.

Conroy, John. *Belfast Diary: War as a Way of Life.* Boston: Beacon Press, 1987.

Corish, Patrick. *The Irish Catholic Experience: A Historical Survey*. Dublin: Gill & Macmillan, 1985.

Coughlan, Anthony. *Fooled Again?* Cork: Mercier Press, 1986.

Crapanzano, Vincent. *Waiting: Whites of South Africa*. New York: Random House, 1985.

Curtin, Chris, Mary Kelly, and Liam O'Dowd, eds. *Culture and Ideology in Ireland*. Galway: Officina Typographica Galway University Press, 1984.

Daly, Cahal B. "Demythologising the Past: No Religious War." Paper presented at the Christian Hope for Ireland Conference, Boston, Massachusetts, November 1988.

———. *War: The Morality, the Reality, the Myth*. Belfast: Queen's University of Belfast, 1984.

Dangerfield, George. *The Damnable Question*. Boston: Little Brown, 1976.

Darby, John. *Intimidation and the Control of Conflict in Northern Ireland*. Dublin: Gill & Macmillan, 1986.

———, ed. *Northern Ireland: The Background to the Conflict*. Belfast: Appletree Press, 1983.

Darby, John, and G. Morris. *Intimidation in Housing*. Northern Ireland Community Delegation Commission Research Paper, Belfast, 1972.

Deane, Seamus. "Civilians and Barbarians." *A Field Day Pamphlet*, no. 3, 1983.

———. "Remembering the Irish Future." *The Crane Bag* 8, no. 1 (1984): 81–92.

Des Pres, Terence. *The Survivor: An Anatomy of Life in the Death Camps*. New York: Oxford University Press, 1976.

Devenny, Danny. "Life in the Cages of the Kesh." *An Phoblacht/Republican News*, 9 May 1981.

Dewar, Michael. *The British Army in Northern Ireland*. London: Arms and Armour Press, 1985.

Donoghue, Denis. " 'Letter from Dublin.' Inside the Maze—Legitimising Heirs to the Men of 1916." *Listener* 106, no. 2725 (3 September 1981), 1–3.

Dooley, Ann. "The Heroic Word: The Reading of Early Irish Sagas." In *The Celtic Consciousness*, edited by Robert O'Driscoll, 155–59. New York: George Braziller, 1981.

Douglas, Mary. *Purity and Danger: An Analysis of the Concepts of Pollution and Taboo*. 1966. Reprint. London: Routledge & Kegan Paul, Ark Paperbacks, 1985.

Easthope, Gary. "Religious War in Northern Ireland." *Sociology* 10, no. 3 (September 1976), 427–49.

Edwards, Ruth Dudley. *Patrick Pearse: The Triumph of Failure*. London: Faber and Faber, 1979.

Elias, Robert. *The Politics of Victimization*. New York: Oxford University Press, 1986.

Elliott, Marianne. "Watchmen in Sion: The Protestant Idea of Liberty." *A Field Day Pamphlet*, no. 8, 1985.

Erikson, Erik H. *In Search of Common Ground: Conversations with Erik Erikson and Hury Newton*. New York: Dell, 1973.

European Commission on Human Rights. Decision of the European Commission (1980) 3-ERREH RR. Strasbourg 1980.

Falconer, Alan D., ed. *Reconciling Memories*. Dublin: The Columba Press, 1988.

Fanning, Ronan. *Independent Ireland*. Dublin: Helicon, 1983.

Fanon, Frantz. *The Wretched of the Earth*. New York: Grove Press, 1968.

Farrell, Michael. *The Orange State*. London: Pluto Press, 1976.

Faul, Denis, and Raymond Murray. *H-Blocks: British Jail for Irish Political Prisoners*. Dungannon, 1977.

Feehan, John. *Bobby Sands and the Tragedy of Northern Ireland*. Sag Harbor, N.Y.: The Permanent Press, 1983.

Flackes, W. D. *Northern Ireland: A Political Directory*. 1980. London: British Broadcasting Corporation, 1983.

Foster, R. F. *Modern Ireland 1600–1972*. London: Penguin Group, 1988.

Fried, Marc. "Grieving for a Lost Home." In *The Urban Condition,* edited by Leonard Duhl. 151–71, New York: Basic Books, 1963.

Gallagher, Eric, and Stanley Worrall. *Christians in Ulster 1968–1980*. Oxford: Oxford University Press, 1982.

Gerassi, John, ed. *Revolutionary Priest: The Complete Writings and Messages of Camilo Torres*. New York: Vintage Books, 1971.

Gibney, Jim. "What Lies Behind the Prisoners' Struggle." *H-Block/Armagh Bulletin* no. 17, 12 June 1981.

Gillman, Peter. "In the Shadow of the Gun—A Deep Concern for Loos and Drains." *London Sunday Times,* 8 May 1983.

Girard, René. *Violence and the Sacred*. Translated by Patrick Gregory. Baltimore: The Johns Hopkins University Press, 1977.

Givant, Michael. "Understanding the Hunger Strike." *New Society* (21 October 1982): 120–22.

Griffin, Victor G. *Anglicans and Irish: What We Believe*. Dublin: APCK, 1976.

———. "Pluralism and Ecumenism State and Church." The JKL Lecture given under the auspices of the Irish School of Ecumenics, 1983.

Hamill, Desmond. *Pig in the Middle: The Army in Northern Ireland 1969–1984*. London: Methuen, 1985.

Harkness, David. *Northern Ireland Since 1920*. Dublin: Helicon Ltd., 1983.

Haslett, E. "The Anglo-Irish Agreement: Northern Ireland Perspectives." Belfast: Unionist Joint Working Party, 1987.

Hauerwas, Stanley. *Suffering Presence*. Notre Dame, Ind.: University of Notre Dame Press, 1986.

Healy, James, S.J. "Notes towards a Study of Irish Hunger Strikes I." *Milltown Studies* no. 8 (Autumn 1981): 43–57.

———. "Notes towards a Study of Irish Hunger Strikes II." *Milltown Studies* no. 9 (Spring 1982): 23–37.

———. "Suffragette Hunger Strikes, 1909–1914." *Horizons* 16 (Summer 1982): 65–76.

———. "The Civil War Hunger Strike—October 1923." *Studies* 71, no. 283 (Autumn 1982): 213–26.

———. "Hunger Strikes Around the World." *Social Studies* 8, no. 1 (Spring/Summer 1984): 81–108.

———. "Martyrs—And Other Heroes." *Doctrine and Life* 34 (July/August 1984): 352–54.

————. "Hunger Strikes: Other Ethical Reflections." *Milltown Studies* no. 15 (Spring 1985): 82–102.

Heskin, Ken. *Northern Ireland: A Psychological Analysis.* New York: Columbia University Press, 1980.

Hickey, John. *Religion and the Northern Ireland Problem.* Dublin: Gill and Macmillan, 1984.

Hopkinson, Michael. *Green against Green: The Irish Civil War.* Dublin: Gill & Macmillan, 1988.

Information on Ireland. "The H-Blocks: An Indictment of British Prison Policy in the North of Ireland." London: Information on Ireland, 1981.

Inglis, Tom. *Moral Monopoly: The Catholic Church in Modern Irish Society.* Dublin: Gill & Macmillan, 1987.

Irish Commission for Justice and Peace. "The H-Block Protest in the Maze Prison, Northern Ireland." Statement issued 13 October 1980.

————. "The Hunger Strike in the Maze Prison, Northern Ireland." Statement issued 3 June 1981.

————. "The Hunger Strike and the Protest in the Maze Prison, Northern Ireland." Statement issued 8 July 1981.

Irish Council of Churches, Board of Community Affairs. "The H-Block Issue." Belfast: Irish Council of Churches, 1980.

Irwin, Steven. "A Decade of Change 1971–1981." Belfast: North Belfast Workshop, n.d.

Jackson, George. *Blood in My Eye.* New York: Random House, 1972.

Janis, Irving L. *Groupthink: Psychological Studies of Policy Decisions and Fiascoes.* 2d ed. Boston: Houghton Mifflin, 1982.

Jeffares, A. Norman, ed. *W. B. Yeats: Selected Plays.* London: Pan Books, 1974.

Jones, Ernest, M.D. *Psycho-Myth, Psycho-History: Essays in Applied Psychoanalysis.* Volume 1. New York: Stonehill Publishing, 1974.

Kearney, Richard. *Transitions: Narrations in Modern Irish Culture.* Manchester: Manchester University Press, 1988.

————, ed. *The Irish Mind.* Dublin: Wolfhound Press, 1985.

————. "The IRA's Strategy of Failure." *The Crane Bag Book of Irish Studies (1977–1981),* edited by M. P. Hederman and R. Kearney, 699–707. Dublin: Blackwater Press, 1982.

————. "Myth and Terror." *The Crane Bag Book of Irish Studies (1977–1981),* edited by M. P. Hederman and R. Kearney, 273–87. Dublin: Blackwater Press, 1982.

————. "Myth and Motherland." *A Field Day Pamphlet,* no. 5, 1984.

————. "Faith and Fatherland." *The Crane Bag* 8, no. 1 (1984): 55–67.

Kee, Robert. *The Most Distressful Country; The Bold Fenian Men;* and *Ourselves Alone* (volumes 1–3 of *The Green Flag*). London: Quartet Books, 1976.

Kelley, Kevin. *The Longest War: Northern Ireland and the IRA.* Dingle, Co. Kerry: Brandon, 1982.

Kenny, Anthony. *The Road to Hillsborough.* Oxford: Pergamon Press, 1986.

Kenny, Vincent. "The Post-Colonial Personality." *The Crane Bag* 9, no. 1 (1985): 70–78.

Kerber, Walter, S.J. "The Politically Motived Hunger Strike: Towards a Verdict in Moral Theology." *Milltown Studies* no. 15 (Spring 1985): 65–81.

Kerrigan, Gene. "Wolf Tone and the Rituals of Republicanism." *Magill*, November 1983, 25–30.

King, Ronald, ed. "The Morality of Hunger Strikes." *The Keys of Peter* no. 8 (July/August 1981): 1–16.

Knutson, Jeanne N. *Victimization and Political Violence: The Sceptre of Our Times.* Uncompleted book MS, 1981.

———. "Report from Belfast: Agony, Rage and the Process of Denial." Paper. University of California, Los Angeles, July 1981.

Laffan, Michael. "Two Irish States." *The Crane Bag* 8, no. 1 (1984): 26–40.

———. "British Exasperation and Neglect." *Irish Times*, 13 November 1985.

———. "Precedent Warns against Great Expectations." *Irish Times*, 14 November 1985.

Lee, Joseph. "The North: An Excuse for Our Own Failures?" *Irish Times*, 11 November 1985.

Levi, Primo. *The Drowned and the Saved.* Translated by Raymond Rosenthal. New York: Summit Books, 1988.

Lifton, Robert Jay. *The Nazi Doctors.* New York: Basic Books, 1986.

Lyons, F. S. L. *Culture and Anarchy in Ireland 1890–1939.* Oxford: Clarendon Press, 1979.

Lyons, H. A. "Psychiatric Sequelae of the Belfast Riots." Reprint. *British Journal of Psychiatry* 118, no. 544 (March 1971).

———. "Depressive Illness and Aggression in Belfast." Reprint. *British Medical Journal* 1 (5 February 1972) 342–45.

———. "Violence in Belfast: A Review of the Psychological Effects." Reprint. *Community Health* 5, no. 163 (1973).

———. "Terrorists' Bombing and the Psychological Sequelae." Reprint. *Journal of the Irish Medical Association* 67, no. 1 (12 January 1974).

———. "Legacy of Violence in Northern Ireland." Reprint. *International Journal of Offender Therapy and Comparative Criminology* 19, No. 3 (1975).

Lyons, H. A., and H. J. Harbinson. "A Comparison of Political and Non-Political Murderers in Northern Ireland, 1974–1984." Reprint. *Medical Science Law* 26, no. 3 (1986).

McAllister, Jim. "Bodenstown 1984." *An Phoblacht/Republican News*, 21 June 1984.

McCabe, Herbert, O.P. "Thoughts on Hunger Strikes." *New Blackfriars* 62 (July/August 1981): 303–10.

MacCana, Proinsias. "Mythology in Early Irish Literature." In *The Celtic Consciousness*, edited by Robert O'Driscoll, 143–54. New York: George Braziller, 1981.

McCartney, R. L. "Liberty and Authority in Ireland." *A Field Day Pamphlet*, no. 9, 1985.

McCormick, Richard A., S.J. "Notes on Moral Theology." *Theological Studies* 43, no. 1 (March 1982): 106–12.

MacCurtin, Margaret. "The Religious Image of Women." *The Crane Bag Book of Irish Studies (1977–1981)*, edited by M. P. Hederman and R. Kearney, 539–43. Dublin: Blackwater Press, 1982.

MacDonagh, Oliver. *States of Mind: A Study of Anglo-Irish Conflict 1780–1980.* London: George Allen & Unwin, 1983.

MacDonald, Michael. *Children of Wrath.* Cambridge, England: Polity Press, 1986.

McEvoy, James. "Catholic Hopes and Protestant Fears." *The Crane Bag* 7, no. 2 (1983): 90–105.

McGuinness, Martin. "Bodenstown '86: We Do Not Fear You—We Are Going to Win." *An Phoblacht/Republican News,* 26 June 1986.

MacIntyre, Alasdair. *Whose Justice? Which Rationality?* Notre Dame, Ind.: University of Notre Dame Press, 1988.

Mack, John. "Nationalism and the Self." *The Psychological Review* 2, nos. 2–3 (Spring 1983): 47–69.

McManus, Sean. "Bodenstown 1985." *An Phoblacht/Republican News,* 27 June 1985.

MacStiofain, Sean. *Revolutionary in Ireland.* Edinburgh: Gordon Cremonesi, 1975.

Marris, Peter. *Loss and Change.* 1974. Revised. London: Routledge & Kegan Paul, 1986.

Metress, Seamus Proinsias. "The Hunger Strike and the Final Struggle." Toledo, Ohio: 1983.

Miller, Ivan W., III, and William H. Norman. "Learned Helplessness in Humans: A Review and Attribution—Theory Model." *Psychological Bulletin* 86, no. 1 (1979): 93–118.

Morrison, Danny. "The Hillsborough Agreement." Bobby Sands commemorative lecture given at Twinbrook, Belfast, 4 May 1986. Dublin: Sinn Fein Publicity Department.

Naipaul, Shiva. *Journey to Nowhere.* New York: Simon and Schuster, 1980.

Nathanson, Sinaia, Joel Brockner, Dan Brenner, Charles Samuelson, Martin Countryman, Mary Lloyd, and Jeffrey Z. Rubin. "Toward the Reduction of Entrapment." *Journal of Applied Social Psychology* 12:3 (1982), 193–208.

Newsinger, John. " 'I Bring Not Peace But A Sword': The Religious Motif in the Irish War of Independence." *Journal of Contemporary History* 13, no. 3 (July 1978): 609–28.

Newton, Huey P. *Revolutionary Suicide.* New York: Harcourt Brace Jovanovich, 1973.

O'Bradaigh, Ruairi. "Presidential Address of Ruairi O'Bradaigh to the 78th Ard-Fheis." Sinn Fein Publicity Department, 31 October 1982.

O'Callaghan, Denis. "Hunger Strikes: Rights and Wrongs," *Irish Press,* 14 November 1980.

———. "A Moral Dilemma." *Irish Times,* 15 June 1981.

O'Callaghan, Margaret. "The Church and Irish Independence." *The Crane Bag* 7, no. 2 (1983): 65–76.

O'Cathasaigh, Tomas. "The Concept of the Hero in Irish Mythology." In *The Irish Mind,* edited by Richard Kearney, 79–90. Dublin: Wolfhound Press, 1985.

O'Driscoll, Robert, ed. Introduction and Epilogue to *The Celtic Consciousness.* New York: George Braziller, 1981.

O'Fiaich, Tomas. "The Clergy and Fenianism, 1860–70." *Irish Ecclesiastical Record,* 109 (February 1968), 81–103.

O'Hare, Rita. " 'Freedom—Ours to be Won:' Bodenstown '87." *An Phoblacht/ Republican News,* 25 June 1987.

O'Higgins, Michael. "Bloody Sunday Revisited." *Magill,* 12 November 1987, 4–6.

O'Malley, Padraig. "Poor Ireland Where the Myths Sweep in to Cloud Reality." *Boston Globe,* 6 May 1981.

———. "An IRA Strategy That's Working." *Boston Globe,* 23 July 1981.

———. "The Precarious Balance Sheet of the New Ireland Forum." *Fortnight,* June 1986, 4–6.

———. *The Uncivil Wars: Ireland Today.* Boston: Houghton Mifflin, 1983.

———. "Ulster: The Marching Season." *The Atlantic,* May 1986, 28–34.

O'Neil, Daniel J. "Three Perennial Themes of Anti-Colonialism: The Irish Case." Denver: University of Denver, Monograph Series in World Affairs, n.d.

O'Neill, Barry. "International Escalation and the Dollar Auction." *Journal of Conflict Resolution* 30, no. 1 (March 1986): 33–50.

O'Toole, Fintan. "The Ballot and the Bullet." *Magill,* 13 November 1986, 9–15.

———. "No Peace for the Dead." *Magill,* August 1987, 40–43.

O'Tuama, Sean. *An Duanaire 1600–1900: Poems of the Dispossessed.* Translated by Thomas Kinsella. 1981. Reprint. Mountrath, Portlaoise: Dolmen Press, 1985.

Pearse, Patrick. *Political Writings and Speeches.* Dublin: Talbot Press, 1962.

Platt, John. "Social Traps." *American Psychologist,* August 1973, 641–51.

Presbyterian Church in Ireland. *The Northern Ireland Situation: Church Statements 1968–1974.* Belfast, 1974.

———. Report to the General Assembly by the Doctrine Committee. *Agreements and Disagreements of Irish Presbyterians and Roman Catholics.* June 1988.

Pruitt, Dean G., and Jeffrey Z. Rubin. *Social Conflict: Escalation, Stalemate, and Settlement.* New York: Random House, 1986.

Republican Prisoners of War. "Questions of History." Dublin: Sinn Fein Education Department, 1987.

Riches, David, ed. *The Anthropology of Violence.* Oxford: Basil Blackwell, 1986.

Robinson, Peter, M.P. "Self-Inflicted: An Exposure of the H-Block Issue." Belfast: Democratic Unionist Party, 1980.

Rubenstein, Richard E. *Alchemists of Revolution: Terrorism in the Modern World.* New York: Basic Books, 1987.

Rubin, Jeffrey Z. "Psychological Traps." *Psychology Today,* March 1981, 52–61.

Rubin, Jeffrey Z., and Joel Brockner. "Factors Affecting Entrapment in Waiting Situations: The Rosencrantz and Guildenstern Effect." *Journal of Personality and Social Psychology* 31, no. 6 (1975): 1054–63.

Rubin, Jeffrey Z., Joel Brockner, Susan Small-Weil, and Sinaia Nathanson. "Factors Affecting Entry into Psychological Traps." *Journal of Conflict Resolution* 24, no. 3 (September 1980): 405–26.

Sands, Bernadette. "My Brother Bobby." *An Phoblacht/Republican News,* 9 May 1981.

Sands, Bobby. *The Diary of Bobby Sands.* Dublin: Sinn Fein Publicity Department, June 1981.

————. *Prison Poems*. Dublin: Sinn Fein Publicity Department, October 1981.

————. *One Day in My Life*. Dublin: Mercier Press, 1982.

————. *Skylark Sing Your Lonely Song*. Dublin: Mercier Press, 1982.

————. "The Birth of a Republican." *Republican News*, 16 December 1978.

Scarry, Elaine. *The Body in Pain*. New York: Oxford University Press, 1985.

Shannon, Elizabeth. *I Am Ireland: Women of the North Speak Out*. Boston: Little Brown, 1989.

Shaw, Francis. "The Canon of Irish History—A Challenge." *Studies* (Summer 1972): 117–53.

Sinn Fein. *The Good Old IRA: Tan War Operations*. Dublin: Sinn Fein Publicity Department, 1985.

————. "The Politics of Revolution: The Main Speeches and Debates from the 1986 Sinn Fein Ard-Fheis." Dublin: Sinn Fein Publicity Department, 1986.

Stewart, A. T. Q. *The Narrow Ground*. London: Faber & Faber, 1977.

Susman, Warren I. " 'Personality' and the Making of Twentieth-Century Culture." In *Culture as History: The Transformation Of American Society in the Twentieth Century*, edited by Warren I. Susman, 271–85. New York: Pantheon Books, 1985.

Symmons, Clive. "The Anglo-Irish Agreement: The Review Process." *Studies* (Autumn 1988): 259–71.

Teger, Allan. *Too Much Invested to Quit*. New York: Pergamon Press, 1980.

Thompson, John. *Religion, Morality and Politics: A Contemporary Analysis of the Northern Ireland Problems*. Presbyterian Church in Northern Ireland, 1986.

Thompson, William Irwin. *The Imagination of an Insurrection*. Oxford: Oxford University Press, 1967.

————. "The Mythic Past and the Present Moment." In *The Celtic Consciousness*, edited by Robert O'Driscoll, 597–609. New York: George Braziller, 1981.

Toibin, Colm. *Letters from the New Island: Martyrs and Metaphors*. Dublin: Raven Arts Press, 1987.

Townshend, Charles. *Political Violence in Ireland*. Oxford: Clarendon Press, 1983.

United Kingdom, Foreign and Commonwealth Office. *Northern Ireland Briefing Pack*. London: Her Majesty's Stationery Office, 1981.

United Kingdom, Northern Ireland Office. *Regimes in Northern Ireland Prisons: Prisoner's Day-to-Day Life with Special Emphasis on Maze and Armagh*. London: Her Majesty's Stationery Office, December, 1980.

————. *H-Blocks: The Reality*. London: Her Majesty's Stationery Office, 1981.

————. *Day to Day Life in Northern Ireland Prisons*. London: Her Majesty's Stationery Office, March 1981.

United Kingdom, Parliament. *Report of a Committee to Consider, in the Context of Civil Liberties and Human Rights, Measures to Deal with Terrorism in Northern Ireland*, chaired by Lord Gardiner. Cmnd. 5847. London: Her Majesty's Stationery Office, January 1975.

Uris, Leon. *Trinity*. New York: Doubleday, 1976.

Volkan, Vamik D. "Psychological Concepts Useful in the Building of Political Foundations Between Nations." *Journal of the Psychoanalytic Association: Track II Diplomacy* 35, no. 4 (1987): 903–35.

Walzer, Michael. *Just and Unjust Wars*. New York: Basic Books, 1977.

Wilson, Andy. "The Hunger Strike in Irish History." MS thesis. Belfast: Queen's University, 1985.

Wright, Frank. *Northern Ireland: A Comparative Analysis.* Dublin: Gill & Macmillan, 1987.

———. "Reconciling the Histories of Protestant and Catholic in Northern Ireland." In *Reconciling Memories,* edited by Alan D. Falconer, 68–83. Dublin: Columba Press, 1988.

Zimbardo, Philip G. "Pathology of Imprisonment." *Society,* April 1972, 4–8.

INDEX

OTHER TITLES

from

BLACKSTAFF PRESS

DESPATCHES FROM BELFAST

DAVID MCKITTRICK

The events of 1985 to 1989 – the signing of the
Anglo-Irish agreement, Unionist attempts to wreck
it, police clashes with extreme loyalists, the
increased ferocity of the IRA's campaign, the
Enniskillen bombing – are now seen by many as a
significant watershed in Northern Ireland politics.

From the pages of the *Independent* and other papers,
Despatches from Belfast presents the best of David
McKittrick's courageous and vivid reports during
that time – providing an invaluable insight into a
crucial period of recent history.

'. . . discerning and balanced writing . . . essential
reading for anyone with the remotest interest in
journalism'
Birmingham Daily News

'succinct and penetrating . . . he reminds us of
events and victims most of us have shamefully
forgotten'
Irish News

'. . . a prose style which is economical, lucid and
free of the ambiguity and cliché which characterise
much coverage of the north. Overlay it all with a
hint of black humour and you have the McKittrick
combination . . . splendid reportage.'
Fortnight

234 × 153mm; 232pp; illus; 0 85640 427 6; pb
£8.95

NORTHERN IRELAND

A POLITICAL DIRECTORY 1968–88

W. D. FLACKES
SYDNEY ELLIOTT

First published in 1980, *Northern Ireland: A Political Directory* has established itself as the foremost reference book in its field. This third edition, completely revised and updated, covers in detail the twenty years since the onset of the current troubles.

With an Introduction and Chronology of Events, Alphabetical Dictionary of people, parties, organisations and key places, and sections on Election Results, Systems of Government in Northern Ireland and the Security System, this is an indispensable guide for anyone with a serious interest in Irish politics.

'No better man to compile a political directory of Northern Ireland . . . impeccably precise in defining political positions of all colours and degrees of stubbornness.'
Sunday Independent

'Immensely useful work by one of the foremost authorities on Northern Ireland and the politics of the region.'
Cork Examiner

198 × 129mm; 448pp; 0 85640 418 7; pb
£9.95

KINGS IN CONFLICT

THE REVOLUTIONARY WAR IN IRELAND AND ITS
AFTERMATH 1689—1750
edited by
W. A. MAGUIRE

The tempestuous events of the late seventeenth
century – at Derry, Enniskillen, the Boyne,
Aughrim, Limerick – and their consequences have
had a fundamental and lasting impact on Irish
history and politics. Exploited as powerful and
emotive symbols of triumph and disaster by
successive generations of Irish people, they have
become difficult to appreciate as historical events in
their own right.

Marking the tercentenary of the battle of the Boyne,
Kings in Conflict is an innovative collection of recent
work by scholars of the period, studying the
dramatic conflicts of the time in a wider European
context – examining the role of France's Louis XIV
in what was effectively a 'war of three kings' rather
than the 'war of two kings' of popular mythology.
Unravelling the tangle of personal, religious,
political and economic motives for William's
intervention in English and Irish affairs, this is a
timely reassessment of a crucial watershed in Irish
and European history.

245 × 182mm; 236pp; illus (b & w and colour); 0 85640 435 7; hb
£14.95

THE BOYNE WATER
THE BATTLE OF THE BOYNE 1690

PETER BERRESFORD ELLIS

In the year 1690 Ireland, still suffering from the effects of Cromwell's colonisation, found itself the pivot of a wider European crisis, with the battle eventually fought at the River Boyne proving decisive of both international and Irish issues. Peter Berresford Ellis's masterly account of the battle and of its causes and consequences makes it plain why, after almost three hundred years, the Boyne remains one of the most potent symbols in Irish politics.

'It throws new light on that encounter and on the men who fought on either side on that scorching July day . . . Well told, the account is enlivened by vivid eye-witness descriptions of the battle and its aftermath.'
Evening Herald

'an admirably impartial account'
Sunday Telegraph

'Although this is a history, it has the readability of a well-written suspense novel, without losing any of the complexity of life.'
Irish Democrat

'Thoroughly researched, competently put together and fluently written. It can be recommended without reserve.'
British Book News

First paperback edition

198 × 129mm; 176pp; illus; 0 85640 419 5; pb
£5.95